Ouran High School

Host Club™

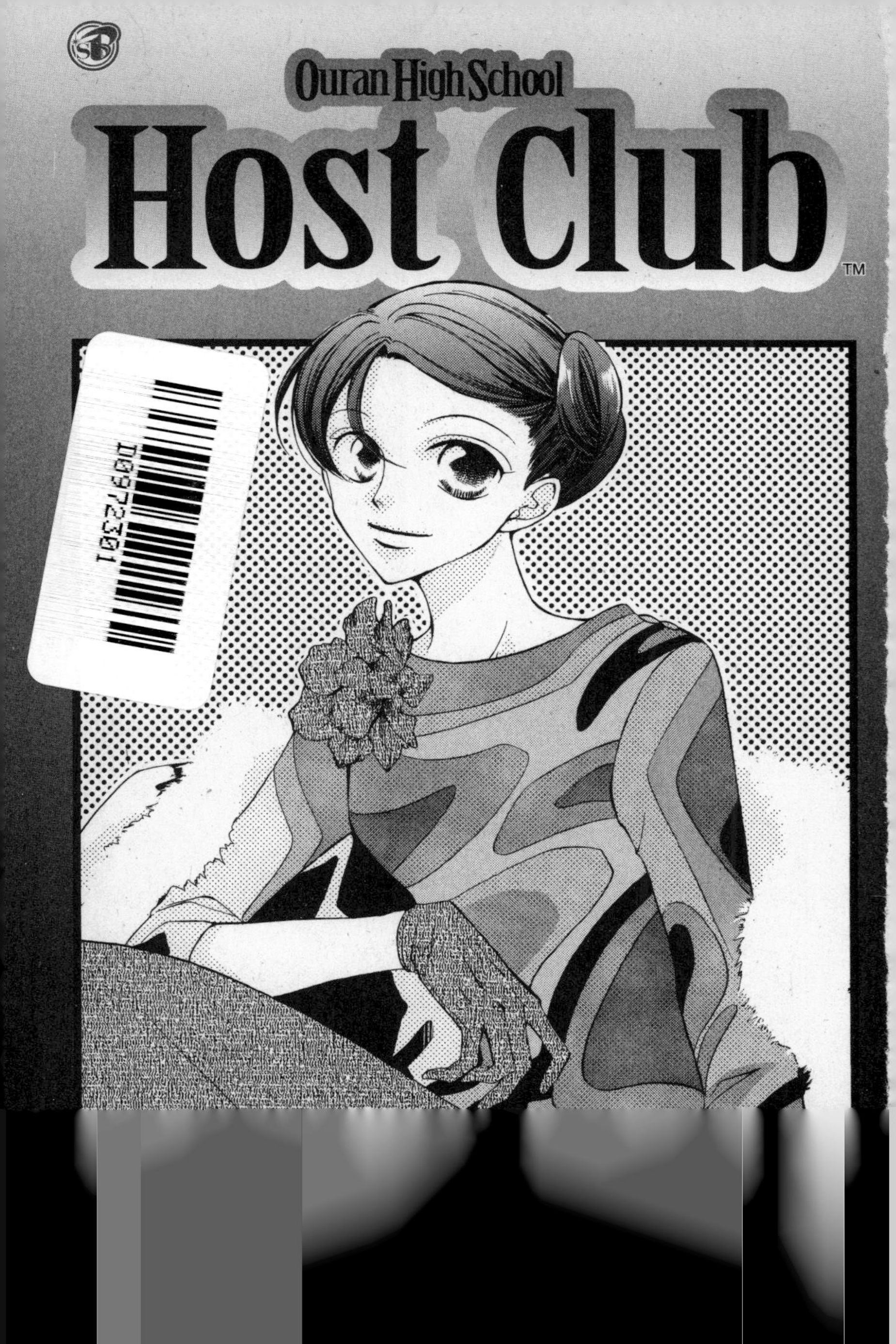

Ouran High School

Host Club™

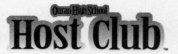

Vol. 6

CONTENTS

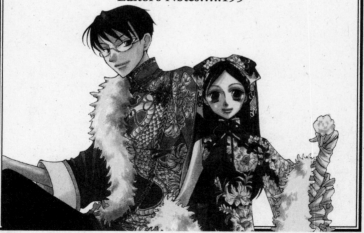

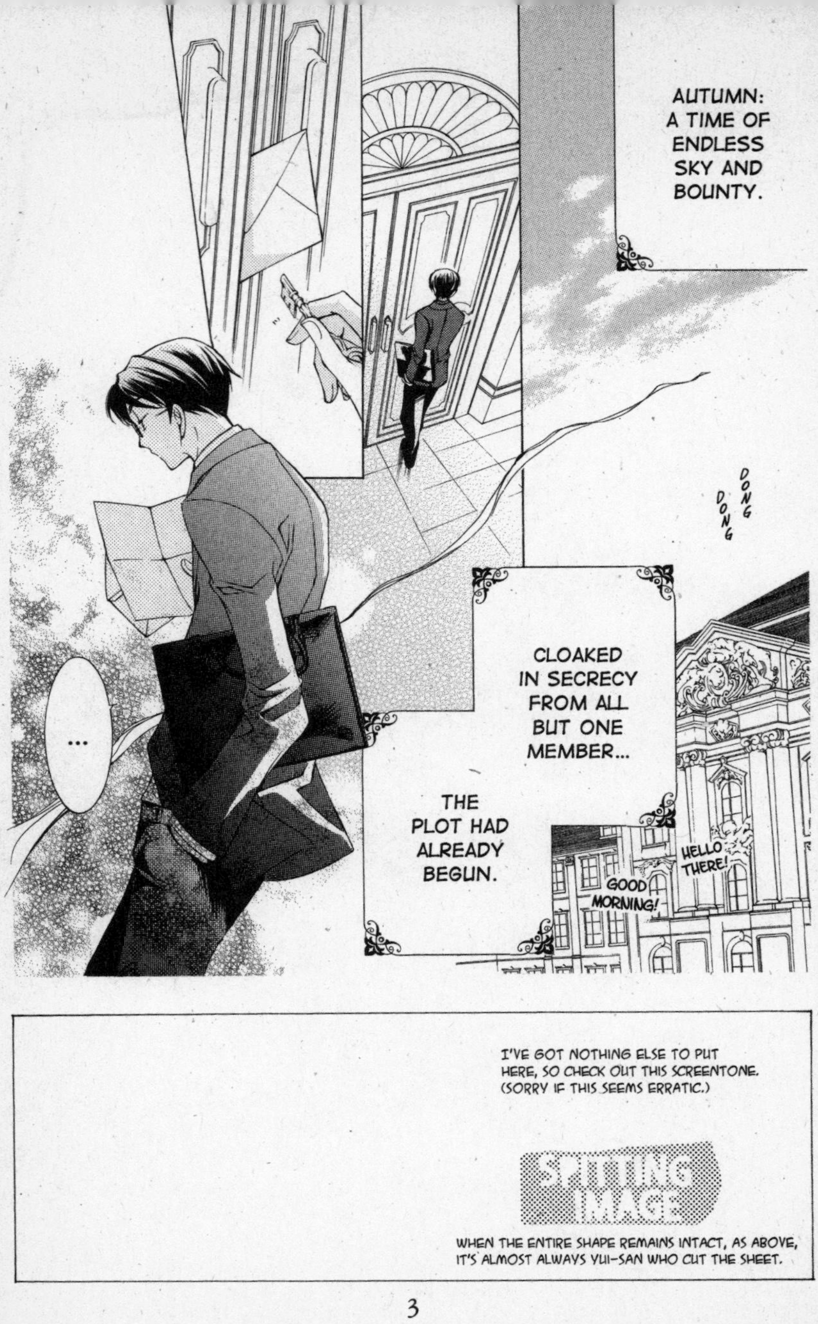
AUTUMN: A TIME OF ENDLESS SKY AND BOUNTY.
DONG DONG
CLOAKED IN SECRECY FROM ALL BUT ONE MEMBER...
THE PLOT HAD ALREADY BEGUN.
HELLO THERE!
GOOD MORNING!
...

I'VE GOT NOTHING ELSE TO PUT HERE, SO CHECK OUT THIS SCREENTONE. (SORRY IF THIS SEEMS ERRATIC.)

SPITTING IMAGE

WHEN THE ENTIRE SHAPE REMAINS INTACT, AS ABOVE, IT'S ALMOST ALWAYS YUI-SAN WHO CUT THE SHEET.

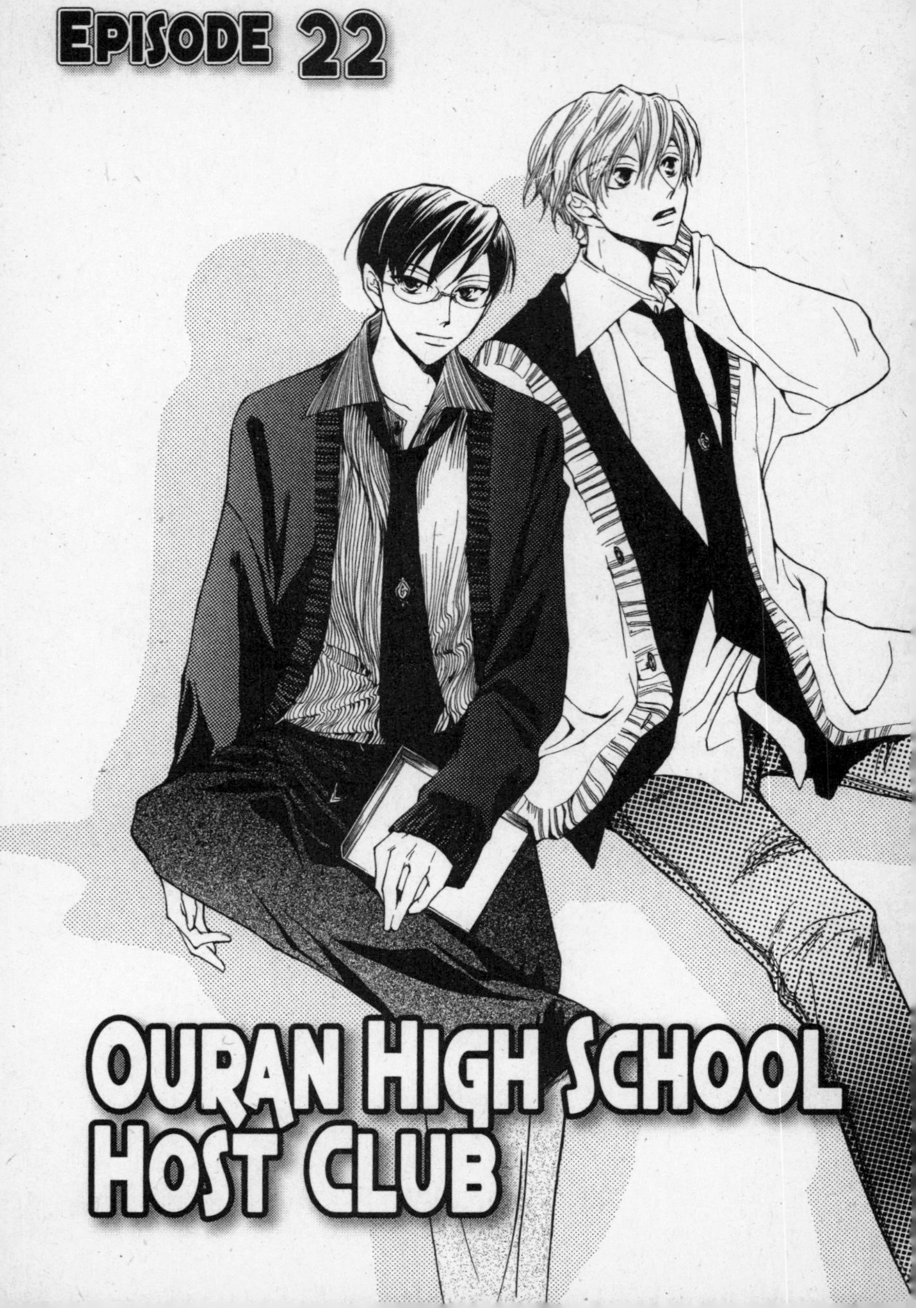
Episode 22
Ouran High School
Host Club

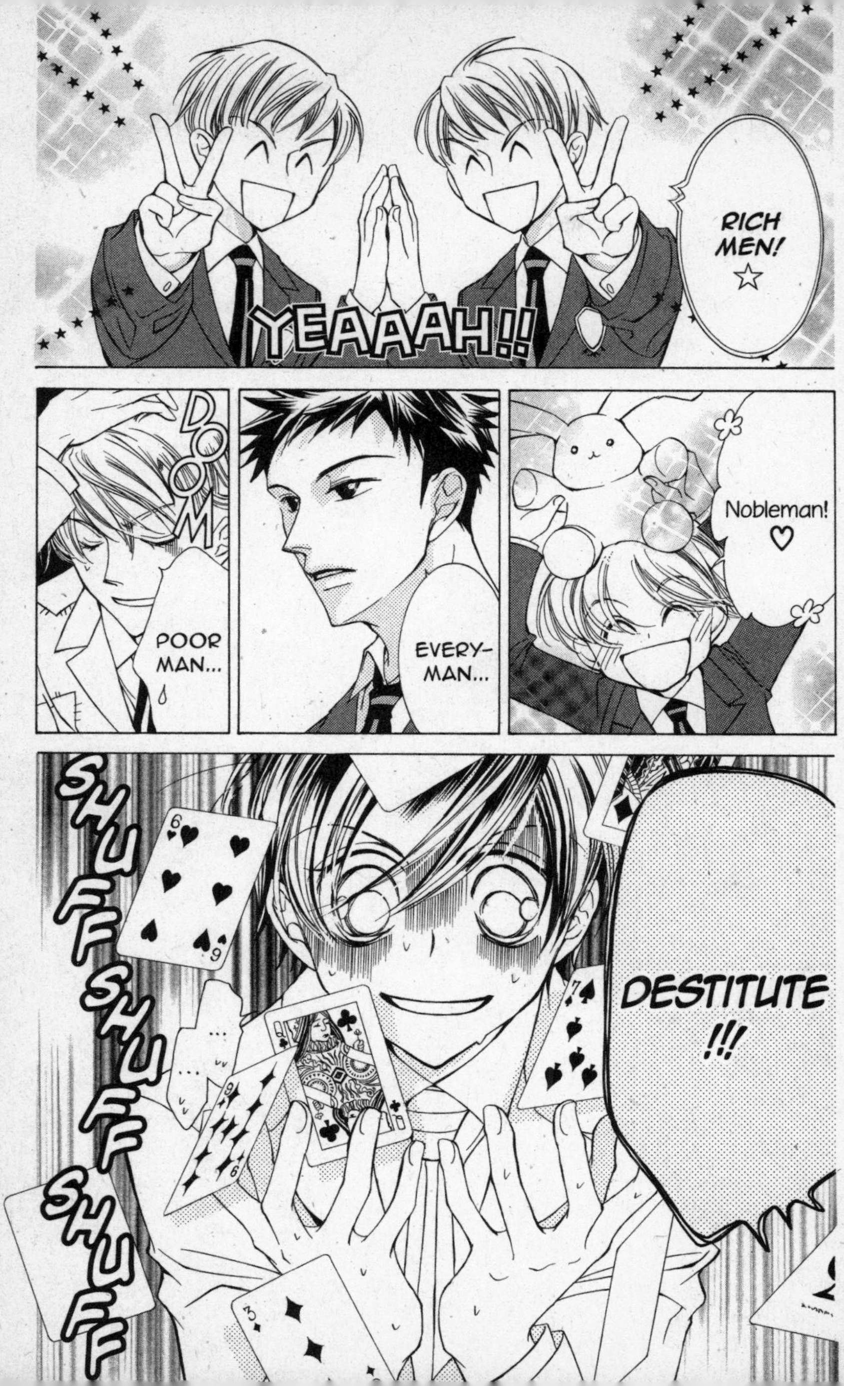
RICH MEN! ☆
YEAAAH!!
Nobleman! ♡
EVERY-MAN...
DOOM
POOR MAN...
DESTITUTE !!!
... ...
SHUFF SHUFF SHUFF

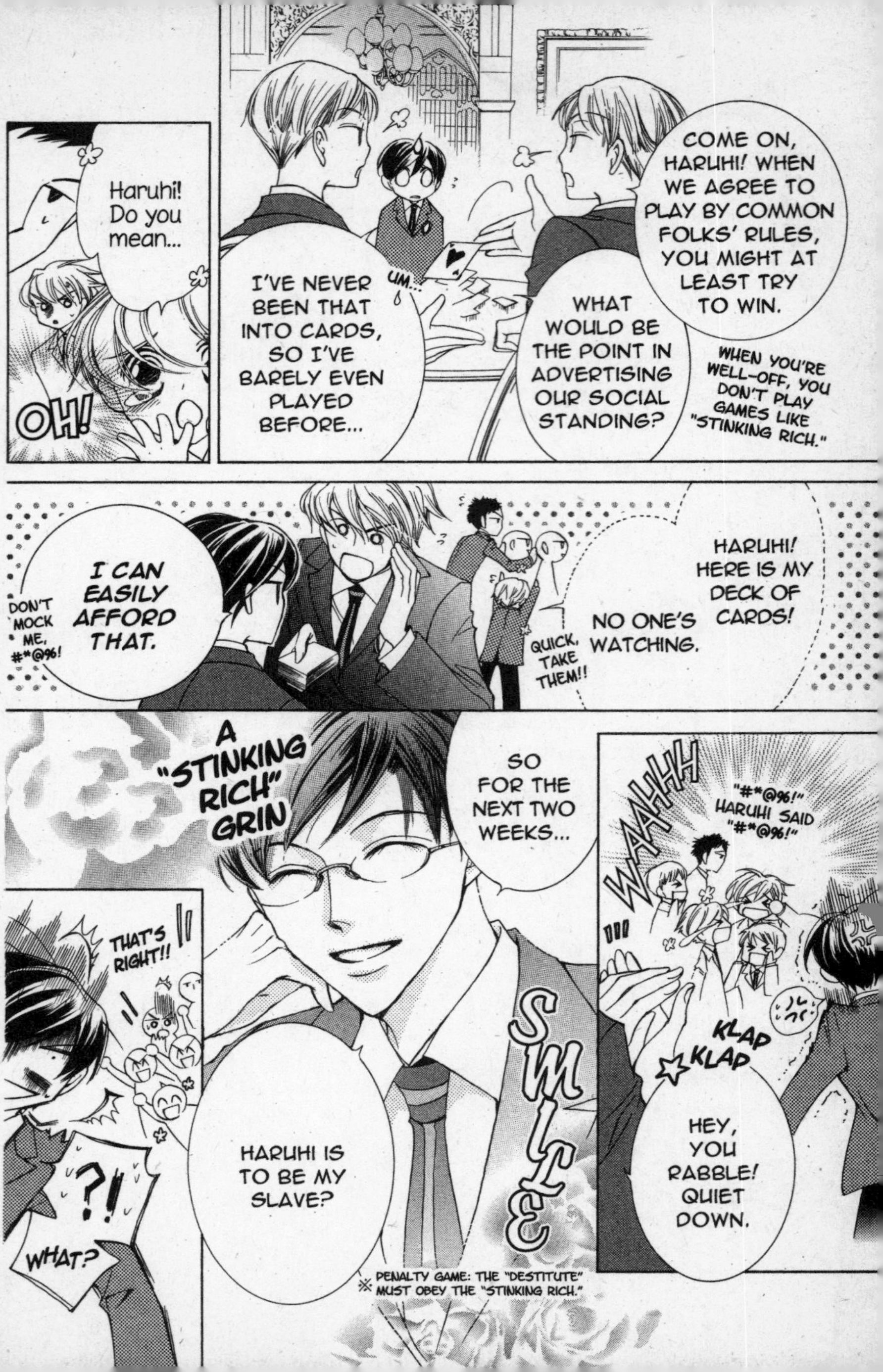
COME ON, HARUHI! WHEN WE AGREE TO PLAY BY COMMON FOLKS' RULES, YOU MIGHT AT LEAST TRY TO WIN.
WHEN YOU'RE WELL-OFF, YOU DON'T PLAY GAMES LIKE "STINKING RICH."
WHAT WOULD BE THE POINT IN ADVERTISING OUR SOCIAL STANDING?
UM...
I'VE NEVER BEEN THAT INTO CARDS, SO I'VE BARELY EVEN PLAYED BEFORE...
Haruhi! Do you mean...
OH!
HARUHI! HERE IS MY DECK OF CARDS!
NO ONE'S WATCHING.
QUICK, TAKE THEM!!
I CAN EASILY AFFORD THAT.
DON'T MOCK ME, #*@%!
WAAHHH
"#*@%!" HARUHI SAID "#*@%!"
KLAP KLAP
HEY, YOU RABBLE! QUIET DOWN.
A "STINKING RICH" GRIN
SO FOR THE NEXT TWO WEEKS...
HARUHI IS TO BE MY SLAVE?
SMILE
※ PENALTY GAME: THE "DESTITUTE" MUST OBEY THE "STINKING RICH."
THAT'S RIGHT!!
?!
WHAT?

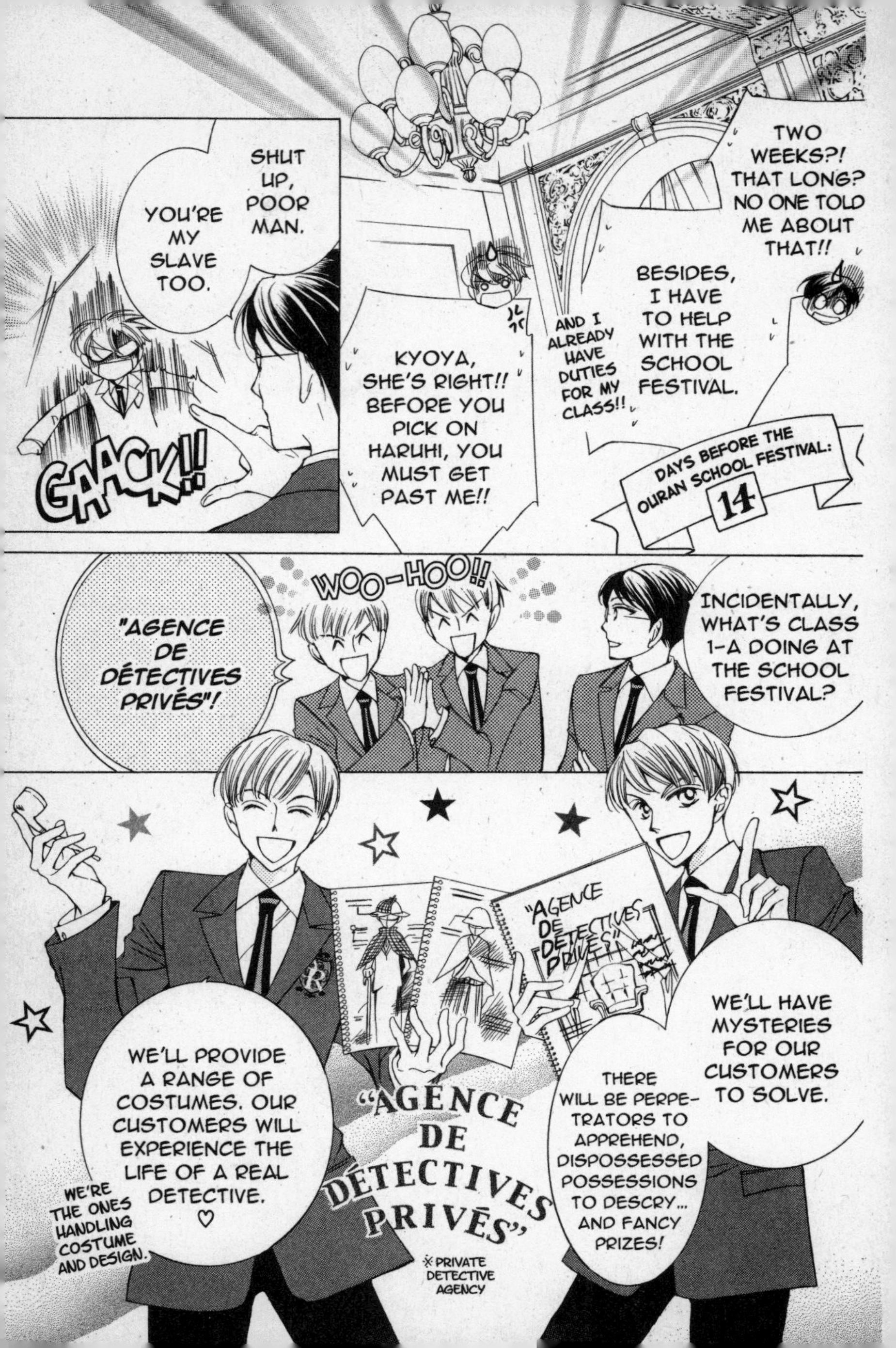
TWO WEEKS?! THAT LONG? NO ONE TOLD ME ABOUT THAT!!
BESIDES, I HAVE TO HELP WITH THE SCHOOL FESTIVAL.
AND I ALREADY HAVE DUTIES FOR MY CLASS!!
KYOYA, SHE'S RIGHT!! BEFORE YOU PICK ON HARUHI, YOU MUST GET PAST ME!!
DAYS BEFORE THE OURAN SCHOOL FESTIVAL: 14
SHUT UP, POOR MAN.
YOU'RE MY SLAVE TOO.
GAACK!!
INCIDENTALLY, WHAT'S CLASS 1-A DOING AT THE SCHOOL FESTIVAL?
WOO-HOO!!
"AGENCE DE DÉTECTIVES PRIVÉS"!
WE'LL HAVE MYSTERIES FOR OUR CUSTOMERS TO SOLVE.
THERE WILL BE PERPETRATORS TO APPREHEND, DISPOSSESSED POSSESSIONS TO DESCRY... AND FANCY PRIZES!
"AGENCE DE DÉTECTIVES PRIVÉS"
"AGENCE DE DÉTECTIVES PRIVÉS"
※PRIVATE DETECTIVE AGENCY
WE'LL PROVIDE A RANGE OF COSTUMES. OUR CUSTOMERS WILL EXPERIENCE THE LIFE OF A REAL DETECTIVE. ♡
WE'RE THE ONES HANDLING COSTUME AND DESIGN.

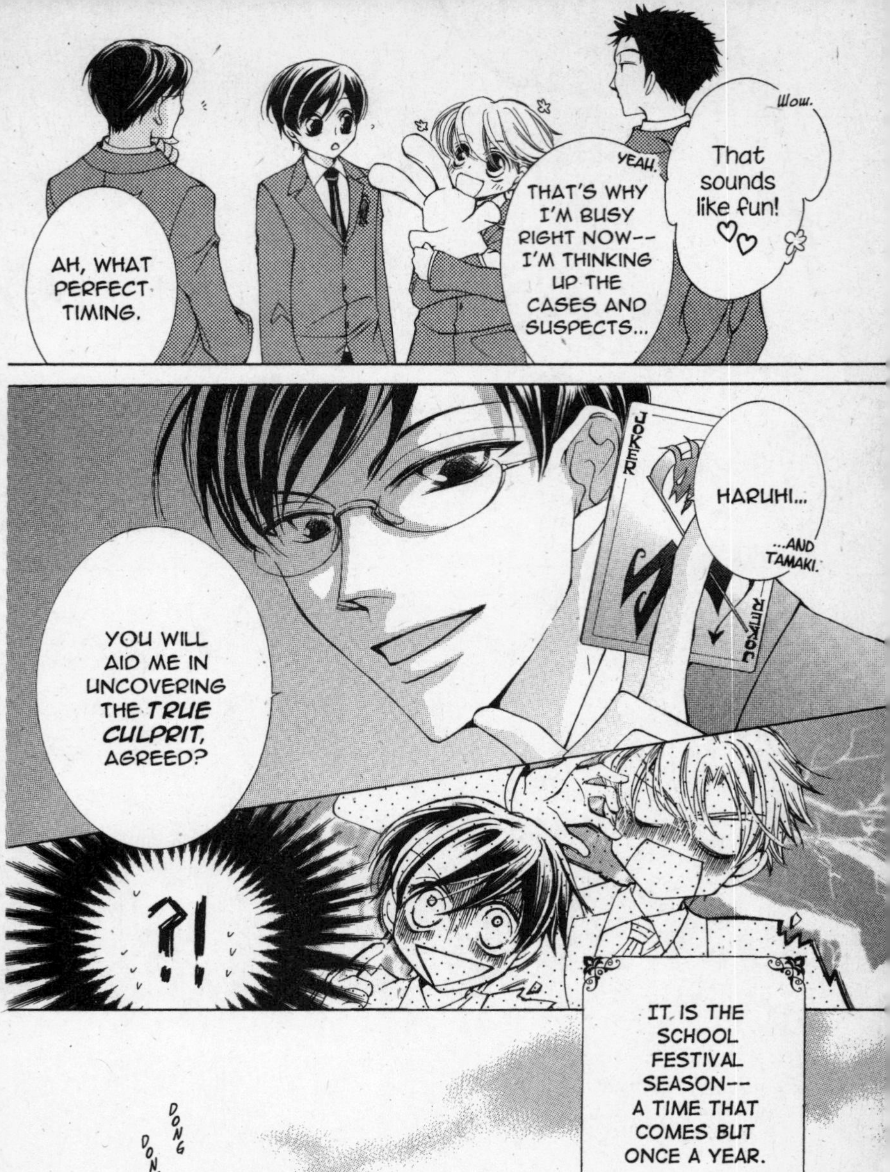
Wow.
That sounds like fun! ♡♡
YEAH.
THAT'S WHY I'M BUSY RIGHT NOW-- I'M THINKING UP THE CASES AND SUSPECTS...
AH, WHAT PERFECT TIMING.
JOKER
HARUHI...
...AND TAMAKI.
YOU WILL AID ME IN UNCOVERING THE TRUE CULPRIT, AGREED?
?!
IT IS THE SCHOOL FESTIVAL SEASON-- A TIME THAT COMES BUT ONCE A YEAR.
DONG
DONG

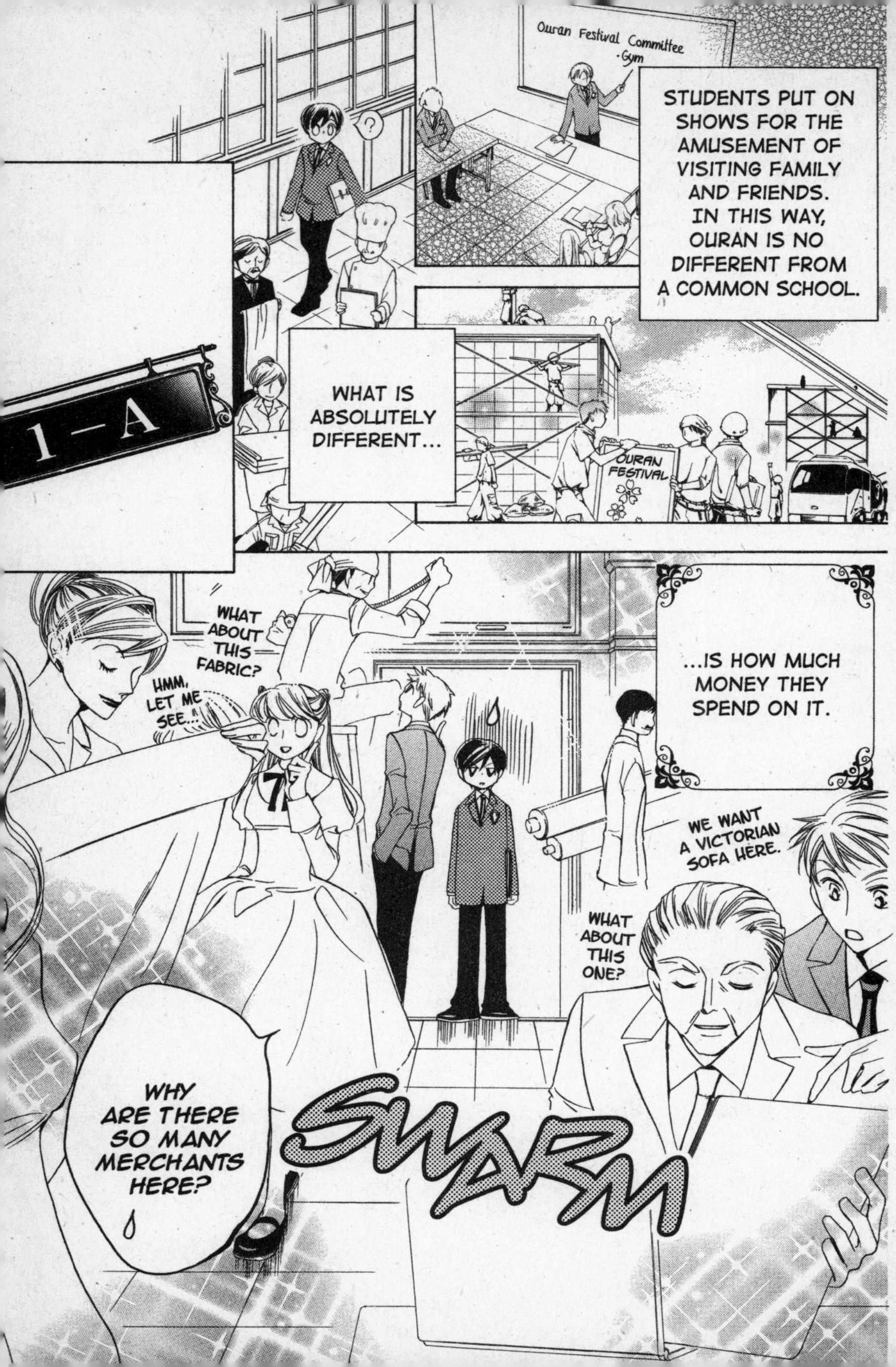
Ouran Festival Committee
· Gym
STUDENTS PUT ON SHOWS FOR THE AMUSEMENT OF VISITING FAMILY AND FRIENDS. IN THIS WAY, OURAN IS NO DIFFERENT FROM A COMMON SCHOOL.
?
OURAN FESTIVAL
WHAT IS ABSOLUTELY DIFFERENT...
1-A
...IS HOW MUCH MONEY THEY SPEND ON IT.
WE WANT A VICTORIAN SOFA HERE.
WHAT ABOUT THIS ONE?
WHAT ABOUT THIS FABRIC?
HMM, LET ME SEE...
SWARM
WHY ARE THERE SO MANY MERCHANTS HERE?

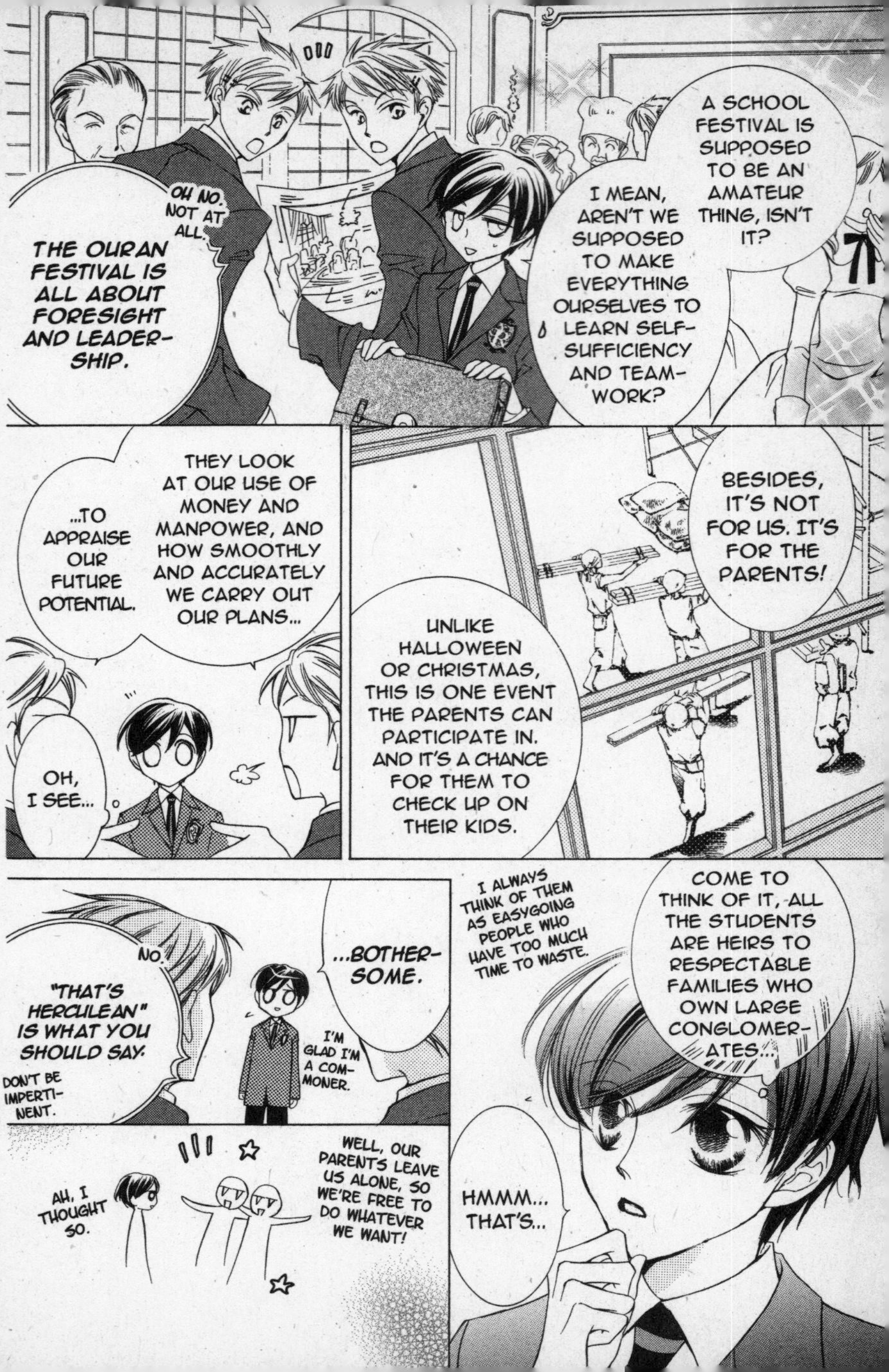
A SCHOOL FESTIVAL IS SUPPOSED TO BE AN AMATEUR THING, ISN'T IT?
I MEAN, AREN'T WE SUPPOSED TO MAKE EVERYTHING OURSELVES TO LEARN SELF-SUFFICIENCY AND TEAM-WORK?
OH NO. NOT AT ALL.
THE OURAN FESTIVAL IS ALL ABOUT FORESIGHT AND LEADER-SHIP.
BESIDES, IT'S NOT FOR US. IT'S FOR THE PARENTS!
UNLIKE HALLOWEEN OR CHRISTMAS, THIS IS ONE EVENT THE PARENTS CAN PARTICIPATE IN. AND IT'S A CHANCE FOR THEM TO CHECK UP ON THEIR KIDS.
THEY LOOK AT OUR USE OF MONEY AND MANPOWER, AND HOW SMOOTHLY AND ACCURATELY WE CARRY OUT OUR PLANS...
...TO APPRAISE OUR FUTURE POTENTIAL.
OH, I SEE...
COME TO THINK OF IT, ALL THE STUDENTS ARE HEIRS TO RESPECTABLE FAMILIES WHO OWN LARGE CONGLOMER-ATES...
I ALWAYS THINK OF THEM AS EASYGOING PEOPLE WHO HAVE TOO MUCH TIME TO WASTE.
HMMM... THAT'S...
...BOTHER-SOME.
I'M GLAD I'M A COM-MONER.
NO.
"THAT'S HERCULEAN" IS WHAT YOU SHOULD SAY.
DON'T BE IMPERTI-NENT.
WELL, OUR PARENTS LEAVE US ALONE, SO WE'RE FREE TO DO WHATEVER WE WANT!
AH, I THOUGHT SO.

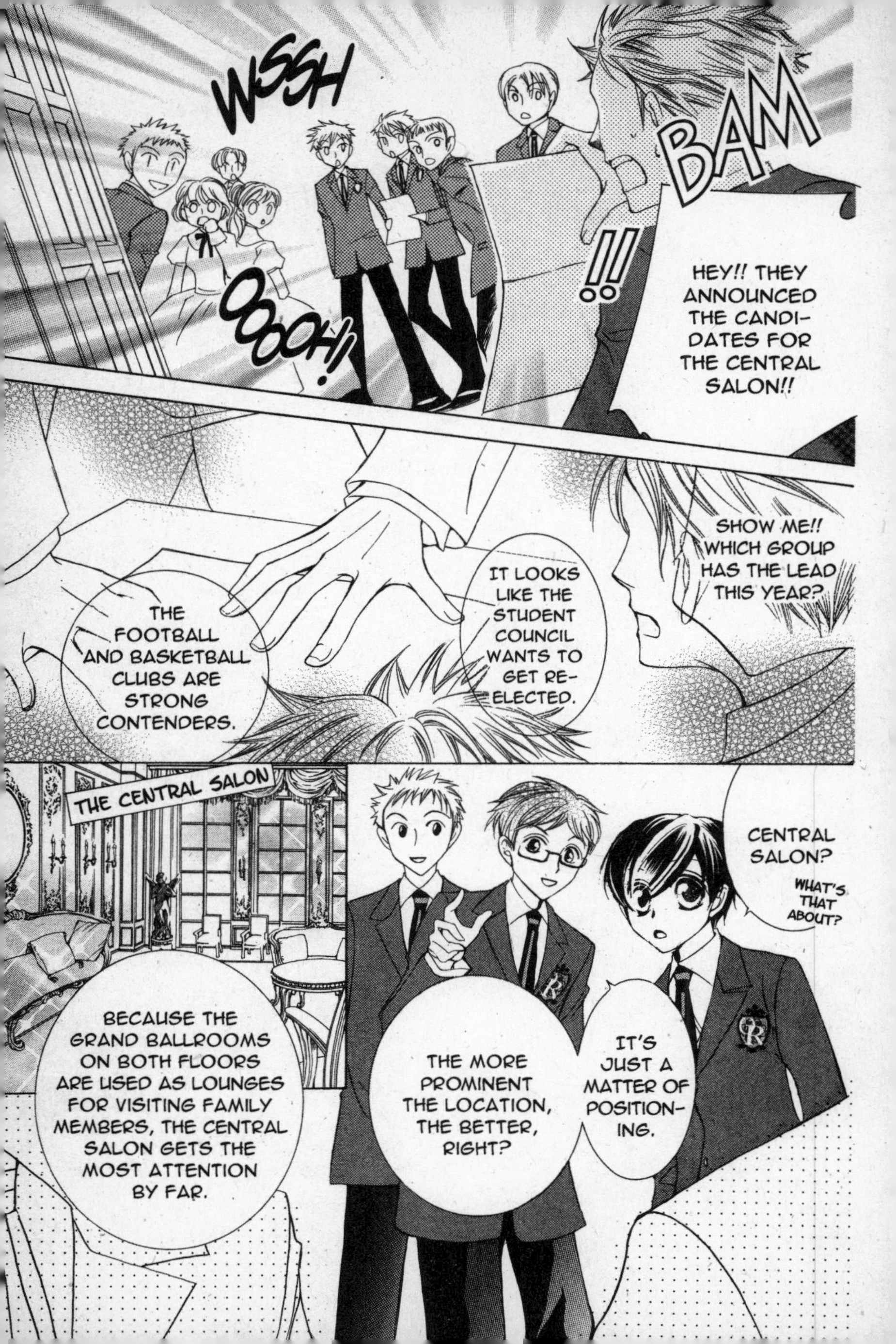
BAM
HEY!! THEY ANNOUNCED THE CANDIDATES FOR THE CENTRAL SALON!!
!!
WSSH
OOOOH!!
SHOW ME!! WHICH GROUP HAS THE LEAD THIS YEAR?
IT LOOKS LIKE THE STUDENT COUNCIL WANTS TO GET RE-ELECTED.
THE FOOTBALL AND BASKETBALL CLUBS ARE STRONG CONTENDERS.
CENTRAL SALON?
WHAT'S THAT ABOUT?
IT'S JUST A MATTER OF POSITIONING.
THE MORE PROMINENT THE LOCATION, THE BETTER, RIGHT?
THE CENTRAL SALON
BECAUSE THE GRAND BALLROOMS ON BOTH FLOORS ARE USED AS LOUNGES FOR VISITING FAMILY MEMBERS, THE CENTRAL SALON GETS THE MOST ATTENTION BY FAR.

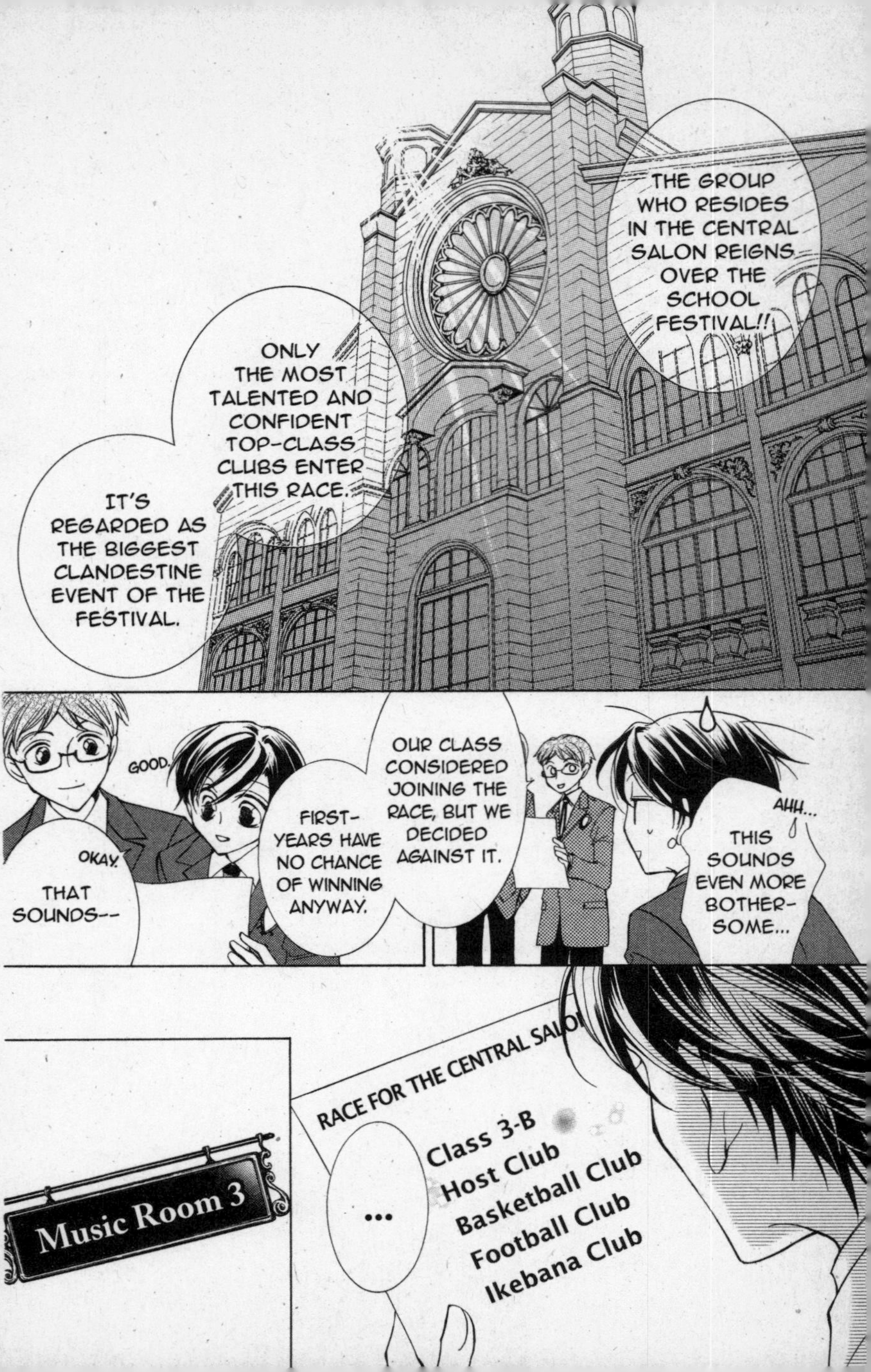
THE GROUP WHO RESIDES IN THE CENTRAL SALON REIGNS OVER THE SCHOOL FESTIVAL!!
ONLY THE MOST TALENTED AND CONFIDENT TOP-CLASS CLUBS ENTER THIS RACE.
IT'S REGARDED AS THE BIGGEST CLANDESTINE EVENT OF THE FESTIVAL.
OUR CLASS CONSIDERED JOINING THE RACE, BUT WE DECIDED AGAINST IT.
AHH...
THIS SOUNDS EVEN MORE BOTHER-SOME...
FIRST-YEARS HAVE NO CHANCE OF WINNING ANYWAY.
GOOD.
OKAY.
THAT SOUNDS--
RACE FOR THE CENTRAL SALO
Class 3-B
Host Club
Basketball Club
Football Club
Ikebana Club
...
Music Room 3

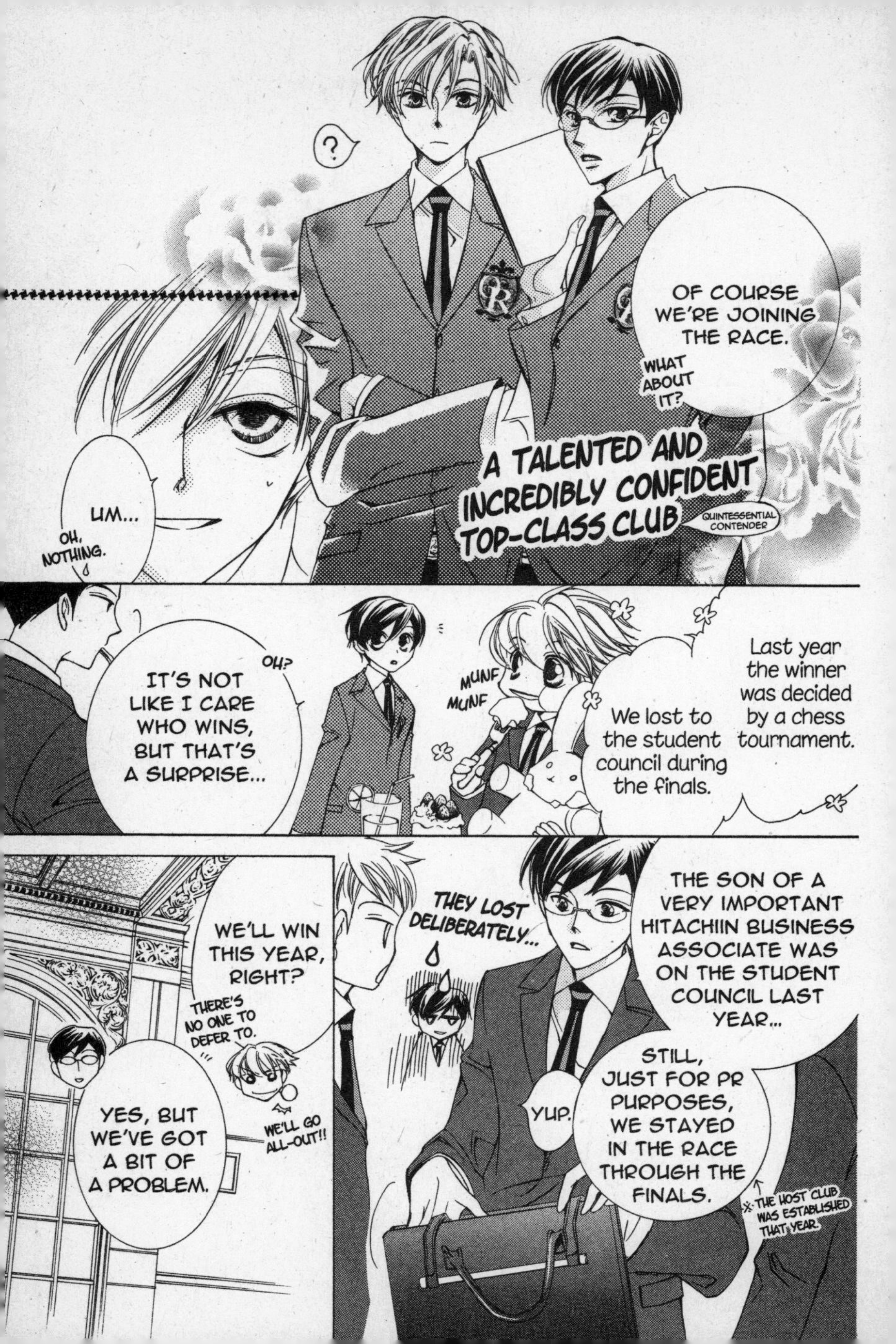
OF COURSE WE'RE JOINING THE RACE.
WHAT ABOUT IT?
A TALENTED AND INCREDIBLY CONFIDENT TOP-CLASS CLUB
QUINTESSENTIAL CONTENDER
UM...
OH, NOTHING.
Last year the winner was decided by a chess tournament.
We lost to the student council during the finals.
MUNF MUNF
OH?
IT'S NOT LIKE I CARE WHO WINS, BUT THAT'S A SURPRISE...
THE SON OF A VERY IMPORTANT HITACHIIN BUSINESS ASSOCIATE WAS ON THE STUDENT COUNCIL LAST YEAR...
THEY LOST DELIBERATELY...
STILL, JUST FOR PR PURPOSES, WE STAYED IN THE RACE THROUGH THE FINALS.
※THE HOST CLUB WAS ESTABLISHED THAT YEAR.
YUP.
WE'LL WIN THIS YEAR, RIGHT?
THERE'S NO ONE TO DEFER TO.
YES, BUT WE'VE GOT A BIT OF A PROBLEM.
WE'LL GO ALL-OUT!!

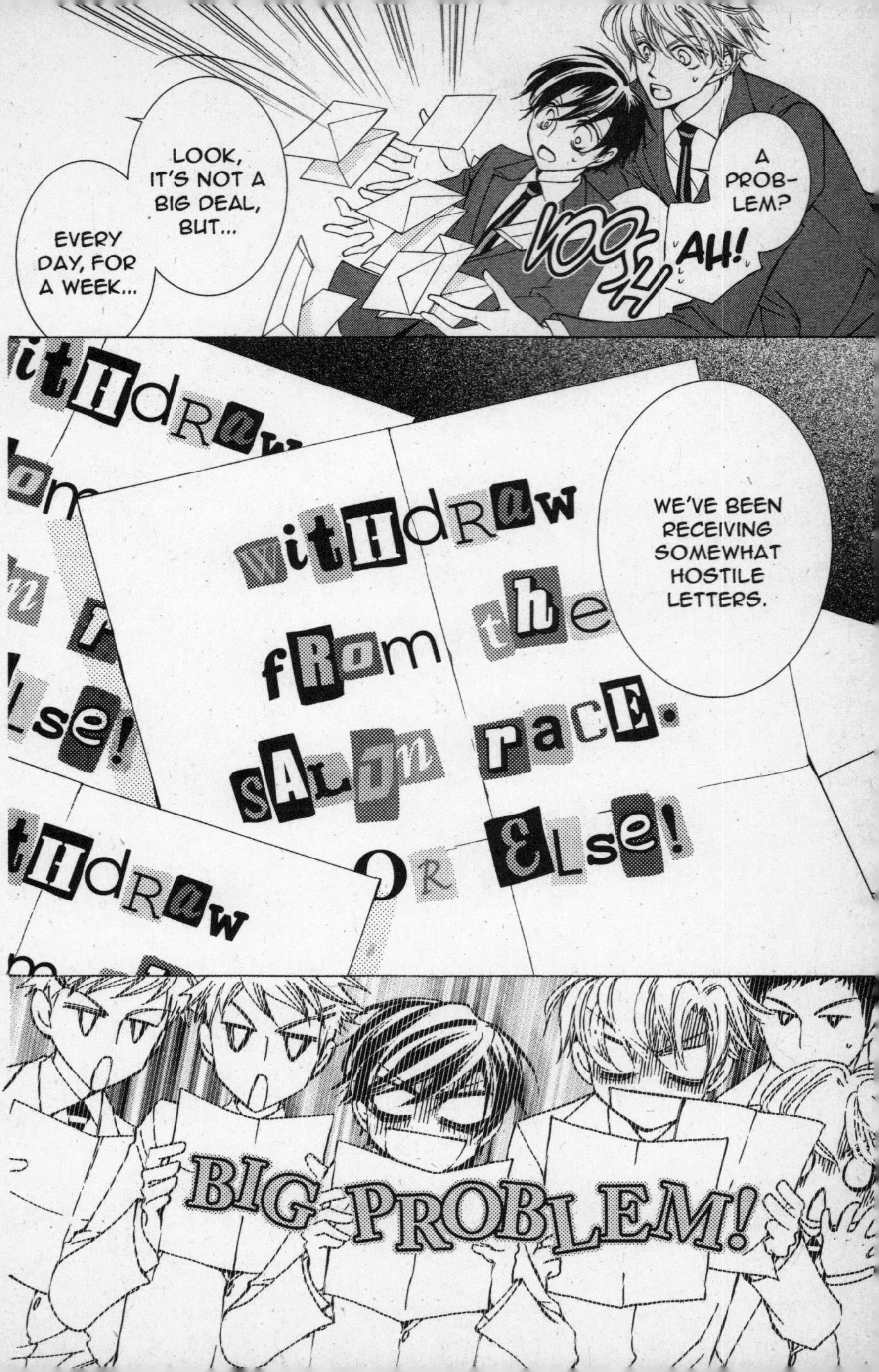
A PROBLEM?
AH!
WOOSH
LOOK, IT'S NOT A BIG DEAL, BUT...
EVERY DAY, FOR A WEEK...
WE'VE BEEN RECEIVING SOMEWHAT HOSTILE LETTERS.
WITHDRAW FROM THE SALON RACE. OR ELSE!
BIG PROBLEM!

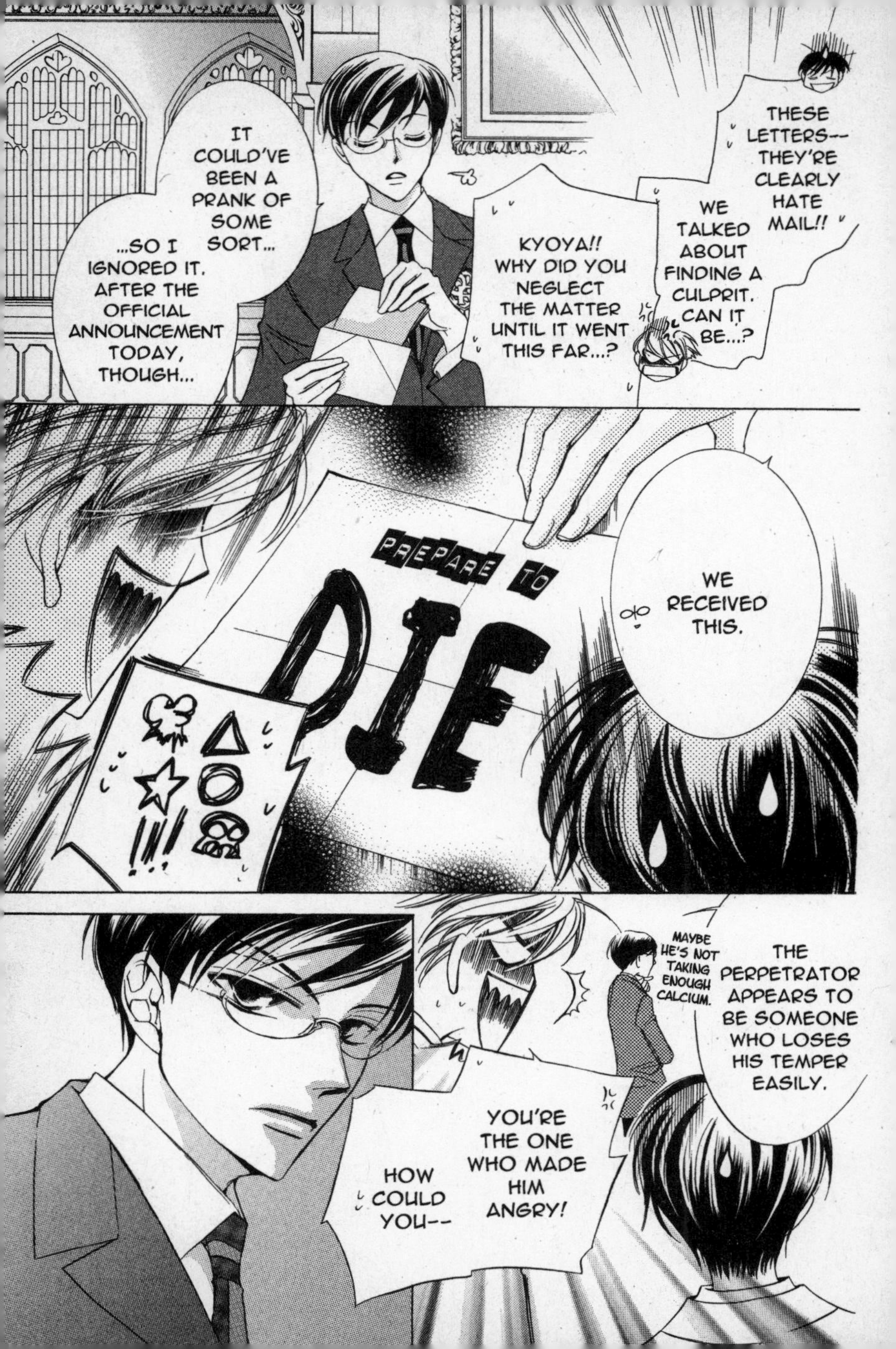
THESE LETTERS-- THEY'RE CLEARLY HATE MAIL!!
WE TALKED ABOUT FINDING A CULPRIT. CAN IT BE...?
KYOYA!! WHY DID YOU NEGLECT THE MATTER UNTIL IT WENT THIS FAR...?
IT COULD'VE BEEN A PRANK OF SOME SORT...
...SO I IGNORED IT. AFTER THE OFFICIAL ANNOUNCEMENT TODAY, THOUGH...
WE RECEIVED THIS.
PREPARE TO
DIE
THE PERPETRATOR APPEARS TO BE SOMEONE WHO LOSES HIS TEMPER EASILY.
MAYBE HE'S NOT TAKING ENOUGH CALCIUM.
YOU'RE THE ONE WHO MADE HIM ANGRY!
HOW COULD YOU--

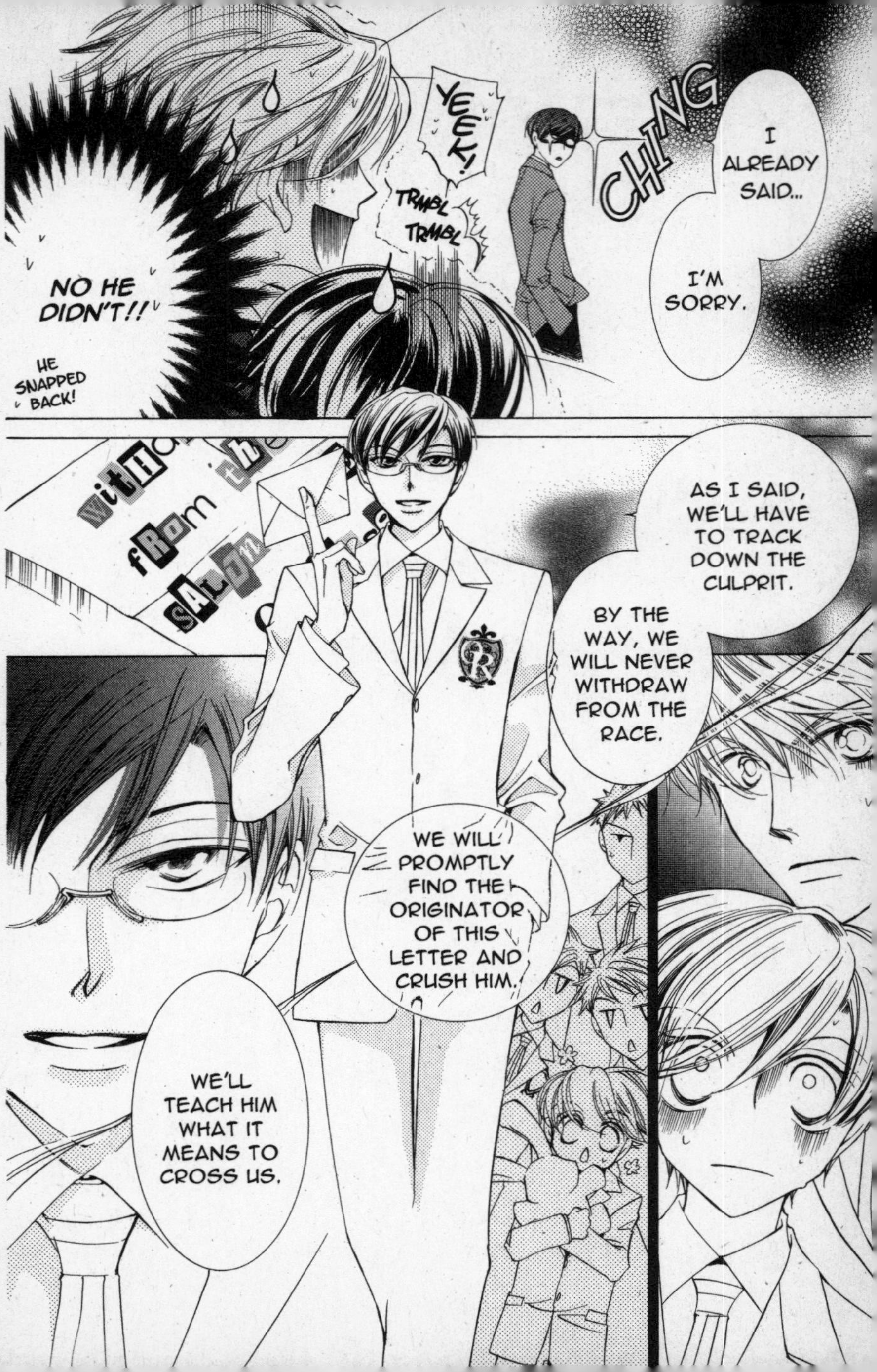

I ALREADY SAID...
I'M SORRY.
CHING
YEEK!
TRMBL TRMBL
NO HE DIDN'T!!
HE SNAPPED BACK!
AS I SAID, WE'LL HAVE TO TRACK DOWN THE CULPRIT.
BY THE WAY, WE WILL NEVER WITHDRAW FROM THE RACE.
WE WILL PROMPTLY FIND THE ORIGINATOR OF THIS LETTER AND CRUSH HIM.
WE'LL TEACH HIM WHAT IT MEANS TO CROSS US.

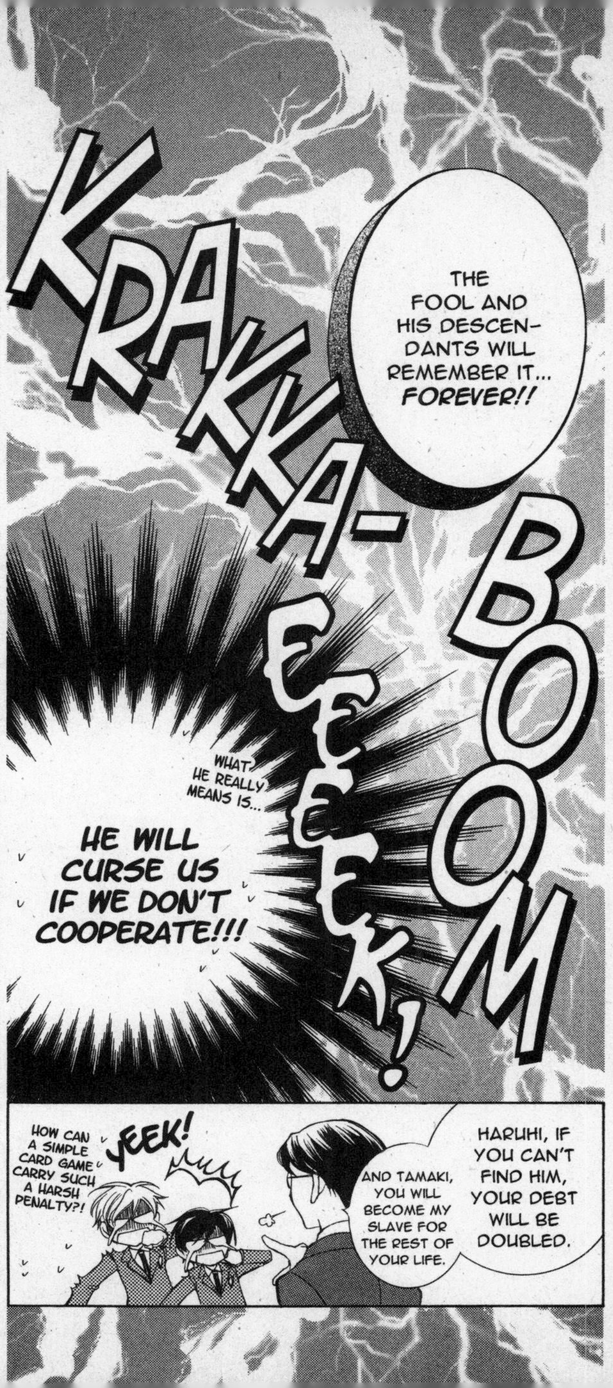
THE FOOL AND HIS DESCEN-DANTS WILL REMEMBER IT... FOREVER!!
KRAKKA-BOOM
EEEEEK!
WHAT HE REALLY MEANS IS...
HE WILL CURSE US IF WE DON'T COOPERATE!!!
HARUHI, IF YOU CAN'T FIND HIM, YOUR DEBT WILL BE DOUBLED.
AND TAMAKI, YOU WILL BECOME MY SLAVE FOR THE REST OF YOUR LIFE.
YEEK!
HOW CAN A SIMPLE CARD GAME CARRY SUCH A HARSH PENALTY?!

✿ HELLO, EVERYONE!! THIS IS HATORI. IT'S VOLUME 6. THIS WILL BE THE LAST BOOK OF MY 20s. (I GET A LOT OF MAIL ASKING FOR MY AGE, SO THIS IS MY CASUAL WAY OF DIVULGING IT.) I'LL BE 30 VERY SOON! PLEASE CONTINUE TO READ ME EVEN THEN.

✿ FOR A WHILE AFTER MY DEBUT, I DREAMED OF PUBLISHING AT LEAST ONE VOLUME BEFORE I TURNED 30. THAT'S HOW LONG AND HARD IT IS FOR A NEW MANGA-KA TO GET PUBLISHED. I WOUND UP WITH EIGHT WHOLE BOOKS. IT FEELS LIKE A DREAM... IT'S ALL THANKS TO YOU!!

THANK YOU VERY MUCH!!

WELL, WHEN I STARTED OFF, I DIDN'T EVEN DREAM OF DRAWING SOMETHING LIKE HOST CLUB...

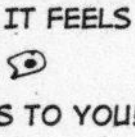

EYES ON THE PAST...

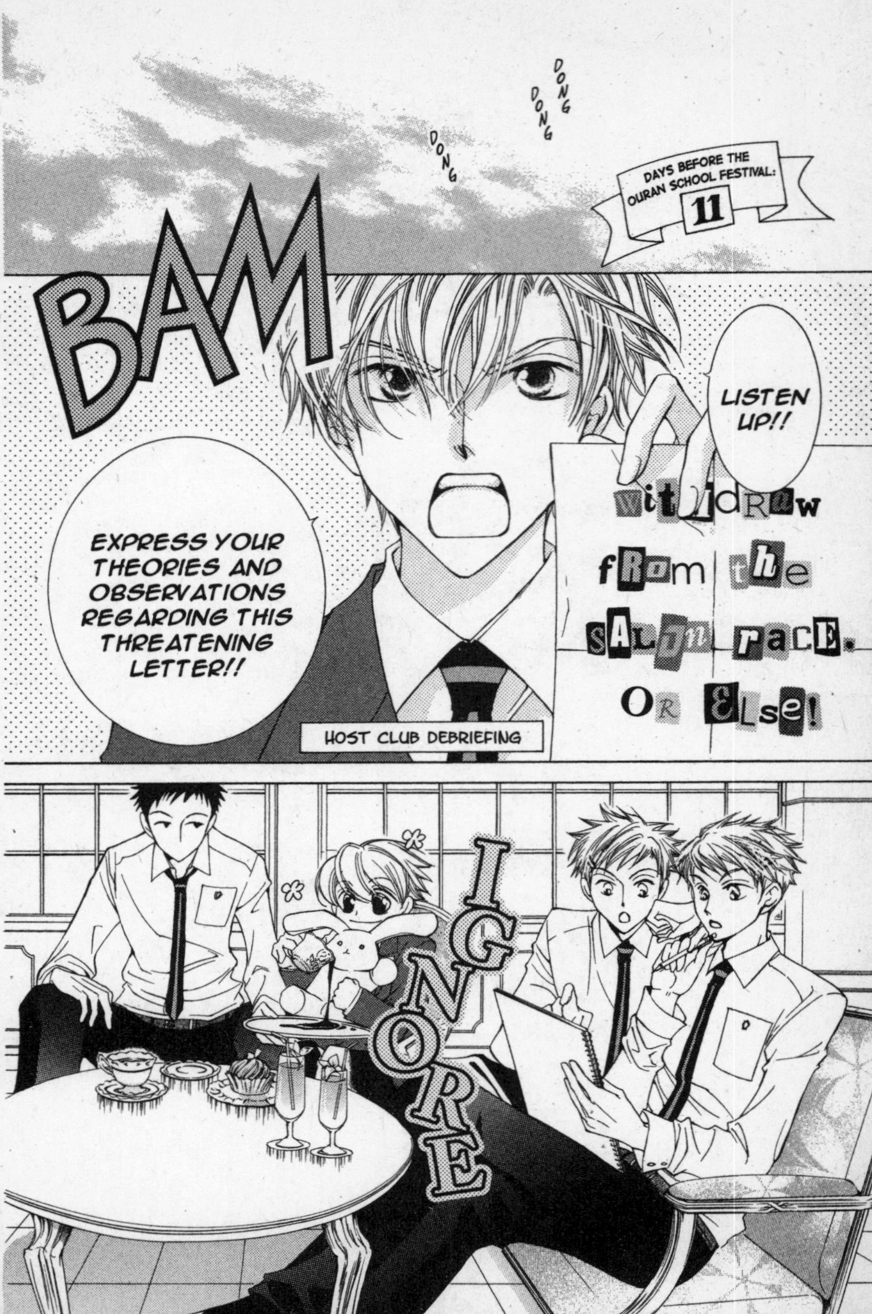
DONG DONG
DONG
DAYS BEFORE THE OURAN SCHOOL FESTIVAL: 11
LISTEN UP!!
Withdraw from the salon race. Or else!
BAM
EXPRESS YOUR THEORIES AND OBSERVATIONS REGARDING THIS THREATENING LETTER!!
HOST CLUB DEBRIEFING
IGNORE

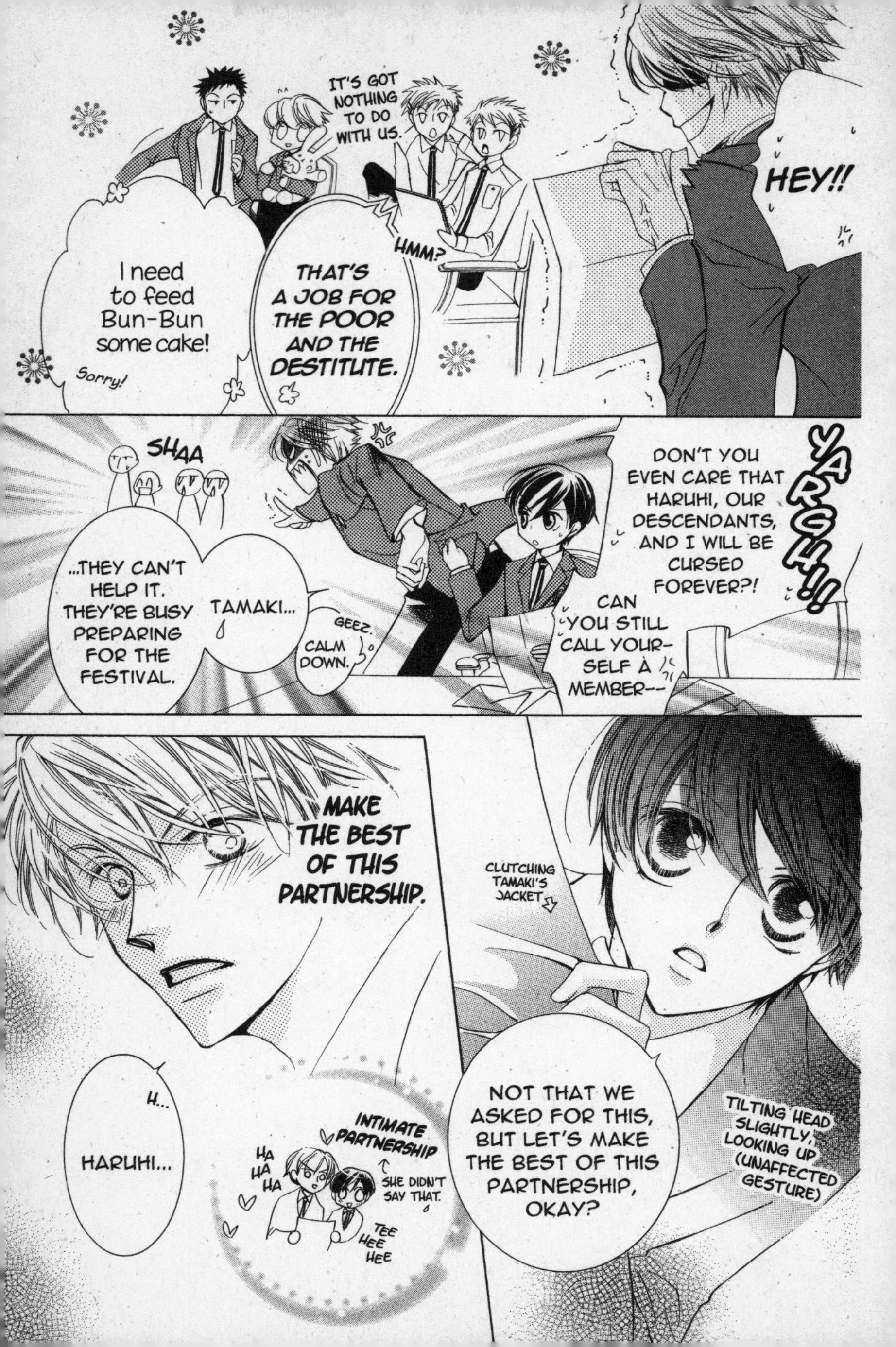
HEY!!
IT'S GOT NOTHING TO DO WITH US.
HMM?
THAT'S A JOB FOR THE POOR AND THE DESTITUTE.
I need to feed Bun-Bun some cake!
Sorry!
YARGH!!
DON'T YOU EVEN CARE THAT HARUHI, OUR DESCENDANTS, AND I WILL BE CURSED FOREVER?!
CAN YOU STILL CALL YOURSELF A MEMBER--
GEEZ.
CALM DOWN.
TAMAKI...
SHAA
...THEY CAN'T HELP IT. THEY'RE BUSY PREPARING FOR THE FESTIVAL.
CLUTCHING TAMAKI'S JACKET
TILTING HEAD SLIGHTLY, LOOKING UP (UNAFFECTED GESTURE)
NOT THAT WE ASKED FOR THIS, BUT LET'S MAKE THE BEST OF THIS PARTNERSHIP, OKAY?
MAKE THE BEST OF THIS PARTNERSHIP.
INTIMATE PARTNERSHIP
HA HA HA
SHE DIDN'T SAY THAT.
TEE HEE HEE
H...
HARUHI...

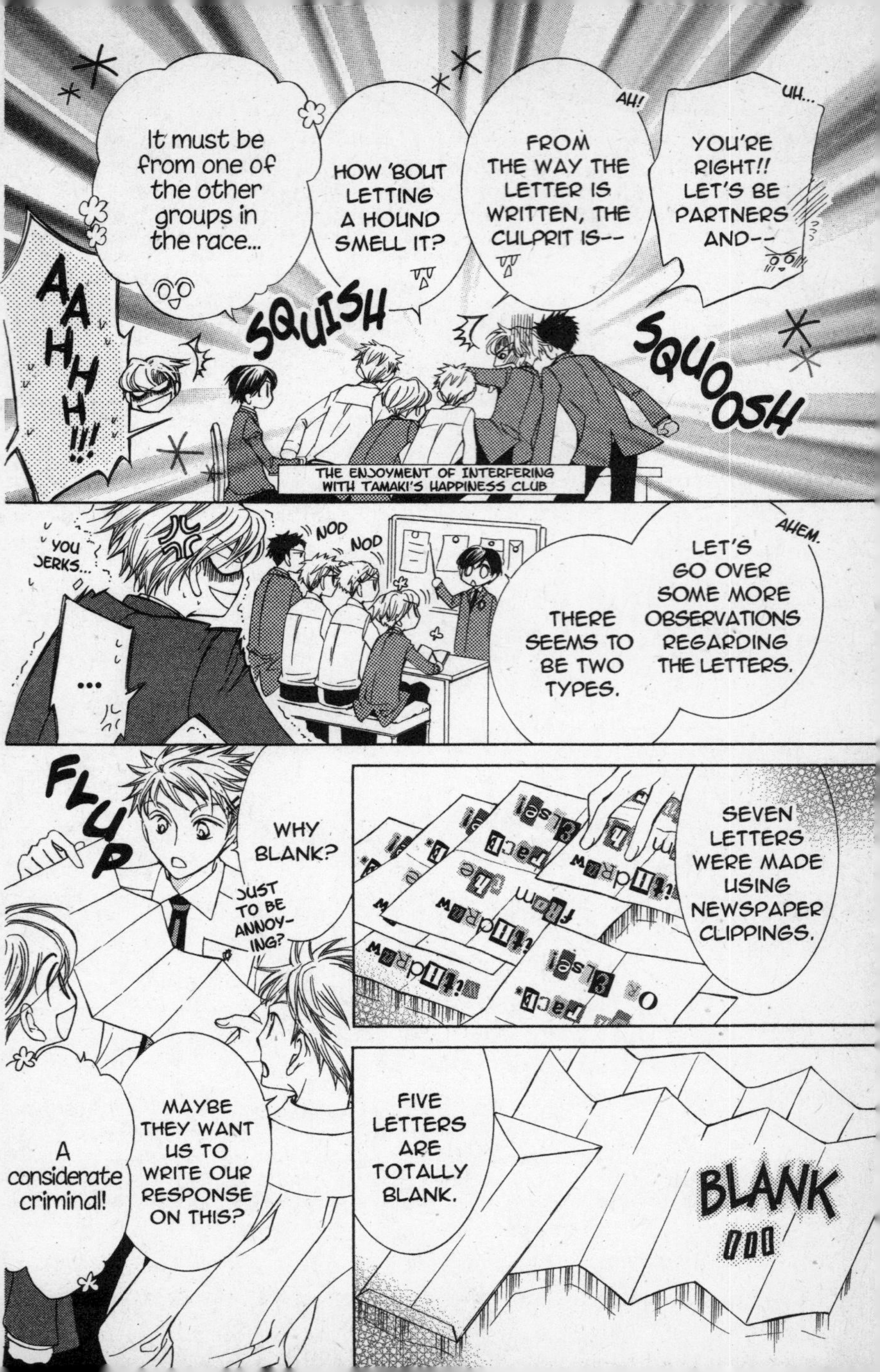
UH...
YOU'RE RIGHT!! LET'S BE PARTNERS AND--
AH!
FROM THE WAY THE LETTER IS WRITTEN, THE CULPRIT IS--
HOW 'BOUT LETTING A HOUND SMELL IT?
It must be from one of the other groups in the race...
SQUOOSH
SQUISH
AAHHH!!!
THE ENJOYMENT OF INTERFERING WITH TAMAKI'S HAPPINESS CLUB
AHEM.
LET'S GO OVER SOME MORE OBSERVATIONS REGARDING THE LETTERS.
THERE SEEMS TO BE TWO TYPES.
NOD
NOD
YOU JERKS...
...
SEVEN LETTERS WERE MADE USING NEWSPAPER CLIPPINGS.
BLANK
FIVE LETTERS ARE TOTALLY BLANK.
FLUP
WHY BLANK?
JUST TO BE ANNOYING?
MAYBE THEY WANT US TO WRITE OUR RESPONSE ON THIS?
A considerate criminal!

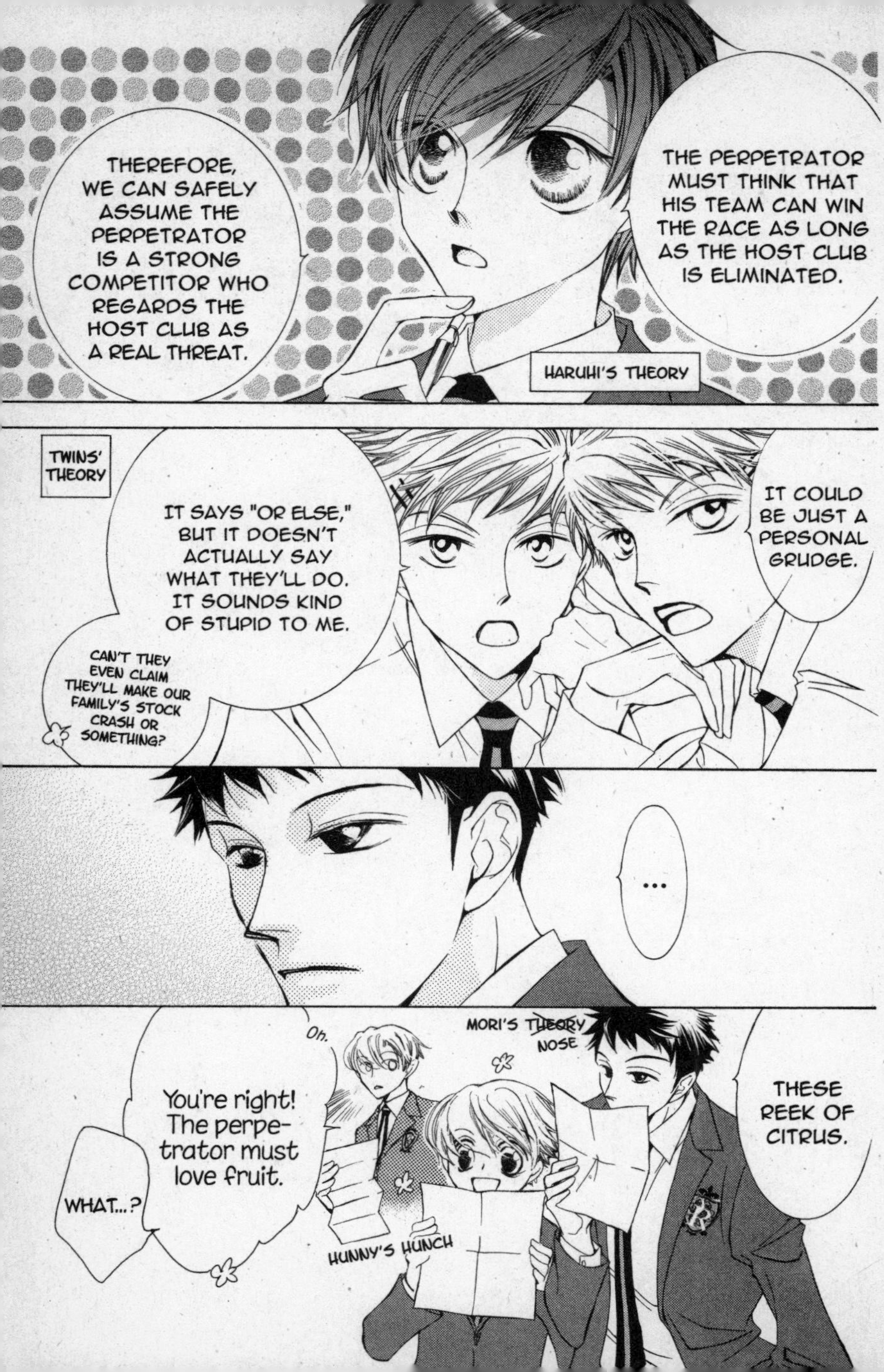

THE PERPETRATOR MUST THINK THAT HIS TEAM CAN WIN THE RACE AS LONG AS THE HOST CLUB IS ELIMINATED.
THEREFORE, WE CAN SAFELY ASSUME THE PERPETRATOR IS A STRONG COMPETITOR WHO REGARDS THE HOST CLUB AS A REAL THREAT.
HARUHI'S THEORY
IT COULD BE JUST A PERSONAL GRUDGE.
TWINS' THEORY
IT SAYS "OR ELSE," BUT IT DOESN'T ACTUALLY SAY WHAT THEY'LL DO. IT SOUNDS KIND OF STUPID TO ME.
CAN'T THEY EVEN CLAIM THEY'LL MAKE OUR FAMILY'S STOCK CRASH OR SOMETHING?
...
THESE REEK OF CITRUS.
MORI'S ~~THEORY~~ NOSE
Oh.
You're right! The perpe-trator must love fruit.
HUNNY'S HUNCH
WHAT...?

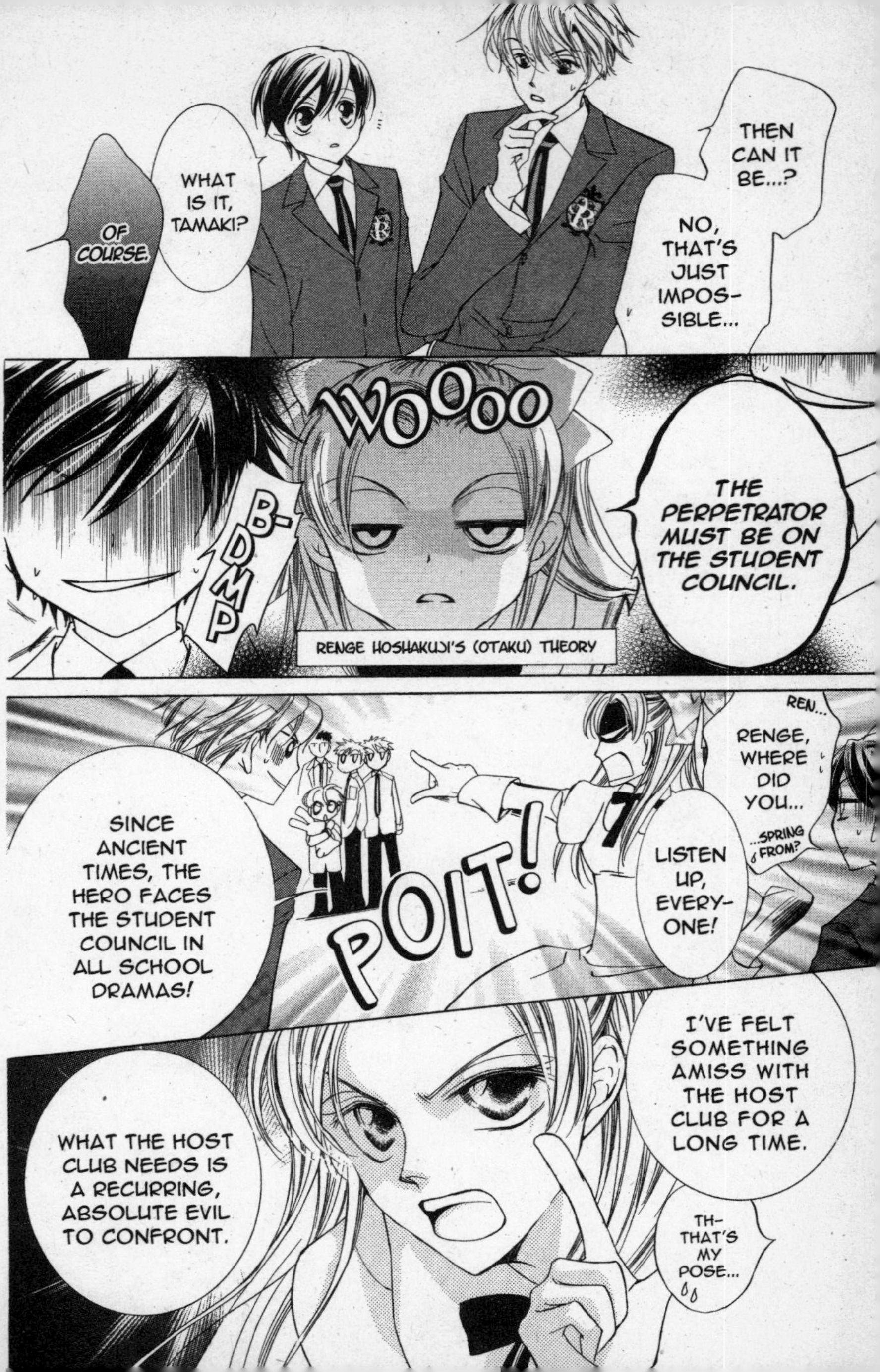
THEN CAN IT BE...?
NO, THAT'S JUST IMPOS-SIBLE...
WHAT IS IT, TAMAKI?
OF COURSE.
THE PERPETRATOR MUST BE ON THE STUDENT COUNCIL.
WOOOO
B-DMP
RENGE HOSHAKUJI'S (OTAKU) THEORY
REN...
RENGE, WHERE DID YOU...
...SPRING FROM?
LISTEN UP, EVERY-ONE!
POIT!
SINCE ANCIENT TIMES, THE HERO FACES THE STUDENT COUNCIL IN ALL SCHOOL DRAMAS!
I'VE FELT SOMETHING AMISS WITH THE HOST CLUB FOR A LONG TIME.
TH- THAT'S MY POSE...
WHAT THE HOST CLUB NEEDS IS A RECURRING, ABSOLUTE EVIL TO CONFRONT.

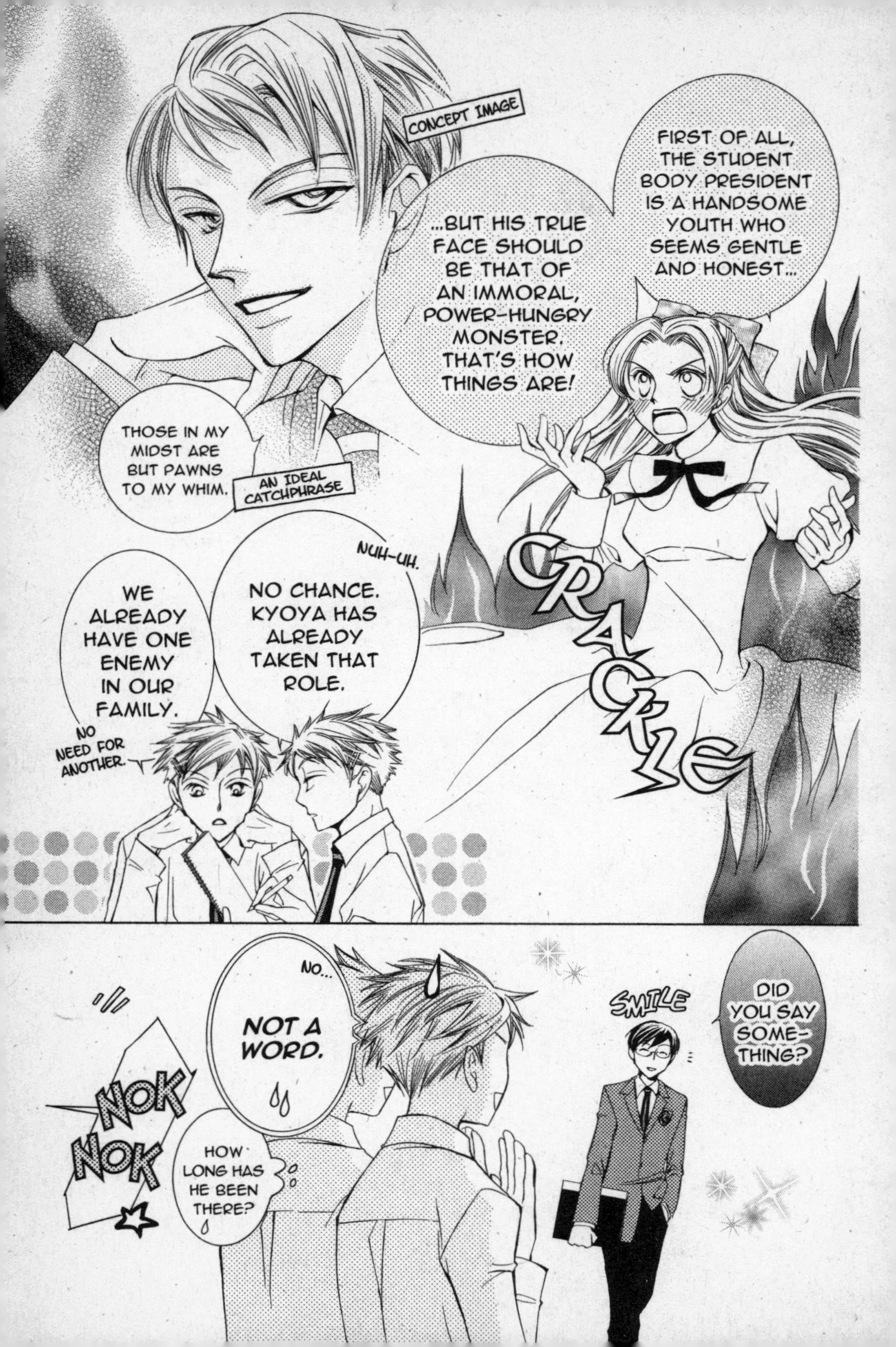
FIRST OF ALL, THE STUDENT BODY PRESIDENT IS A HANDSOME YOUTH WHO SEEMS GENTLE AND HONEST...
...BUT HIS TRUE FACE SHOULD BE THAT OF AN IMMORAL, POWER-HUNGRY MONSTER. THAT'S HOW THINGS ARE!
CONCEPT IMAGE
THOSE IN MY MIDST ARE BUT PAWNS TO MY WHIM.
AN IDEAL CATCHPHRASE
CRACKLE
NUH-UH.
NO CHANCE. KYOYA HAS ALREADY TAKEN THAT ROLE.
WE ALREADY HAVE ONE ENEMY IN OUR FAMILY.
NO NEED FOR ANOTHER.
DID YOU SAY SOME-THING?
SMILE
NO...
NOT A WORD.
HOW LONG HAS HE BEEN THERE?
NOK NOK

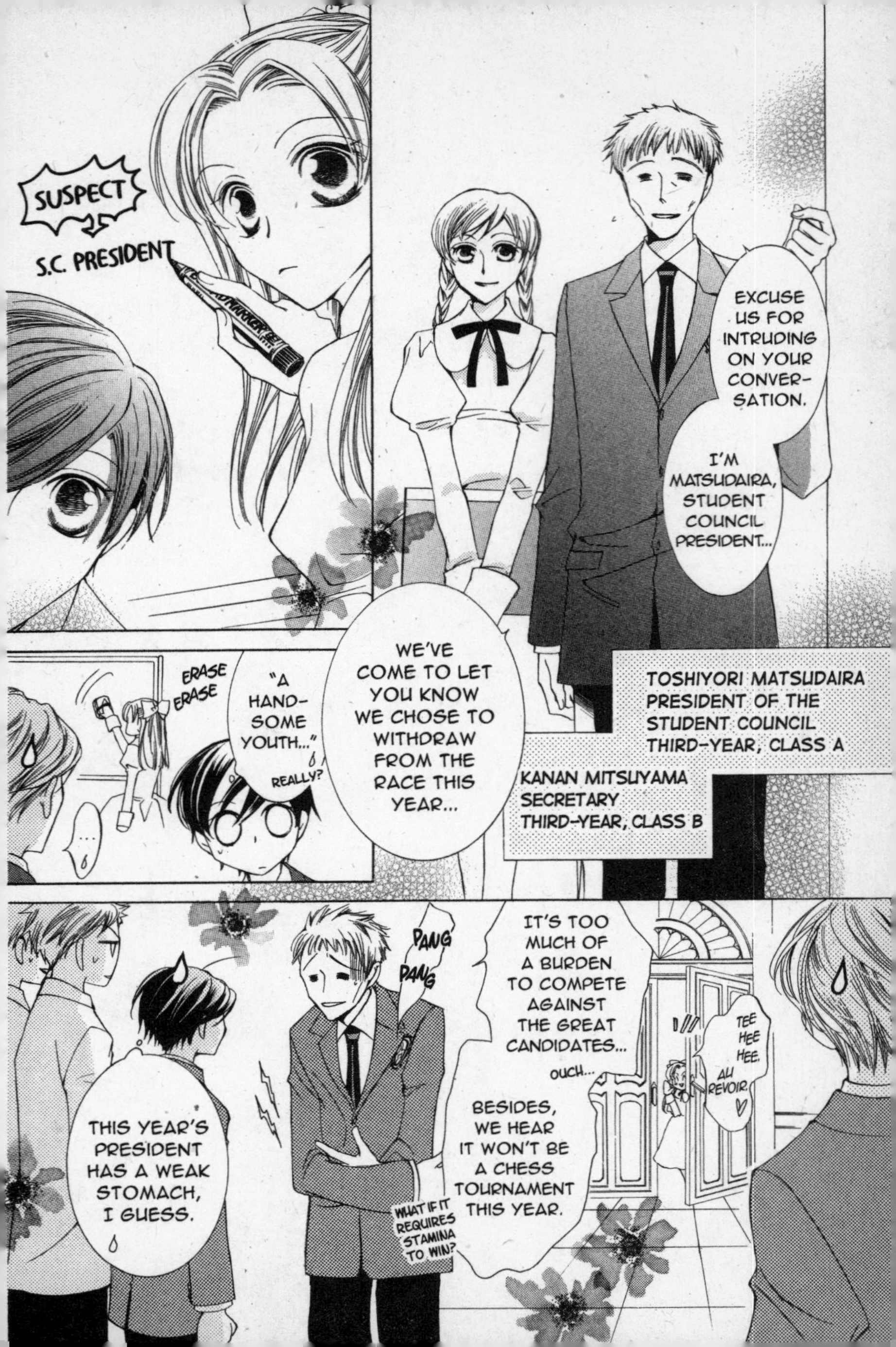
EXCUSE US FOR INTRUDING ON YOUR CONVERSATION.
I'M MATSUDAIRA, STUDENT COUNCIL PRESIDENT...
TOSHIYORI MATSUDAIRA PRESIDENT OF THE STUDENT COUNCIL THIRD-YEAR, CLASS A
KANAN MITSUYAMA SECRETARY THIRD-YEAR, CLASS B
WE'VE COME TO LET YOU KNOW WE CHOSE TO WITHDRAW FROM THE RACE THIS YEAR...
SUSPECT
S.C. PRESIDENT
"A HAND-SOME YOUTH..."
ERASE ERASE
REALLY?
...
IT'S TOO MUCH OF A BURDEN TO COMPETE AGAINST THE GREAT CANDIDATES...
OUCH...
TEE HEE HEE.
AU REVOIR
BESIDES, WE HEAR IT WON'T BE A CHESS TOURNAMENT THIS YEAR.
WHAT IF IT REQUIRES STAMINA TO WIN?
PANG
PANG
THIS YEAR'S PRESIDENT HAS A WEAK STOMACH, I GUESS.

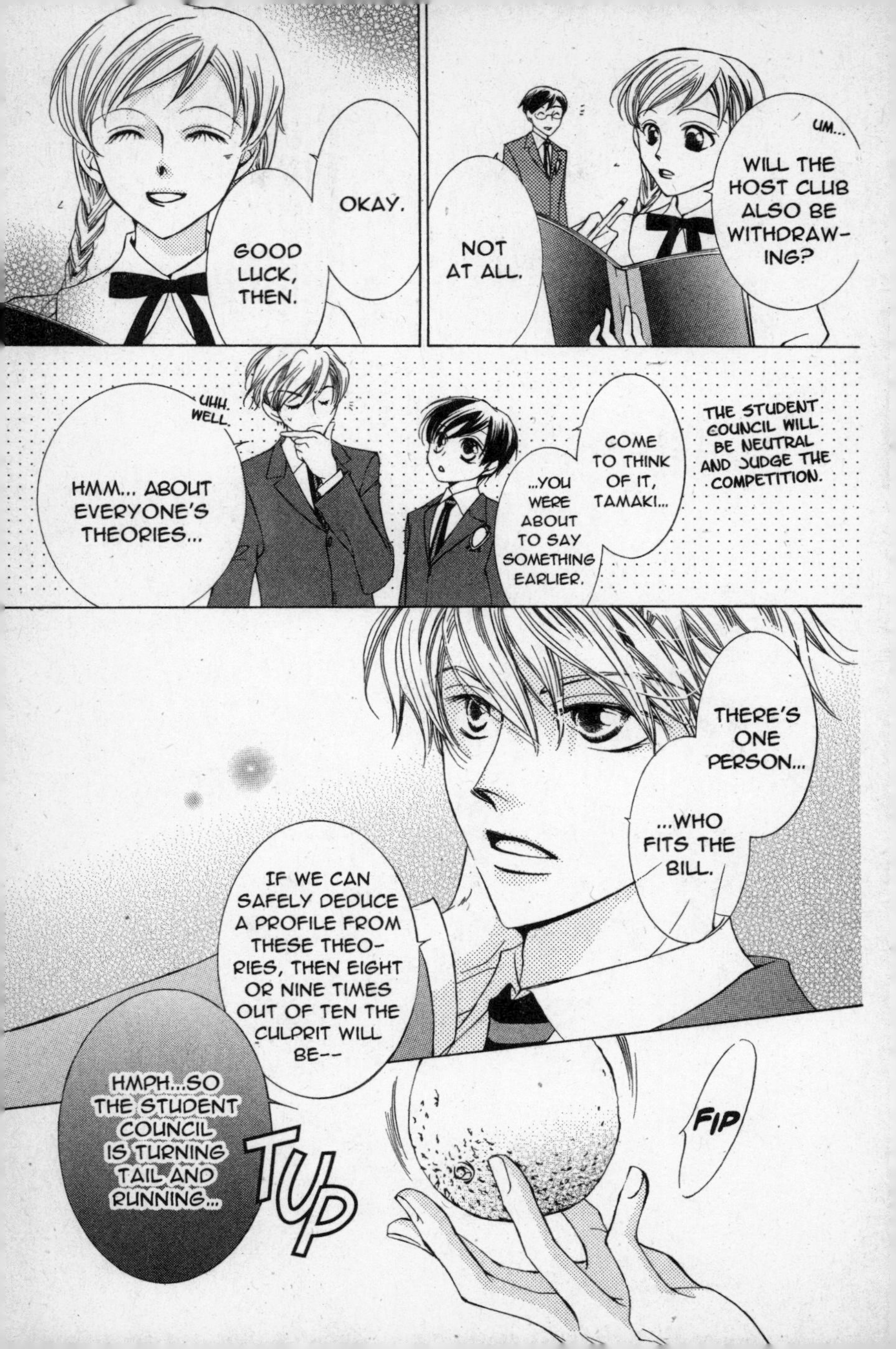
UM...
WILL THE HOST CLUB ALSO BE WITHDRAW-ING?
NOT AT ALL.
OKAY.
GOOD LUCK, THEN.
THE STUDENT COUNCIL WILL BE NEUTRAL AND JUDGE THE COMPETITION.
COME TO THINK OF IT, TAMAKI...
...YOU WERE ABOUT TO SAY SOMETHING EARLIER.
UHH. WELL.
HMM... ABOUT EVERYONE'S THEORIES...
THERE'S ONE PERSON...
...WHO FITS THE BILL.
IF WE CAN SAFELY DEDUCE A PROFILE FROM THESE THEO-RIES, THEN EIGHT OR NINE TIMES OUT OF TEN THE CULPRIT WILL BE--
FIP
TUP
HMPH...SO THE STUDENT COUNCIL IS TURNING TAIL AND RUNNING...

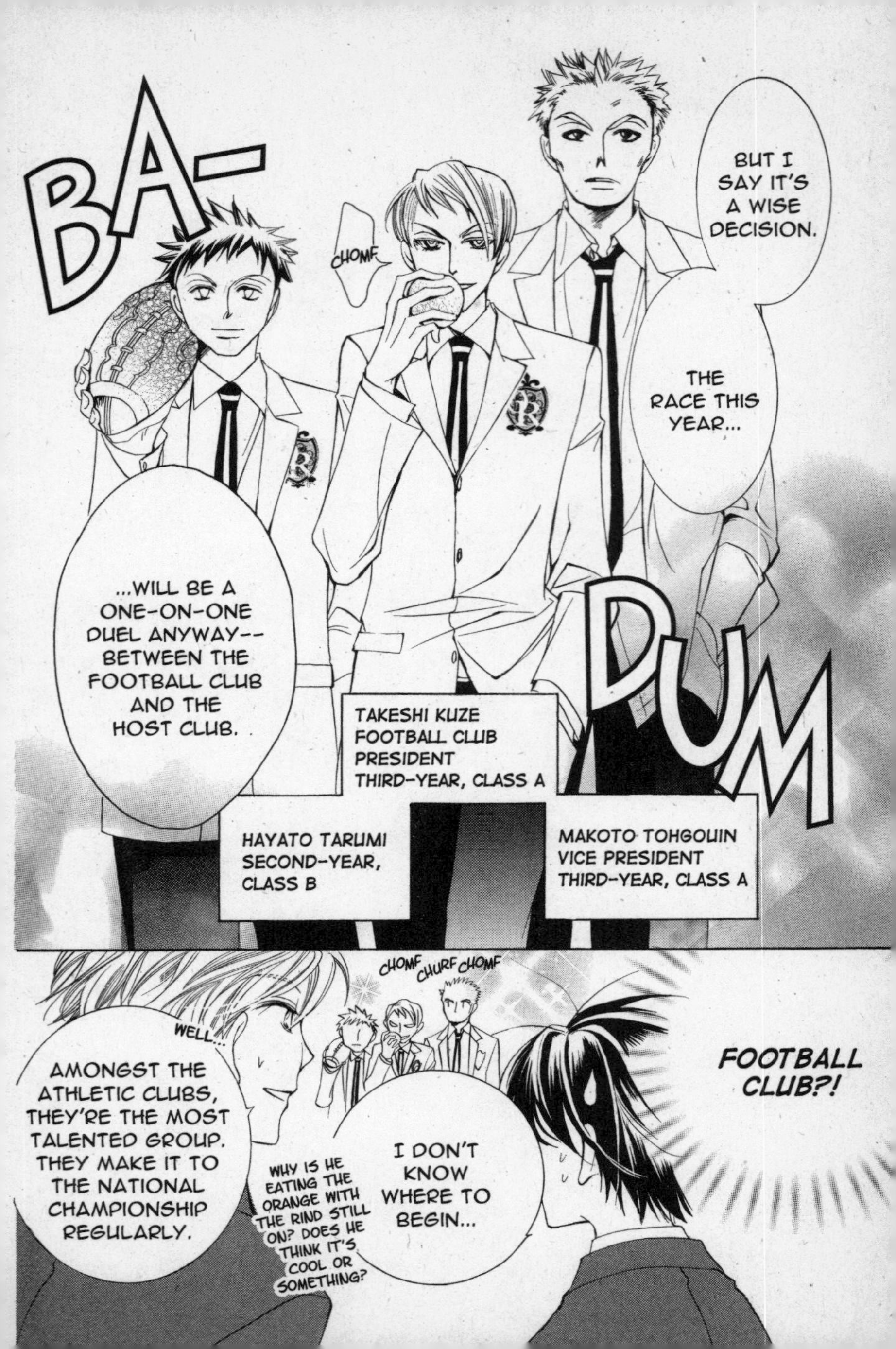
BUT I SAY IT'S A WISE DECISION.
THE RACE THIS YEAR...
CHOMF
BA-
DUM
...WILL BE A ONE-ON-ONE DUEL ANYWAY-- BETWEEN THE FOOTBALL CLUB AND THE HOST CLUB.
TAKESHI KUZE FOOTBALL CLUB PRESIDENT THIRD-YEAR, CLASS A
MAKOTO TOHGOUIN VICE PRESIDENT THIRD-YEAR, CLASS A
HAYATO TARUMI SECOND-YEAR, CLASS B
FOOTBALL CLUB?!
CHOMF CHURF CHOMF
I DON'T KNOW WHERE TO BEGIN...
WHY IS HE EATING THE ORANGE WITH THE RIND STILL ON? DOES HE THINK IT'S COOL OR SOMETHING?
WELL...
AMONGST THE ATHLETIC CLUBS, THEY'RE THE MOST TALENTED GROUP. THEY MAKE IT TO THE NATIONAL CHAMPIONSHIP REGULARLY.

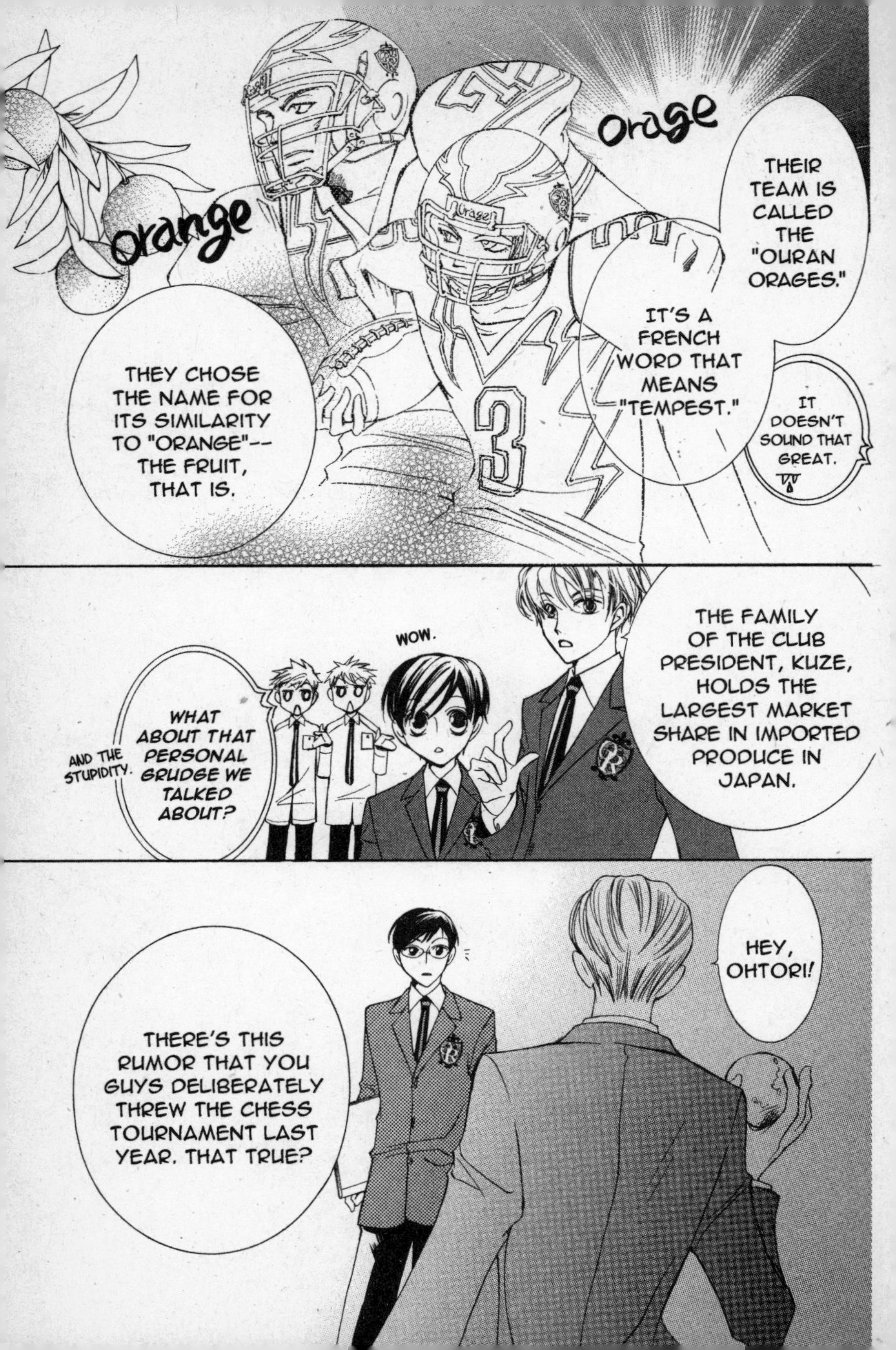
Orage
THEIR TEAM IS CALLED THE "OURAN ORAGES."
IT'S A FRENCH WORD THAT MEANS "TEMPEST."
IT DOESN'T SOUND THAT GREAT.
Orange
THEY CHOSE THE NAME FOR ITS SIMILARITY TO "ORANGE"-- THE FRUIT, THAT IS.
THE FAMILY OF THE CLUB PRESIDENT, KUZE, HOLDS THE LARGEST MARKET SHARE IN IMPORTED PRODUCE IN JAPAN.
WOW.
WHAT ABOUT THAT PERSONAL GRUDGE WE TALKED ABOUT?
AND THE STUPIDITY.
HEY, OHTORI!
THERE'S THIS RUMOR THAT YOU GUYS DELIBERATELY THREW THE CHESS TOURNAMENT LAST YEAR. THAT TRUE?

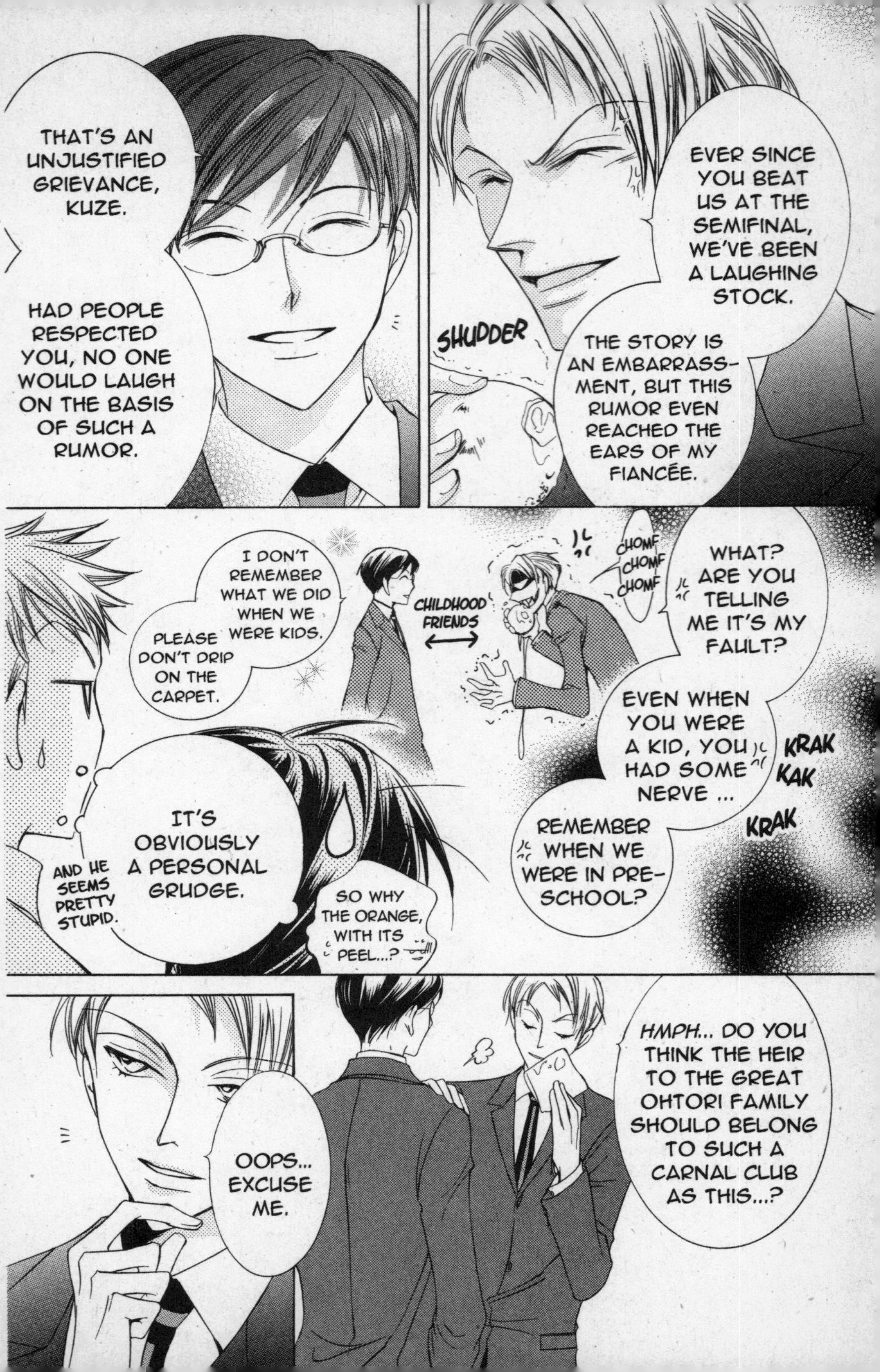
EVER SINCE YOU BEAT US AT THE SEMIFINAL, WE'VE BEEN A LAUGHING STOCK.
SHUDDER
THE STORY IS AN EMBARRASS-MENT, BUT THIS RUMOR EVEN REACHED THE EARS OF MY FIANCÉE.
THAT'S AN UNJUSTIFIED GRIEVANCE, KUZE.
HAD PEOPLE RESPECTED YOU, NO ONE WOULD LAUGH ON THE BASIS OF SUCH A RUMOR.
CHOMF CHOMF CHOMF
WHAT? ARE YOU TELLING ME IT'S MY FAULT?
EVEN WHEN YOU WERE A KID, YOU HAD SOME NERVE ...
KRAK KAK
KRAK
REMEMBER WHEN WE WERE IN PRE-SCHOOL?
I DON'T REMEMBER WHAT WE DID WHEN WE WERE KIDS.
CHILDHOOD FRIENDS
PLEASE DON'T DRIP ON THE CARPET.
SO WHY THE ORANGE, WITH ITS PEEL...?
IT'S OBVIOUSLY A PERSONAL GRUDGE.
AND HE SEEMS PRETTY STUPID.
HMPH... DO YOU THINK THE HEIR TO THE GREAT OHTORI FAMILY SHOULD BELONG TO SUCH A CARNAL CLUB AS THIS...?
OOPS... EXCUSE ME.

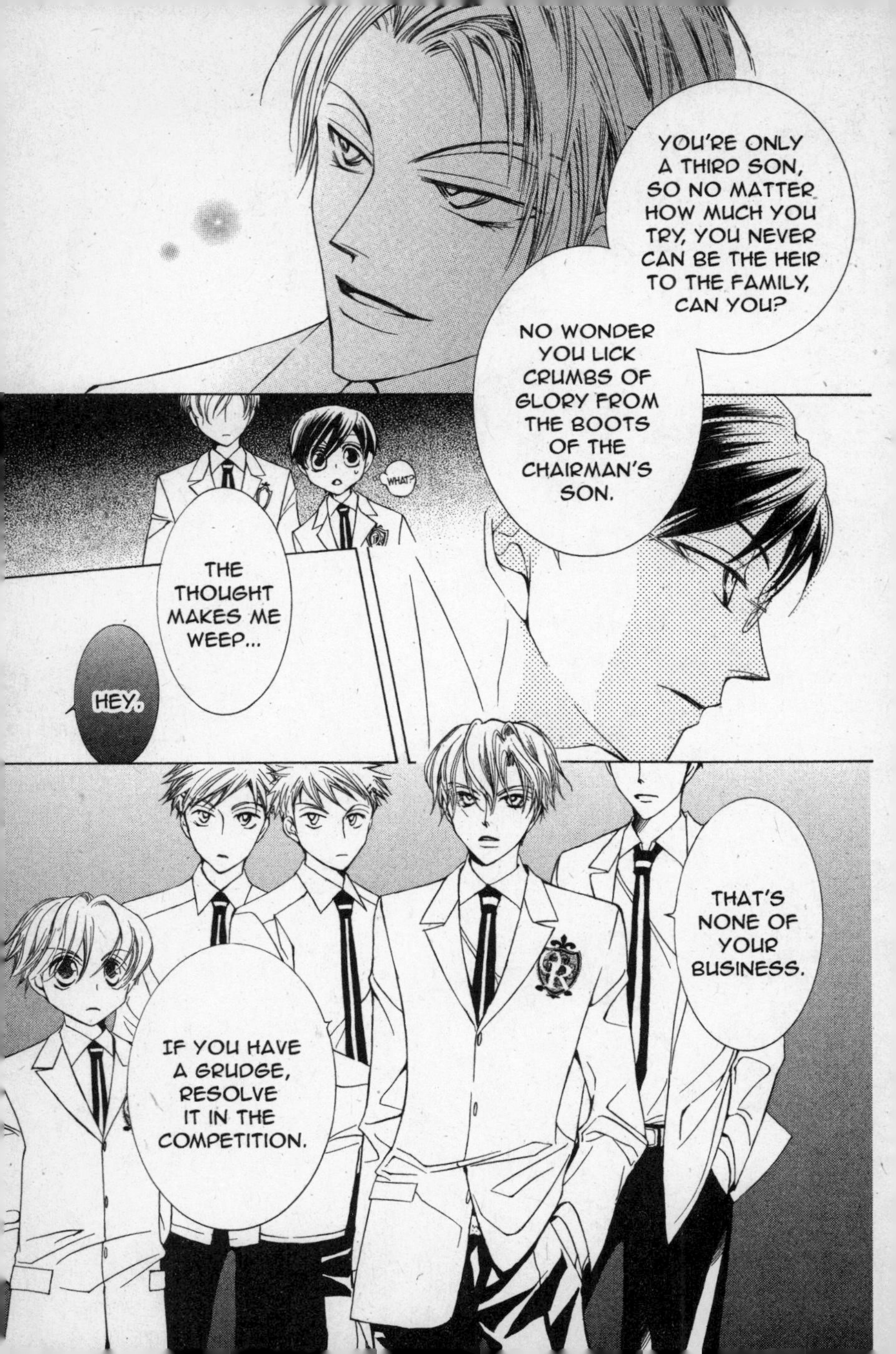

YOU'RE ONLY A THIRD SON, SO NO MATTER HOW MUCH YOU TRY, YOU NEVER CAN BE THE HEIR TO THE FAMILY, CAN YOU?
NO WONDER YOU LICK CRUMBS OF GLORY FROM THE BOOTS OF THE CHAIRMAN'S SON.
THE THOUGHT MAKES ME WEEP...
WHAT?
HEY.
THAT'S NONE OF YOUR BUSINESS.
IF YOU HAVE A GRUDGE, RESOLVE IT IN THE COMPETITION.

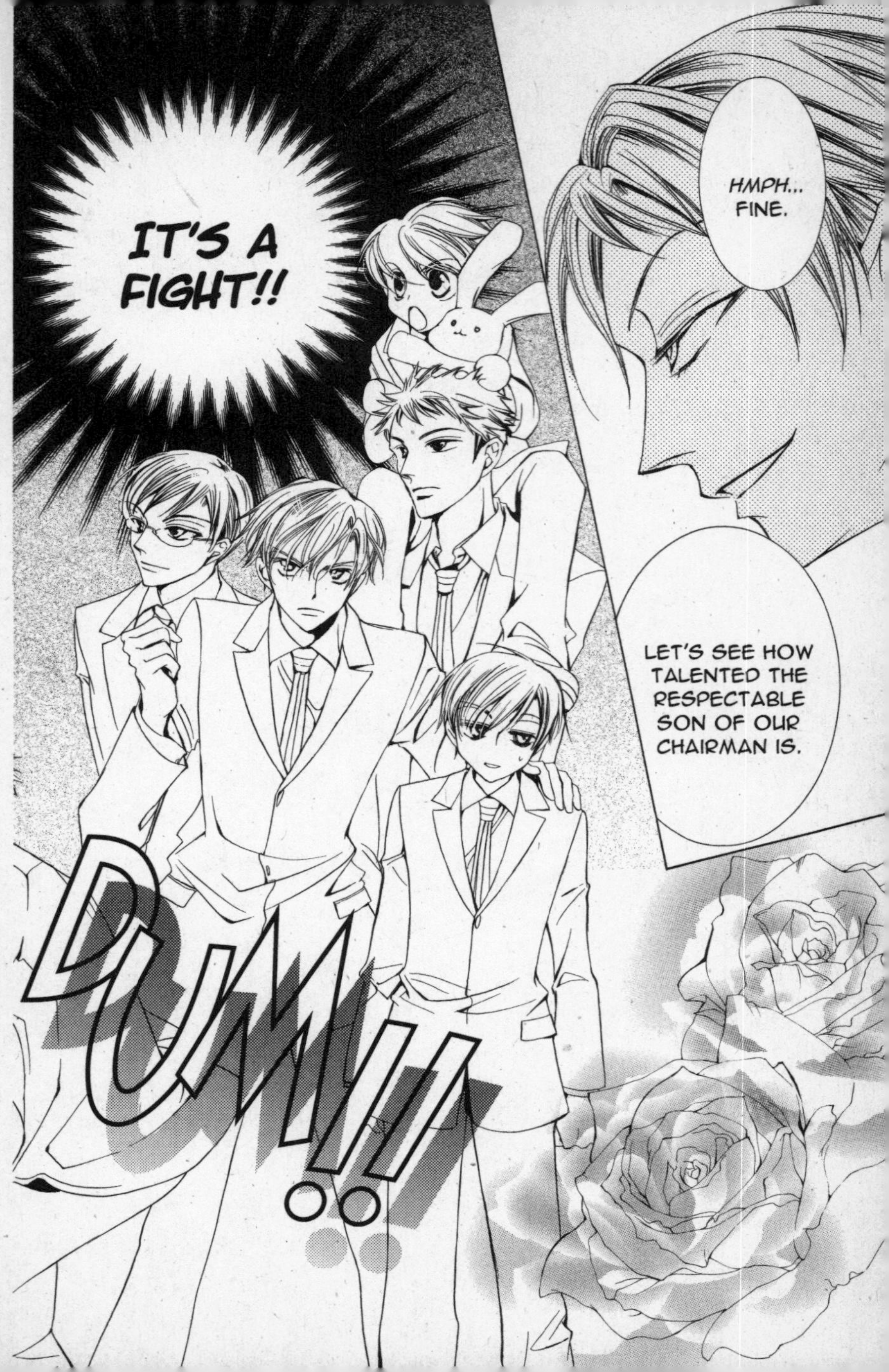
HMPH... FINE.
LET'S SEE HOW TALENTED THE RESPECTABLE SON OF OUR CHAIRMAN IS.
IT'S A FIGHT!!
DUN!!

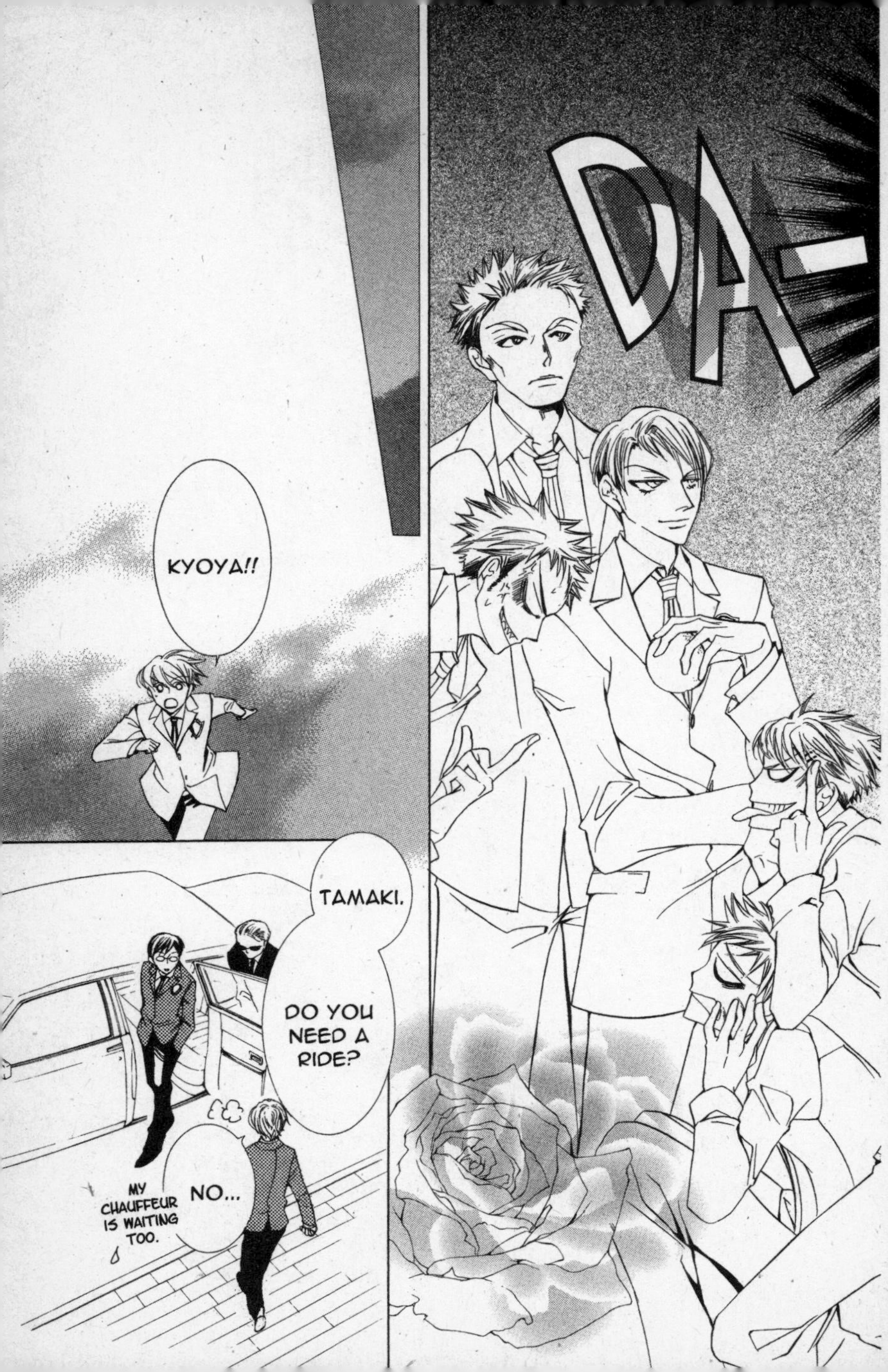
DA-
KYOYA!!
TAMAKI.
DO YOU NEED A RIDE?
NO...
MY CHAUFFEUR IS WAITING TOO.

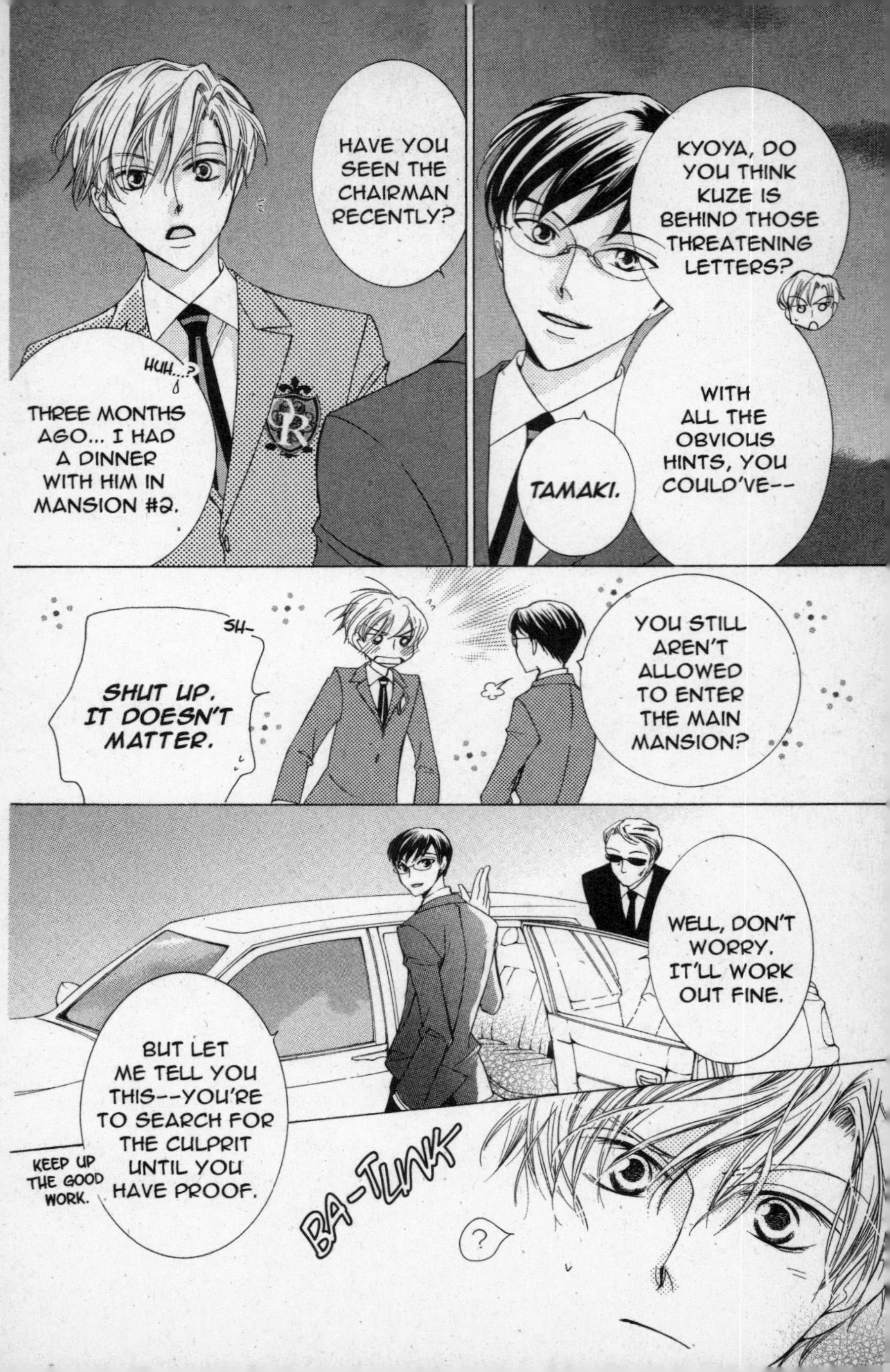
KYOYA, DO YOU THINK KUZE IS BEHIND THOSE THREATENING LETTERS?
WITH ALL THE OBVIOUS HINTS, YOU COULD'VE--
TAMAKI.
HAVE YOU SEEN THE CHAIRMAN RECENTLY?
HUH...?
THREE MONTHS AGO... I HAD A DINNER WITH HIM IN MANSION #2.
YOU STILL AREN'T ALLOWED TO ENTER THE MAIN MANSION?
SH-
SHUT UP. IT DOESN'T MATTER.
WELL, DON'T WORRY. IT'LL WORK OUT FINE.
BUT LET ME TELL YOU THIS--YOU'RE TO SEARCH FOR THE CULPRIT UNTIL YOU HAVE PROOF.
KEEP UP THE GOOD WORK.
BA-TUNK
?

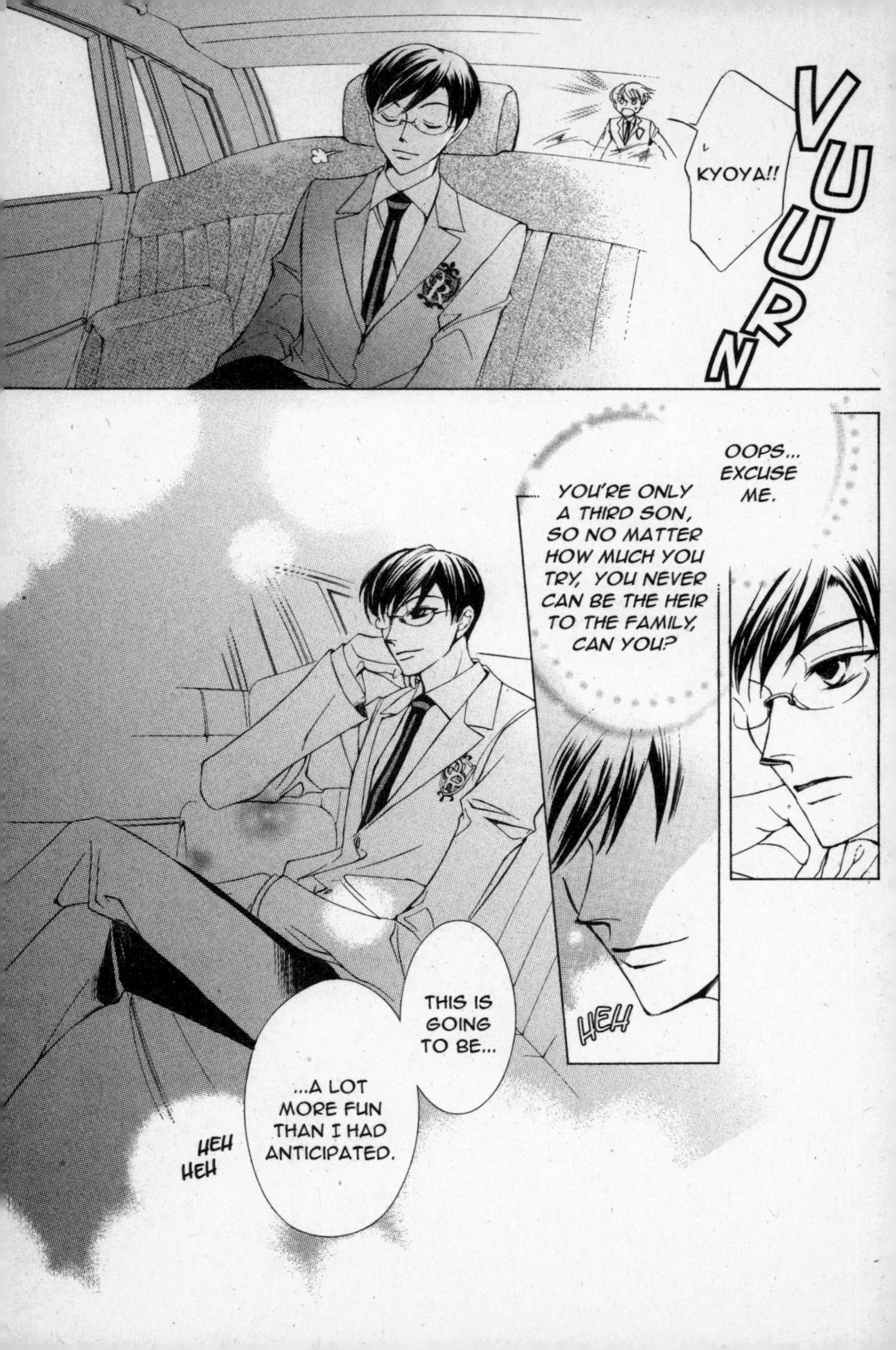
VUURN
KYOYA!!
OOPS... EXCUSE ME.
YOU'RE ONLY A THIRD SON, SO NO MATTER HOW MUCH YOU TRY, YOU NEVER CAN BE THE HEIR TO THE FAMILY, CAN YOU?
HEH
THIS IS GOING TO BE...
...A LOT MORE FUN THAN I HAD ANTICIPATED.
HEH HEH

Q: Eating Order

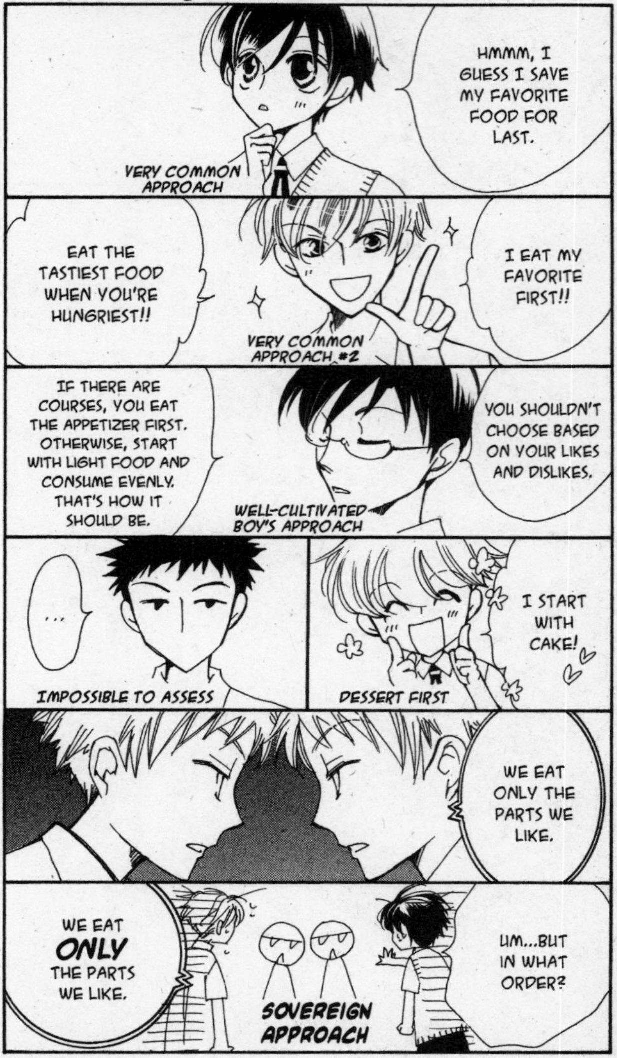
HMMM, I GUESS I SAVE MY FAVORITE FOOD FOR LAST.
VERY COMMON APPROACH
I EAT MY FAVORITE FIRST!!
EAT THE TASTIEST FOOD WHEN YOU'RE HUNGRIEST!!
VERY COMMON APPROACH #2
YOU SHOULDN'T CHOOSE BASED ON YOUR LIKES AND DISLIKES.
IF THERE ARE COURSES, YOU EAT THE APPETIZER FIRST. OTHERWISE, START WITH LIGHT FOOD AND CONSUME EVENLY. THAT'S HOW IT SHOULD BE.
WELL-CULTIVATED BOY'S APPROACH
I START WITH CAKE!
DESSERT FIRST
...
IMPOSSIBLE TO ASSESS
WE EAT ONLY THE PARTS WE LIKE.
UM...BUT IN WHAT ORDER?
WE EAT ONLY THE PARTS WE LIKE.
SOVEREIGN APPROACH

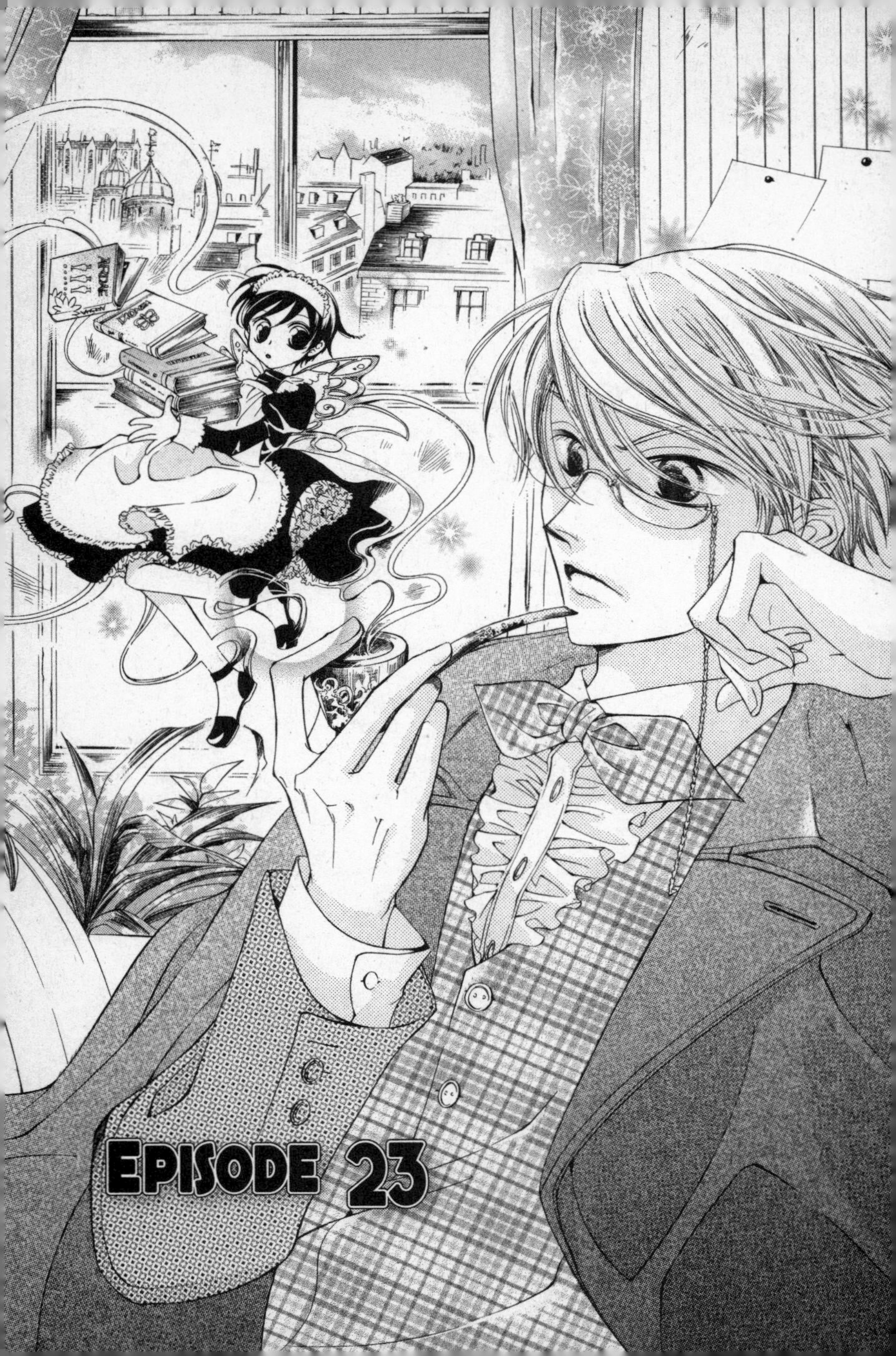
EPISODE 23

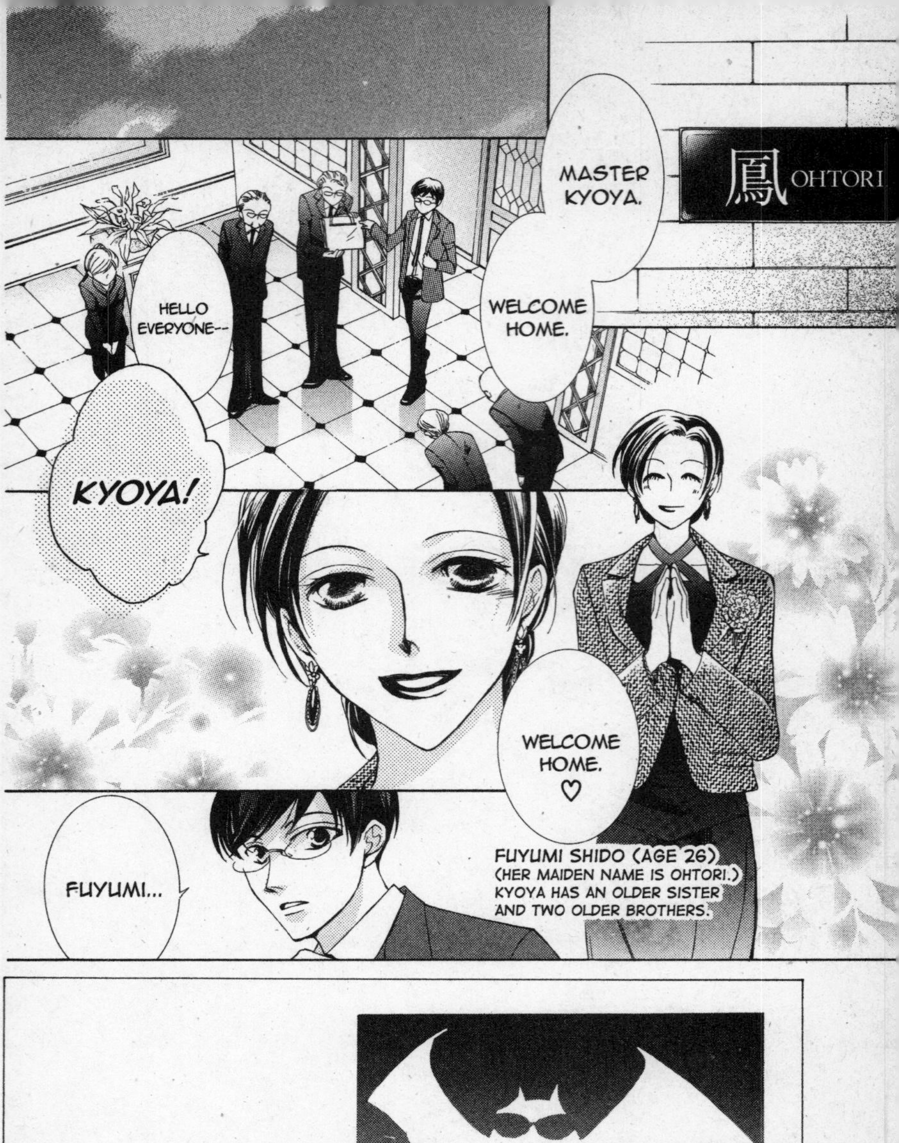
鳳 OHTORI
MASTER KYOYA.
WELCOME HOME.
HELLO EVERYONE--
KYOYA!
WELCOME HOME. ♡
FUYUMI SHIDO (AGE 26) (HER MAIDEN NAME IS OHTORI.) KYOYA HAS AN OLDER SISTER AND TWO OLDER BROTHERS.
FUYUMI...

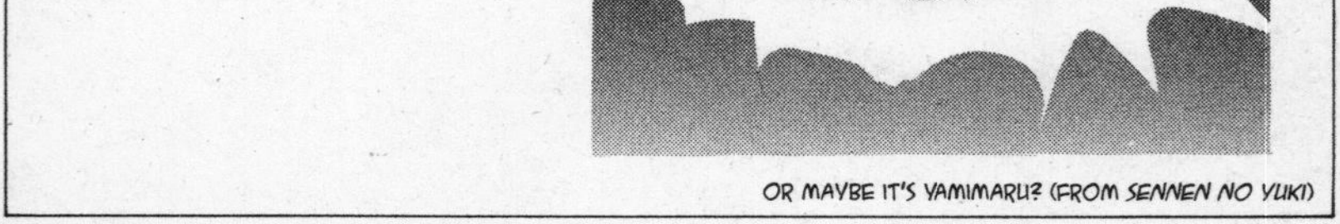

OR MAYBE IT'S YAMIMARU? (FROM SENNEN NO YUKI)

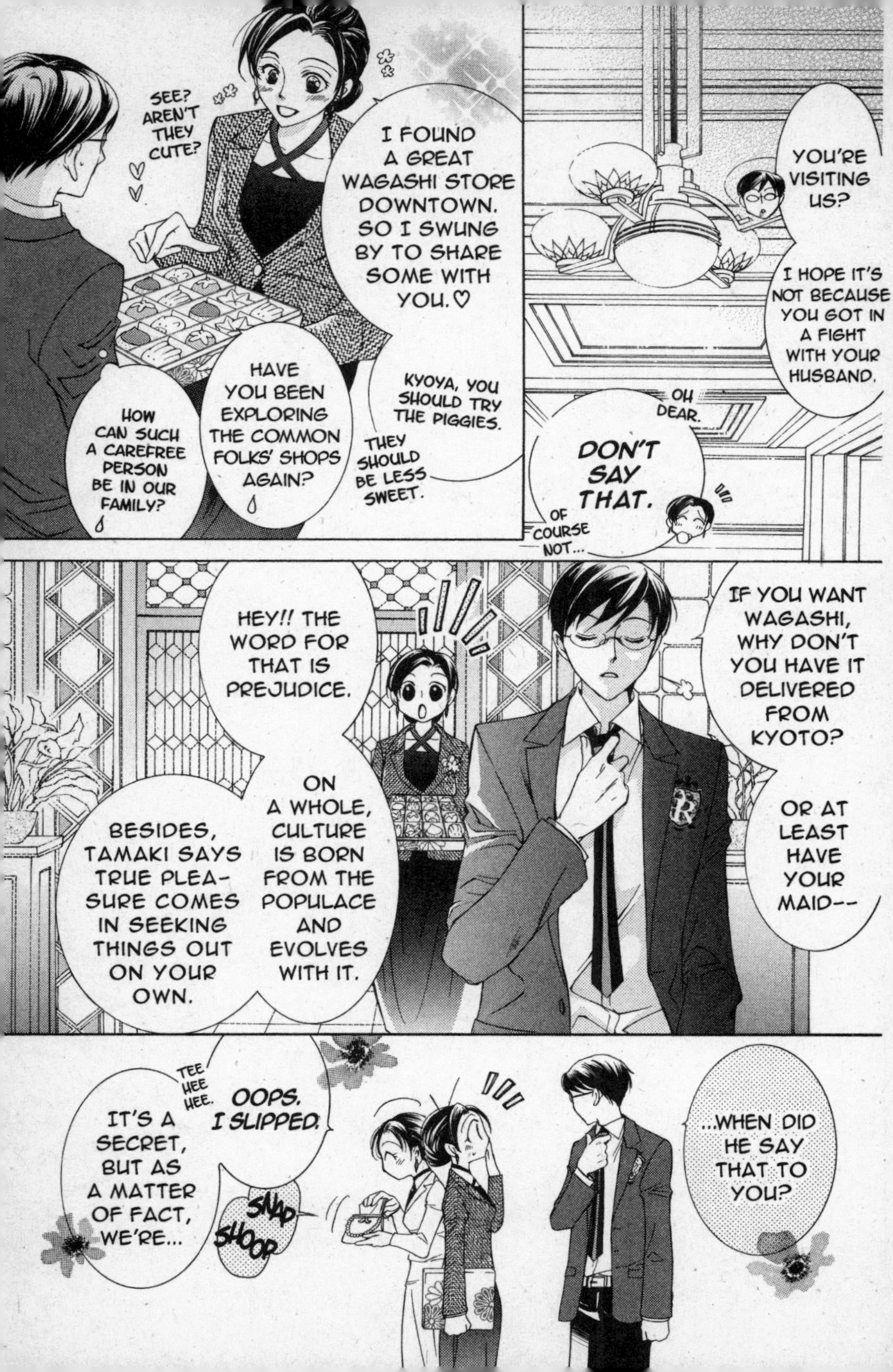

YOU'RE VISITING US?
I HOPE IT'S NOT BECAUSE YOU GOT IN A FIGHT WITH YOUR HUSBAND.
OH DEAR.
DON'T SAY THAT.
OF COURSE NOT...
I FOUND A GREAT WAGASHI STORE DOWNTOWN. SO I SWUNG BY TO SHARE SOME WITH YOU.♡
SEE? AREN'T THEY CUTE?
KYOYA, YOU SHOULD TRY THE PIGGIES.
THEY SHOULD BE LESS SWEET.
HAVE YOU BEEN EXPLORING THE COMMON FOLKS' SHOPS AGAIN?
HOW CAN SUCH A CAREFREE PERSON BE IN OUR FAMILY?
IF YOU WANT WAGASHI, WHY DON'T YOU HAVE IT DELIVERED FROM KYOTO?
OR AT LEAST HAVE YOUR MAID--
HEY!! THE WORD FOR THAT IS PREJUDICE.
ON A WHOLE, CULTURE IS BORN FROM THE POPULACE AND EVOLVES WITH IT.
BESIDES, TAMAKI SAYS TRUE PLEA-SURE COMES IN SEEKING THINGS OUT ON YOUR OWN.
...WHEN DID HE SAY THAT TO YOU?
OOPS. I SLIPPED.
TEE HEE HEE.
SNAP
SHOOP
IT'S A SECRET, BUT AS A MATTER OF FACT, WE'RE...

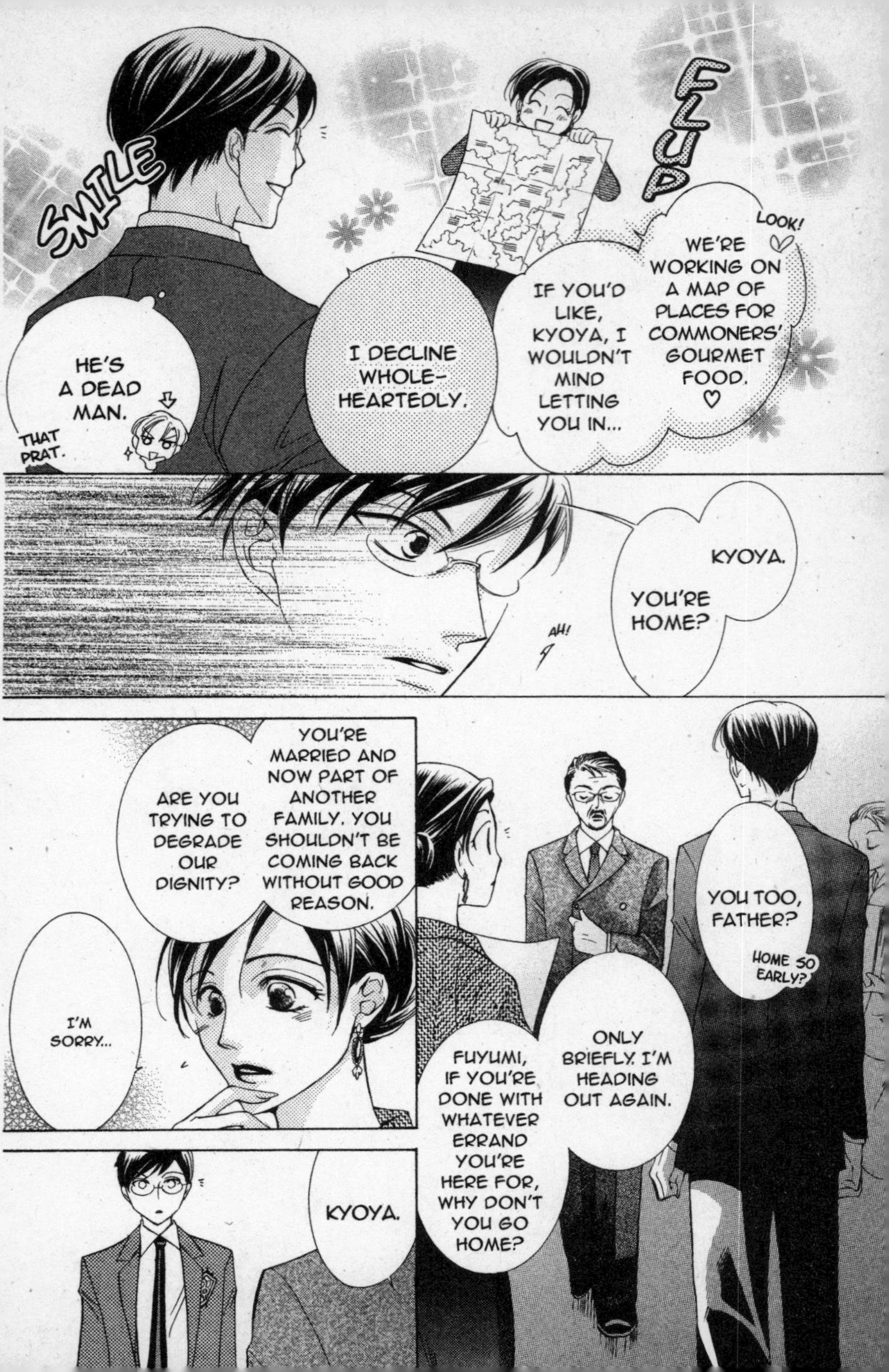
FLUD
LOOK!
WE'RE WORKING ON A MAP OF PLACES FOR COMMONERS' GOURMET FOOD. ♡
IF YOU'D LIKE, KYOYA, I WOULDN'T MIND LETTING YOU IN...
I DECLINE WHOLE-HEARTEDLY.
SMILE
HE'S A DEAD MAN.
THAT PRAT.
KYOYA.
YOU'RE HOME?
AH!
YOU TOO, FATHER?
HOME SO EARLY?
ONLY BRIEFLY. I'M HEADING OUT AGAIN.
FUYUMI, IF YOU'RE DONE WITH WHATEVER ERRAND YOU'RE HERE FOR, WHY DON'T YOU GO HOME?
YOU'RE MARRIED AND NOW PART OF ANOTHER FAMILY. YOU SHOULDN'T BE COMING BACK WITHOUT GOOD REASON.
ARE YOU TRYING TO DEGRADE OUR DIGNITY?
I'M SORRY...
KYOYA.

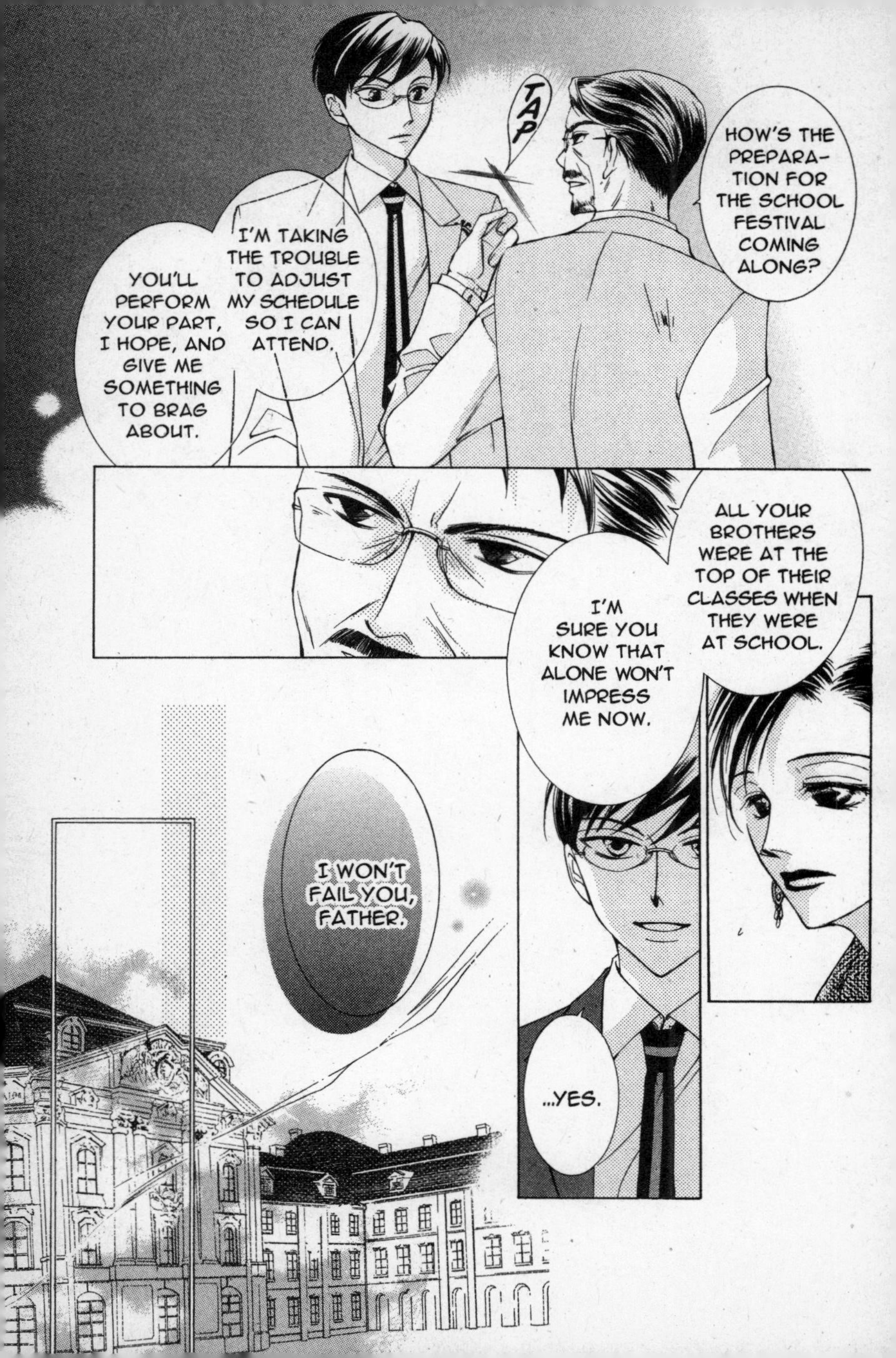
HOW'S THE PREPARATION FOR THE SCHOOL FESTIVAL COMING ALONG?
TAP
I'M TAKING THE TROUBLE TO ADJUST MY SCHEDULE SO I CAN ATTEND.
YOU'LL PERFORM YOUR PART, I HOPE, AND GIVE ME SOMETHING TO BRAG ABOUT.
ALL YOUR BROTHERS WERE AT THE TOP OF THEIR CLASSES WHEN THEY WERE AT SCHOOL.
I'M SURE YOU KNOW THAT ALONE WON'T IMPRESS ME NOW.
...YES.
I WON'T FAIL YOU, FATHER.

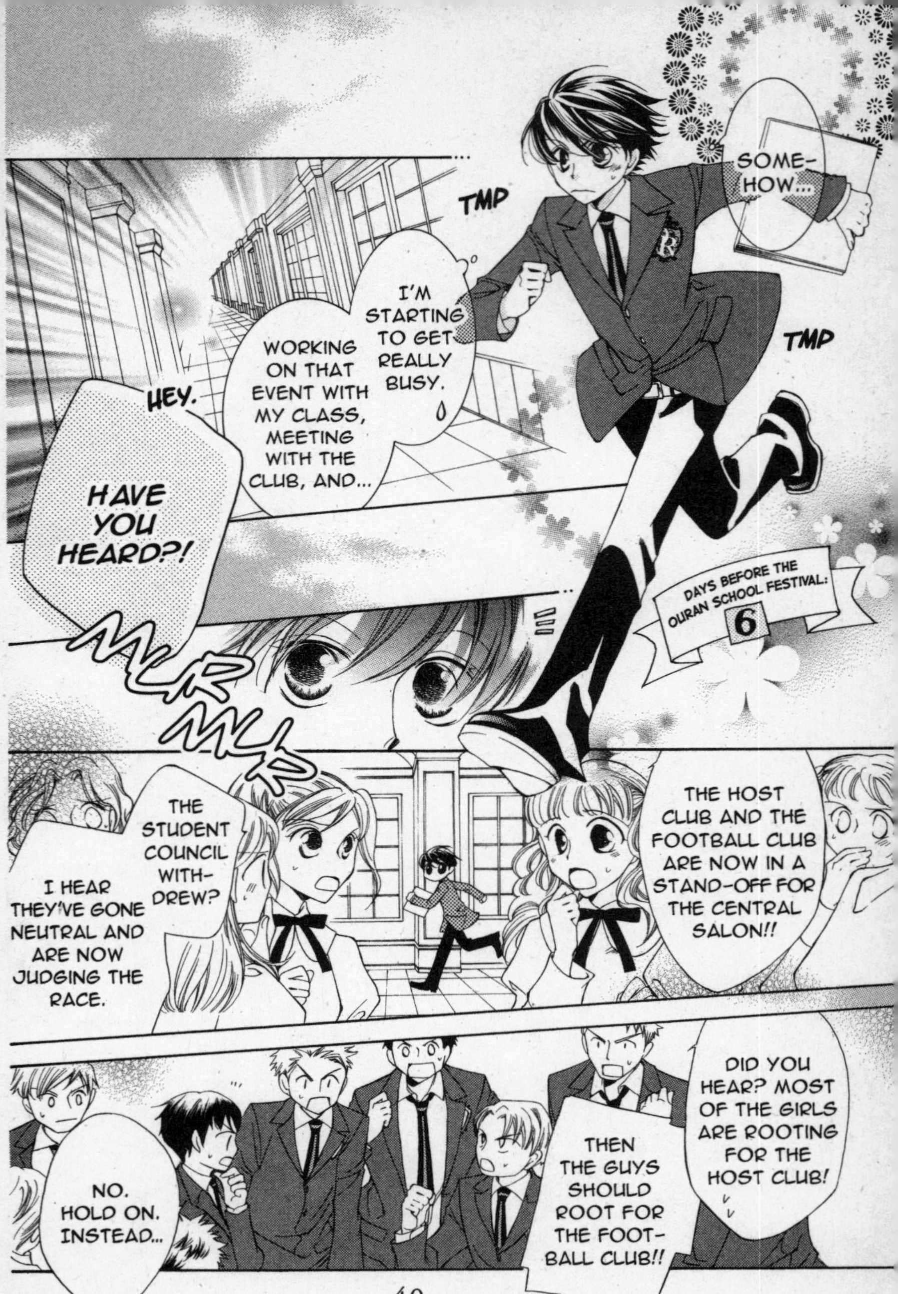
SOME-HOW...
TMP
I'M STARTING TO GET REALLY BUSY.
WORKING ON THAT EVENT WITH MY CLASS, MEETING WITH THE CLUB, AND...
TMP
HEY.
HAVE YOU HEARD?!
DAYS BEFORE THE OURAN SCHOOL FESTIVAL: 6
MUR MUR
THE HOST CLUB AND THE FOOTBALL CLUB ARE NOW IN A STAND-OFF FOR THE CENTRAL SALON!!
THE STUDENT COUNCIL WITH-DREW?
I HEAR THEY'VE GONE NEUTRAL AND ARE NOW JUDGING THE RACE.
DID YOU HEAR? MOST OF THE GIRLS ARE ROOTING FOR THE HOST CLUB!
THEN THE GUYS SHOULD ROOT FOR THE FOOT-BALL CLUB!!
NO. HOLD ON. INSTEAD...

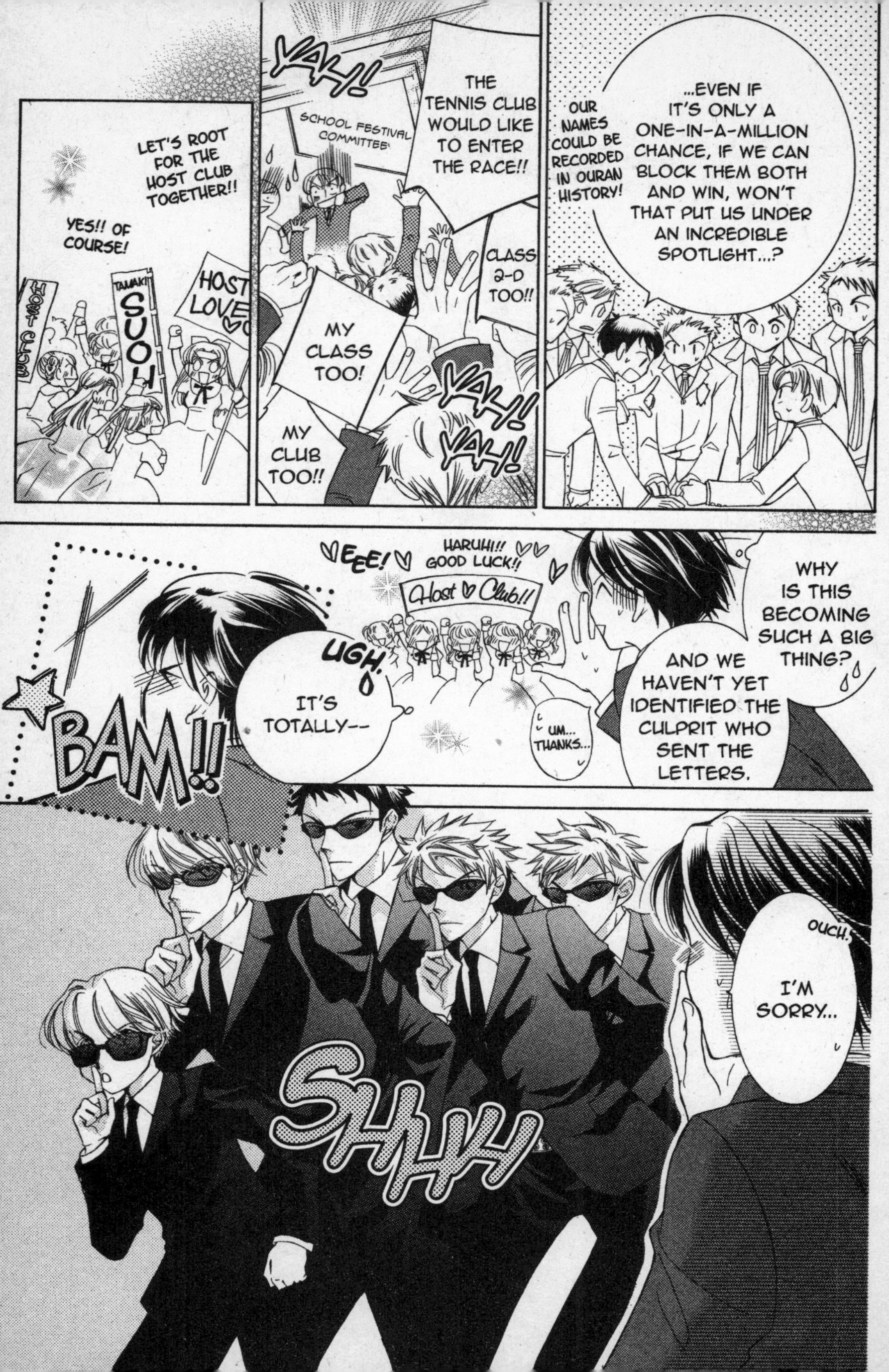
...EVEN IF IT'S ONLY A ONE-IN-A-MILLION CHANCE, IF WE CAN BLOCK THEM BOTH AND WIN, WON'T THAT PUT US UNDER AN INCREDIBLE SPOTLIGHT...?
OUR NAMES COULD BE RECORDED IN OURAN HISTORY!
YAH!
SCHOOL FESTIVAL COMMITTEE
THE TENNIS CLUB WOULD LIKE TO ENTER THE RACE!!
CLASS 2-D TOO!!
MY CLASS TOO!
YAH! YAH!
MY CLUB TOO!!
LET'S ROOT FOR THE HOST CLUB TOGETHER!!
YES!! OF COURSE!
HOST LOVE
TAMAKI SUOH
HOST CLUB
WHY IS THIS BECOMING SUCH A BIG THING?
AND WE HAVEN'T YET IDENTIFIED THE CULPRIT WHO SENT THE LETTERS.
HARUHI!! GOOD LUCK!!
EEE!
Host Club!!
UM... THANKS...
UGH.
IT'S TOTALLY--
BAM!!
OUCH.
I'M SORRY...
SHHH

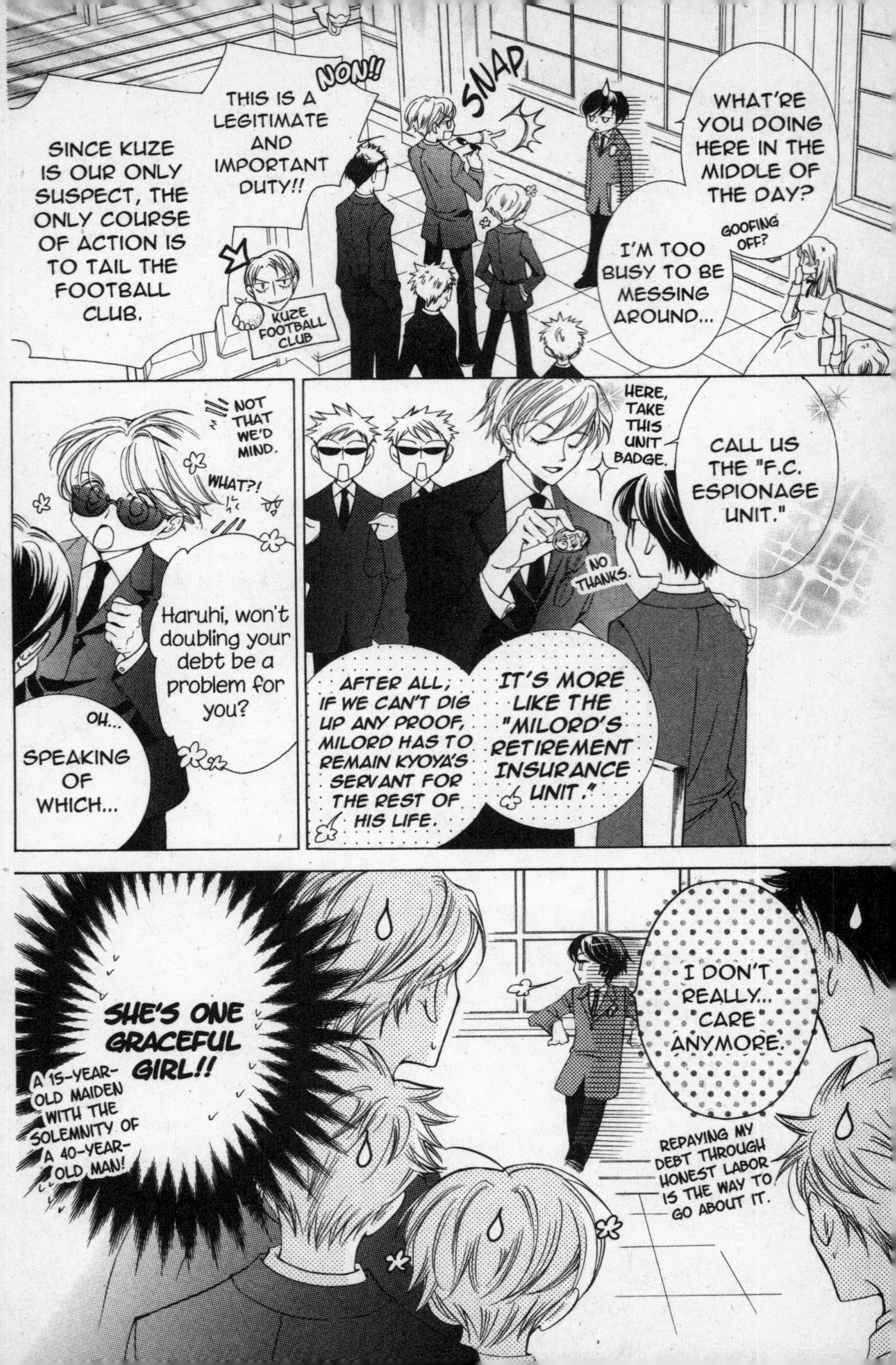

WHAT'RE YOU DOING HERE IN THE MIDDLE OF THE DAY?
GOOFING OFF?
I'M TOO BUSY TO BE MESSING AROUND...
SNAP
NON!!
THIS IS A LEGITIMATE AND IMPORTANT DUTY!!
SINCE KUZE IS OUR ONLY SUSPECT, THE ONLY COURSE OF ACTION IS TO TAIL THE FOOTBALL CLUB.
KUZE FOOTBALL CLUB
CALL US THE "F.C. ESPIONAGE UNIT."
HERE, TAKE THIS UNIT BADGE.
NO THANKS.
IT'S MORE LIKE THE "MILORD'S RETIREMENT INSURANCE UNIT."
AFTER ALL, IF WE CAN'T DIG UP ANY PROOF, MILORD HAS TO REMAIN KYOYA'S SERVANT FOR THE REST OF HIS LIFE.
NOT THAT WE'D MIND.
WHAT?!
Haruhi, won't doubling your debt be a problem for you?
OH...
SPEAKING OF WHICH...
I DON'T REALLY... CARE ANYMORE.
REPAYING MY DEBT THROUGH HONEST LABOR IS THE WAY TO GO ABOUT IT.
SHE'S ONE GRACEFUL GIRL!!
A 15-YEAR-OLD MAIDEN WITH THE SOLEMNITY OF A 40-YEAR-OLD MAN!

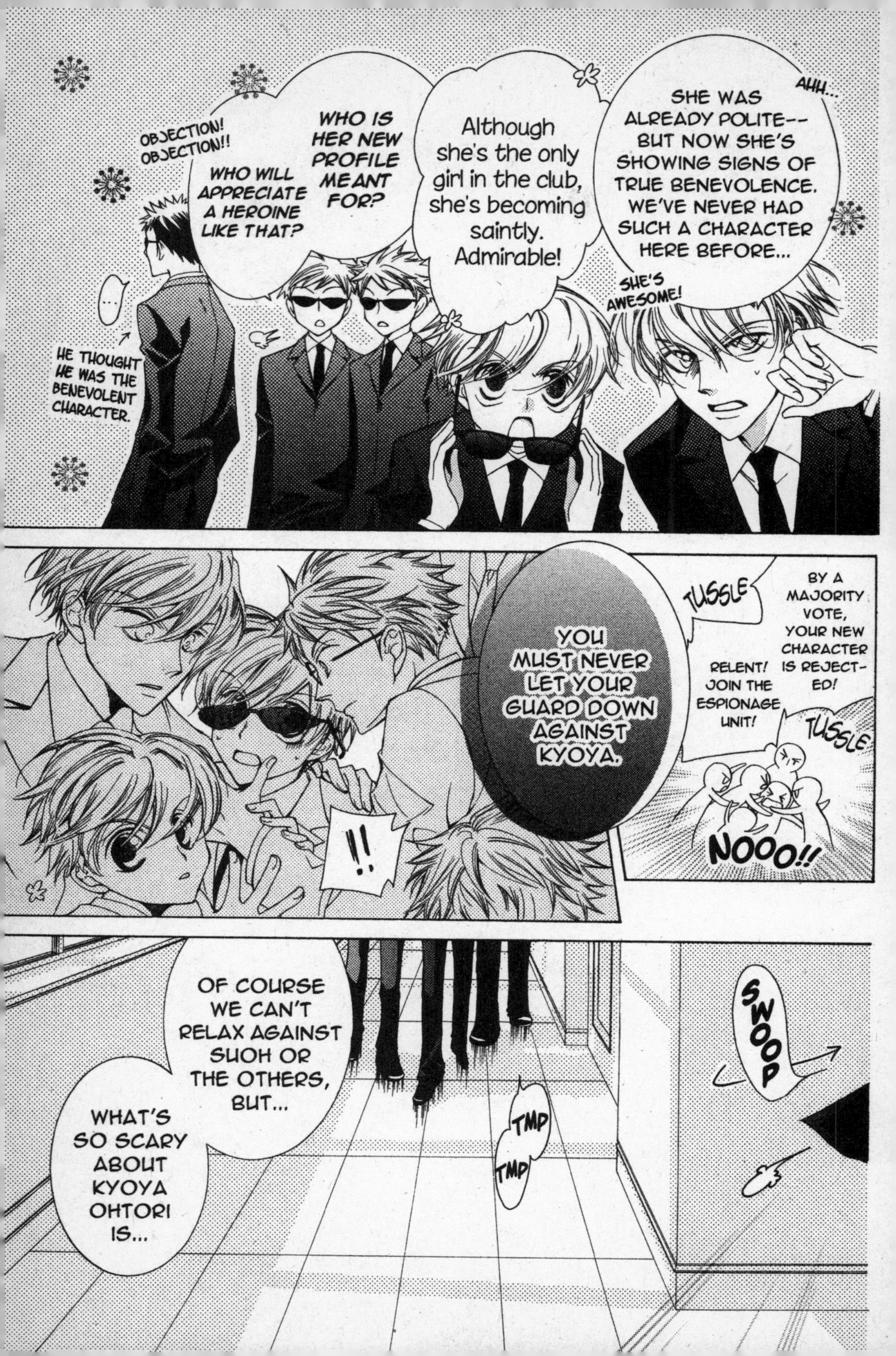

AHH...
SHE WAS ALREADY POLITE-- BUT NOW SHE'S SHOWING SIGNS OF TRUE BENEVOLENCE. WE'VE NEVER HAD SUCH A CHARACTER HERE BEFORE...
SHE'S AWESOME!
Although she's the only girl in the club, she's becoming saintly. Admirable!
WHO IS HER NEW PROFILE MEANT FOR?
OBJECTION! OBJECTION!!
WHO WILL APPRECIATE A HEROINE LIKE THAT?
...
HE THOUGHT HE WAS THE BENEVOLENT CHARACTER.
BY A MAJORITY VOTE, YOUR NEW CHARACTER IS REJECT-ED!
TUSSLE
RELENT! JOIN THE ESPIONAGE UNIT!
TUSSLE
NOOO!!
YOU MUST NEVER LET YOUR GUARD DOWN AGAINST KYOYA.
!!
SWOOP
TMP
TMP
OF COURSE WE CAN'T RELAX AGAINST SUOH OR THE OTHERS, BUT...
WHAT'S SO SCARY ABOUT KYOYA OHTORI IS...

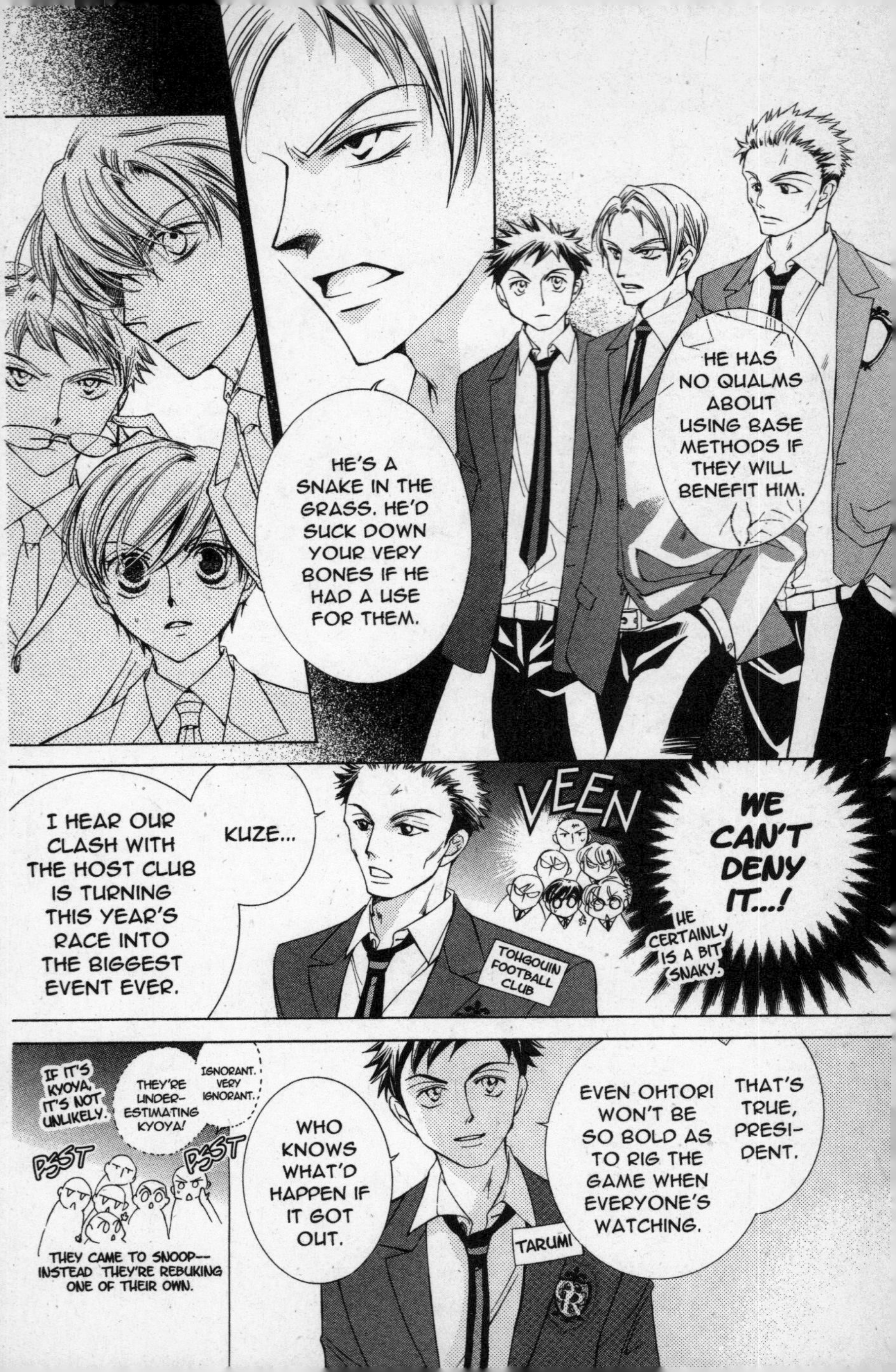
HE HAS NO QUALMS ABOUT USING BASE METHODS IF THEY WILL BENEFIT HIM.
HE'S A SNAKE IN THE GRASS. HE'D SUCK DOWN YOUR VERY BONES IF HE HAD A USE FOR THEM.
WE CAN'T DENY IT...!
HE CERTAINLY IS A BIT SNAKY.
VEEN
TOHGOUIN FOOTBALL CLUB
KUZE...
I HEAR OUR CLASH WITH THE HOST CLUB IS TURNING THIS YEAR'S RACE INTO THE BIGGEST EVENT EVER.
THAT'S TRUE, PRESIDENT.
EVEN OHTORI WON'T BE SO BOLD AS TO RIG THE GAME WHEN EVERYONE'S WATCHING.
TARUMI
WHO KNOWS WHAT'D HAPPEN IF IT GOT OUT.
IGNORANT. VERY IGNORANT.
THEY'RE UNDER-ESTIMATING KYOYA!
IF IT'S KYOYA, IT'S NOT UNLIKELY.
PSST
PSST
THEY CAME TO SNOOP-- INSTEAD THEY'RE REBUKING ONE OF THEIR OWN.

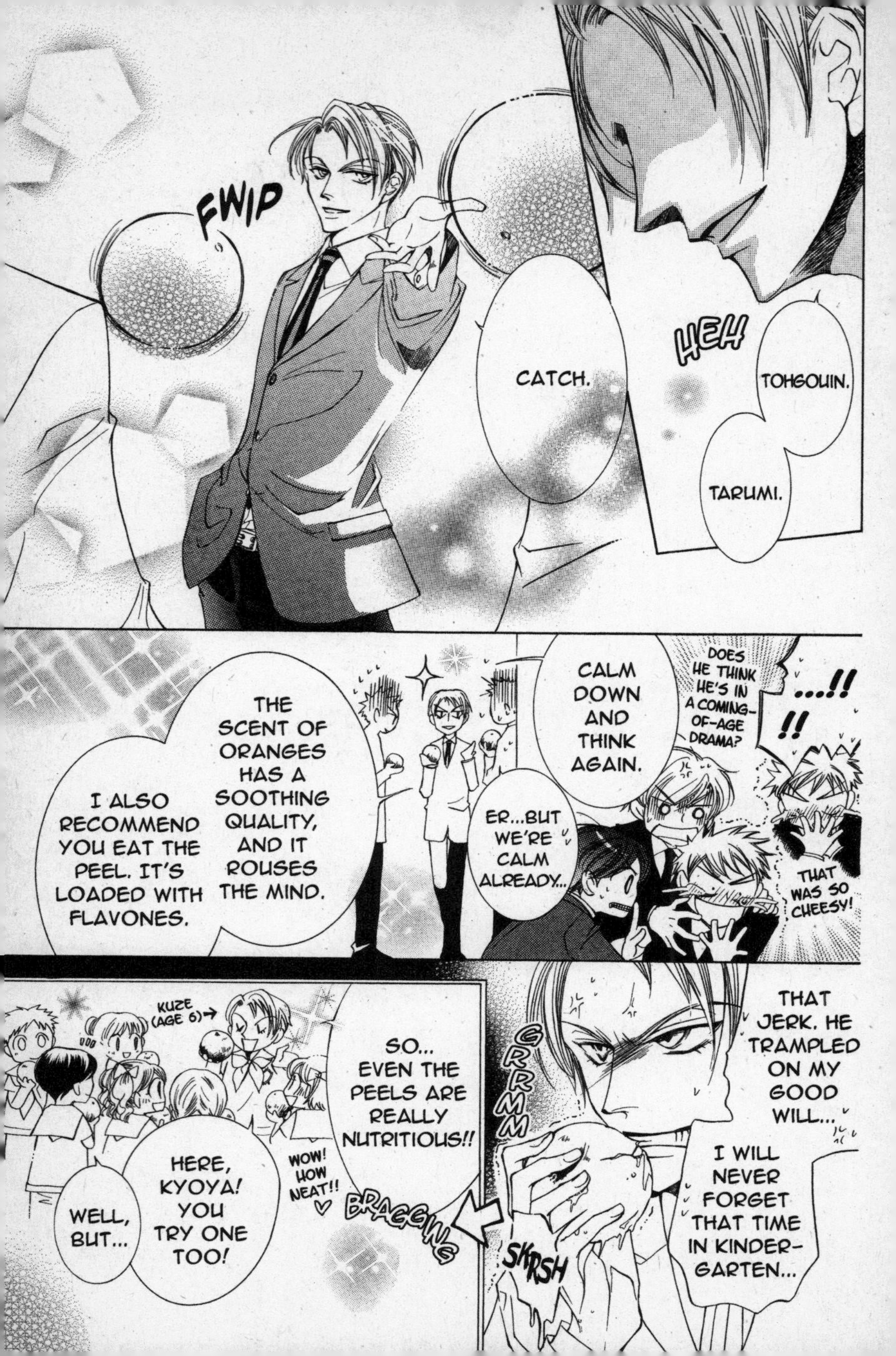
HEH
TOHGOUIN.
TARUMI.
CATCH.
FWIP
...!!
!!
DOES HE THINK HE'S IN A COMING-OF-AGE DRAMA?
CALM DOWN AND THINK AGAIN.
THAT WAS SO CHEESY!
ER...BUT WE'RE CALM ALREADY...
THE SCENT OF ORANGES HAS A SOOTHING QUALITY, AND IT ROUSES THE MIND.
I ALSO RECOMMEND YOU EAT THE PEEL. IT'S LOADED WITH FLAVONES.
THAT JERK. HE TRAMPLED ON MY GOOD WILL...
GRRMM
I WILL NEVER FORGET THAT TIME IN KINDER-GARTEN...
SKRSH
SO... EVEN THE PEELS ARE REALLY NUTRITIOUS!!
KUZE (AGE 6)
WOW! HOW NEAT!!
BRAGGING
HERE, KYOYA! YOU TRY ONE TOO!
WELL, BUT...

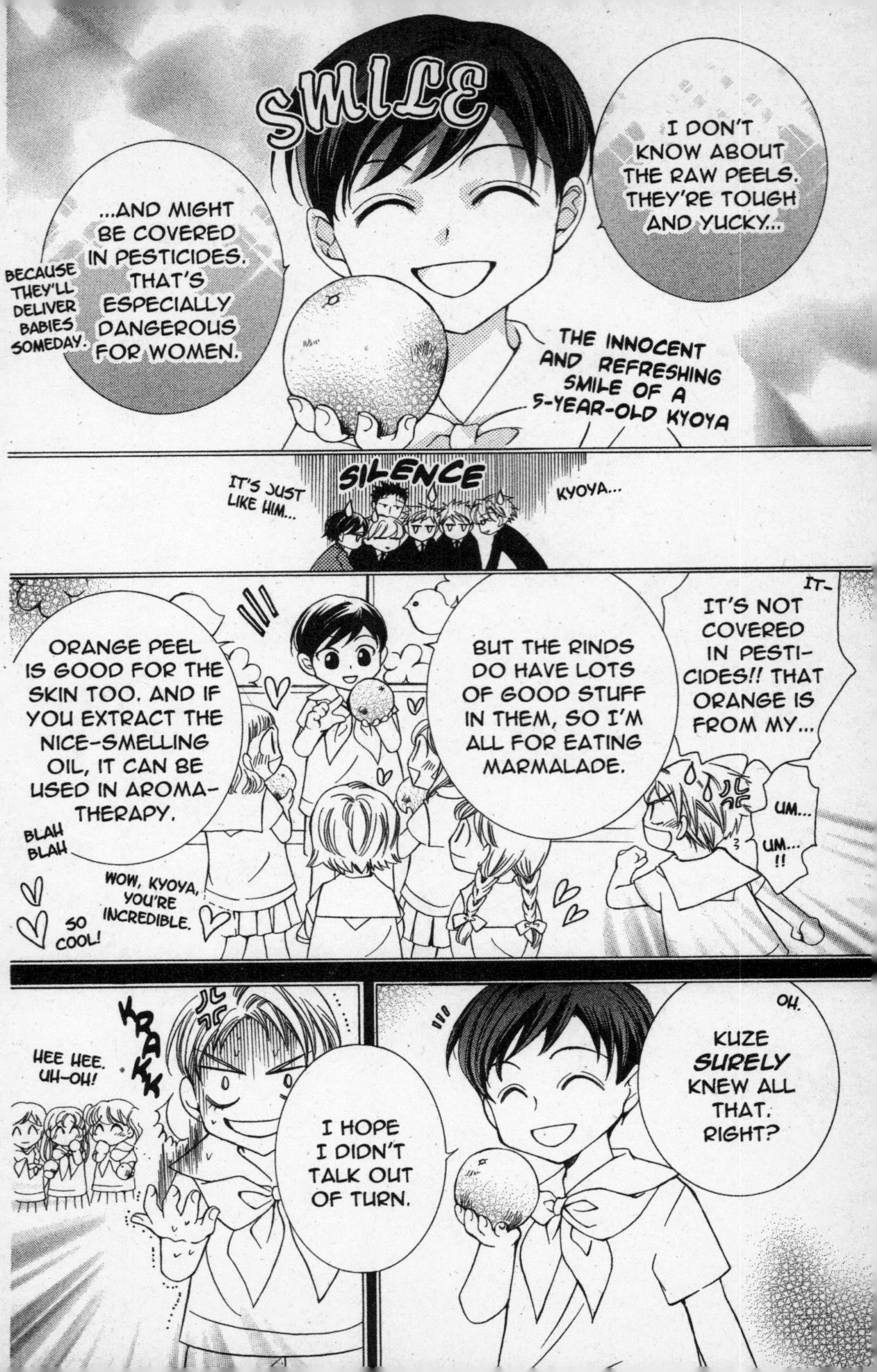
SMILE
I DON'T KNOW ABOUT THE RAW PEELS. THEY'RE TOUGH AND YUCKY...
...AND MIGHT BE COVERED IN PESTICIDES. THAT'S ESPECIALLY DANGEROUS FOR WOMEN.
BECAUSE THEY'LL DELIVER BABIES SOMEDAY.
THE INNOCENT AND REFRESHING SMILE OF A 5-YEAR-OLD KYOYA
KYOYA...
SILENCE
IT'S JUST LIKE HIM...
IT- IT'S NOT COVERED IN PESTICIDES!! THAT ORANGE IS FROM MY...
UM...
UM... !!
BUT THE RINDS DO HAVE LOTS OF GOOD STUFF IN THEM, SO I'M ALL FOR EATING MARMALADE.
ORANGE PEEL IS GOOD FOR THE SKIN TOO. AND IF YOU EXTRACT THE NICE-SMELLING OIL, IT CAN BE USED IN AROMA-THERAPY.
BLAH BLAH
WOW, KYOYA, YOU'RE INCREDIBLE.
SO COOL!
OH.
KUZE *SURELY* KNEW ALL THAT. RIGHT?
I HOPE I DIDN'T TALK OUT OF TURN.
KRAKK
HEE HEE. UH-OH!

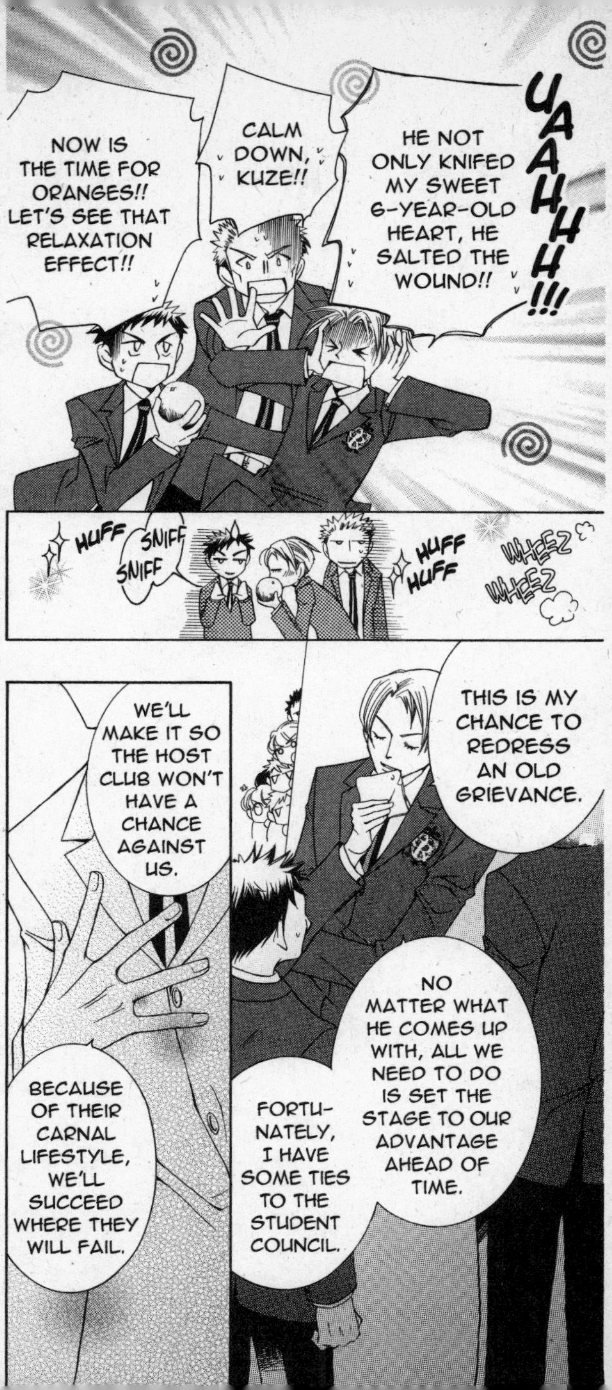
UAAHHHH!!!
HE NOT ONLY KNIFED MY SWEET 6-YEAR-OLD HEART, HE SALTED THE WOUND!!
CALM DOWN, KUZE!!
NOW IS THE TIME FOR ORANGES!! LET'S SEE THAT RELAXATION EFFECT!!
WHEEZ WHEEZ
HUFF HUFF
SNIFF SNIFF
HUFF
THIS IS MY CHANCE TO REDRESS AN OLD GRIEVANCE.
NO MATTER WHAT HE COMES UP WITH, ALL WE NEED TO DO IS SET THE STAGE TO OUR ADVANTAGE AHEAD OF TIME.
FORTUNATELY, I HAVE SOME TIES TO THE STUDENT COUNCIL.
WE'LL MAKE IT SO THE HOST CLUB WON'T HAVE A CHANCE AGAINST US.
BECAUSE OF THEIR CARNAL LIFESTYLE, WE'LL SUCCEED WHERE THEY WILL FAIL.

✿ AFTER I WROTE ABOUT THE 1500 YUNKER ENERGY SUPPLEMENT, I GOT LETTERS TELLING ME OF MORE EXPENSIVE ONES TOO. I DIDN'T KNOW! THANKS! BUT SINCE THEY'RE A LOT MORE EXPENSIVE, I'VE YET TO TRY THEM...

✿ I ALSO GOT A LETTER REGARDING MY BED FACING NORTH: "YOU'D BE BETTER OFF NOT HAVING YOUR BED FACING NORTH. MY FATHER USED TO SLEEP LIKE THAT, AND HE OFTEN SUFFERED FROM SLEEP PARALYSIS."

IN MY CASE, I EXPERIENCE LOADS OF SLEEP PARALYSIS WHEN I SLEEP FACING WEST, SO I NO LONGER SLEEP THAT WAY. BUT MY STAFF HAVE NO TROUBLE DOING IT...

I GUESS EVERYONE'S DIFFERENT...

BUT THANK YOU! THESE DAYS I SLEEP FACING EAST! ☆

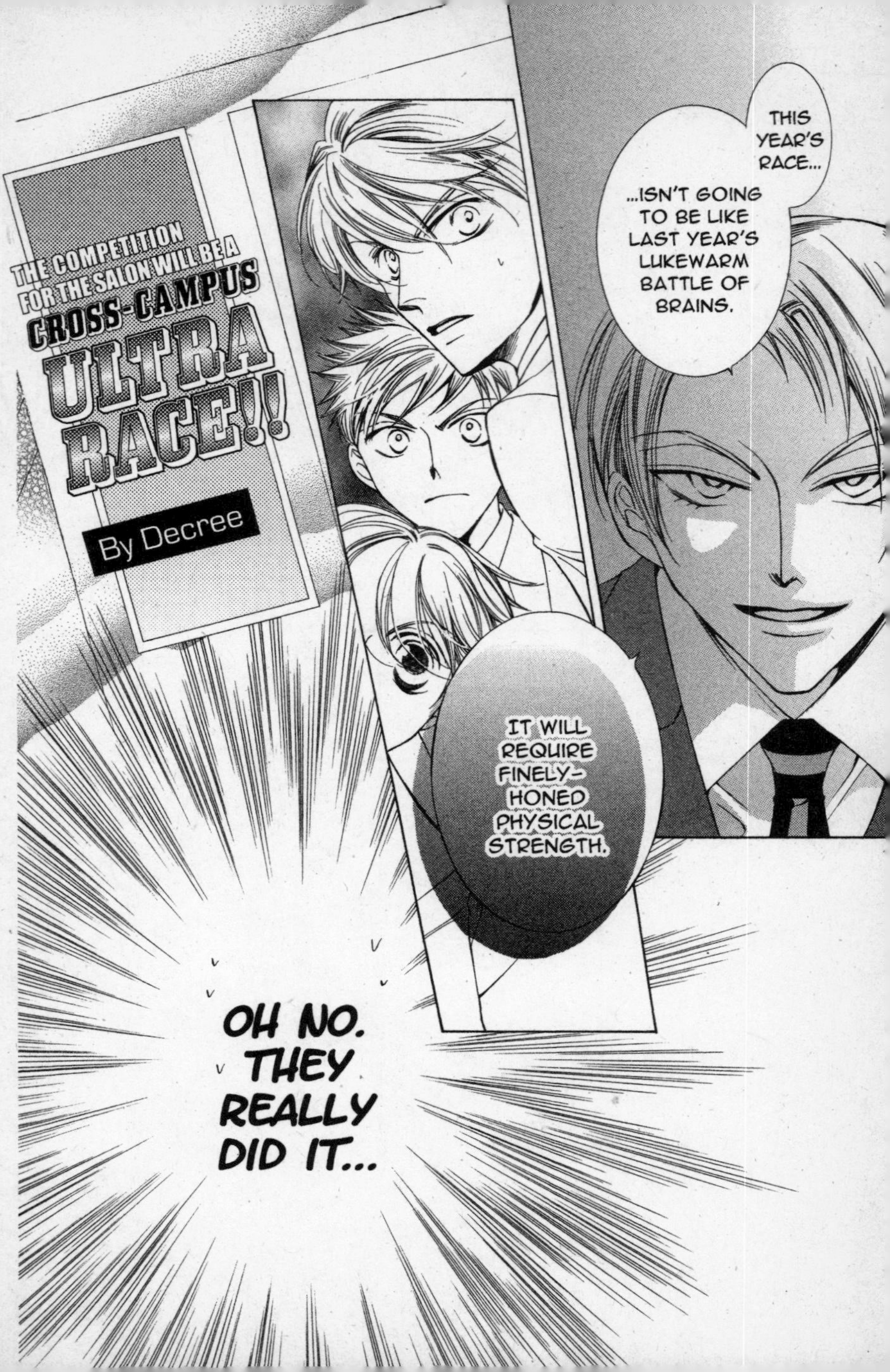
THIS YEAR'S RACE...
...ISN'T GOING TO BE LIKE LAST YEAR'S LUKEWARM BATTLE OF BRAINS.
IT WILL REQUIRE FINELY-HONED PHYSICAL STRENGTH.
THE COMPETITION FOR THE SALON WILL BE A CROSS-CAMPUS ULTRA RACE!!
By Decree
OH NO. THEY REALLY DID IT...

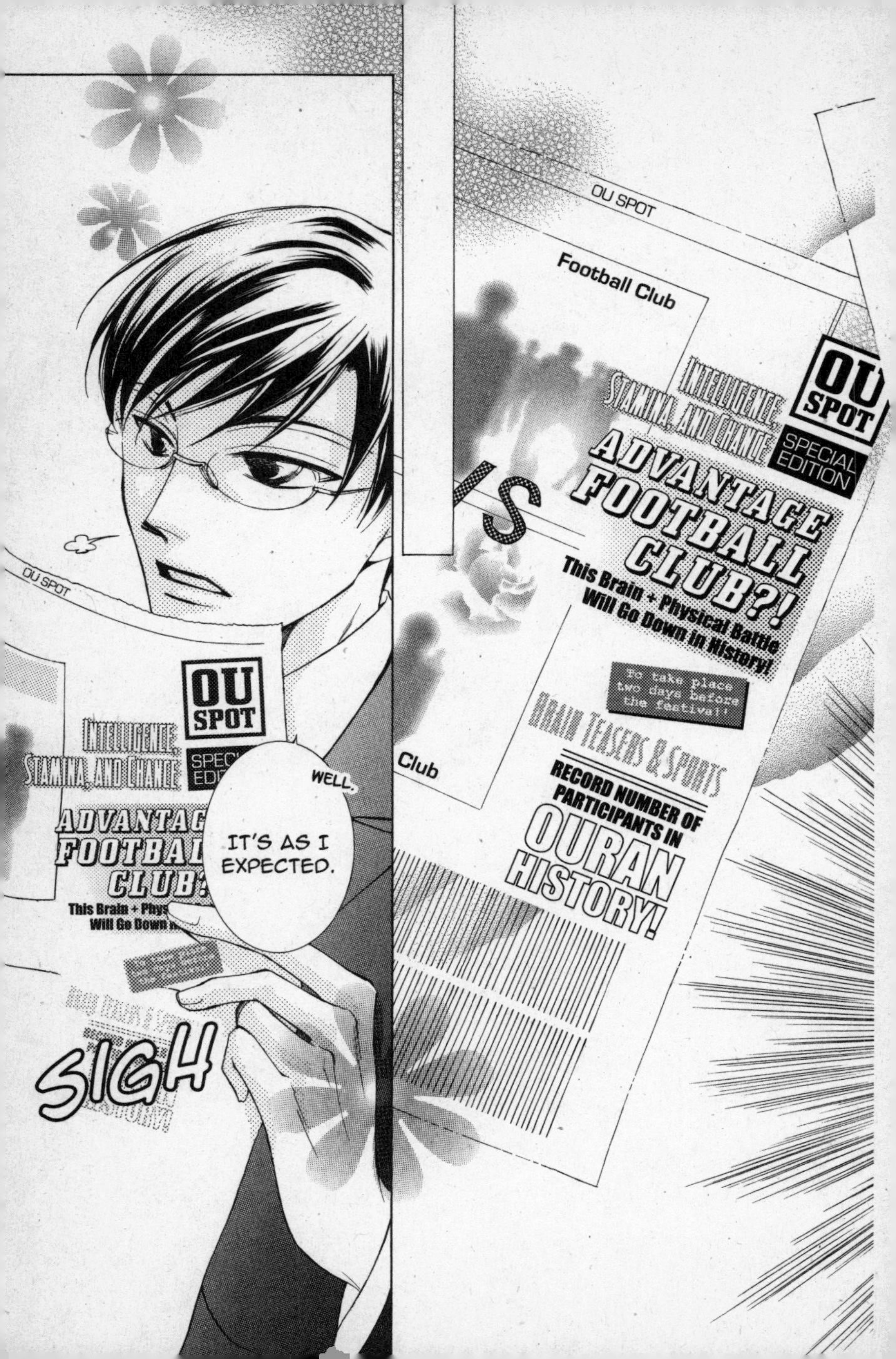
OU SPOT
Football Club
OU SPOT
SPECIAL EDITION
INTELLIGENCE, STAMINA, AND CHANCE
ADVANTAGE FOOTBALL CLUB?!
This Brain + Physical Battle Will Go Down in History!
To take place two days before the festival!
VS
Club
BRAIN TEASERS & SPORTS
RECORD NUMBER OF PARTICIPANTS IN OURAN HISTORY!
WELL.
IT'S AS I EXPECTED.
SIGH

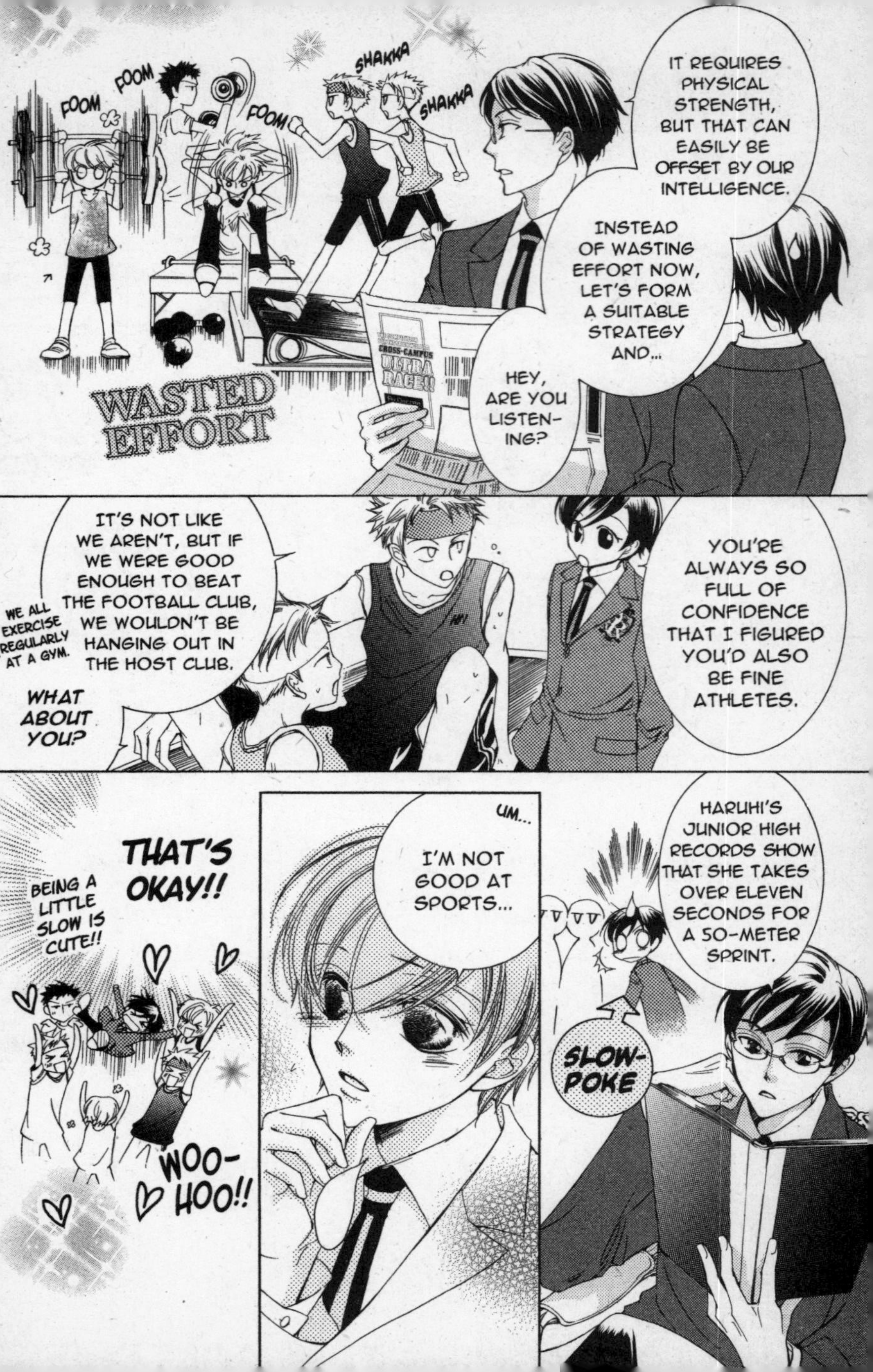
IT REQUIRES PHYSICAL STRENGTH, BUT THAT CAN EASILY BE OFFSET BY OUR INTELLIGENCE.
INSTEAD OF WASTING EFFORT NOW, LET'S FORM A SUITABLE STRATEGY AND...
HEY, ARE YOU LISTENING?
CROSS-CAMPUS ULTRA RACE!!
SHAKKA
SHAKKA
FOOM
FOOM
FOOM
WASTED EFFORT
YOU'RE ALWAYS SO FULL OF CONFIDENCE THAT I FIGURED YOU'D ALSO BE FINE ATHLETES.
IT'S NOT LIKE WE AREN'T, BUT IF WE WERE GOOD ENOUGH TO BEAT THE FOOTBALL CLUB, WE WOULDN'T BE HANGING OUT IN THE HOST CLUB.
WE ALL EXERCISE REGULARLY AT A GYM.
WHAT ABOUT YOU?
HARUHI'S JUNIOR HIGH RECORDS SHOW THAT SHE TAKES OVER ELEVEN SECONDS FOR A 50-METER SPRINT.
SLOW-POKE
UM...
I'M NOT GOOD AT SPORTS...
THAT'S OKAY!!
BEING A LITTLE SLOW IS CUTE!!
WOO-HOO!!

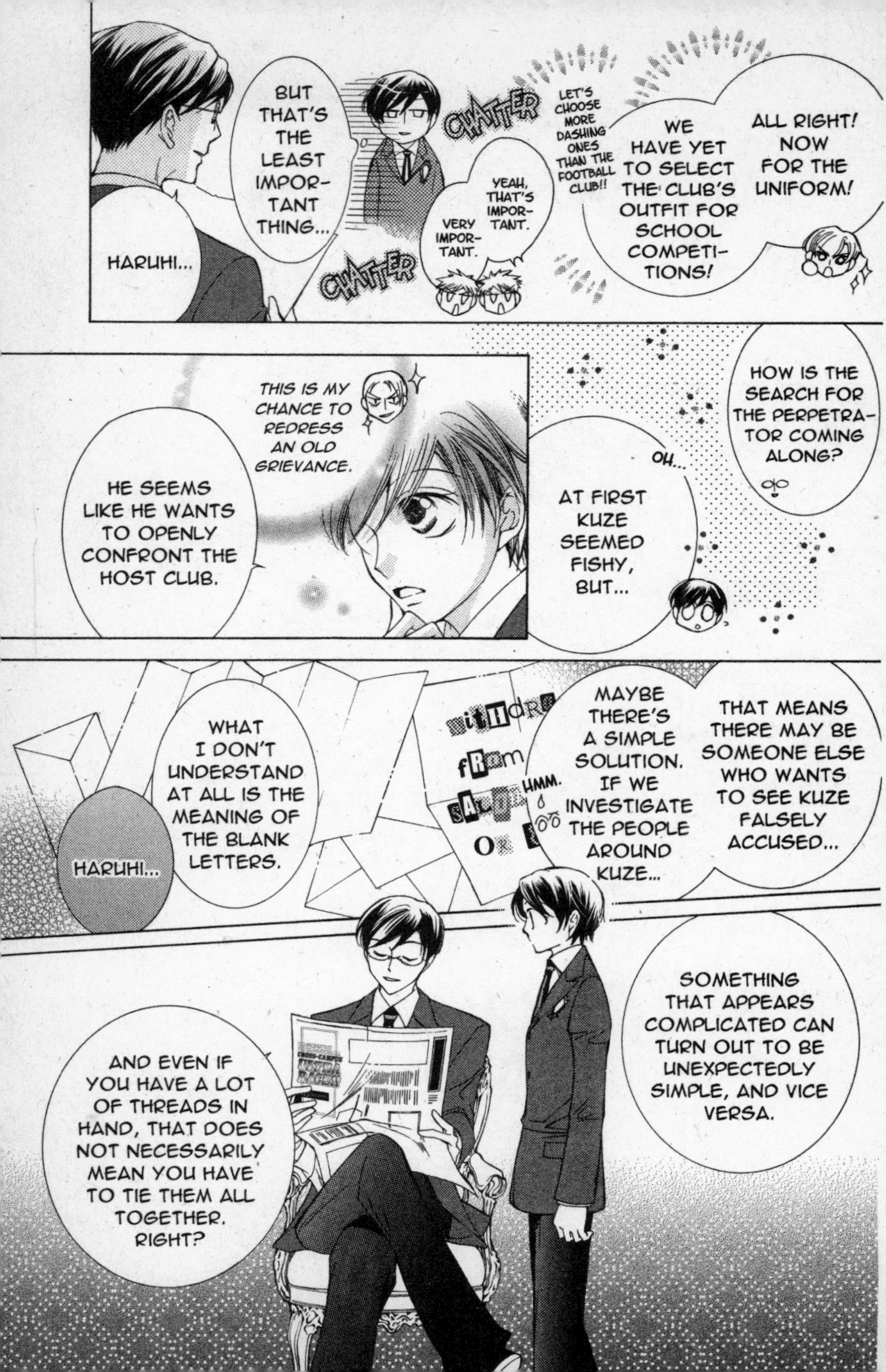
ALL RIGHT! NOW FOR THE UNIFORM!
WE HAVE YET TO SELECT THE CLUB'S OUTFIT FOR SCHOOL COMPETITIONS!
LET'S CHOOSE MORE DASHING ONES THAN THE FOOTBALL CLUB!!
CHATTER
YEAH, THAT'S IMPORTANT.
VERY IMPORTANT.
CHATTER
BUT THAT'S THE LEAST IMPORTANT THING...
HARUHI...
HOW IS THE SEARCH FOR THE PERPETRATOR COMING ALONG?
OH...
AT FIRST KUZE SEEMED FISHY, BUT...
THIS IS MY CHANCE TO REDRESS AN OLD GRIEVANCE.
HE SEEMS LIKE HE WANTS TO OPENLY CONFRONT THE HOST CLUB.
THAT MEANS THERE MAY BE SOMEONE ELSE WHO WANTS TO SEE KUZE FALSELY ACCUSED...
MAYBE THERE'S A SIMPLE SOLUTION. IF WE INVESTIGATE THE PEOPLE AROUND KUZE...
HMM.
WHAT I DON'T UNDERSTAND AT ALL IS THE MEANING OF THE BLANK LETTERS.
HARUHI...
SOMETHING THAT APPEARS COMPLICATED CAN TURN OUT TO BE UNEXPECTEDLY SIMPLE, AND VICE VERSA.
AND EVEN IF YOU HAVE A LOT OF THREADS IN HAND, THAT DOES NOT NECESSARILY MEAN YOU HAVE TO TIE THEM ALL TOGETHER. RIGHT?

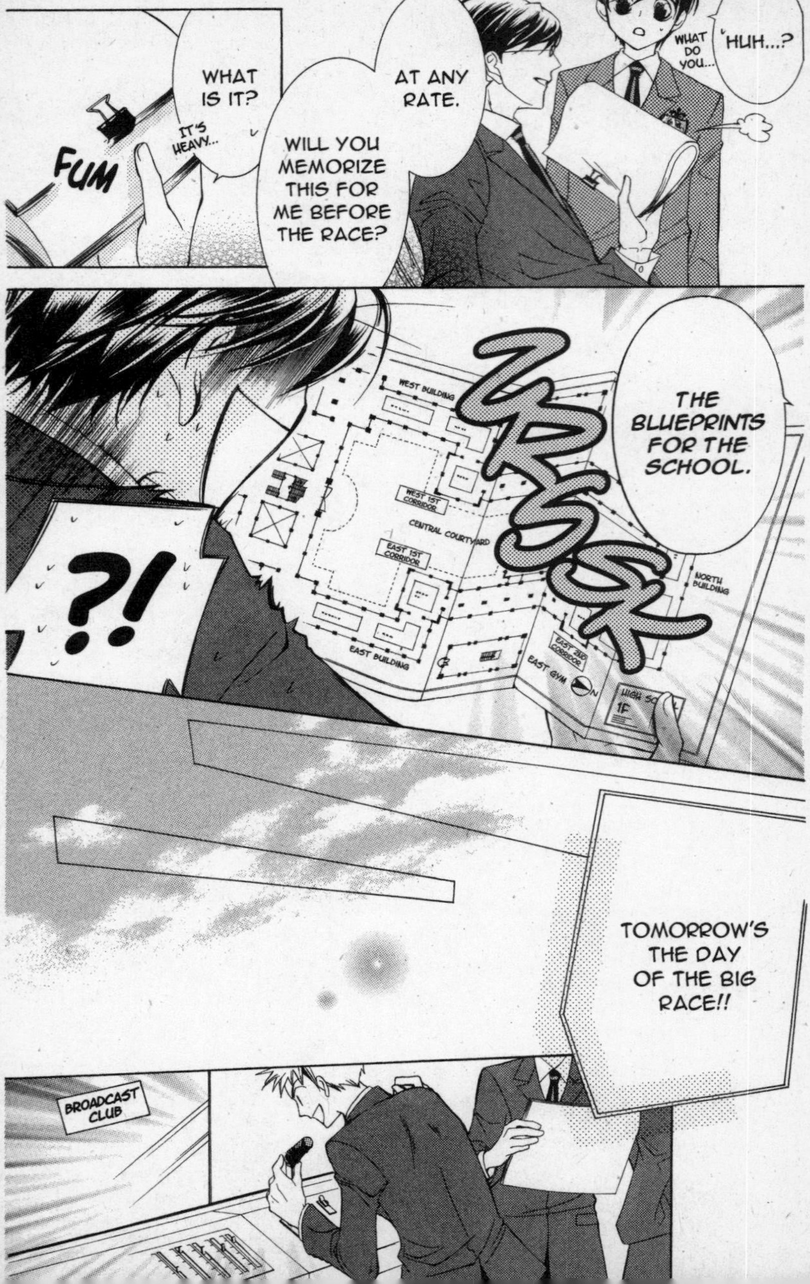
HUH...?
WHAT DO YOU...
AT ANY RATE.
WILL YOU MEMORIZE THIS FOR ME BEFORE THE RACE?
WHAT IS IT?
IT'S HEAVY...
FUM
THE BLUEPRINTS FOR THE SCHOOL.
ZRSK
?!
WEST BUILDING
WEST 1ST CORRIDOR
CENTRAL COURTYARD
EAST 1ST CORRIDOR
NORTH BUILDING
EAST BUILDING
EAST 2ND CORRIDOR
EAST GYM
1F
TOMORROW'S THE DAY OF THE BIG RACE!!
BROADCAST CLUB

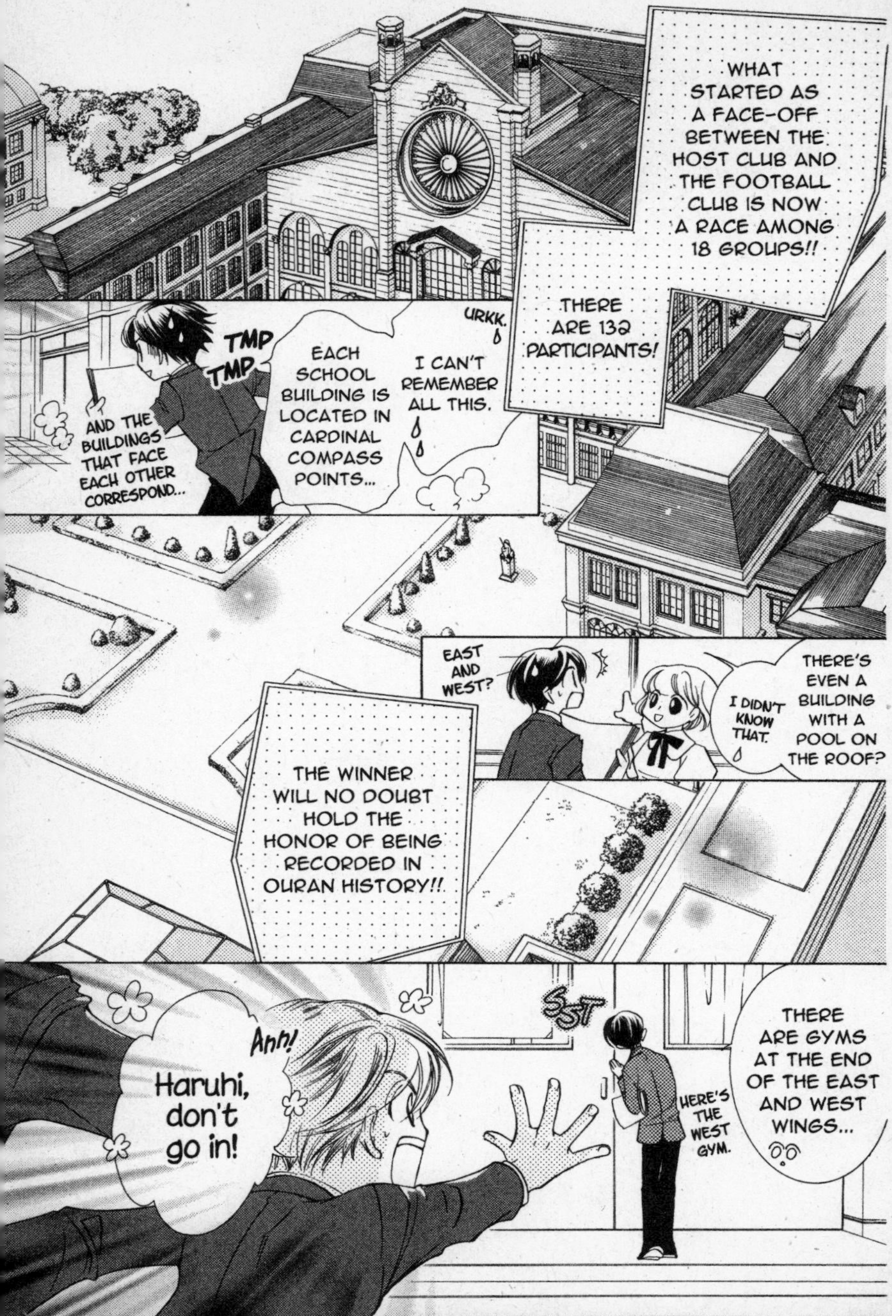
WHAT STARTED AS A FACE-OFF BETWEEN THE HOST CLUB AND THE FOOTBALL CLUB IS NOW A RACE AMONG 18 GROUPS!!
THERE ARE 132 PARTICIPANTS!
URKK.
I CAN'T REMEMBER ALL THIS.
EACH SCHOOL BUILDING IS LOCATED IN CARDINAL COMPASS POINTS...
TMP TMP
AND THE BUILDINGS THAT FACE EACH OTHER CORRESPOND...
THERE'S EVEN A BUILDING WITH A POOL ON THE ROOF?
I DIDN'T KNOW THAT.
EAST AND WEST?
THE WINNER WILL NO DOUBT HOLD THE HONOR OF BEING RECORDED IN OURAN HISTORY!!
THERE ARE GYMS AT THE END OF THE EAST AND WEST WINGS...
HERE'S THE WEST GYM.
SST
Ahh!
Haruhi, don't go in!

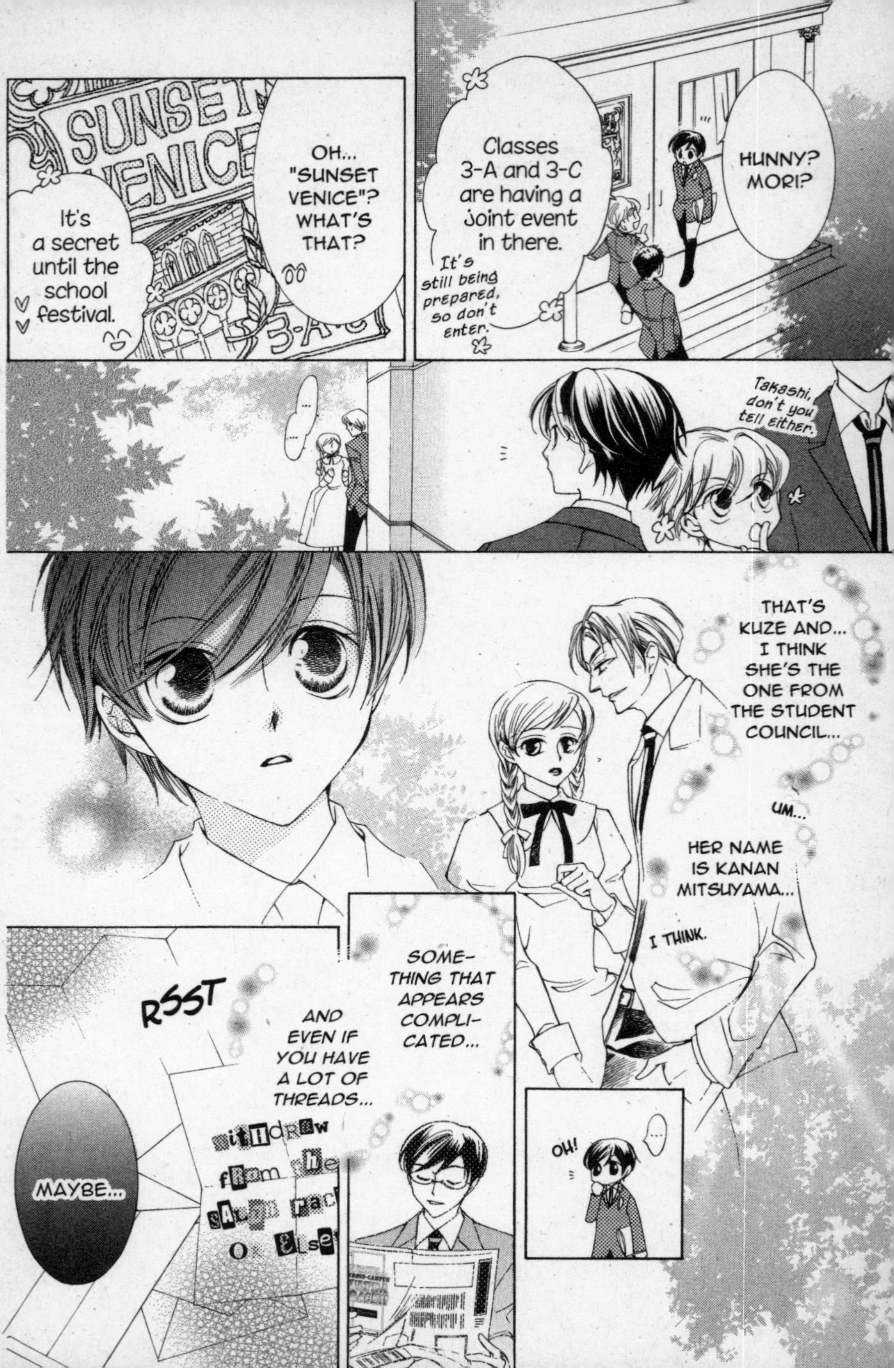
HUNNY? MORI?
Classes 3-A and 3-C are having a joint event in there.
It's still being prepared, so don't enter.
SUNSET VENICE
OH... "SUNSET VENICE"? WHAT'S THAT?
It's a secret until the school festival.
Takashi, don't you tell either.
...
...
THAT'S KUZE AND... I THINK SHE'S THE ONE FROM THE STUDENT COUNCIL...
UM...
HER NAME IS KANAN MITSUYAMA...
I THINK.
...
OH!
SOME-THING THAT APPEARS COMPLI-CATED...
AND EVEN IF YOU HAVE A LOT OF THREADS...
RSST
MAYBE...

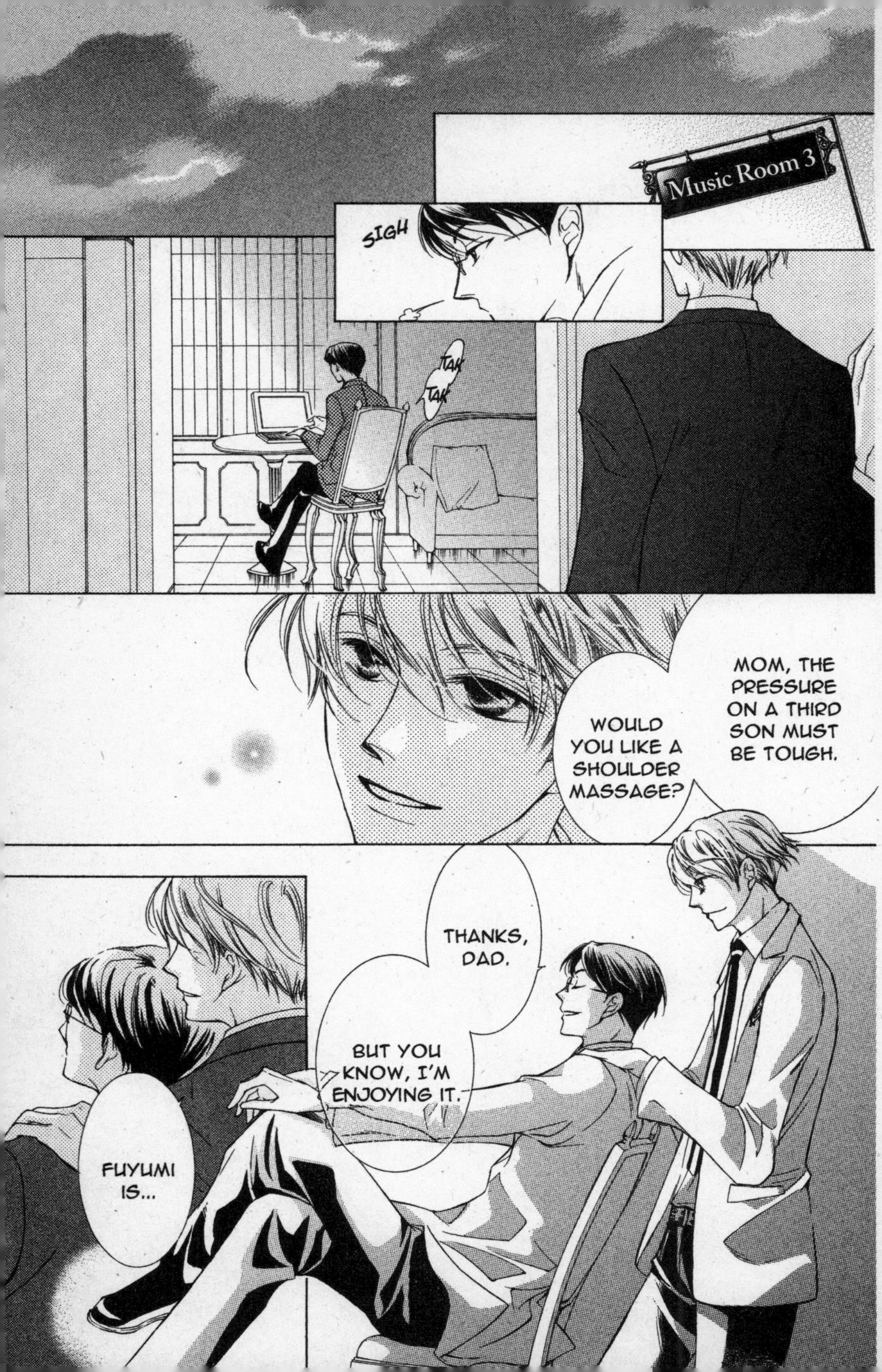
Music Room 3
SIGH
TAK TAK
MOM, THE PRESSURE ON A THIRD SON MUST BE TOUGH.
WOULD YOU LIKE A SHOULDER MASSAGE?
THANKS, DAD.
BUT YOU KNOW, I'M ENJOYING IT.
FUYUMI IS...

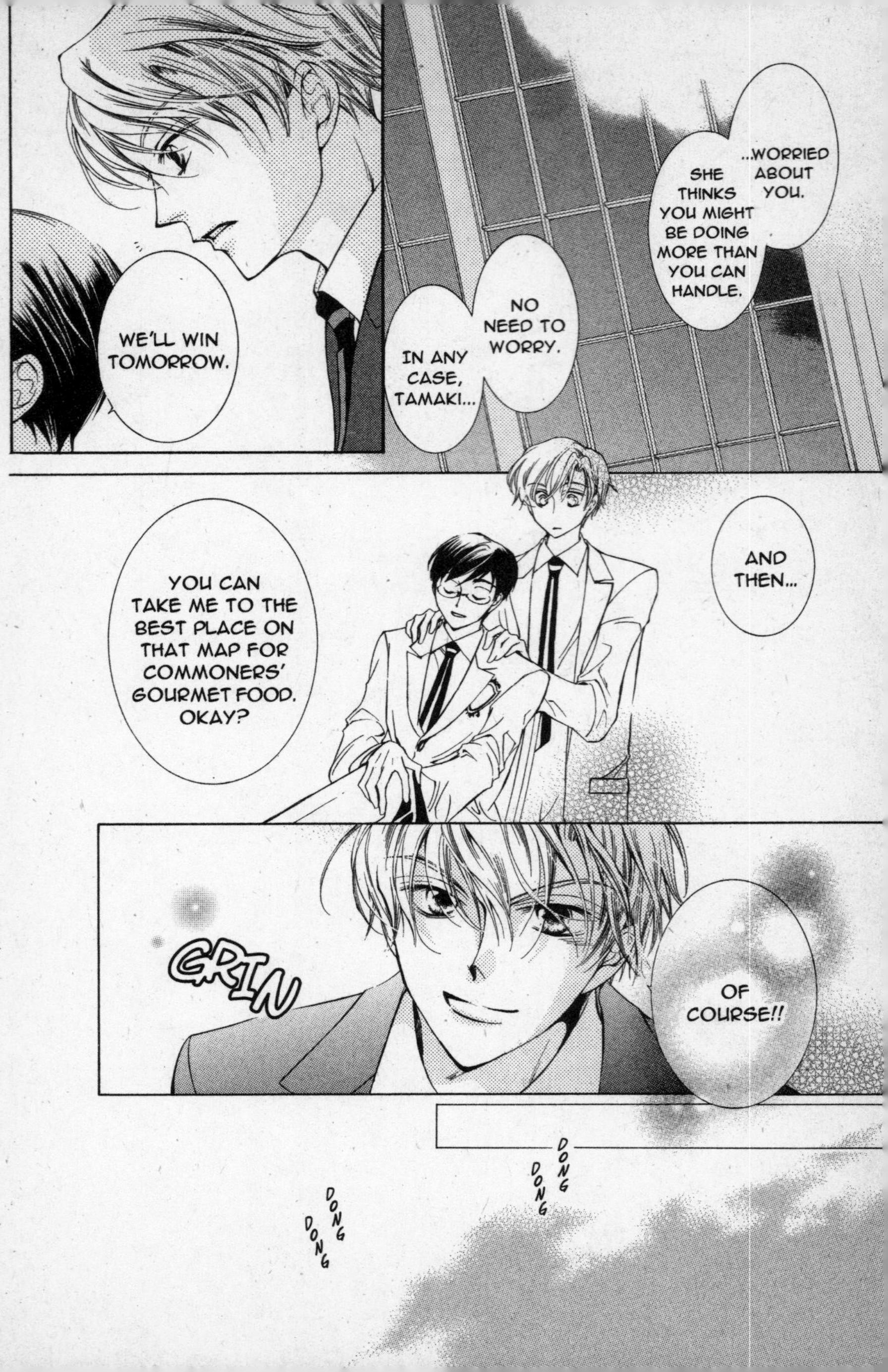

...WORRIED ABOUT YOU.
SHE THINKS YOU MIGHT BE DOING MORE THAN YOU CAN HANDLE.
NO NEED TO WORRY.
IN ANY CASE, TAMAKI...
WE'LL WIN TOMORROW.
AND THEN...
YOU CAN TAKE ME TO THE BEST PLACE ON THAT MAP FOR COMMONERS' GOURMET FOOD. OKAY?
OF COURSE!!
GRIN
DONG DONG
DONG DONG

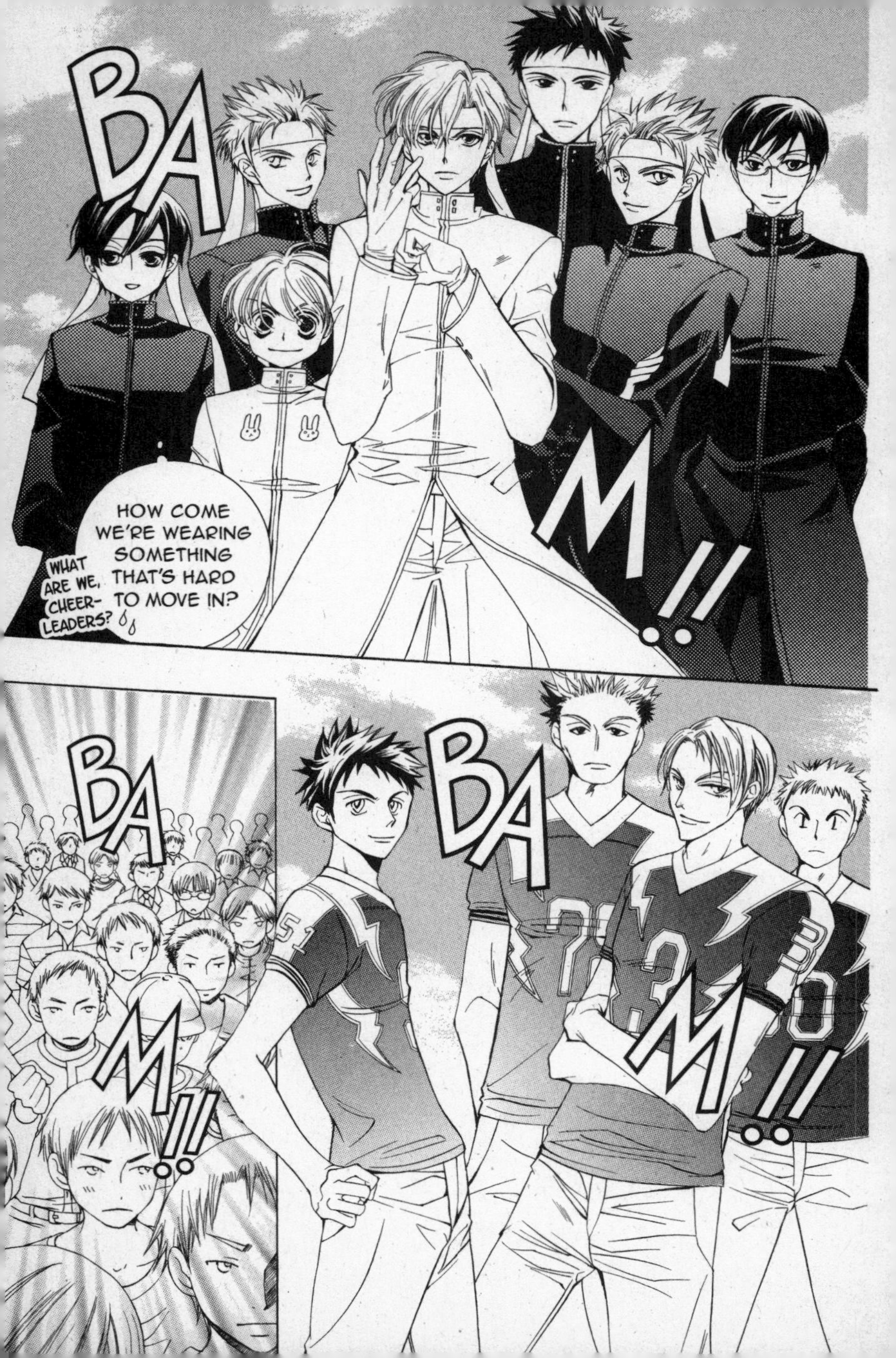
BAM!!
HOW COME WE'RE WEARING SOMETHING THAT'S HARD TO MOVE IN?
WHAT ARE WE, CHEERLEADERS?
BAM!!
BAM!!

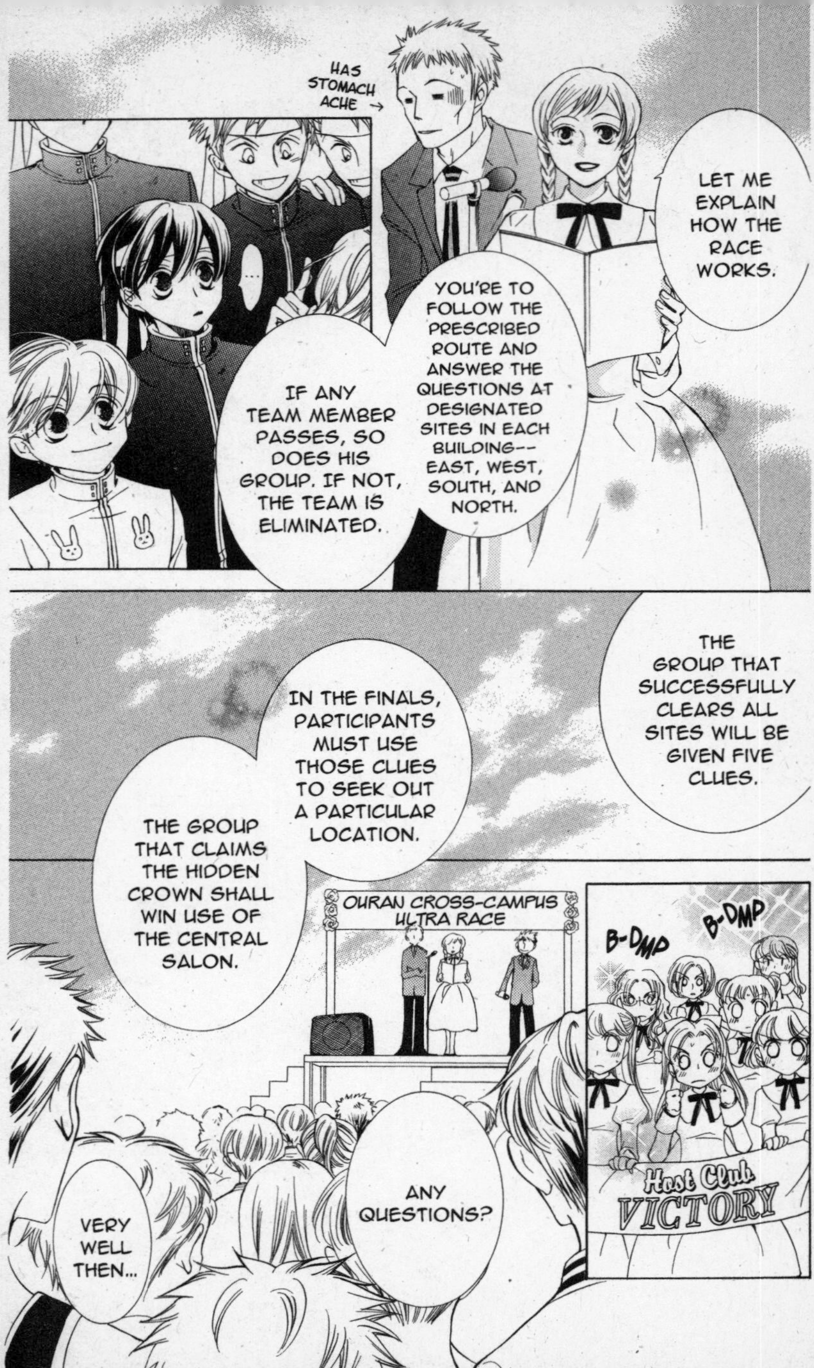
LET ME EXPLAIN HOW THE RACE WORKS.
HAS STOMACH ACHE →
YOU'RE TO FOLLOW THE PRESCRIBED ROUTE AND ANSWER THE QUESTIONS AT DESIGNATED SITES IN EACH BUILDING-- EAST, WEST, SOUTH, AND NORTH.
...
IF ANY TEAM MEMBER PASSES, SO DOES HIS GROUP. IF NOT, THE TEAM IS ELIMINATED.
THE GROUP THAT SUCCESSFULLY CLEARS ALL SITES WILL BE GIVEN FIVE CLUES.
IN THE FINALS, PARTICIPANTS MUST USE THOSE CLUES TO SEEK OUT A PARTICULAR LOCATION.
THE GROUP THAT CLAIMS THE HIDDEN CROWN SHALL WIN USE OF THE CENTRAL SALON.
B-DMP
B-DMP
Host Club VICTORY
OURAN CROSS-CAMPUS ULTRA RACE
ANY QUESTIONS?
VERY WELL THEN...

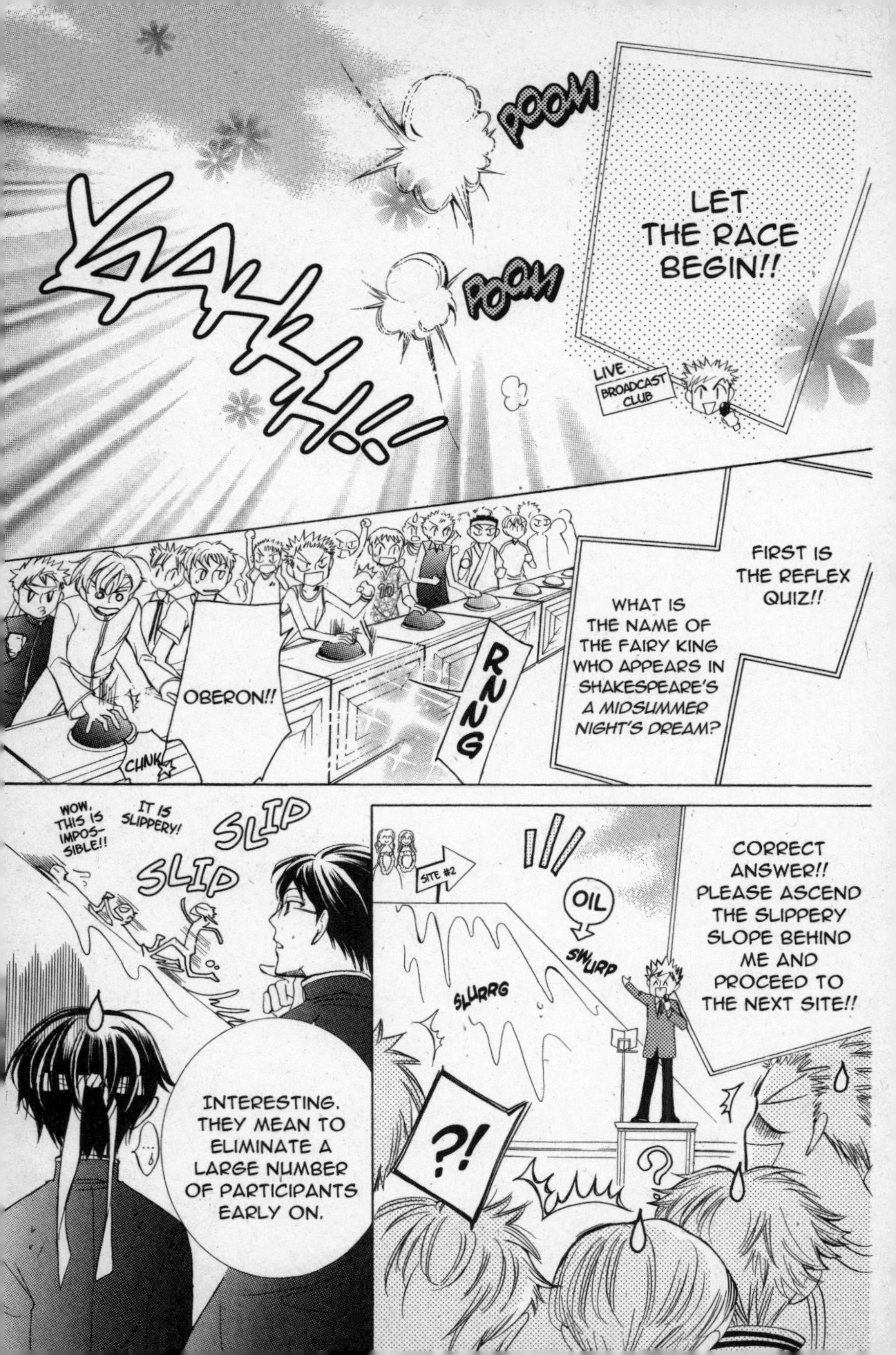
POOM
LET THE RACE BEGIN!!
POOM
LIVE
BROADCAST CLUB
YAAHHH!!
FIRST IS THE REFLEX QUIZ!!
WHAT IS THE NAME OF THE FAIRY KING WHO APPEARS IN SHAKESPEARE'S *A MIDSUMMER NIGHT'S DREAM*?
RNNG
OBERON!!
CHUNK
CORRECT ANSWER!! PLEASE ASCEND THE SLIPPERY SLOPE BEHIND ME AND PROCEED TO THE NEXT SITE!!
OIL
SWURP
SITE #2
SLURRG
?!
?
IT IS SLIPPERY!
WOW, THIS IS IMPOSSIBLE!!
SLIP
SLIP
INTERESTING. THEY MEAN TO ELIMINATE A LARGE NUMBER OF PARTICIPANTS EARLY ON.
...

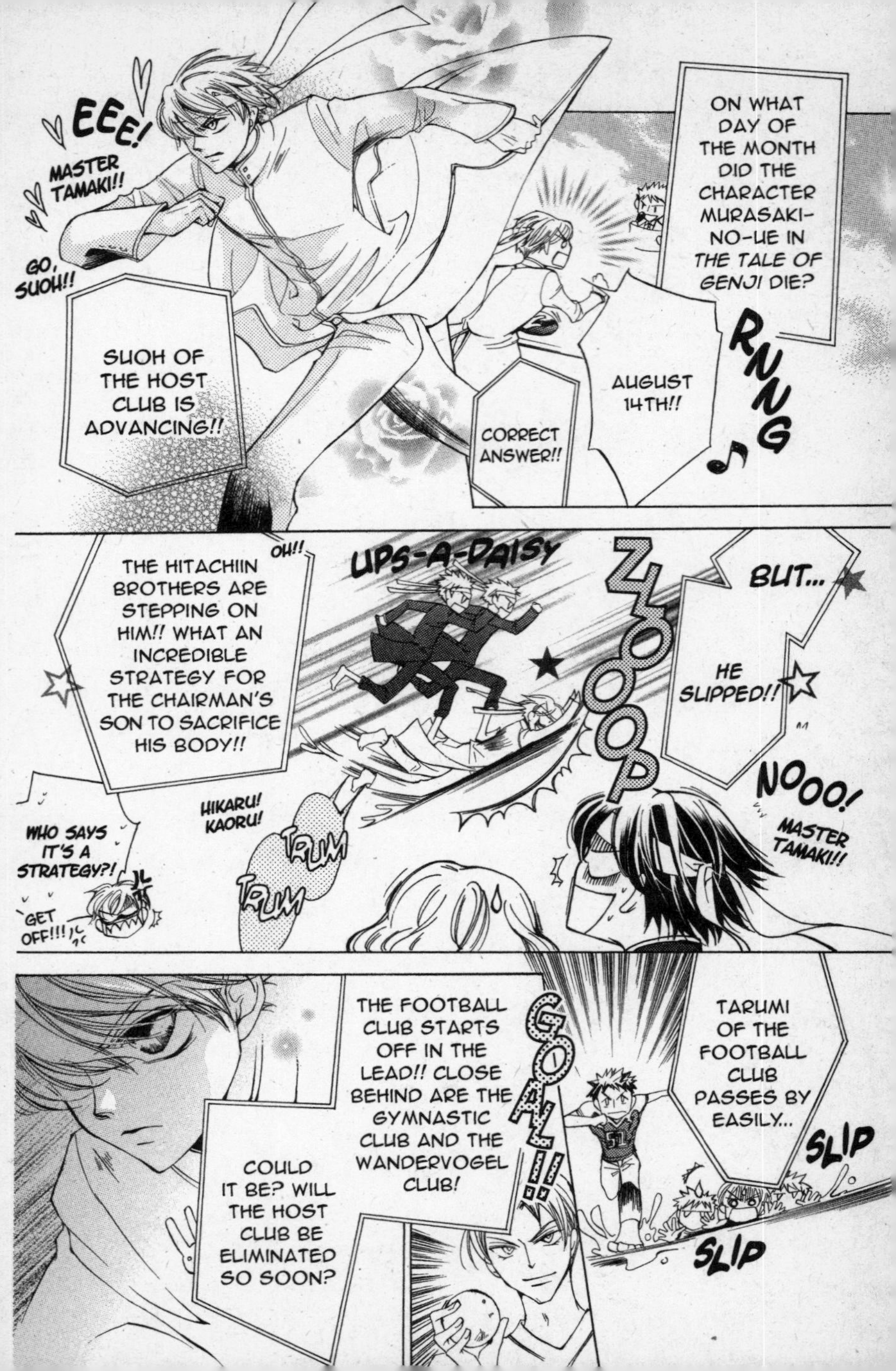

ON WHAT DAY OF THE MONTH DID THE CHARACTER MURASAKI-NO-UE IN THE TALE OF GENJI DIE?
RNNG
AUGUST 14TH!!
CORRECT ANSWER!!
EEE!
MASTER TAMAKI!!
GO, SUOH!!
SUOH OF THE HOST CLUB IS ADVANCING!!
BUT...
HE SLIPPED!!
ZOOOP
NOOO!
MASTER TAMAKI!!
UPS-A-DAISY
OH!!
THE HITACHIIN BROTHERS ARE STEPPING ON HIM!! WHAT AN INCREDIBLE STRATEGY FOR THE CHAIRMAN'S SON TO SACRIFICE HIS BODY!!
HIKARU! KAORU!
TRUM
TRUM
WHO SAYS IT'S A STRATEGY?!
GET OFF!!!
TARUMI OF THE FOOTBALL CLUB PASSES BY EASILY...
SLIP
SLIP
GOAL!!
THE FOOTBALL CLUB STARTS OFF IN THE LEAD!! CLOSE BEHIND ARE THE GYMNASTIC CLUB AND THE WANDERVOGEL CLUB!
COULD IT BE? WILL THE HOST CLUB BE ELIMINATED SO SOON?

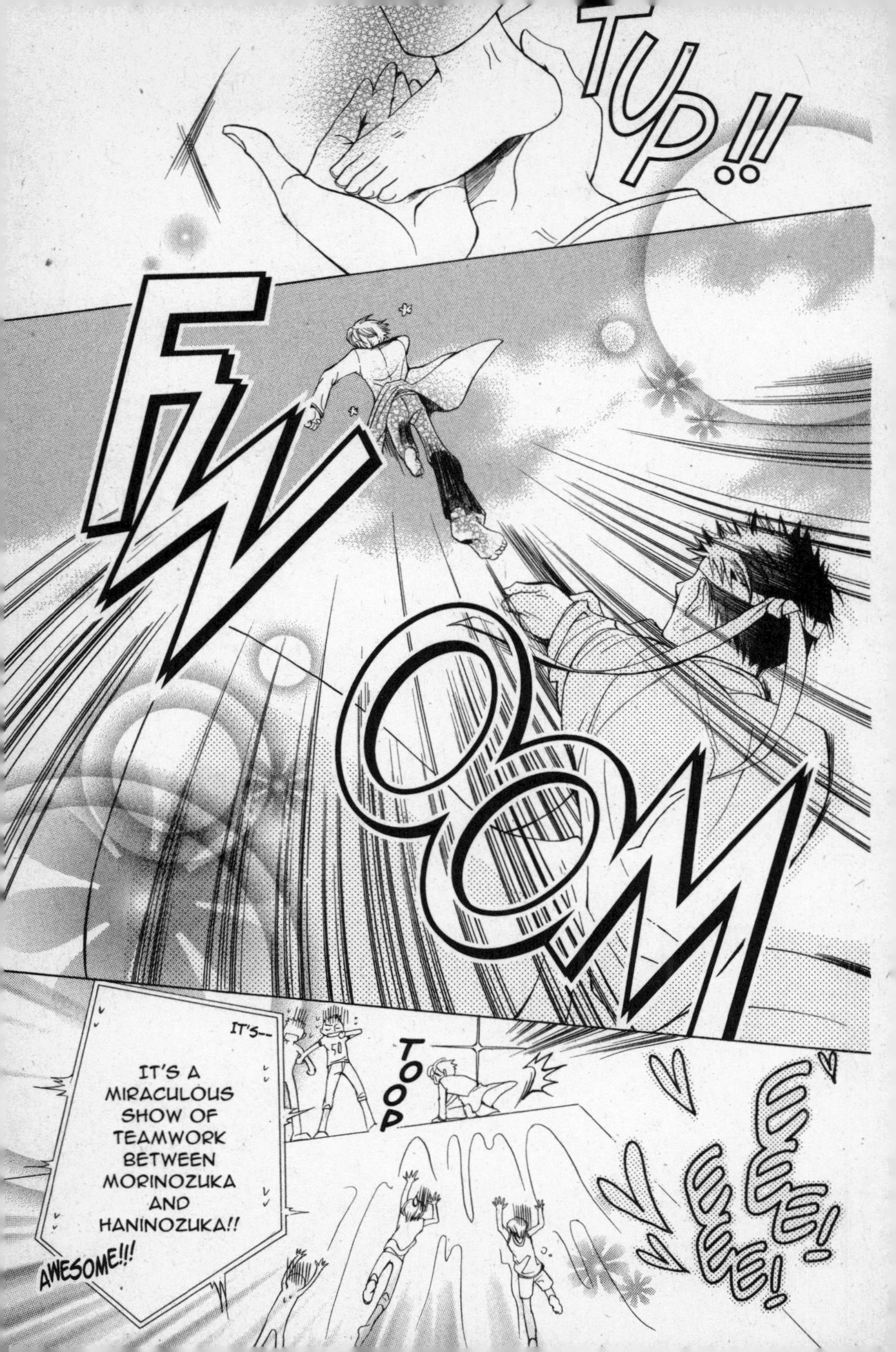
TUP!!
FWOOM
EEEE!
EEEE!
TOOP
IT'S--
IT'S A MIRACULOUS SHOW OF TEAMWORK BETWEEN MORINOZUKA AND HANINOZUKA!!
AWESOME!!!

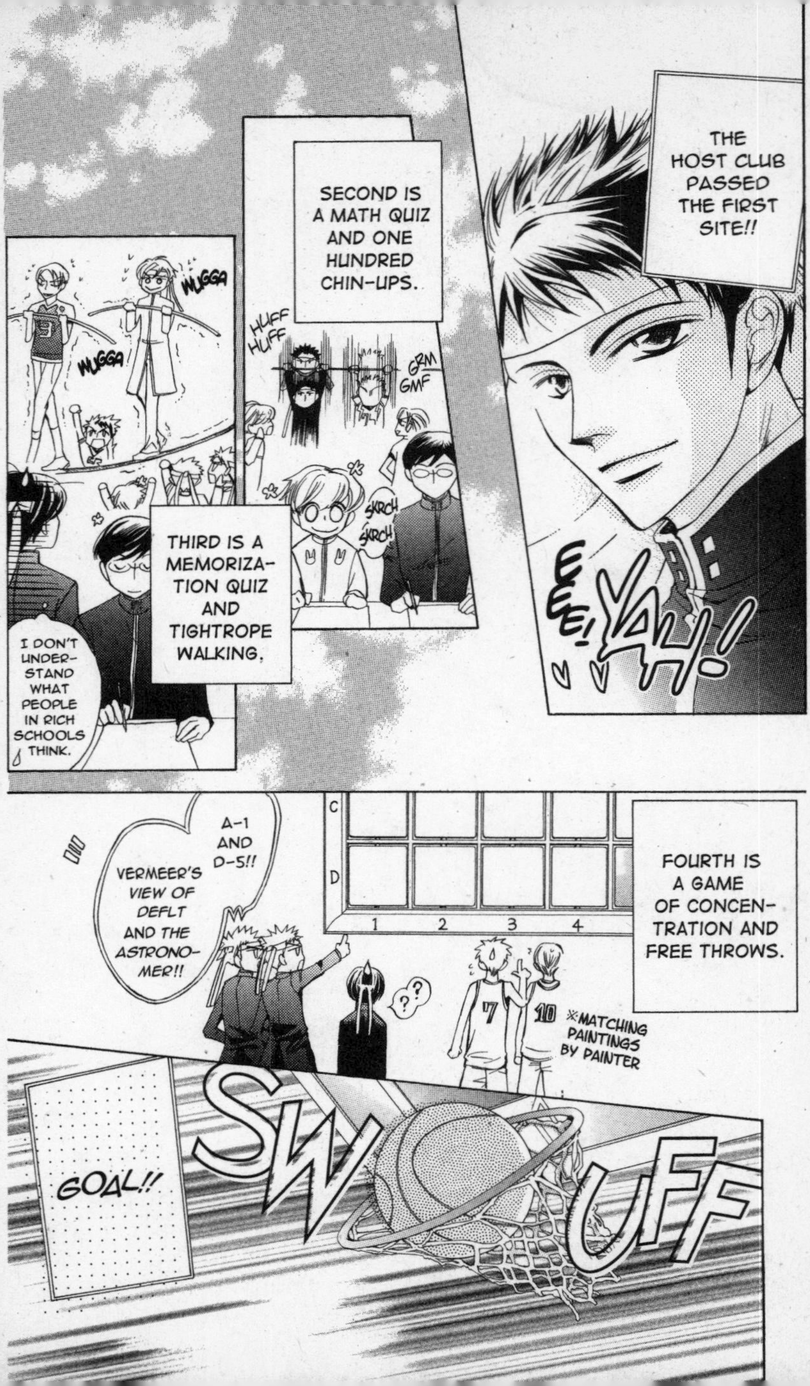
THE HOST CLUB PASSED THE FIRST SITE!!
EEE! YAH!
SECOND IS A MATH QUIZ AND ONE HUNDRED CHIN-UPS.
HUFF HUFF
GRM GMF
SKRCH SKRCH
MUGGA
MUGGA
THIRD IS A MEMORIZATION QUIZ AND TIGHTROPE WALKING.
I DON'T UNDERSTAND WHAT PEOPLE IN RICH SCHOOLS THINK.
FOURTH IS A GAME OF CONCENTRATION AND FREE THROWS.
C
D
1 2 3 4
A-1 AND D-5!!
VERMEER'S VIEW OF DEFLT AND THE ASTRONOMER!!
※MATCHING PAINTINGS BY PAINTER
SWUFF
GOAL!!

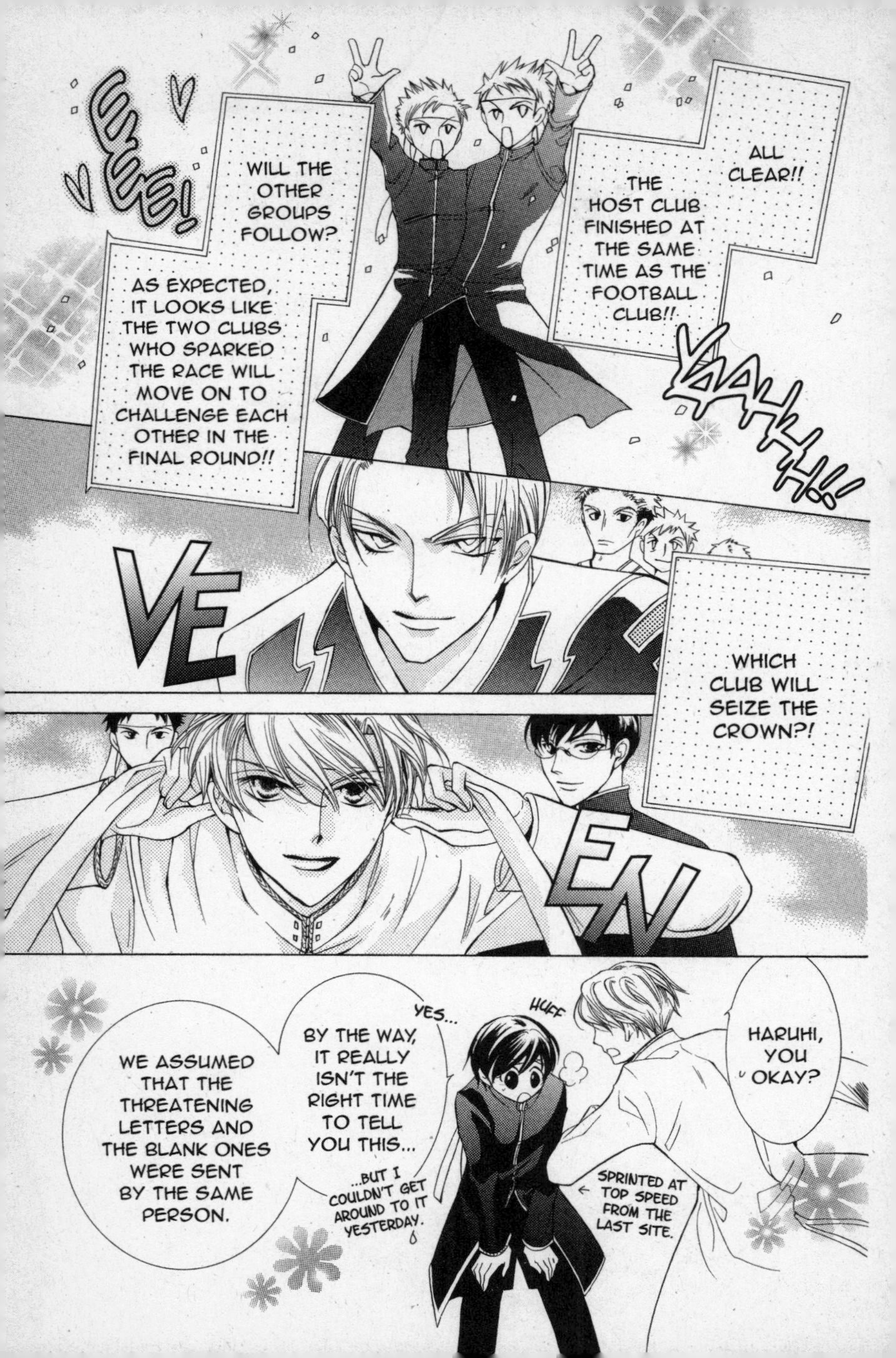
ALL CLEAR!!
THE HOST CLUB FINISHED AT THE SAME TIME AS THE FOOTBALL CLUB!!
YAAHHH!!
WILL THE OTHER GROUPS FOLLOW?
AS EXPECTED, IT LOOKS LIKE THE TWO CLUBS WHO SPARKED THE RACE WILL MOVE ON TO CHALLENGE EACH OTHER IN THE FINAL ROUND!!
WHICH CLUB WILL SEIZE THE CROWN?!
VE
EN
HARUHI, YOU OKAY?
HUFF
YES...
SPRINTED AT TOP SPEED FROM THE LAST SITE.
BY THE WAY, IT REALLY ISN'T THE RIGHT TIME TO TELL YOU THIS...
...BUT I COULDN'T GET AROUND TO IT YESTERDAY.
WE ASSUMED THAT THE THREATENING LETTERS AND THE BLANK ONES WERE SENT BY THE SAME PERSON.

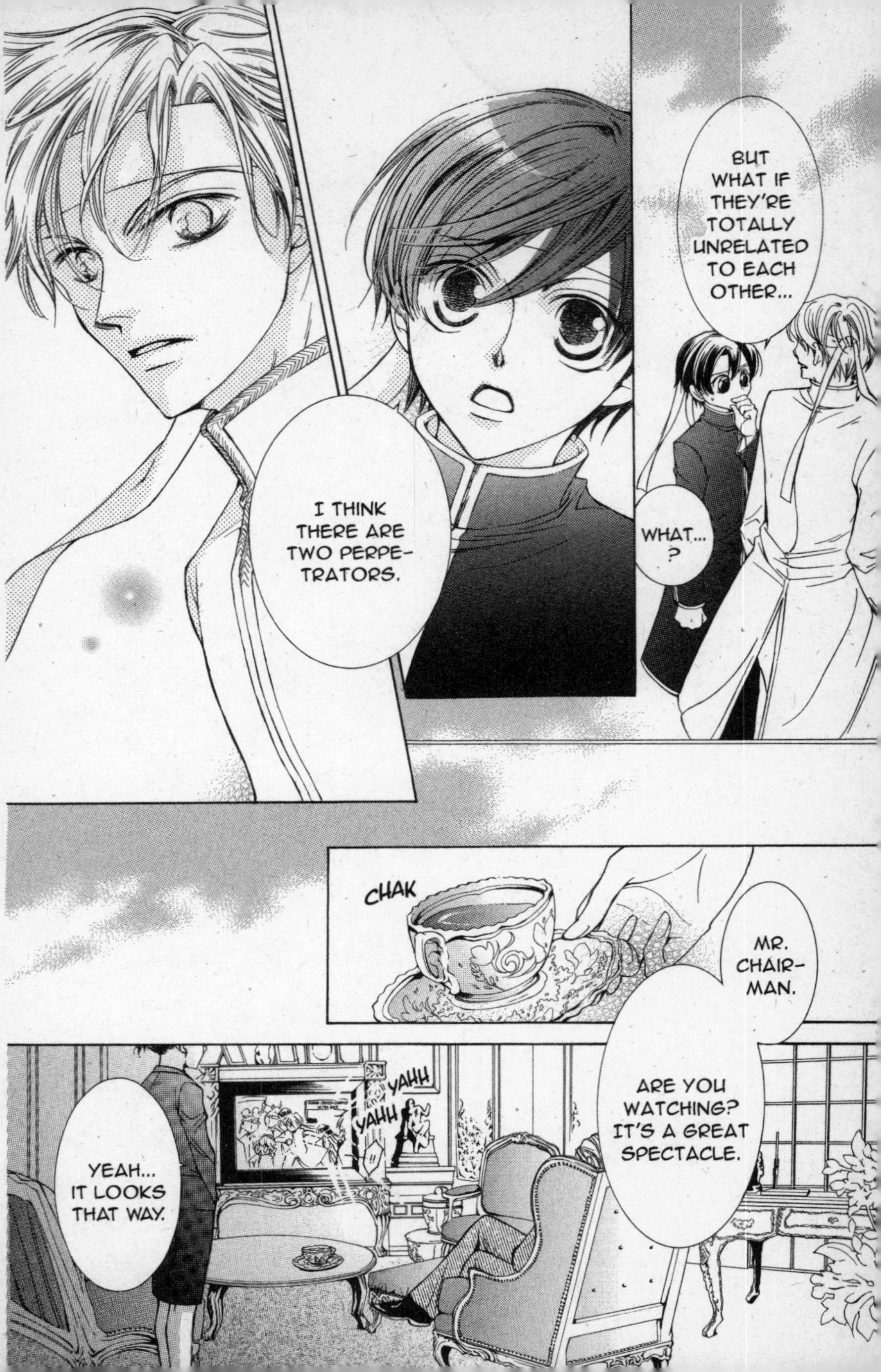
BUT WHAT IF THEY'RE TOTALLY UNRELATED TO EACH OTHER...
WHAT... ?
I THINK THERE ARE TWO PERPE-TRATORS.
MR. CHAIR-MAN.
CHAK
ARE YOU WATCHING? IT'S A GREAT SPECTACLE.
YAHH
YAHH
YEAH... IT LOOKS THAT WAY.

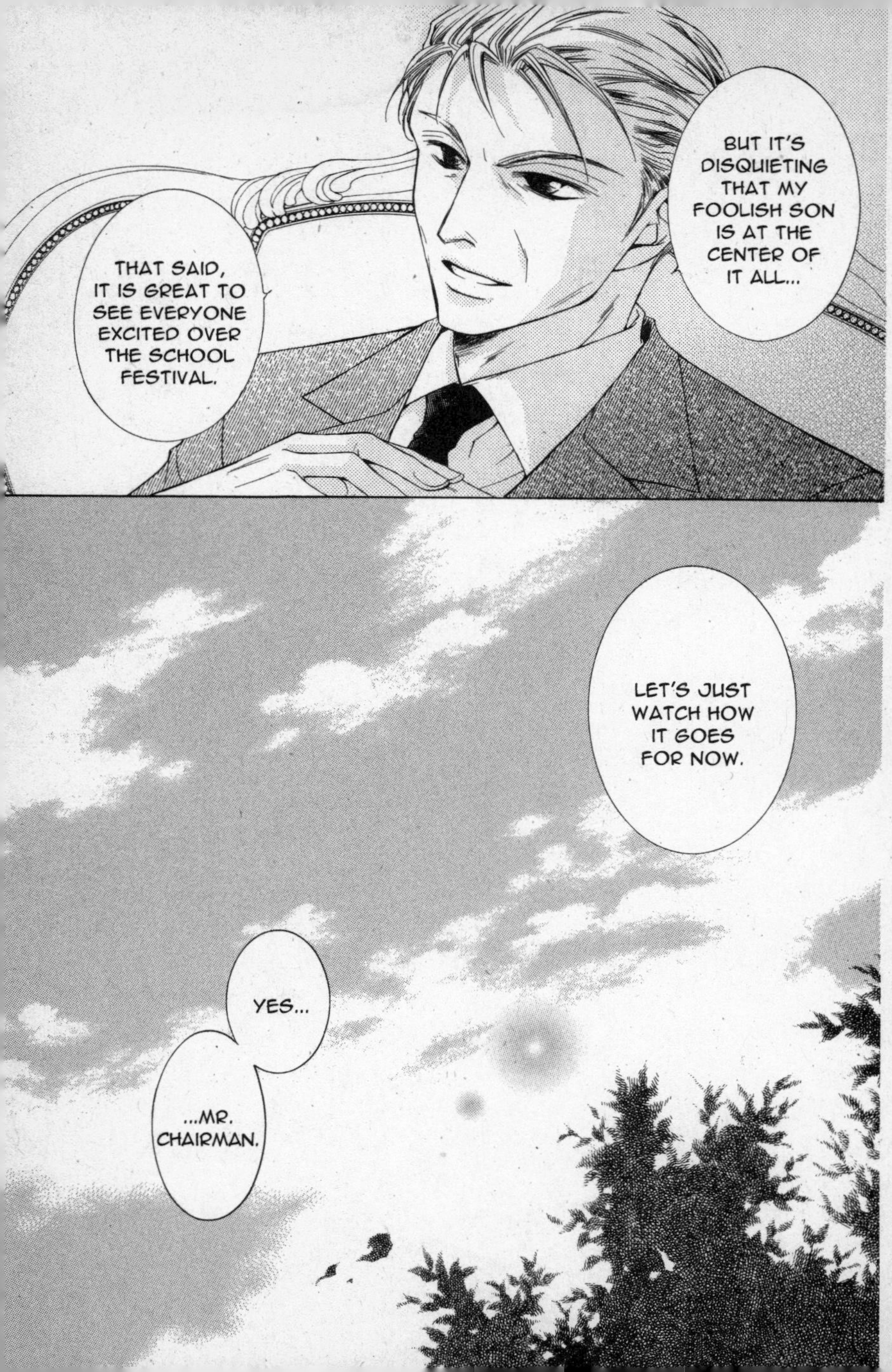
BUT IT'S DISQUIETING THAT MY FOOLISH SON IS AT THE CENTER OF IT ALL...
THAT SAID, IT IS GREAT TO SEE EVERYONE EXCITED OVER THE SCHOOL FESTIVAL.
LET'S JUST WATCH HOW IT GOES FOR NOW.
YES...
...MR. CHAIRMAN.

Great Detective Tamaki and Pipe Fairy

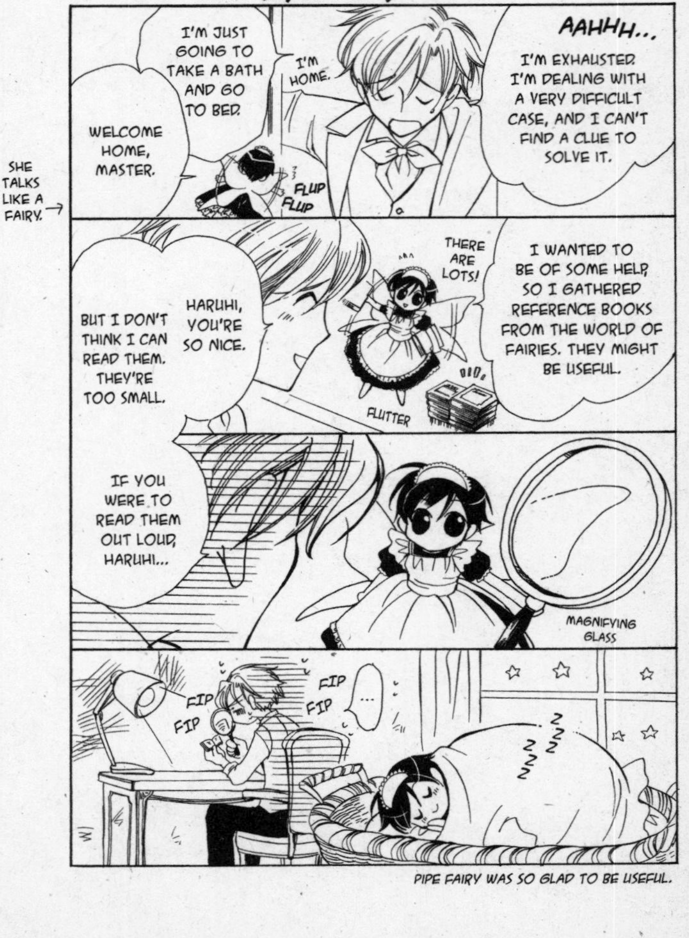
AAHHH...
I'M EXHAUSTED. I'M DEALING WITH A VERY DIFFICULT CASE, AND I CAN'T FIND A CLUE TO SOLVE IT.
I'M HOME.
I'M JUST GOING TO TAKE A BATH AND GO TO BED.
FLUP FLUP
WELCOME HOME, MASTER.
SHE TALKS LIKE A FAIRY.
I WANTED TO BE OF SOME HELP, SO I GATHERED REFERENCE BOOKS FROM THE WORLD OF FAIRIES. THEY MIGHT BE USEFUL.
THERE ARE LOTS!
FLUTTER
HARUHI, YOU'RE SO NICE.
BUT I DON'T THINK I CAN READ THEM. THEY'RE TOO SMALL.
MAGNIFYING GLASS
IF YOU WERE TO READ THEM OUT LOUD, HARUHI...
Z Z Z
...
FIP FIP
FIP FIP

PIPE FAIRY WAS SO GLAD TO BE USEFUL.

Episode 24

B□H
Go up and sink
Tenjiku
KCN
Between the Holy Mother and Angel

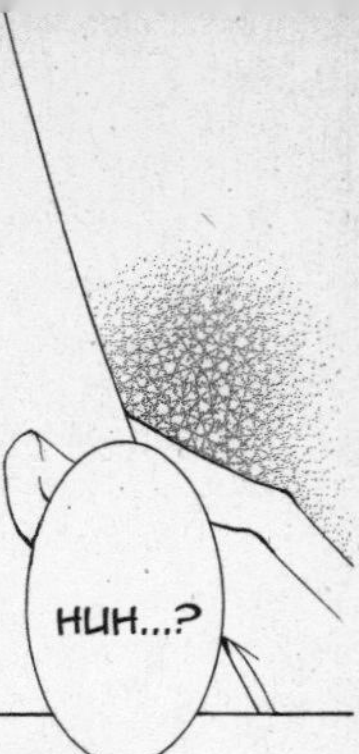
HUH...?

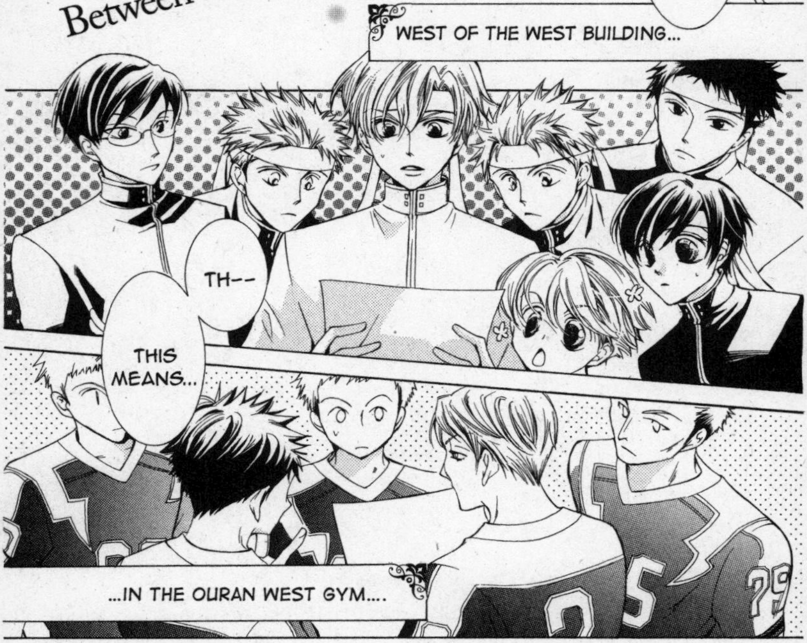
WEST OF THE WEST BUILDING...
TH--
THIS MEANS...
...IN THE OURAN WEST GYM....

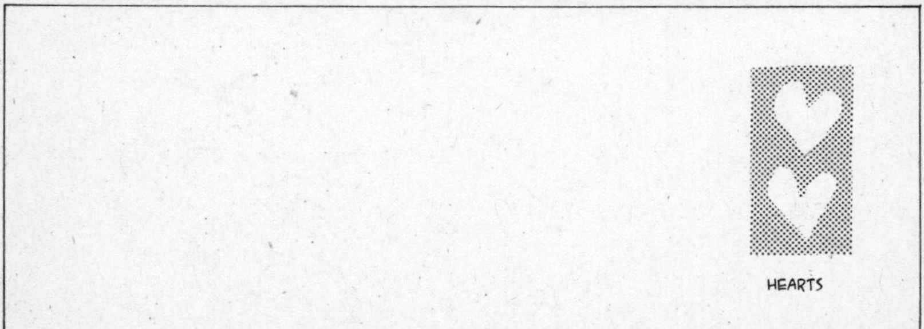
HEARTS

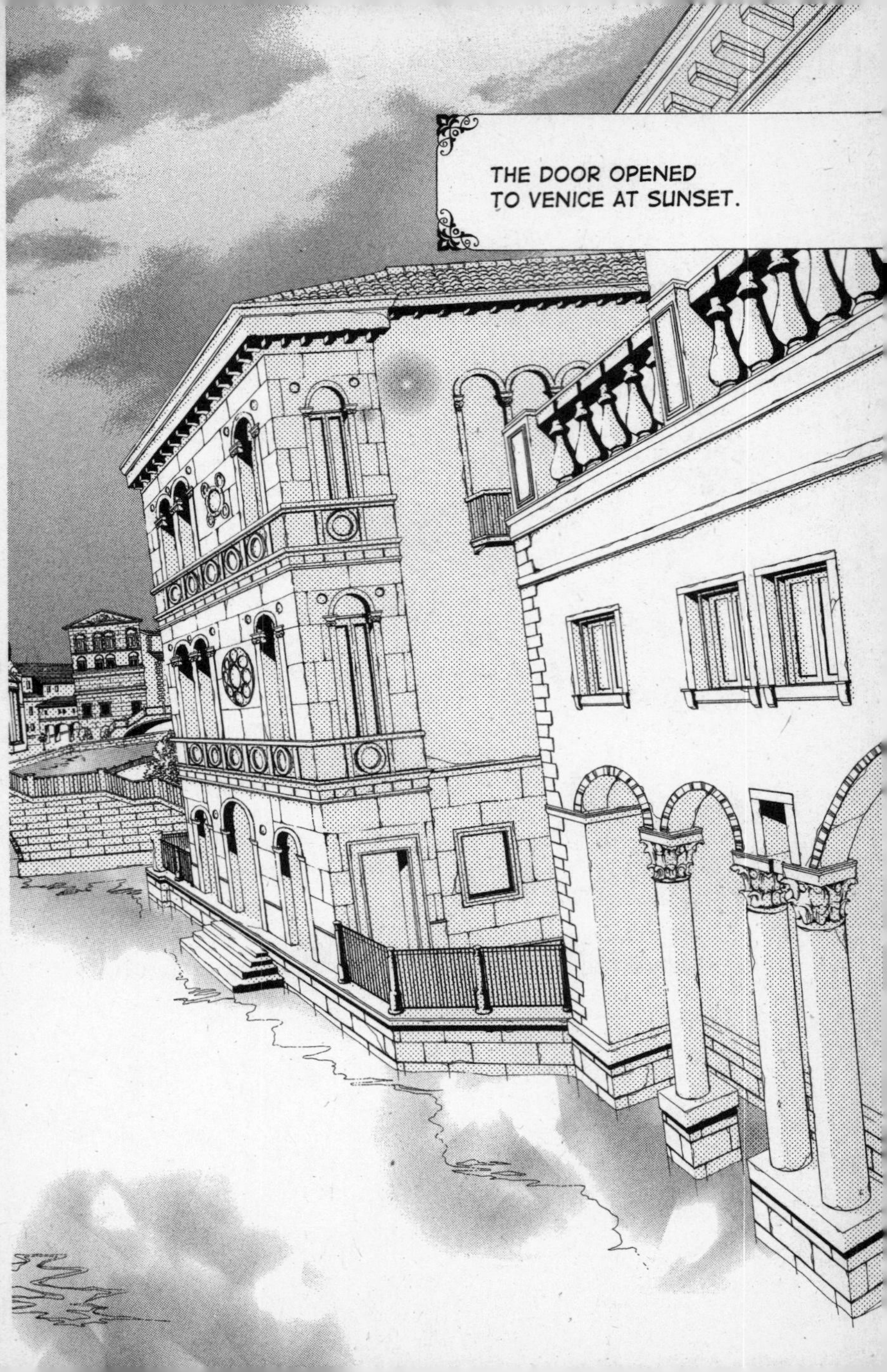
THE DOOR OPENED TO VENICE AT SUNSET.

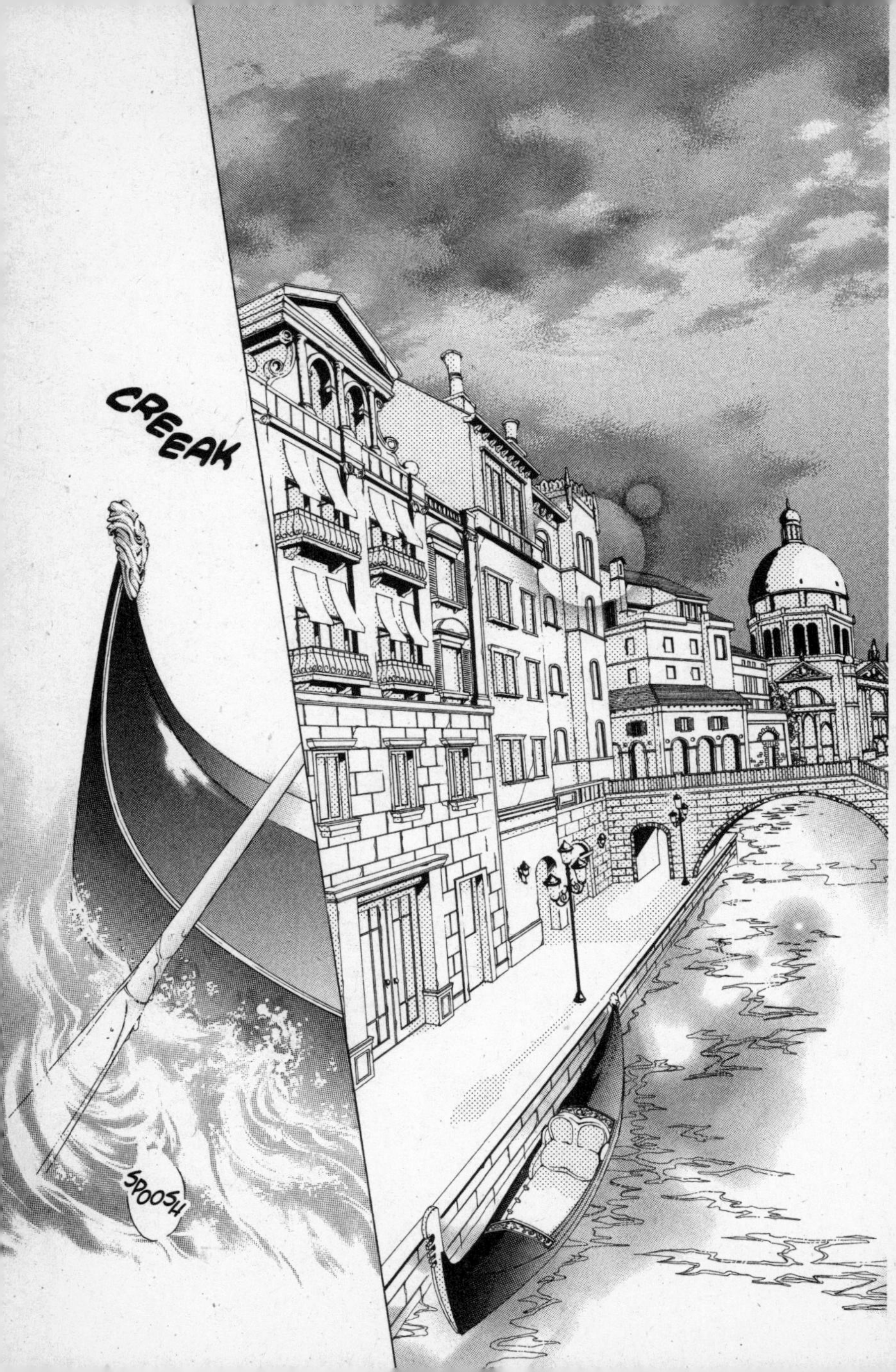
CREEAK
SPOOSH

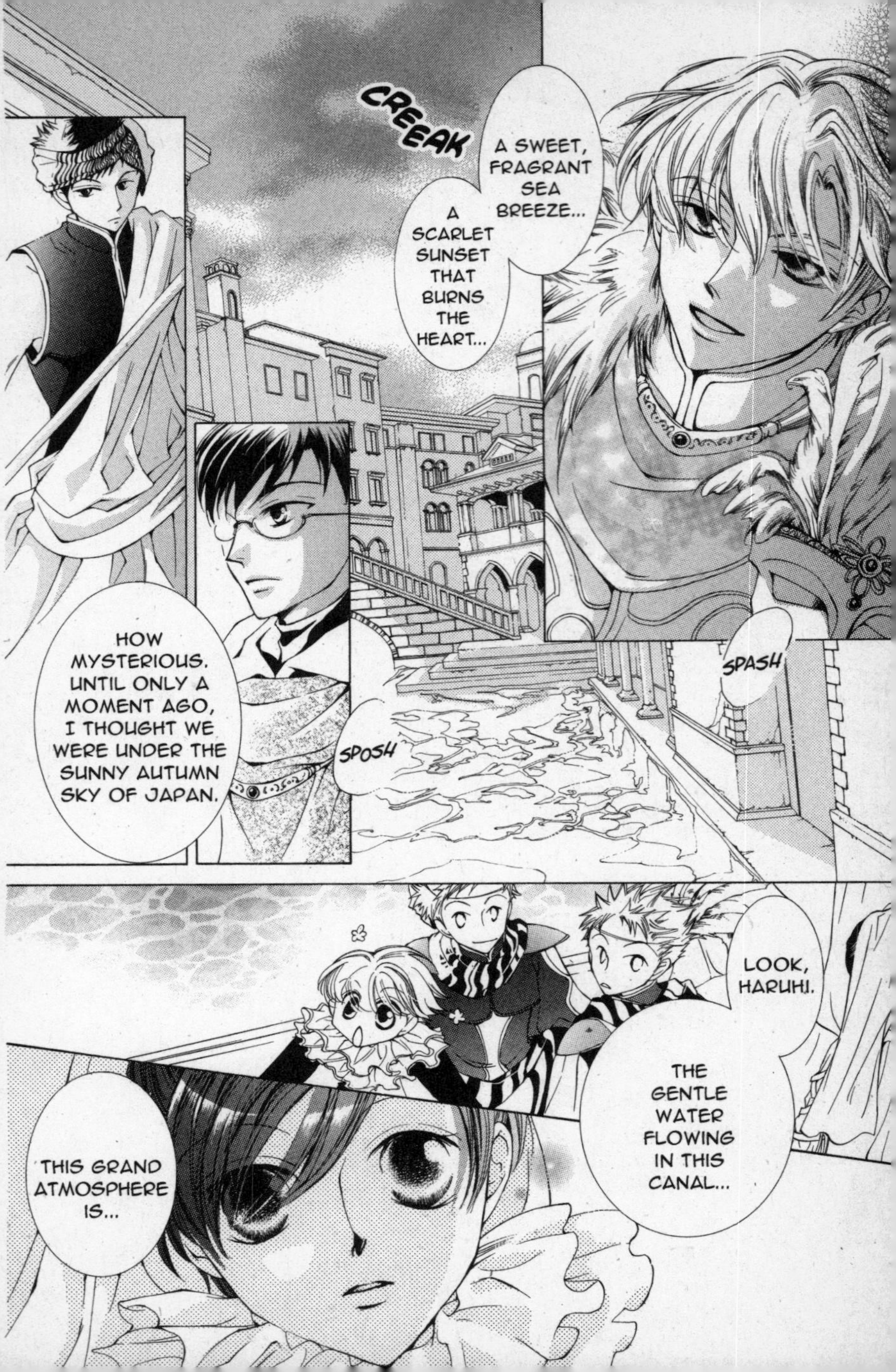
A SWEET, FRAGRANT SEA BREEZE...
A SCARLET SUNSET THAT BURNS THE HEART...
CREEAK
SPASH
SPOSH
HOW MYSTERIOUS. UNTIL ONLY A MOMENT AGO, I THOUGHT WE WERE UNDER THE SUNNY AUTUMN SKY OF JAPAN.
LOOK, HARUHI.
THE GENTLE WATER FLOWING IN THIS CANAL...
THIS GRAND ATMOSPHERE IS...

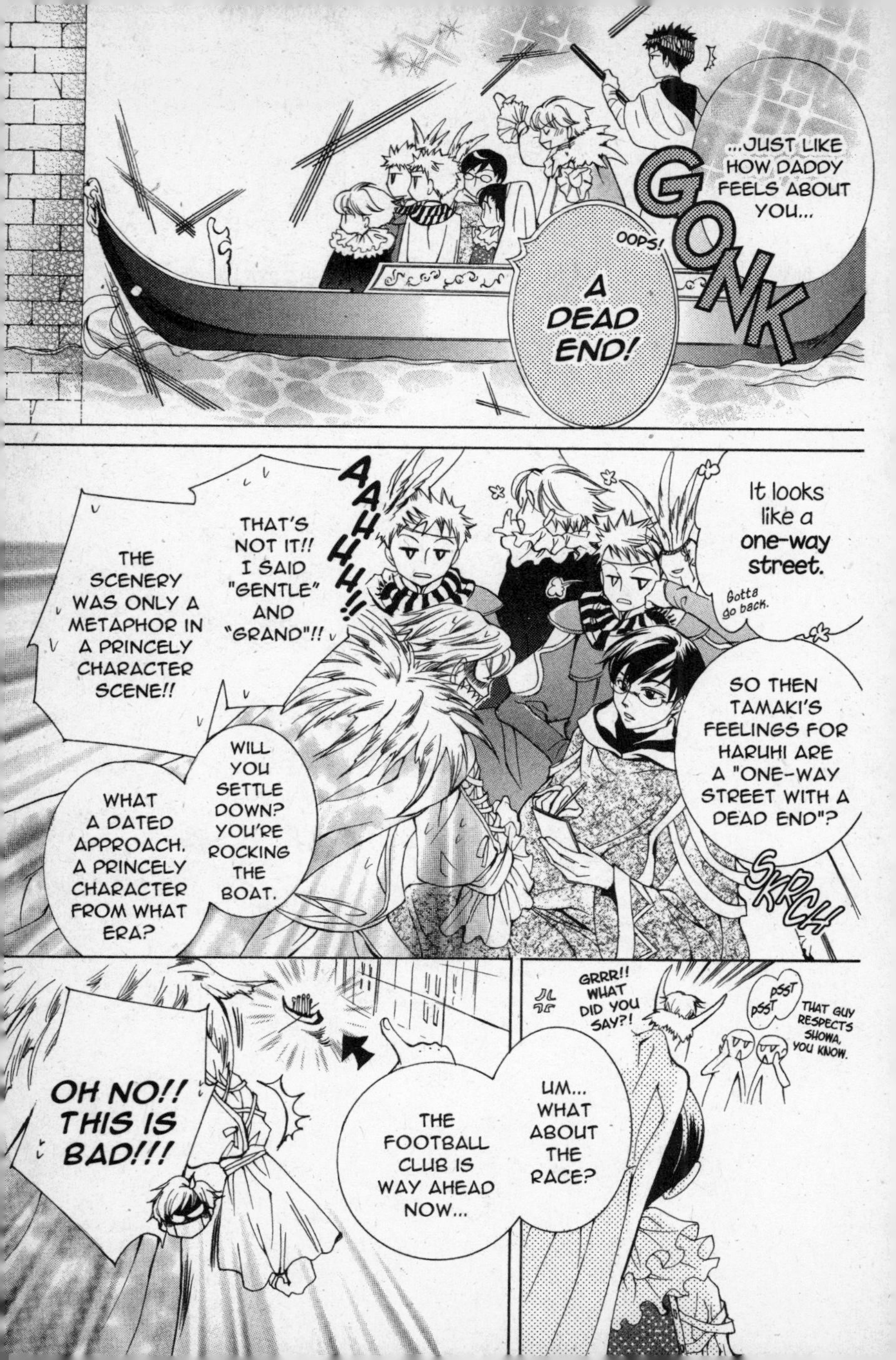
...JUST LIKE HOW DADDY FEELS ABOUT YOU...
GONK
OOPS!
A DEAD END!
It looks like a **one-way street.**
Gotta go back.
SO THEN TAMAKI'S FEELINGS FOR HARUHI ARE A "ONE-WAY STREET WITH A DEAD END"?
SKRCH
AAHHHH!!
THAT'S NOT IT!! I SAID "GENTLE" AND "GRAND"!!
THE SCENERY WAS ONLY A METAPHOR IN A PRINCELY CHARACTER SCENE!!
WILL YOU SETTLE DOWN? YOU'RE ROCKING THE BOAT.
WHAT A DATED APPROACH. A PRINCELY CHARACTER FROM WHAT ERA?
GRRR!! WHAT DID YOU SAY?!
PSST PSST
THAT GUY RESPECTS SHOWA, YOU KNOW.
UM... WHAT ABOUT THE RACE?
THE FOOTBALL CLUB IS WAY AHEAD NOW...
OH NO!! THIS IS BAD!!!

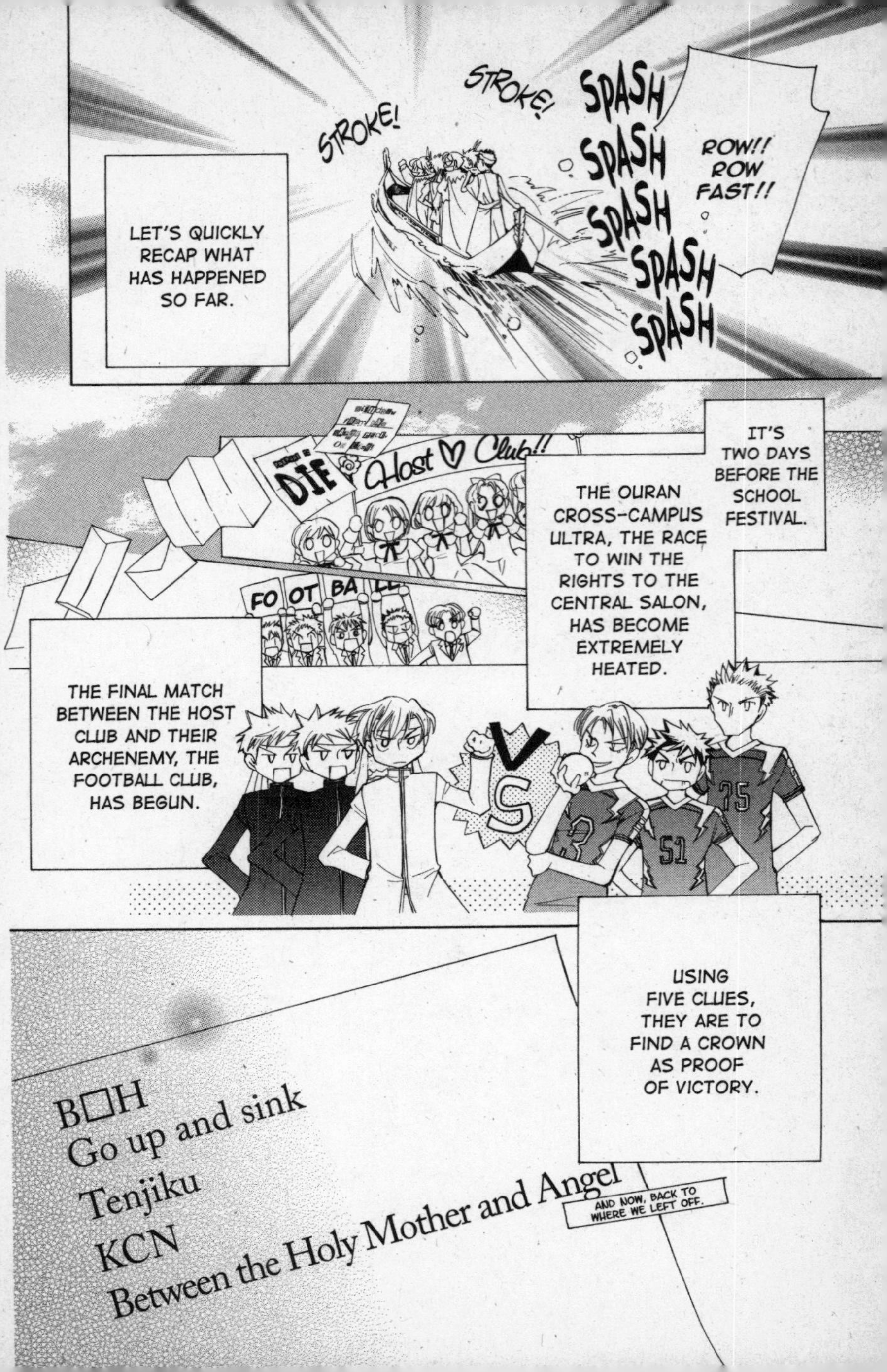
ROW!! ROW FAST!!
SPASH SPASH SPASH SPASH SPASH
STROKE!
STROKE!
LET'S QUICKLY RECAP WHAT HAS HAPPENED SO FAR.
IT'S TWO DAYS BEFORE THE SCHOOL FESTIVAL.
THE OURAN CROSS-CAMPUS ULTRA, THE RACE TO WIN THE RIGHTS TO THE CENTRAL SALON, HAS BECOME EXTREMELY HEATED.
Host ♡ Club!!
DIE
FO OT BA LL
THE FINAL MATCH BETWEEN THE HOST CLUB AND THEIR ARCHENEMY, THE FOOTBALL CLUB, HAS BEGUN.
VS
51
75
USING FIVE CLUES, THEY ARE TO FIND A CROWN AS PROOF OF VICTORY.
B□H
Go up and sink
Tenjiku
KCN
Between the Holy Mother and Angel
AND NOW, BACK TO WHERE WE LEFT OFF.

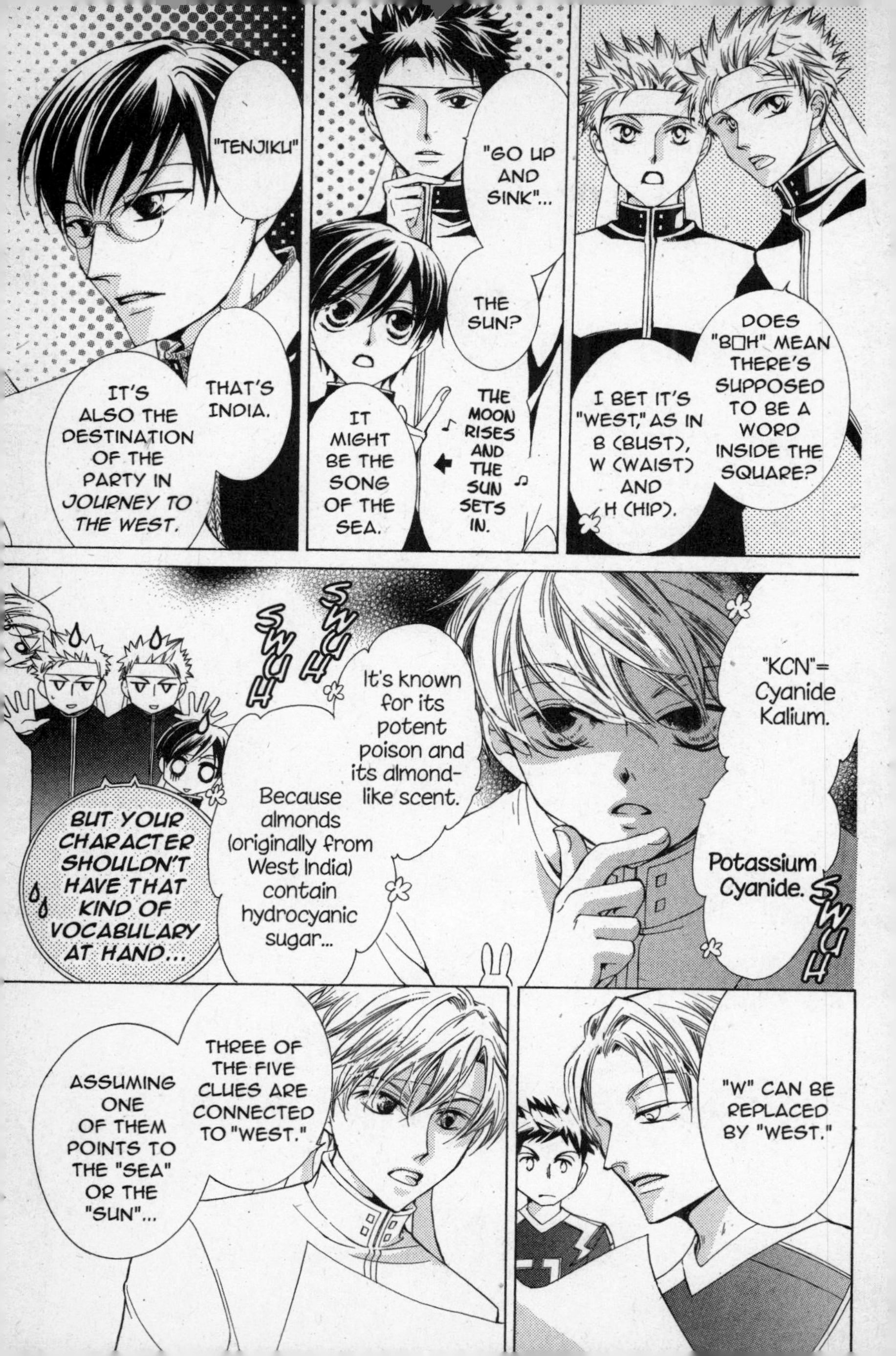
DOES "B□H" MEAN THERE'S SUPPOSED TO BE A WORD INSIDE THE SQUARE?
I BET IT'S "WEST," AS IN B (BUST), W (WAIST) AND H (HIP).
"GO UP AND SINK"...
THE SUN?
THE MOON RISES AND THE SUN SETS IN.
IT MIGHT BE THE SONG OF THE SEA.
"TENJIKU"
THAT'S INDIA.
IT'S ALSO THE DESTINATION OF THE PARTY IN *JOURNEY TO THE WEST.*
"KCN"= Cyanide Kalium.
Potassium Cyanide.
SWUH
It's known for its potent poison and its almond-like scent.
Because almonds (originally from West India) contain hydrocyanic sugar...
SWUH
SWUH
BUT YOUR CHARACTER SHOULDN'T HAVE THAT KIND OF VOCABULARY AT HAND...
"W" CAN BE REPLACED BY "WEST."
THREE OF THE FIVE CLUES ARE CONNECTED TO "WEST."
ASSUMING ONE OF THEM POINTS TO THE "SEA" OR THE "SUN"...

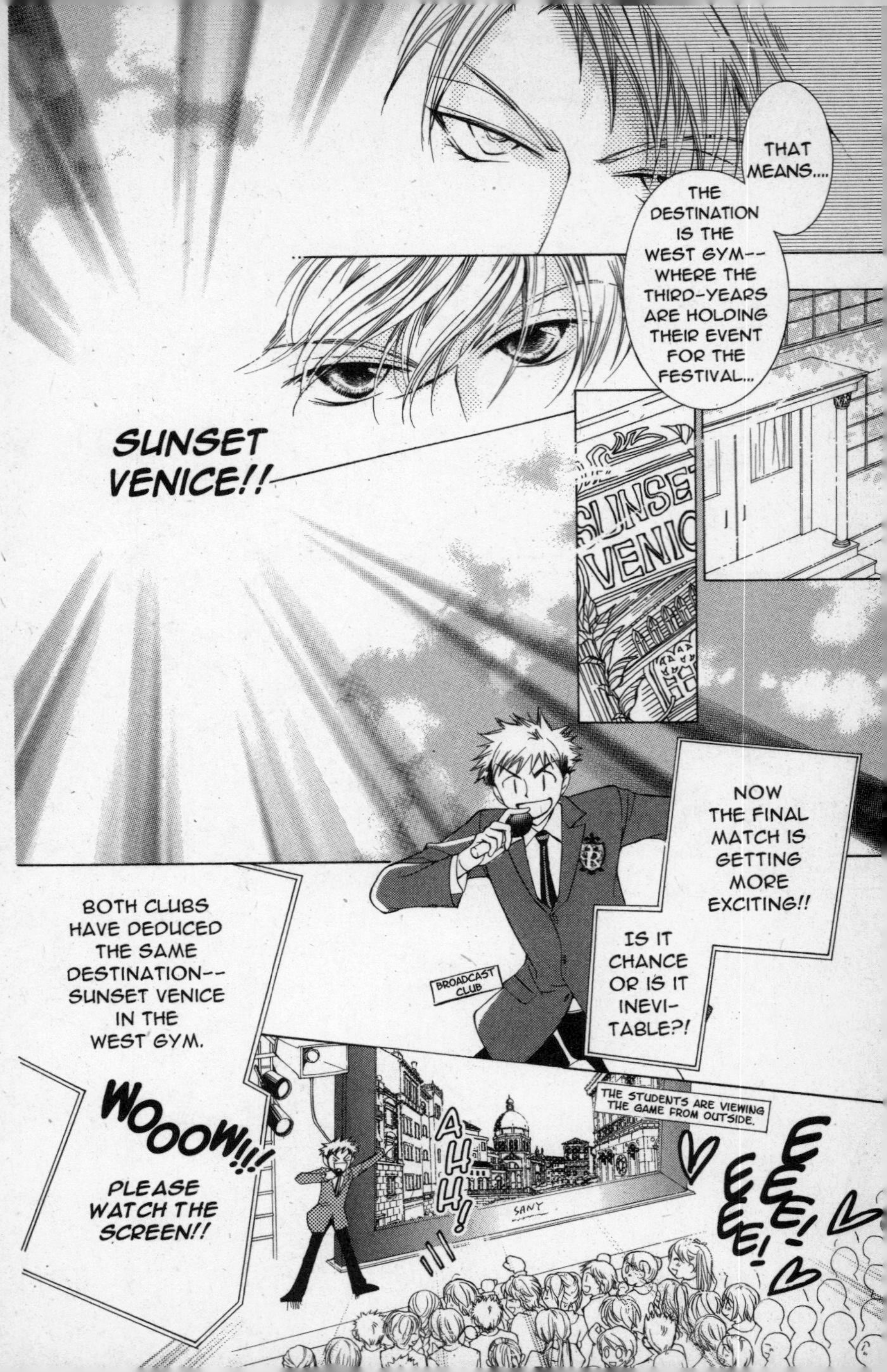
THAT MEANS....
THE DESTINATION IS THE WEST GYM-- WHERE THE THIRD-YEARS ARE HOLDING THEIR EVENT FOR THE FESTIVAL...
SUNSET VENICE!!
NOW THE FINAL MATCH IS GETTING MORE EXCITING!!
IS IT CHANCE OR IS IT INEVI-TABLE?!
BROADCAST CLUB
BOTH CLUBS HAVE DEDUCED THE SAME DESTINATION-- SUNSET VENICE IN THE WEST GYM.
THE STUDENTS ARE VIEWING THE GAME FROM OUTSIDE.
EEEE!
EEE!
AHH!
WOOOW!!!
PLEASE WATCH THE SCREEN!!

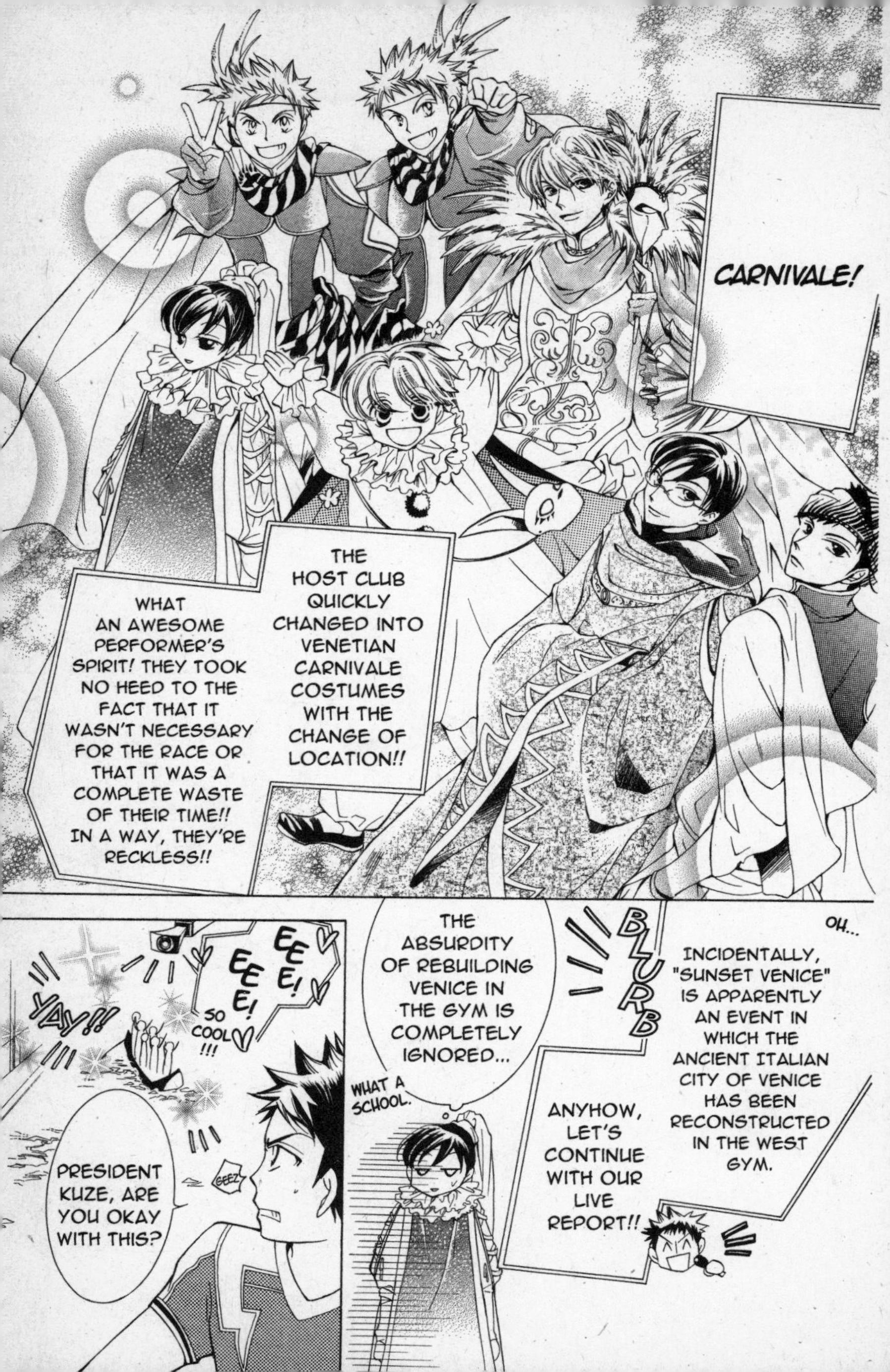
CARNIVALE!
THE HOST CLUB QUICKLY CHANGED INTO VENETIAN CARNIVALE COSTUMES WITH THE CHANGE OF LOCATION!!
WHAT AN AWESOME PERFORMER'S SPIRIT! THEY TOOK NO HEED TO THE FACT THAT IT WASN'T NECESSARY FOR THE RACE OR THAT IT WAS A COMPLETE WASTE OF THEIR TIME!! IN A WAY, THEY'RE RECKLESS!!
OH...
INCIDENTALLY, "SUNSET VENICE" IS APPARENTLY AN EVENT IN WHICH THE ANCIENT ITALIAN CITY OF VENICE HAS BEEN RECONSTRUCTED IN THE WEST GYM.
BLURB
ANYHOW, LET'S CONTINUE WITH OUR LIVE REPORT!!
THE ABSURDITY OF REBUILDING VENICE IN THE GYM IS COMPLETELY IGNORED...
WHAT A SCHOOL.
EEE!
EEE!
SO COOL!!!
YAY!!
GEEZ
PRESIDENT KUZE, ARE YOU OKAY WITH THIS?

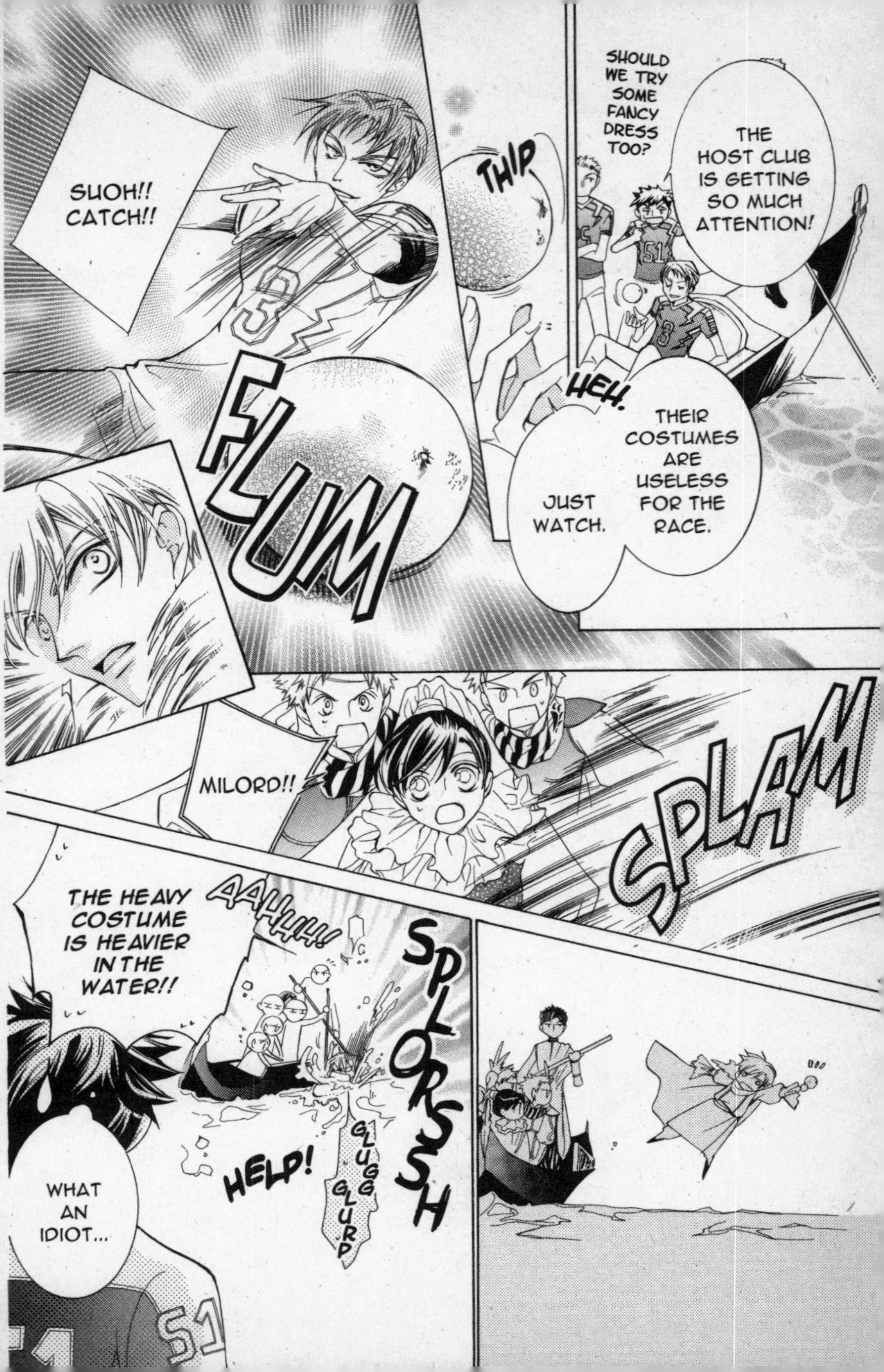
THE HOST CLUB IS GETTING SO MUCH ATTENTION!
SHOULD WE TRY SOME FANCY DRESS TOO?
HEH.
THEIR COSTUMES ARE USELESS FOR THE RACE.
JUST WATCH.
THIP
SUOH!! CATCH!!
FLUM
SPLAM
MILORD!!
SPLORSSH
GLUGG GLUGG GLURP
AAHHH!
HELP!
THE HEAVY COSTUME IS HEAVIER IN THE WATER!!
WHAT AN IDIOT...

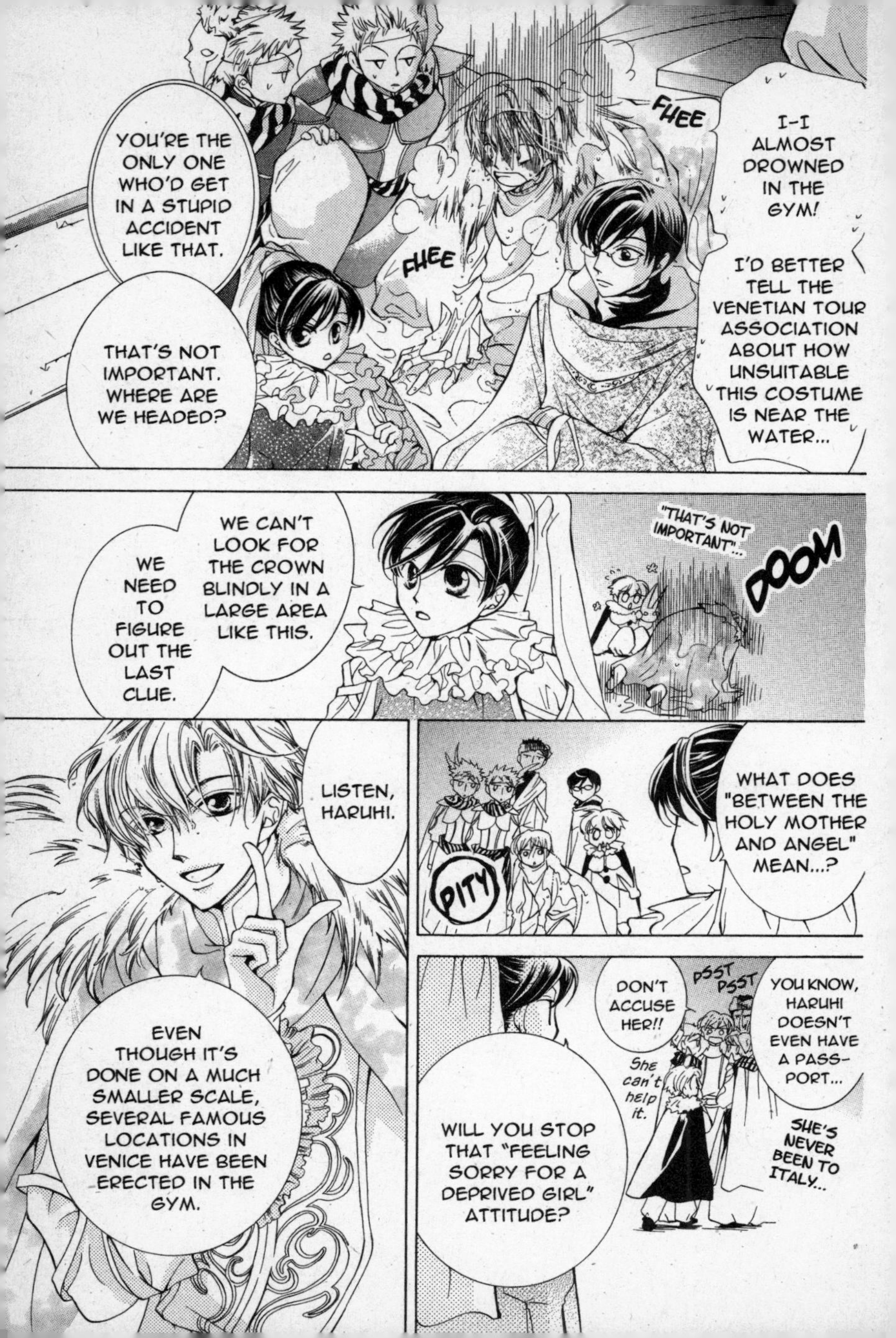
FHEE
I-I ALMOST DROWNED IN THE GYM!
I'D BETTER TELL THE VENETIAN TOUR ASSOCIATION ABOUT HOW UNSUITABLE THIS COSTUME IS NEAR THE WATER...
YOU'RE THE ONLY ONE WHO'D GET IN A STUPID ACCIDENT LIKE THAT.
FHEE
THAT'S NOT IMPORTANT. WHERE ARE WE HEADED?
"THAT'S NOT IMPORTANT"...
DOOM
WE CAN'T LOOK FOR THE CROWN BLINDLY IN A LARGE AREA LIKE THIS.
WE NEED TO FIGURE OUT THE LAST CLUE.
WHAT DOES "BETWEEN THE HOLY MOTHER AND ANGEL" MEAN...?
PITY
YOU KNOW, HARUHI DOESN'T EVEN HAVE A PASS-PORT...
PSST PSST
DON'T ACCUSE HER!!
SHE'S NEVER BEEN TO ITALY...
She can't help it.
WILL YOU STOP THAT "FEELING SORRY FOR A DEPRIVED GIRL" ATTITUDE?
LISTEN, HARUHI.
EVEN THOUGH IT'S DONE ON A MUCH SMALLER SCALE, SEVERAL FAMOUS LOCATIONS IN VENICE HAVE BEEN ERECTED IN THE GYM.

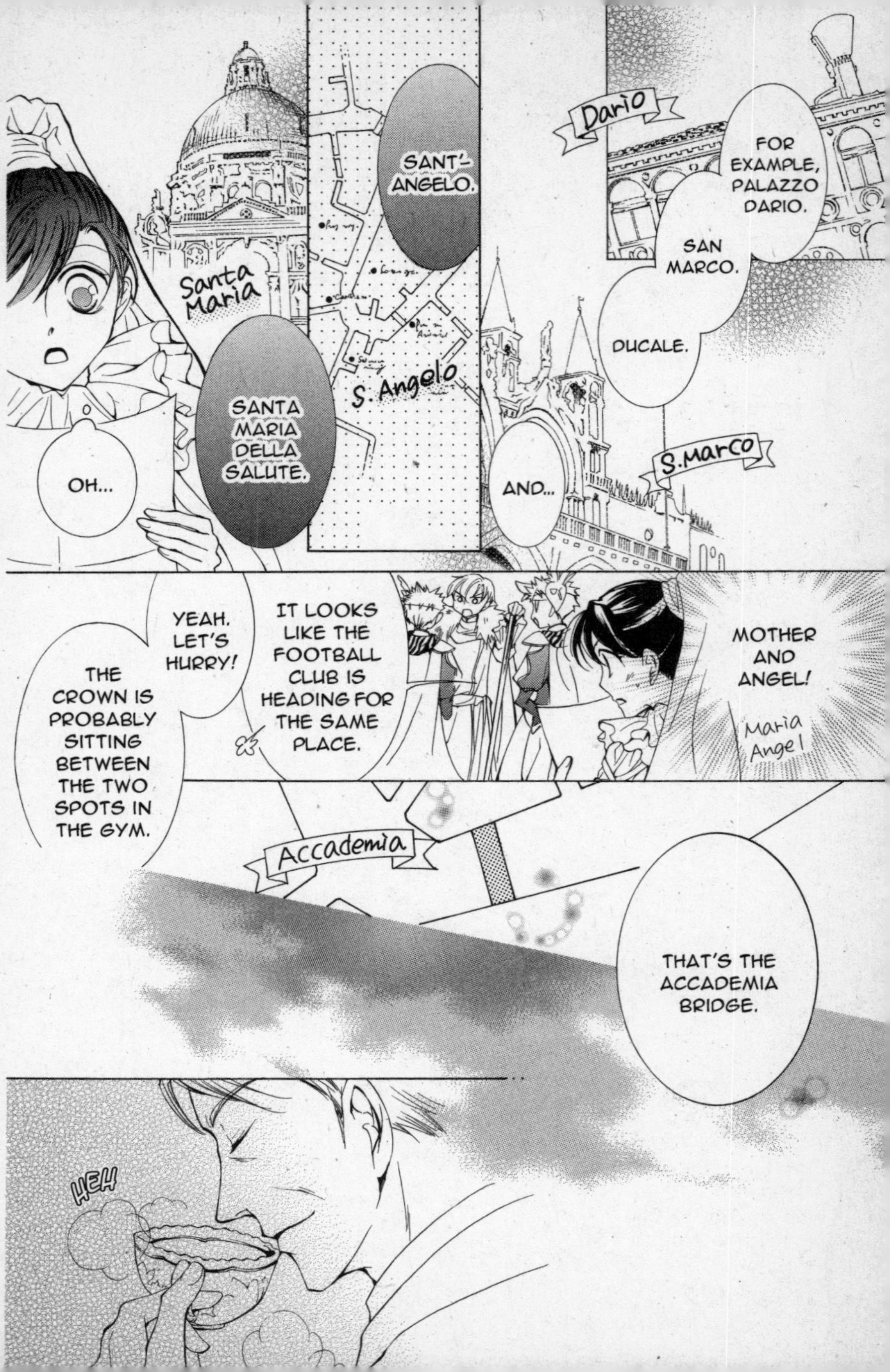
Dario
FOR EXAMPLE, PALAZZO DARIO.
SAN MARCO.
DUCALE.
S.Marco
AND...
SANT'-ANGELO.
S. Angelo
Santa Maria
SANTA MARIA DELLA SALUTE.
OH...
MOTHER AND ANGEL!
Maria Angel
IT LOOKS LIKE THE FOOTBALL CLUB IS HEADING FOR THE SAME PLACE.
YEAH. LET'S HURRY!
THE CROWN IS PROBABLY SITTING BETWEEN THE TWO SPOTS IN THE GYM.
Accademia
THAT'S THE ACCADEMIA BRIDGE.
HEH

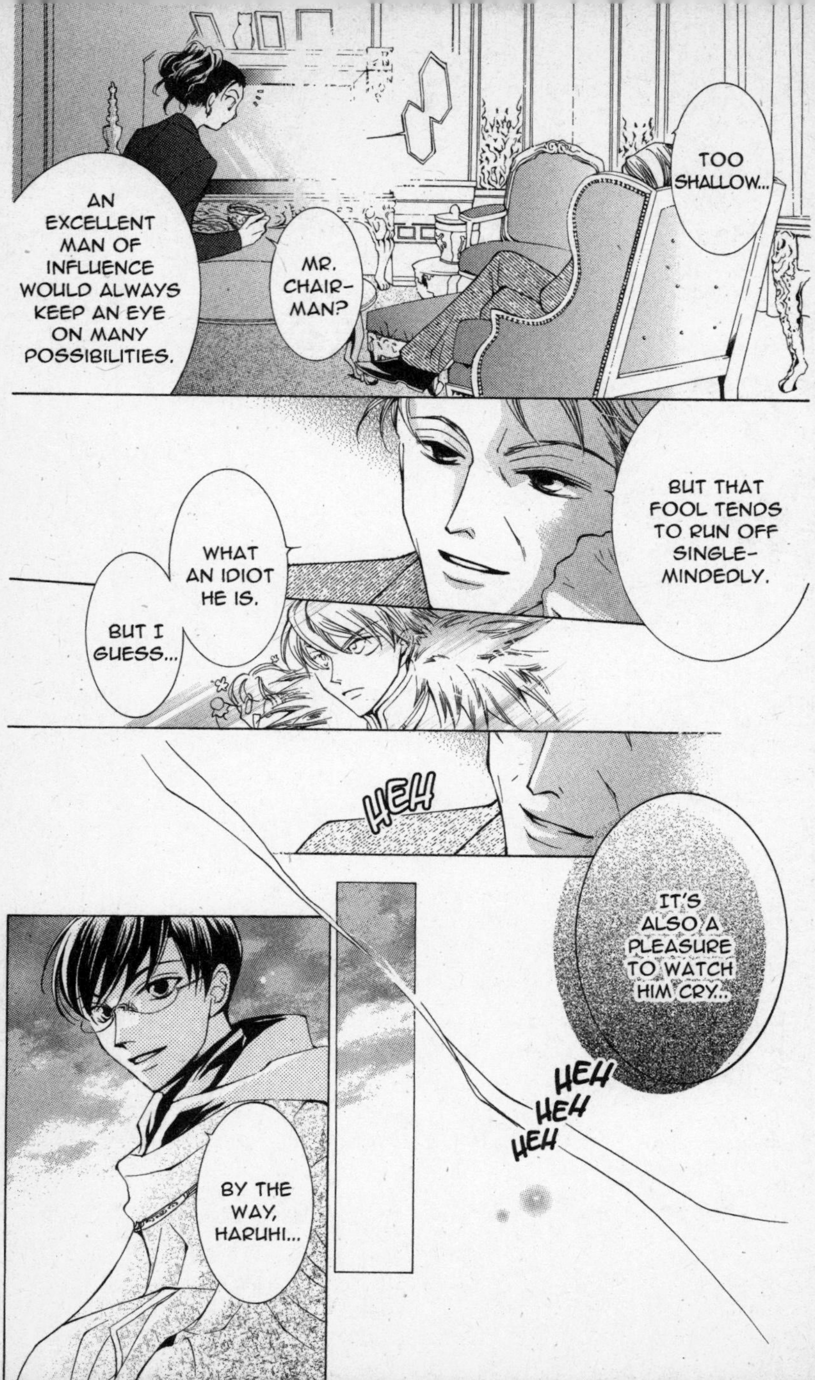
TOO SHALLOW...
MR. CHAIR-MAN?
AN EXCELLENT MAN OF INFLUENCE WOULD ALWAYS KEEP AN EYE ON MANY POSSIBILITIES.
BUT THAT FOOL TENDS TO RUN OFF SINGLE-MINDEDLY.
WHAT AN IDIOT HE IS.
BUT I GUESS...
HEH
IT'S ALSO A PLEASURE TO WATCH HIM CRY...
HEH HEH HEH
BY THE WAY, HARUHI...

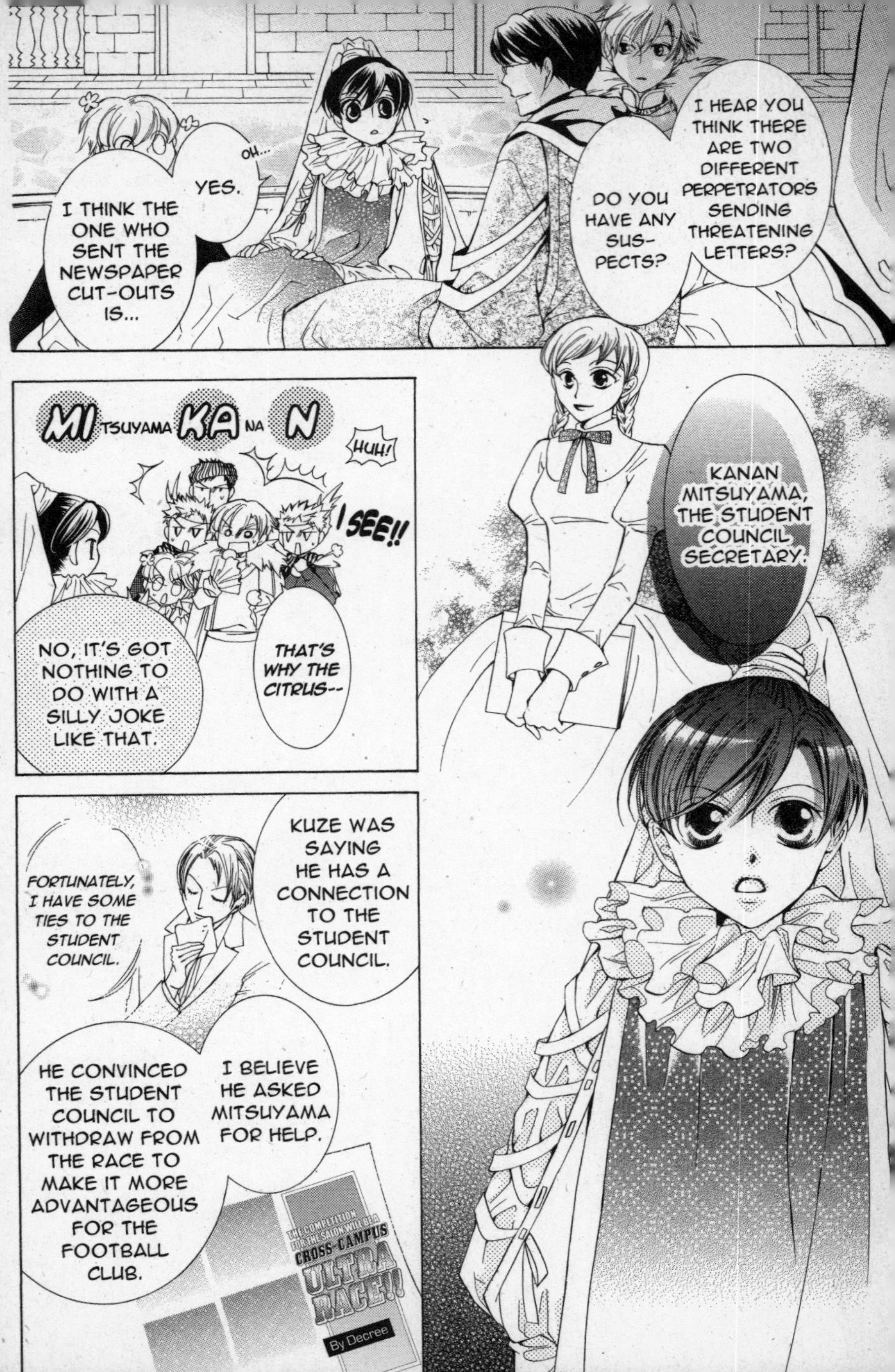
I HEAR YOU THINK THERE ARE TWO DIFFERENT PERPETRATORS SENDING THREATENING LETTERS?
DO YOU HAVE ANY SUS-PECTS?
OH...
YES.
I THINK THE ONE WHO SENT THE NEWSPAPER CUT-OUTS IS...
KANAN MITSUYAMA, THE STUDENT COUNCIL SECRETARY.
MItsuyama KAnaN
HUH!
I SEE!!
THAT'S WHY THE CITRUS--
NO, IT'S GOT NOTHING TO DO WITH A SILLY JOKE LIKE THAT.
KUZE WAS SAYING HE HAS A CONNECTION TO THE STUDENT COUNCIL.
FORTUNATELY, I HAVE SOME TIES TO THE STUDENT COUNCIL.
I BELIEVE HE ASKED MITSUYAMA FOR HELP.
HE CONVINCED THE STUDENT COUNCIL TO WITHDRAW FROM THE RACE TO MAKE IT MORE ADVANTAGEOUS FOR THE FOOTBALL CLUB.
THE COMPETITION FOR THE SALON WILL BE A CROSS-CAMPUS ULTRA RACE!!
By Decree

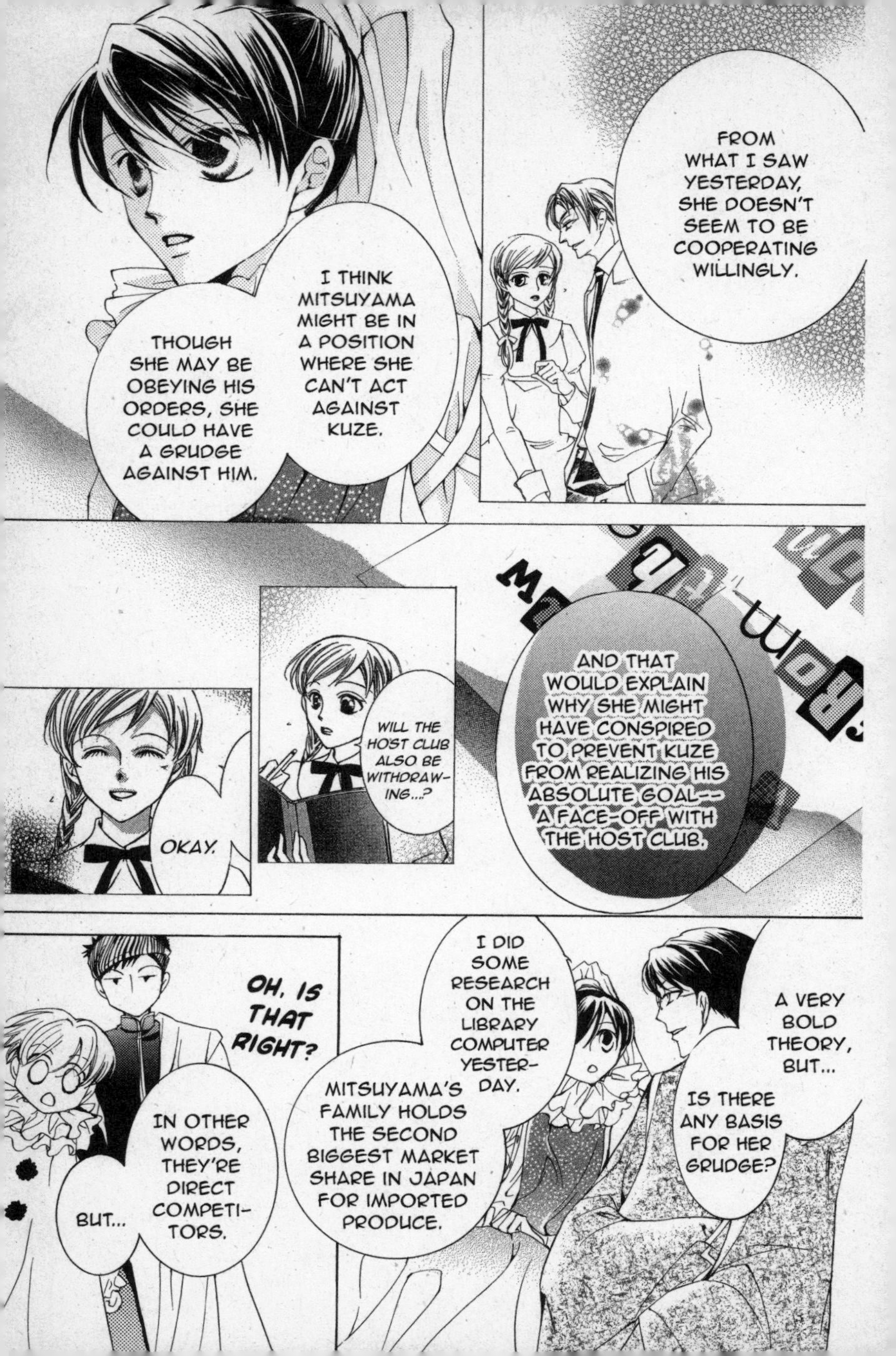
FROM WHAT I SAW YESTERDAY, SHE DOESN'T SEEM TO BE COOPERATING WILLINGLY.
I THINK MITSUYAMA MIGHT BE IN A POSITION WHERE SHE CAN'T ACT AGAINST KUZE.
THOUGH SHE MAY BE OBEYING HIS ORDERS, SHE COULD HAVE A GRUDGE AGAINST HIM.
AND THAT WOULD EXPLAIN WHY SHE MIGHT HAVE CONSPIRED TO PREVENT KUZE FROM REALIZING HIS ABSOLUTE GOAL-- A FACE-OFF WITH THE HOST CLUB.
WILL THE HOST CLUB ALSO BE WITHDRAWING...?
OKAY.
A VERY BOLD THEORY, BUT...
IS THERE ANY BASIS FOR HER GRUDGE?
I DID SOME RESEARCH ON THE LIBRARY COMPUTER YESTERDAY.
MITSUYAMA'S FAMILY HOLDS THE SECOND BIGGEST MARKET SHARE IN JAPAN FOR IMPORTED PRODUCE.
OH, IS THAT RIGHT?
IN OTHER WORDS, THEY'RE DIRECT COMPETITORS.
BUT...

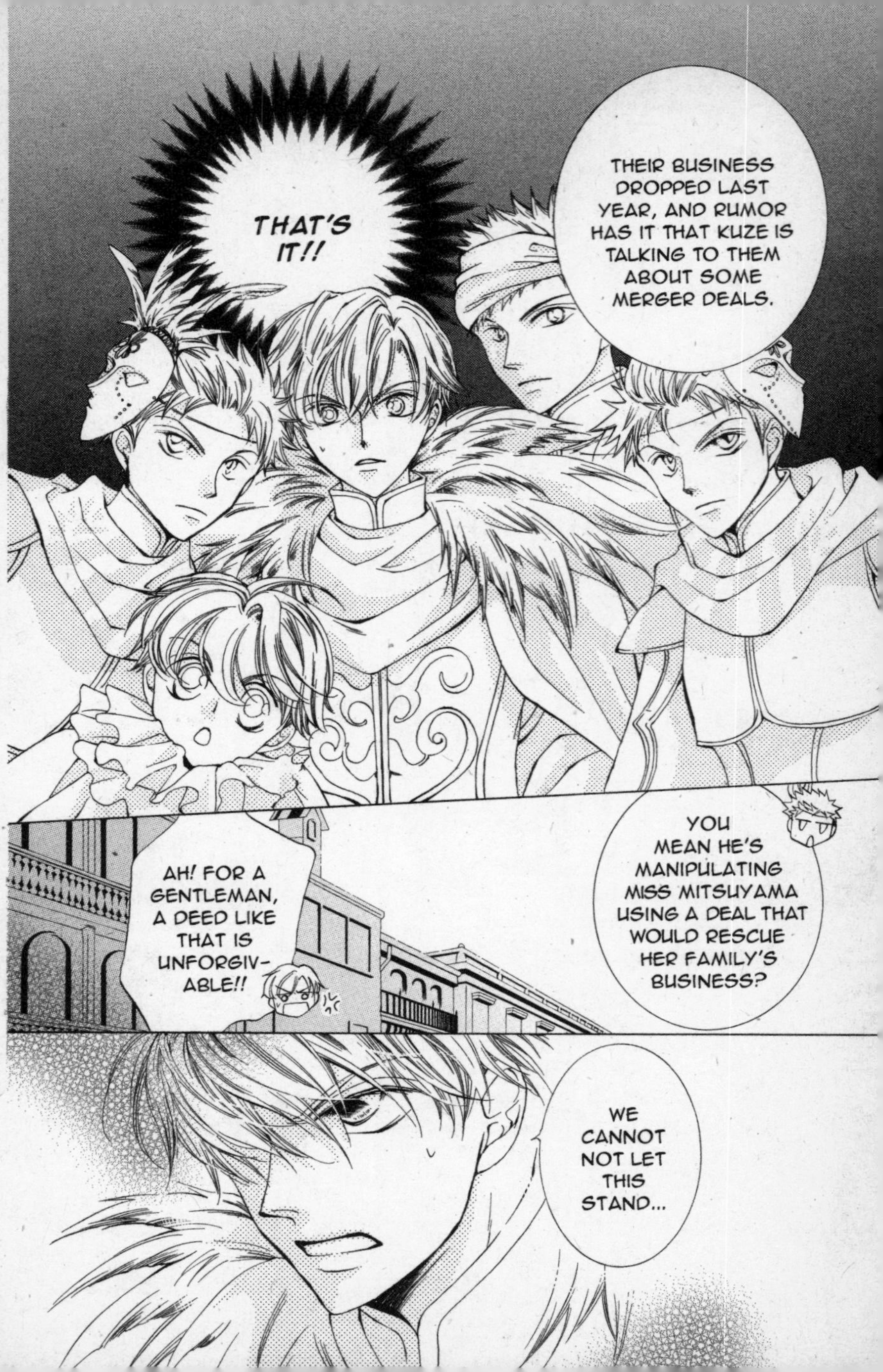
THEIR BUSINESS DROPPED LAST YEAR, AND RUMOR HAS IT THAT KUZE IS TALKING TO THEM ABOUT SOME MERGER DEALS.
THAT'S IT!!
YOU MEAN HE'S MANIPULATING MISS MITSUYAMA USING A DEAL THAT WOULD RESCUE HER FAMILY'S BUSINESS?
AH! FOR A GENTLEMAN, A DEED LIKE THAT IS UNFORGIV-ABLE!!
WE CANNOT NOT LET THIS STAND...

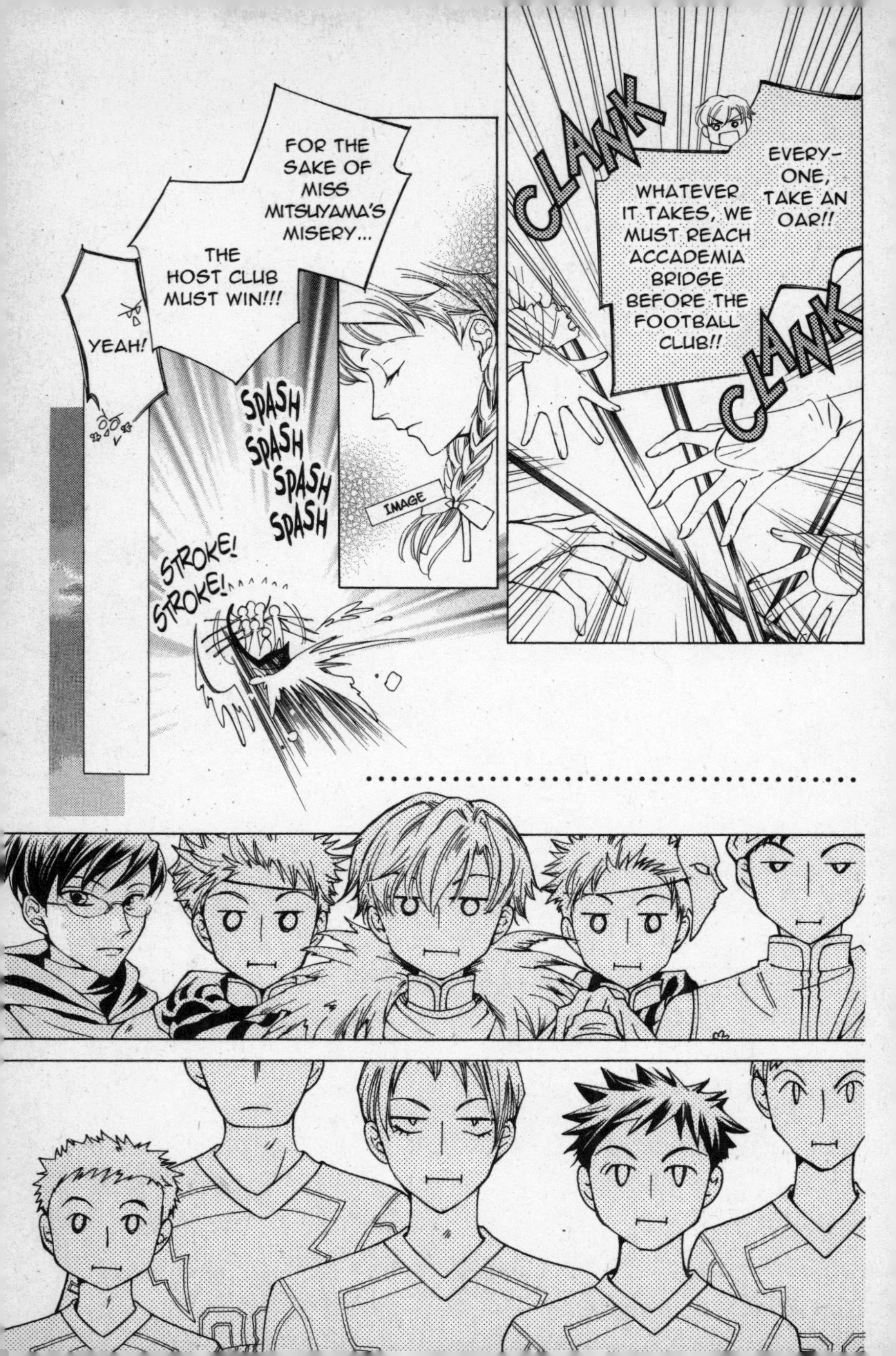
CLANK
EVERY-ONE, TAKE AN OAR!!
WHATEVER IT TAKES, WE MUST REACH ACCADEMIA BRIDGE BEFORE THE FOOTBALL CLUB!!
CLANK
FOR THE SAKE OF MISS MITSUYAMA'S MISERY...
THE HOST CLUB MUST WIN!!!
YEAH!
IMAGE
SPASH SPASH SPASH SPASH
STROKE! STROKE!

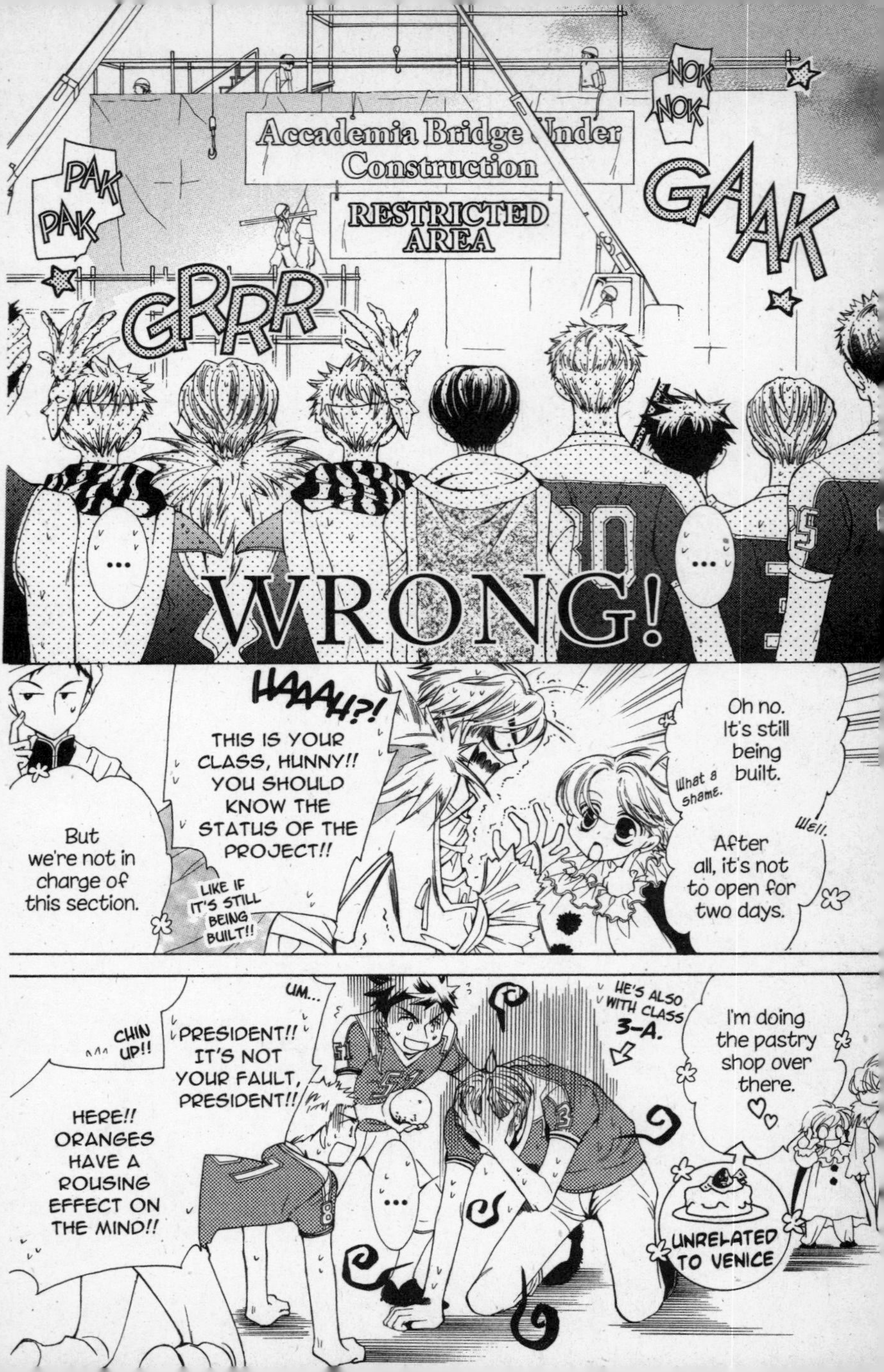
NOK NOK
GAAK
Accademia Bridge Under Construction
RESTRICTED AREA
PAK PAK
GRRR
...
...
WRONG!
Oh no. It's still being built.
What a shame.
Well.
After all, it's not to open for two days.
HAAAH?!
THIS IS YOUR CLASS, HUNNY!! YOU SHOULD KNOW THE STATUS OF THE PROJECT!!
LIKE IF IT'S STILL BEING BUILT!!
But we're not in charge of this section.
I'm doing the pastry shop over there.
UNRELATED TO VENICE
HE'S ALSO WITH CLASS 3-A.
UM...
PRESIDENT!! IT'S NOT YOUR FAULT, PRESIDENT!!
...
CHIN UP!!
HERE!! ORANGES HAVE A ROUSING EFFECT ON THE MIND!!

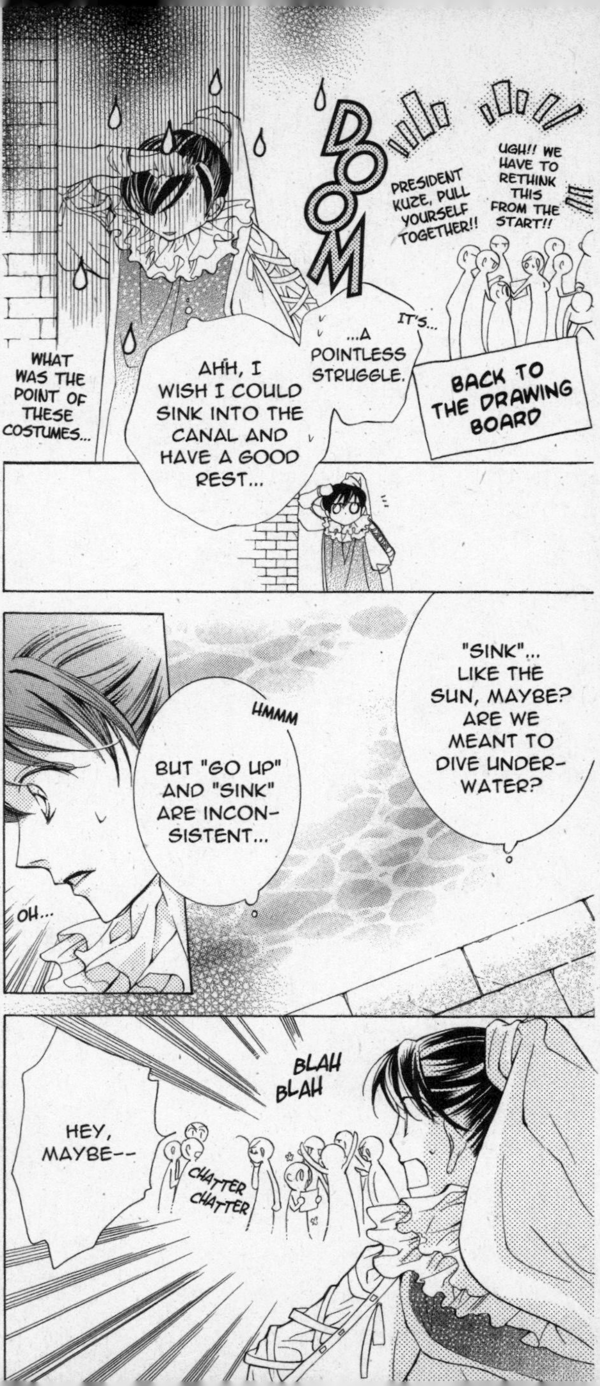
DOOM
UGH!! WE HAVE TO RETHINK THIS FROM THE START!!
PRESIDENT KUZE, PULL YOURSELF TOGETHER!!
BACK TO THE DRAWING BOARD
IT'S...
...A POINTLESS STRUGGLE.
WHAT WAS THE POINT OF THESE COSTUMES...
AHH, I WISH I COULD SINK INTO THE CANAL AND HAVE A GOOD REST...
"SINK"... LIKE THE SUN, MAYBE? ARE WE MEANT TO DIVE UNDER-WATER?
HMMM
BUT "GO UP" AND "SINK" ARE INCON-SISTENT...
OH...
BLAH BLAH
CHATTER CHATTER
HEY, MAYBE--

✿ IT'S ABOUT TIME I ANSWER SOME OF THE QUESTIONS IN THE LETTERS I RECEIVE.

Q1.
ARE YOU A DOG-TYPE OR A CAT-TYPE?

A. I'M A DOG-TYPE. I LOVE DOGGIES!! THE DOG I USED TO HAVE WAS A MUTT, AND IT HAD A VERY COOL NAME: CHOJURO. IF I REMEMBER CORRECTLY, IT WAS MY FRIEND WHO NAMED IT. BUT WHEN I ASKED, MY FRIEND SAID I CAME UP WITH THAT NAME. SO I ACTUALLY DON'T KNOW WHO NAMED THE MUTT AFTER A PEAR. I JUST KNOW IT WASN'T ME.

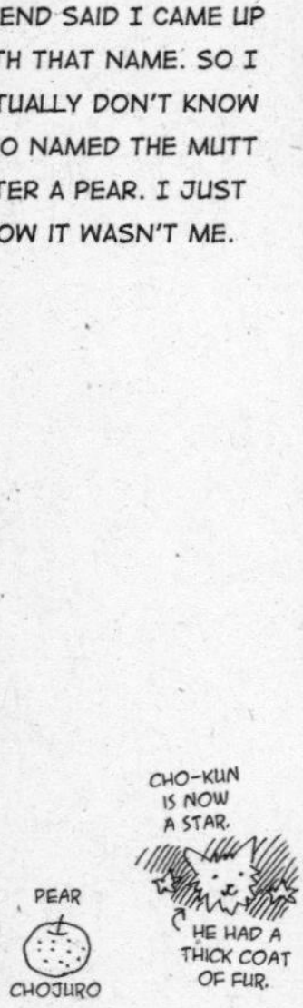
CHO-KUN IS NOW A STAR.
PEAR
CHOJURO
HE HAD A THICK COAT OF FUR.

I LIKE CATS TOO, BUT THEY KEEP BITING ME...

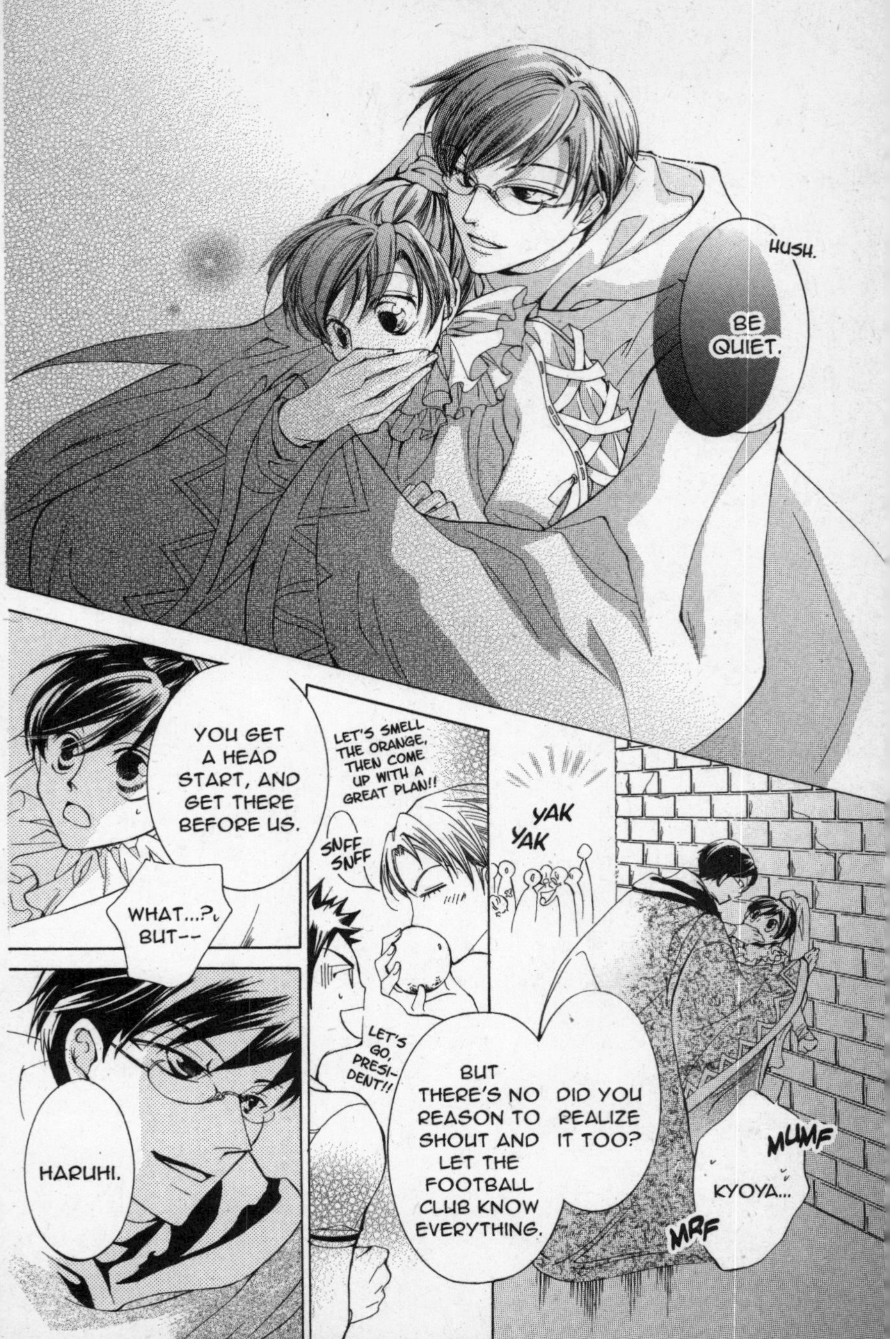
HUSH.
BE QUIET.
MUMF
KYOYA...
MRF
DID YOU REALIZE IT TOO?
BUT THERE'S NO REASON TO SHOUT AND LET THE FOOTBALL CLUB KNOW EVERYTHING.
YAK YAK
LET'S SMELL THE ORANGE, THEN COME UP WITH A GREAT PLAN!!
SNFF SNFF
LET'S GO, PRESIDENT!!
YOU GET A HEAD START, AND GET THERE BEFORE US.
WHAT...? BUT--
HARUHI.

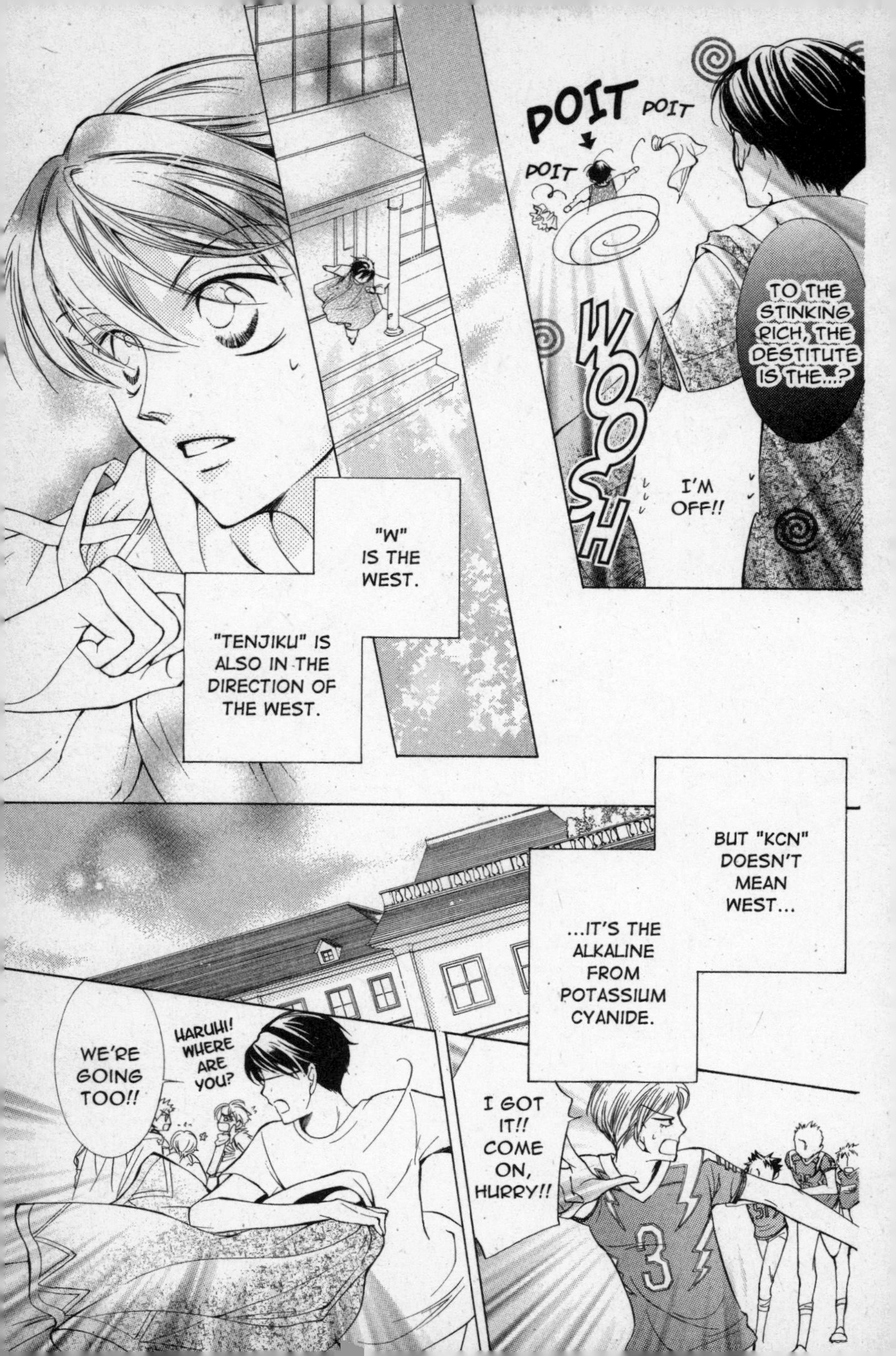
POIT POIT
POIT
TO THE STINKING RICH, THE DESTITUTE IS THE...?
WOOSH
I'M OFF!!
"W" IS THE WEST.
"TENJIKU" IS ALSO IN THE DIRECTION OF THE WEST.
BUT "KCN" DOESN'T MEAN WEST...
...IT'S THE ALKALINE FROM POTASSIUM CYANIDE.
I GOT IT!! COME ON, HURRY!!
HARUHI! WHERE ARE YOU?
WE'RE GOING TOO!!

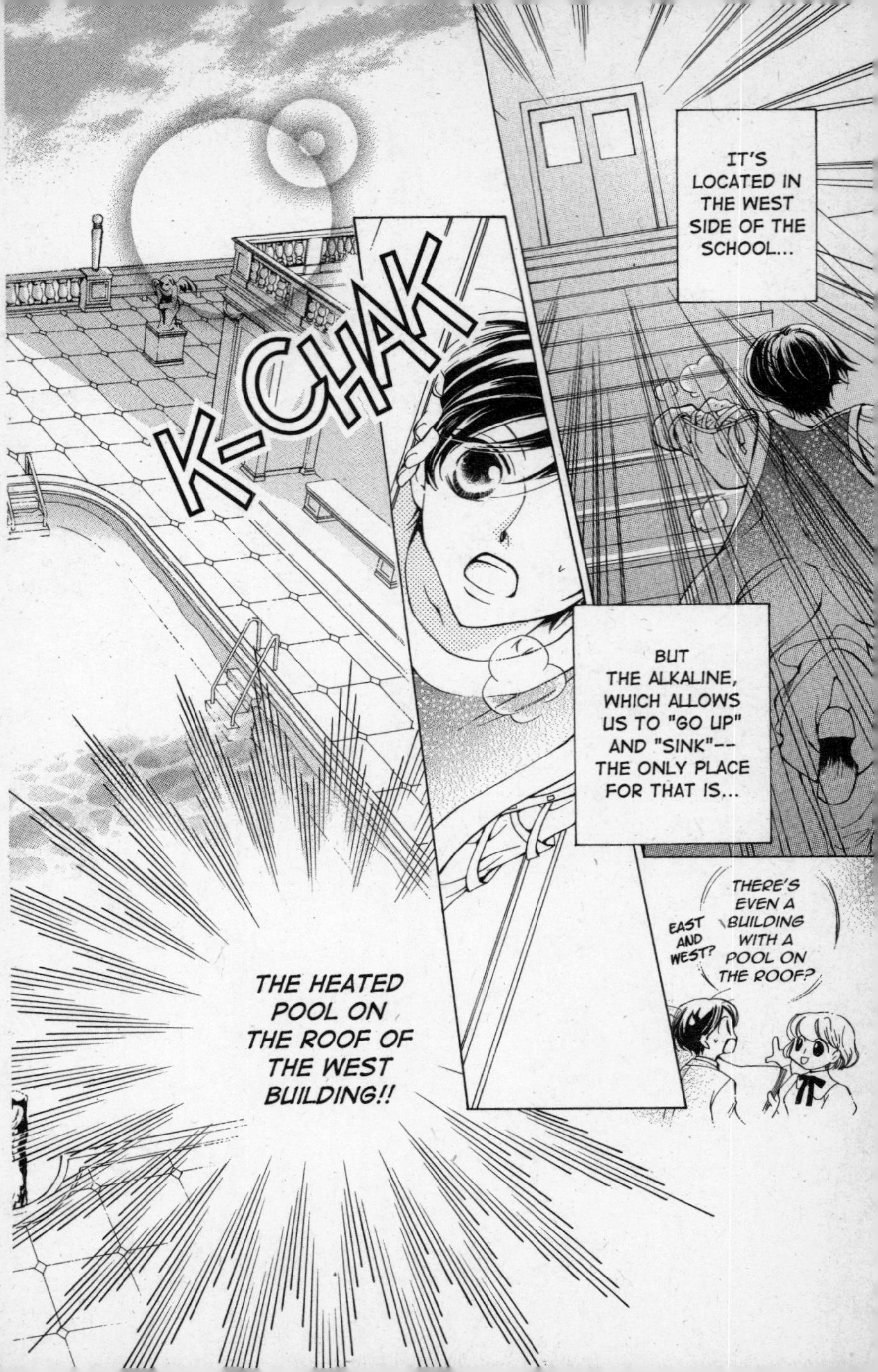
IT'S LOCATED IN THE WEST SIDE OF THE SCHOOL...
BUT THE ALKALINE, WHICH ALLOWS US TO "GO UP" AND "SINK"-- THE ONLY PLACE FOR THAT IS...
THERE'S EVEN A BUILDING WITH A POOL ON THE ROOF?
EAST AND WEST?
K-CHAK
THE HEATED POOL ON THE ROOF OF THE WEST BUILDING!!

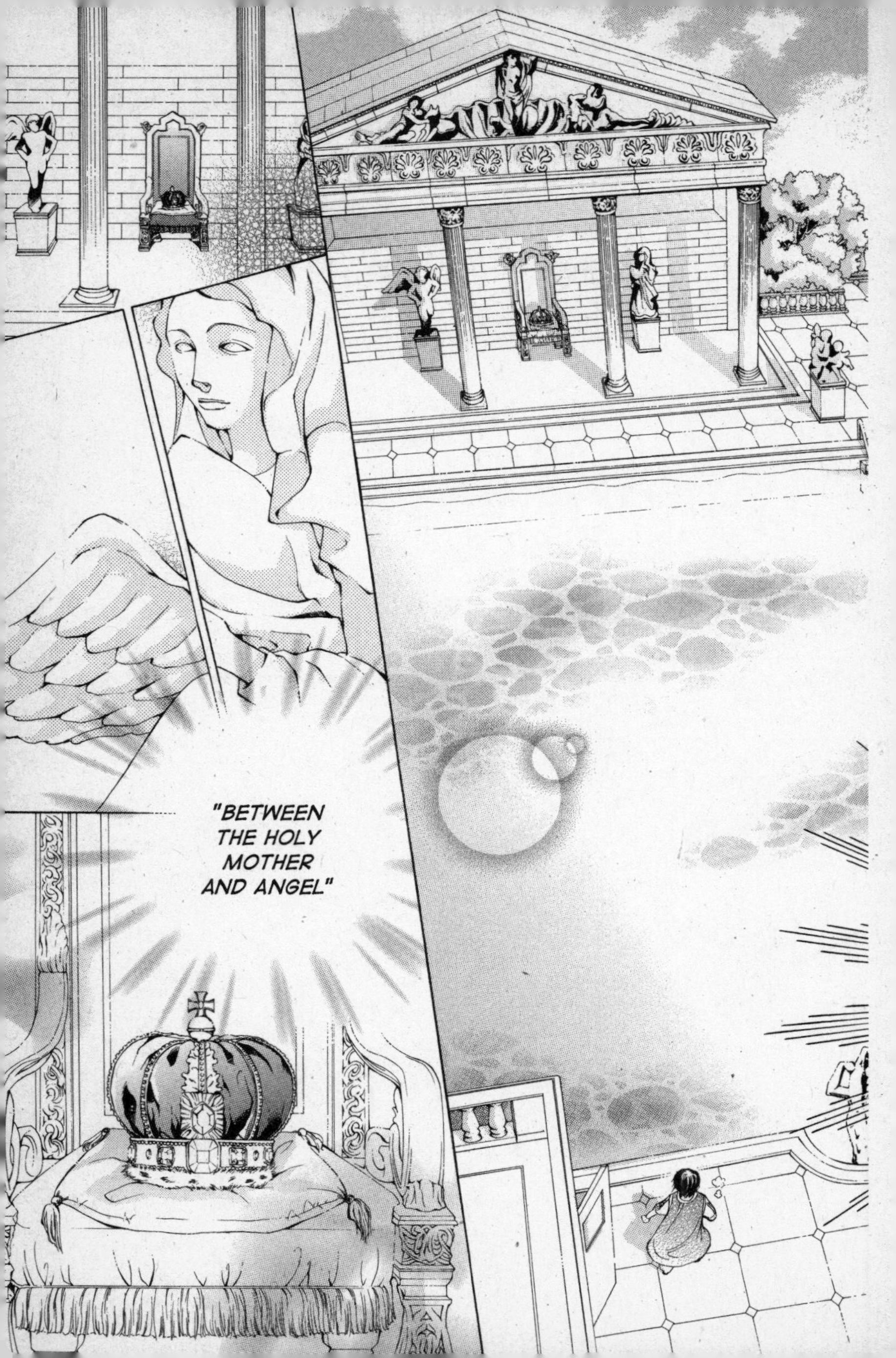
"BETWEEN THE HOLY MOTHER AND ANGEL"

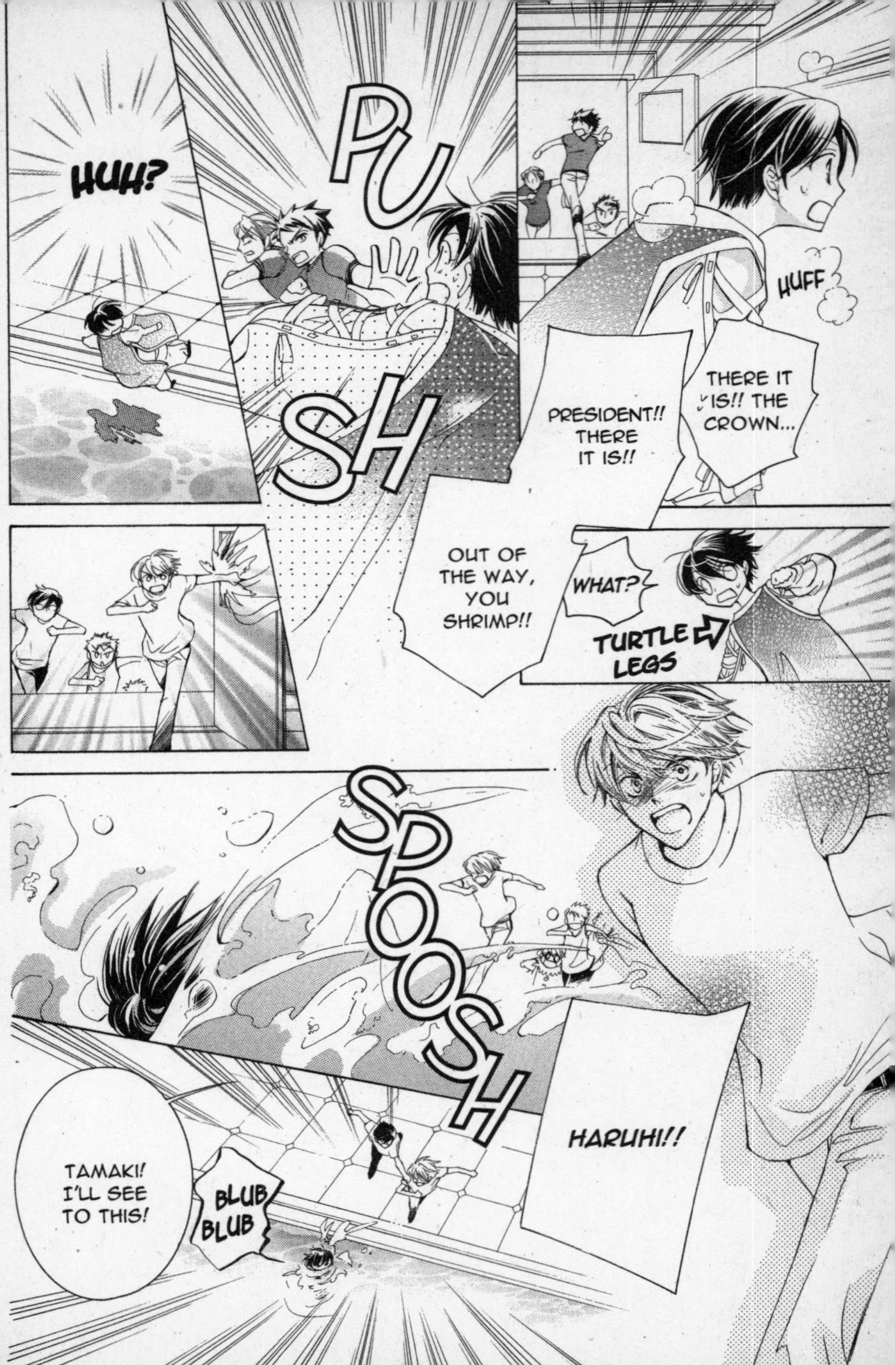
HUFF
THERE IT IS!! THE CROWN...
PRESIDENT!! THERE IT IS!!
OUT OF THE WAY, YOU SHRIMP!!
PUSH
HUH?
WHAT?
TURTLE LEGS
HARUHI!!
SPOOSH
BLUB BLUB
TAMAKI! I'LL SEE TO THIS!

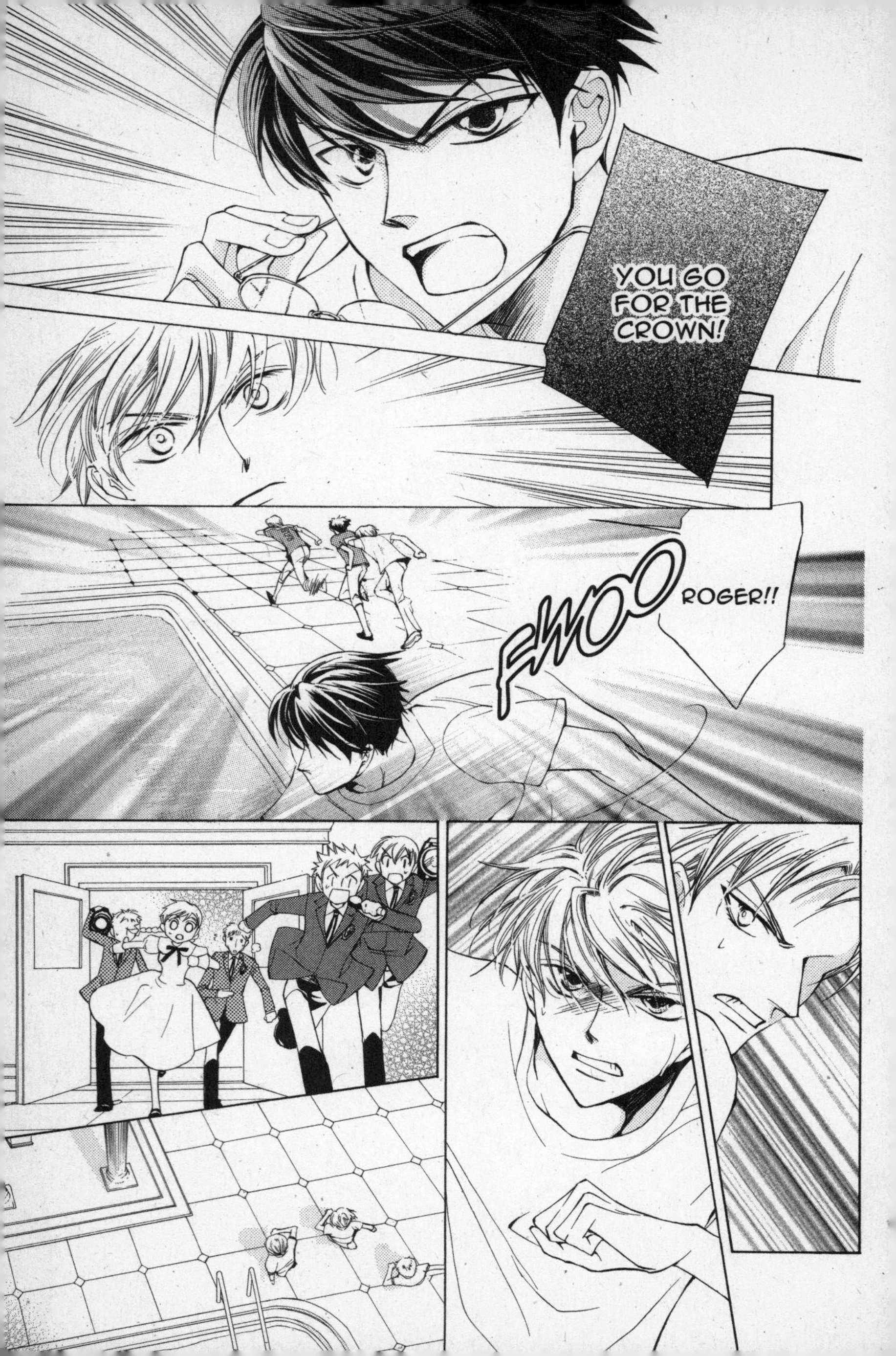
YOU GO FOR THE CROWN!
ROGER!!
FWOO

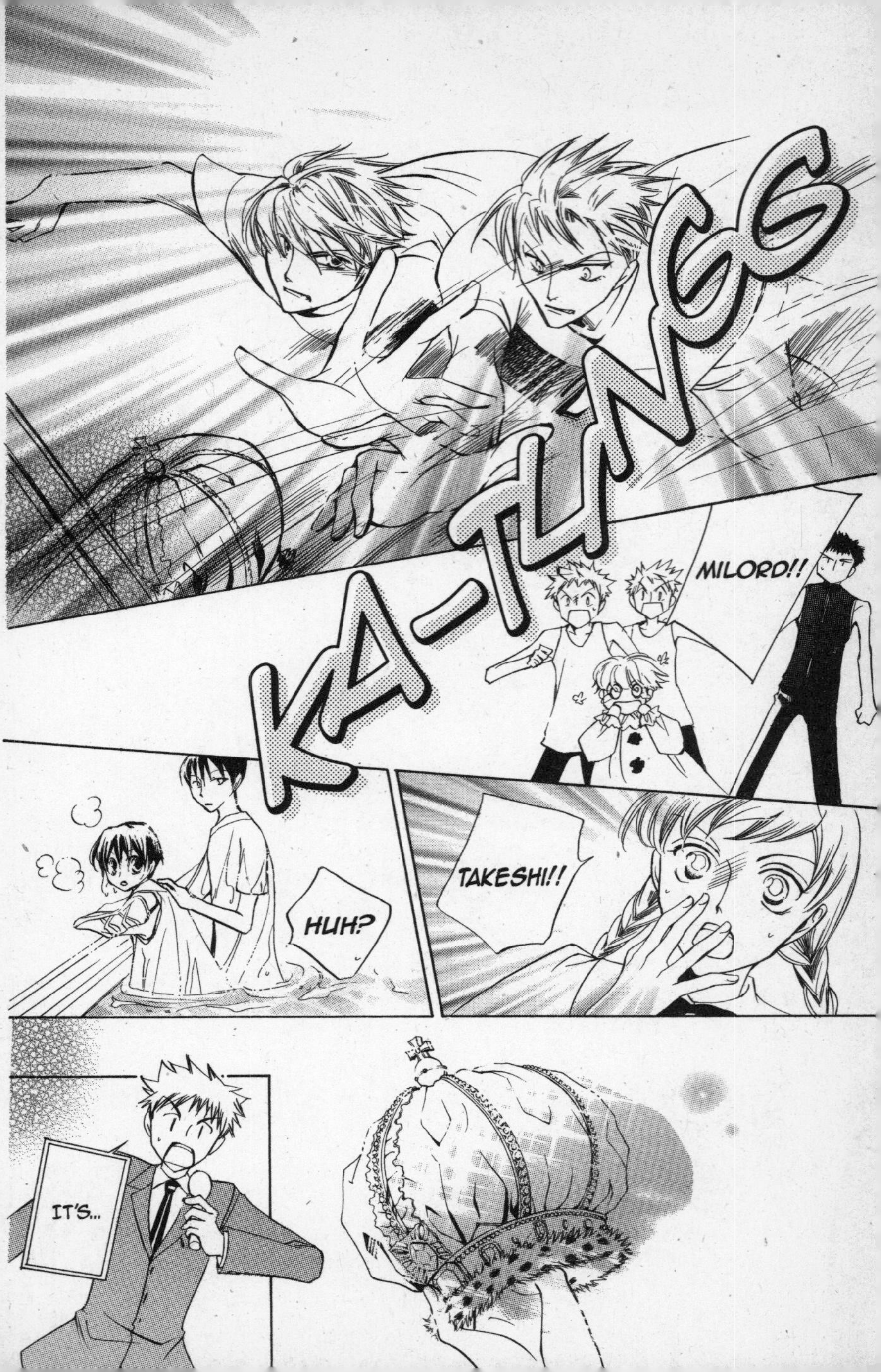
KA-TUNGG
MILORD!!
TAKESHI!!
HUH?
IT'S...

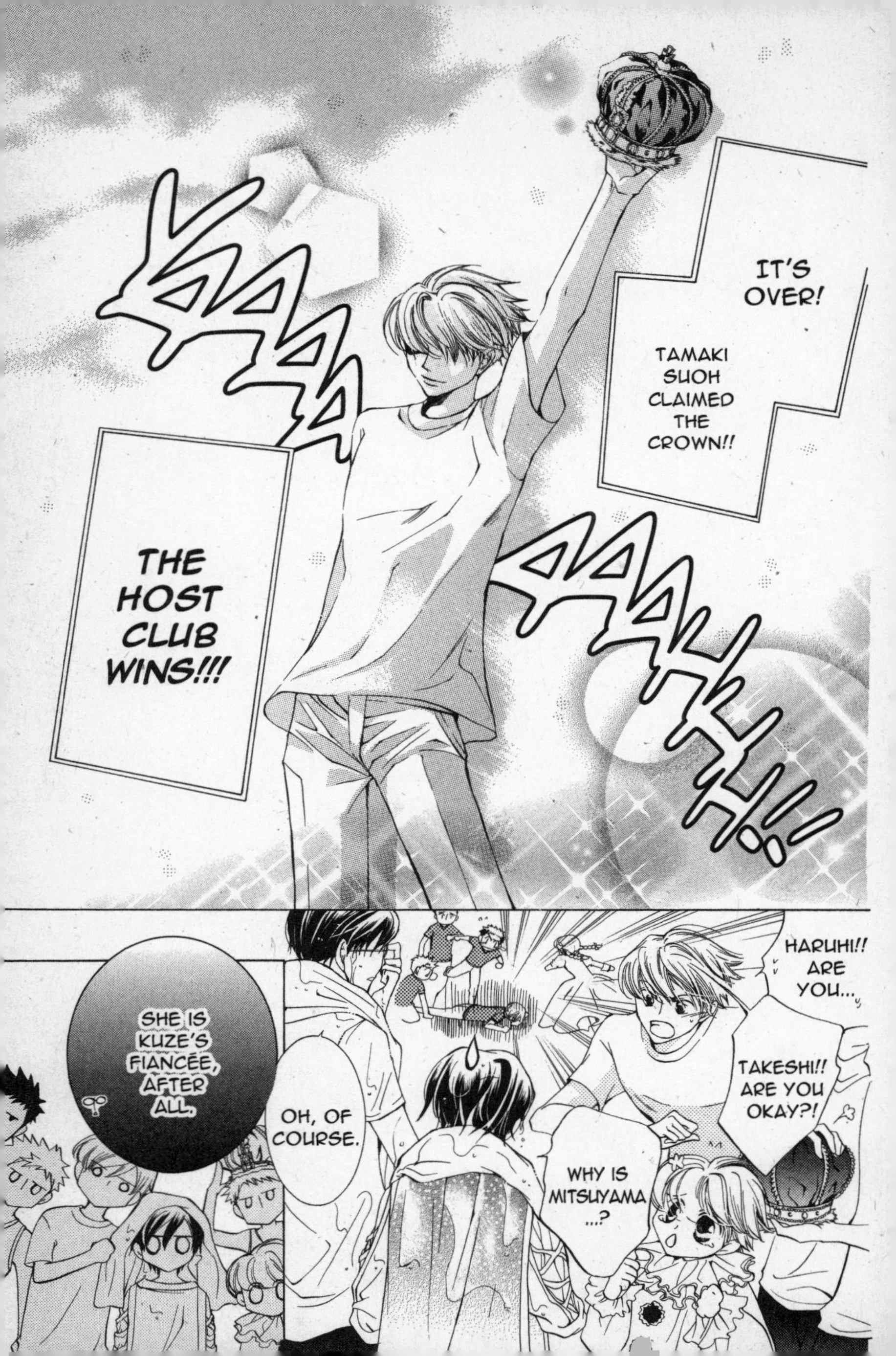
IT'S OVER!
TAMAKI SUOH CLAIMED THE CROWN!!
YAAAA
AAAHH!!
THE HOST CLUB WINS!!!
HARUHI!! ARE YOU...
TAKESHI!! ARE YOU OKAY?!
WHY IS MITSUYAMA ...?
OH, OF COURSE.
SHE IS KUZE'S FIANCÉE, AFTER ALL.

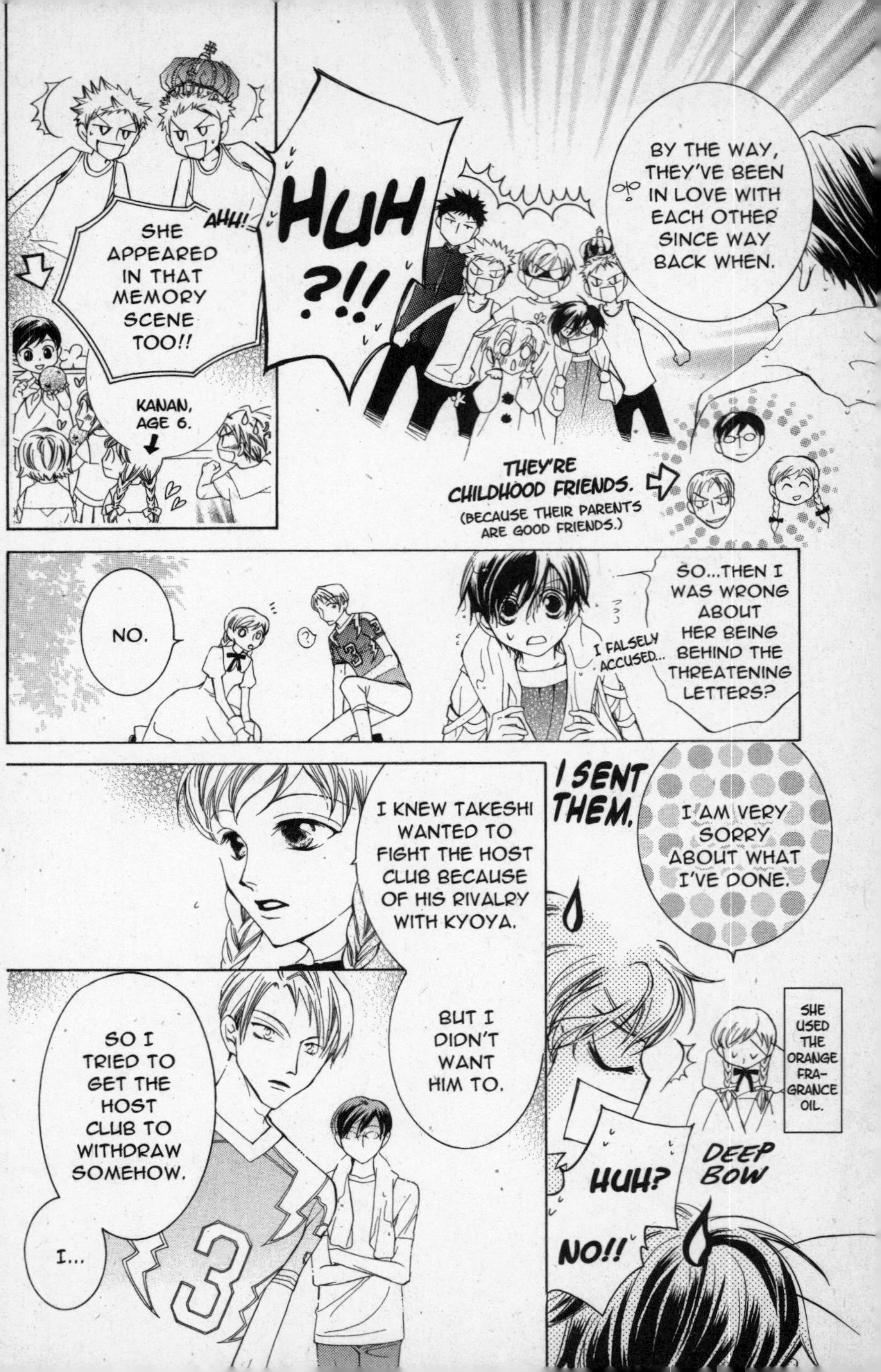
BY THE WAY, THEY'VE BEEN IN LOVE WITH EACH OTHER SINCE WAY BACK WHEN.
HUH?!!
THEY'RE CHILDHOOD FRIENDS.
(BECAUSE THEIR PARENTS ARE GOOD FRIENDS.)
AHH!
SHE APPEARED IN THAT MEMORY SCENE TOO!!
KANAN, AGE 6.
SO...THEN I WAS WRONG ABOUT HER BEING BEHIND THE THREATENING LETTERS?
I FALSELY ACCUSED...
NO.
I SENT THEM.
I AM VERY SORRY ABOUT WHAT I'VE DONE.
SHE USED THE ORANGE FRA-GRANCE OIL.
DEEP BOW
HUH?
NO!!
I KNEW TAKESHI WANTED TO FIGHT THE HOST CLUB BECAUSE OF HIS RIVALRY WITH KYOYA.
BUT I DIDN'T WANT HIM TO.
SO I TRIED TO GET THE HOST CLUB TO WITHDRAW SOMEHOW.
I...

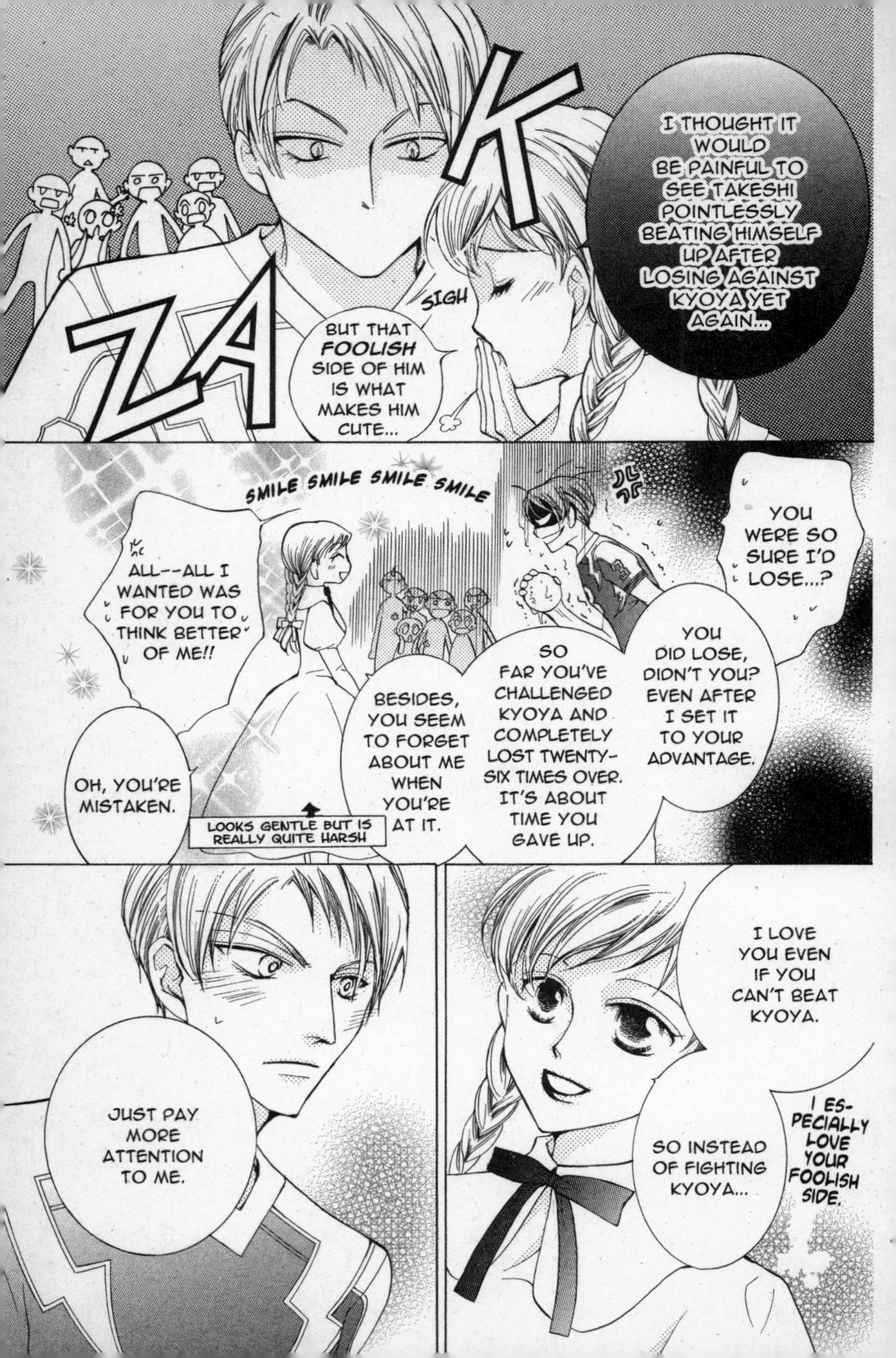
I THOUGHT IT WOULD BE PAINFUL TO SEE TAKESHI POINTLESSLY BEATING HIMSELF UP AFTER LOSING AGAINST KYOYA YET AGAIN...
ZA
K
SIGH
BUT THAT FOOLISH SIDE OF HIM IS WHAT MAKES HIM CUTE...
YOU WERE SO SURE I'D LOSE...?
YOU DID LOSE, DIDN'T YOU? EVEN AFTER I SET IT TO YOUR ADVANTAGE.
SO FAR YOU'VE CHALLENGED KYOYA AND COMPLETELY LOST TWENTY-SIX TIMES OVER. IT'S ABOUT TIME YOU GAVE UP.
BESIDES, YOU SEEM TO FORGET ABOUT ME WHEN YOU'RE AT IT.
SMILE SMILE SMILE SMILE
ALL--ALL I WANTED WAS FOR YOU TO THINK BETTER OF ME!!
OH, YOU'RE MISTAKEN.
LOOKS GENTLE BUT IS REALLY QUITE HARSH
I LOVE YOU EVEN IF YOU CAN'T BEAT KYOYA.
I ESPECIALLY LOVE YOUR FOOLISH SIDE.
SO INSTEAD OF FIGHTING KYOYA...
JUST PAY MORE ATTENTION TO ME.

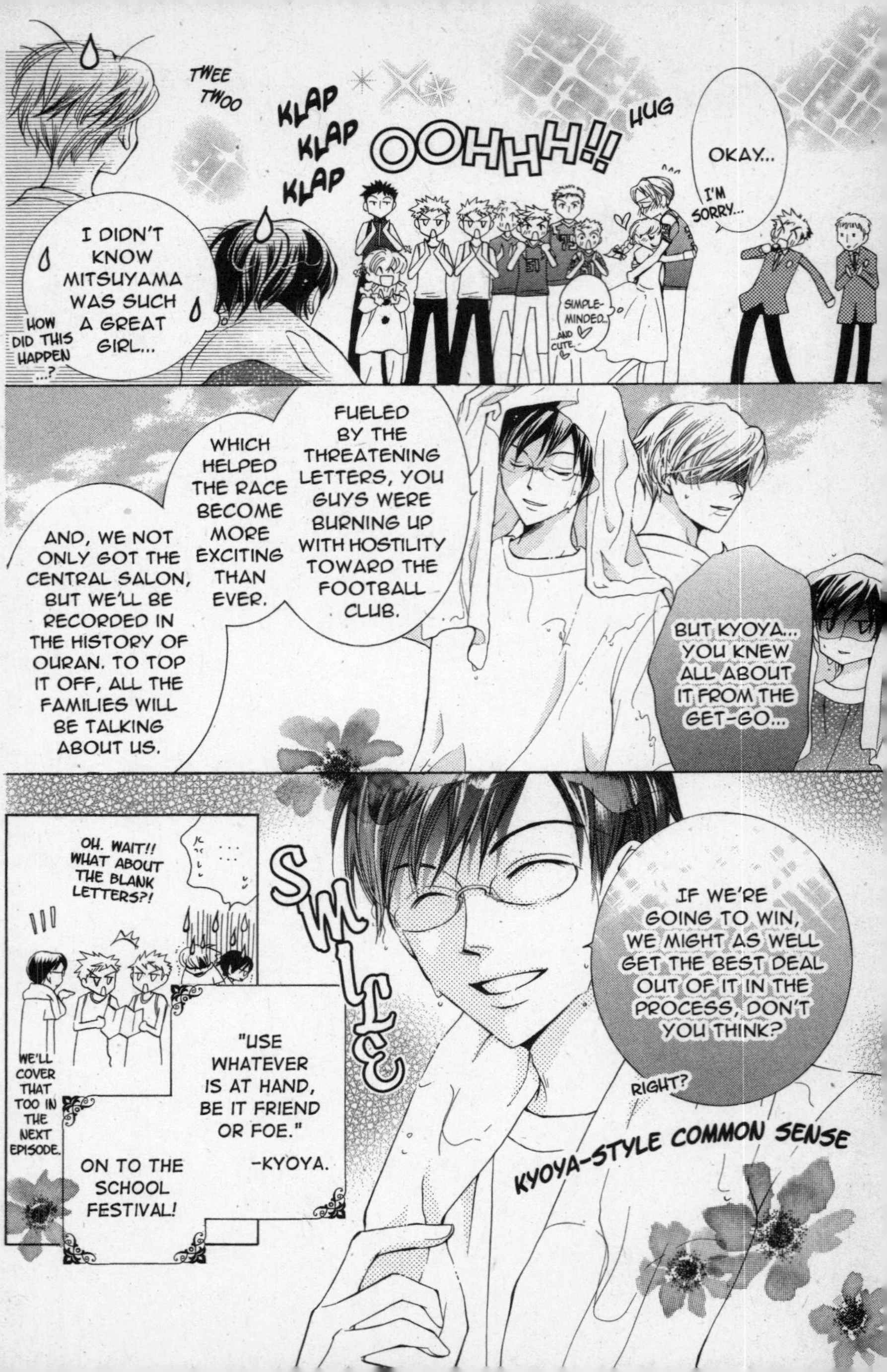
OKAY... I'M SORRY...
HUG
OOHHH!!
KLAP KLAP KLAP
TWEE TWOO
SIMPLE-MINDED... ...AND CUTE
I DIDN'T KNOW MITSUYAMA WAS SUCH A GREAT GIRL...
HOW DID THIS HAPPEN...?
BUT KYOYA... YOU KNEW ALL ABOUT IT FROM THE GET-GO...
FUELED BY THE THREATENING LETTERS, YOU GUYS WERE BURNING UP WITH HOSTILITY TOWARD THE FOOTBALL CLUB.
WHICH HELPED THE RACE BECOME MORE EXCITING THAN EVER.
AND, WE NOT ONLY GOT THE CENTRAL SALON, BUT WE'LL BE RECORDED IN THE HISTORY OF OURAN. TO TOP IT OFF, ALL THE FAMILIES WILL BE TALKING ABOUT US.
IF WE'RE GOING TO WIN, WE MIGHT AS WELL GET THE BEST DEAL OUT OF IT IN THE PROCESS, DON'T YOU THINK?
RIGHT?
KYOYA-STYLE COMMON SENSE
SMILE
OH. WAIT!! WHAT ABOUT THE BLANK LETTERS?!
WE'LL COVER THAT TOO IN THE NEXT EPISODE.
"USE WHATEVER IS AT HAND, BE IT FRIEND OR FOE." -KYOYA.
ON TO THE SCHOOL FESTIVAL!

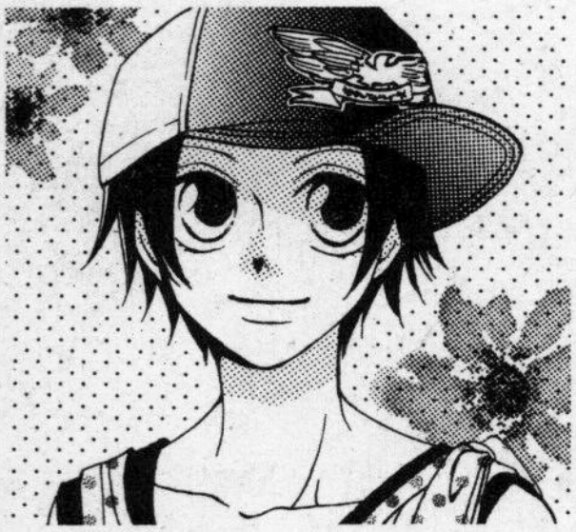
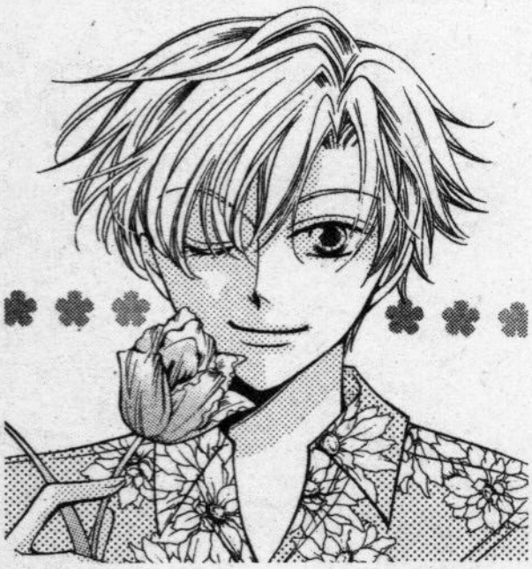

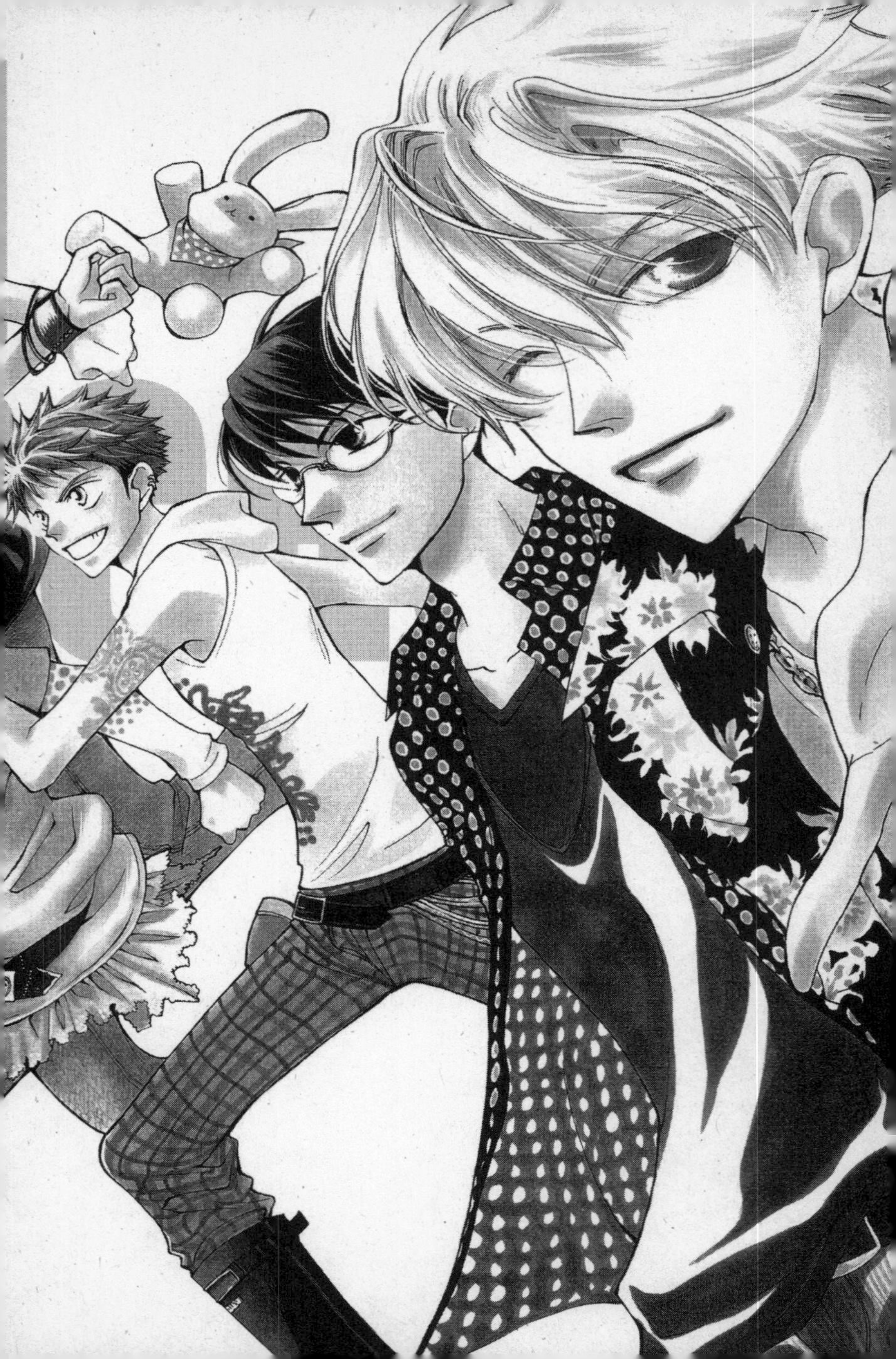

EPISODE 25

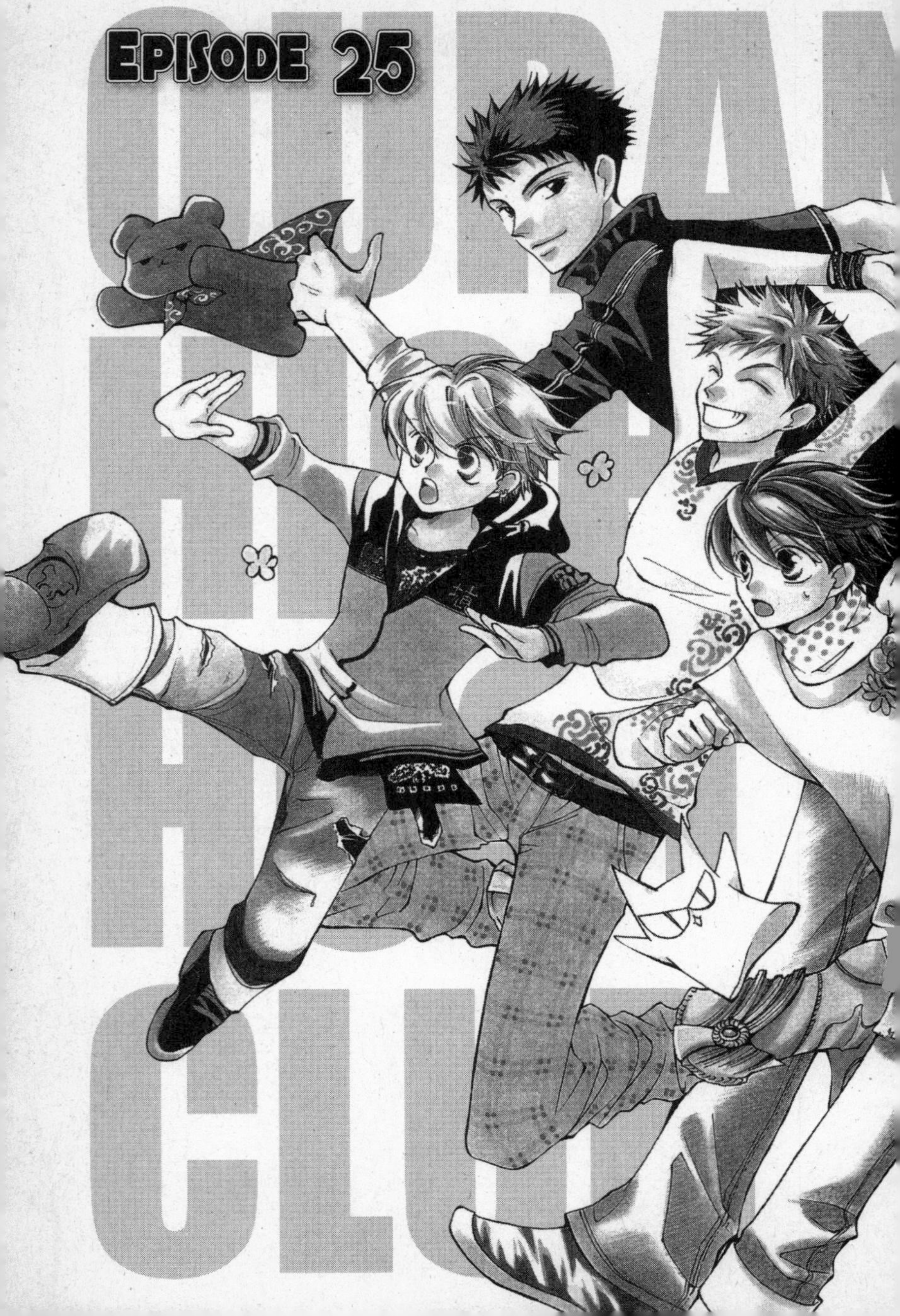

When Master Kyoya Gets Scared

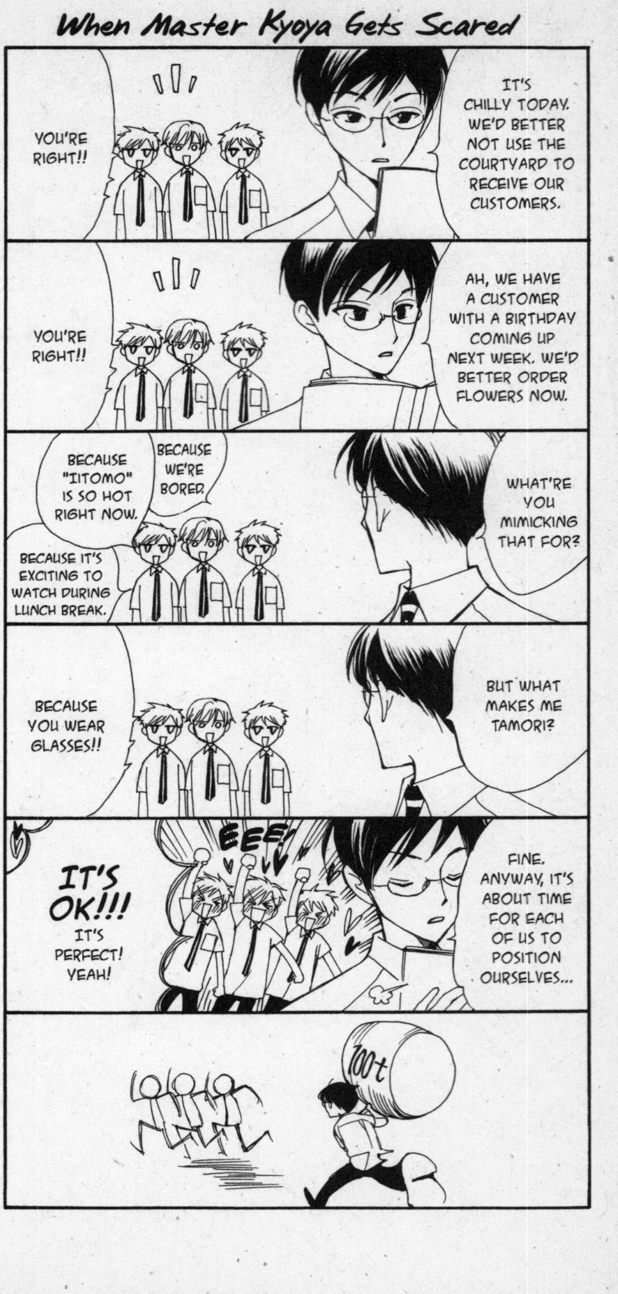
IT'S CHILLY TODAY. WE'D BETTER NOT USE THE COURTYARD TO RECEIVE OUR CUSTOMERS.
YOU'RE RIGHT!!
AH, WE HAVE A CUSTOMER WITH A BIRTHDAY COMING UP NEXT WEEK. WE'D BETTER ORDER FLOWERS NOW.
YOU'RE RIGHT!!
WHAT'RE YOU MIMICKING THAT FOR?
BECAUSE WE'RE BORED.
BECAUSE "IITOMO" IS SO HOT RIGHT NOW.
BECAUSE IT'S EXCITING TO WATCH DURING LUNCH BREAK.
BUT WHAT MAKES ME TAMORI?
BECAUSE YOU WEAR GLASSES!!
FINE. ANYWAY, IT'S ABOUT TIME FOR EACH OF US TO POSITION OURSELVES...
EEE!
IT'S OK!!!
IT'S PERFECT! YEAH!
100t

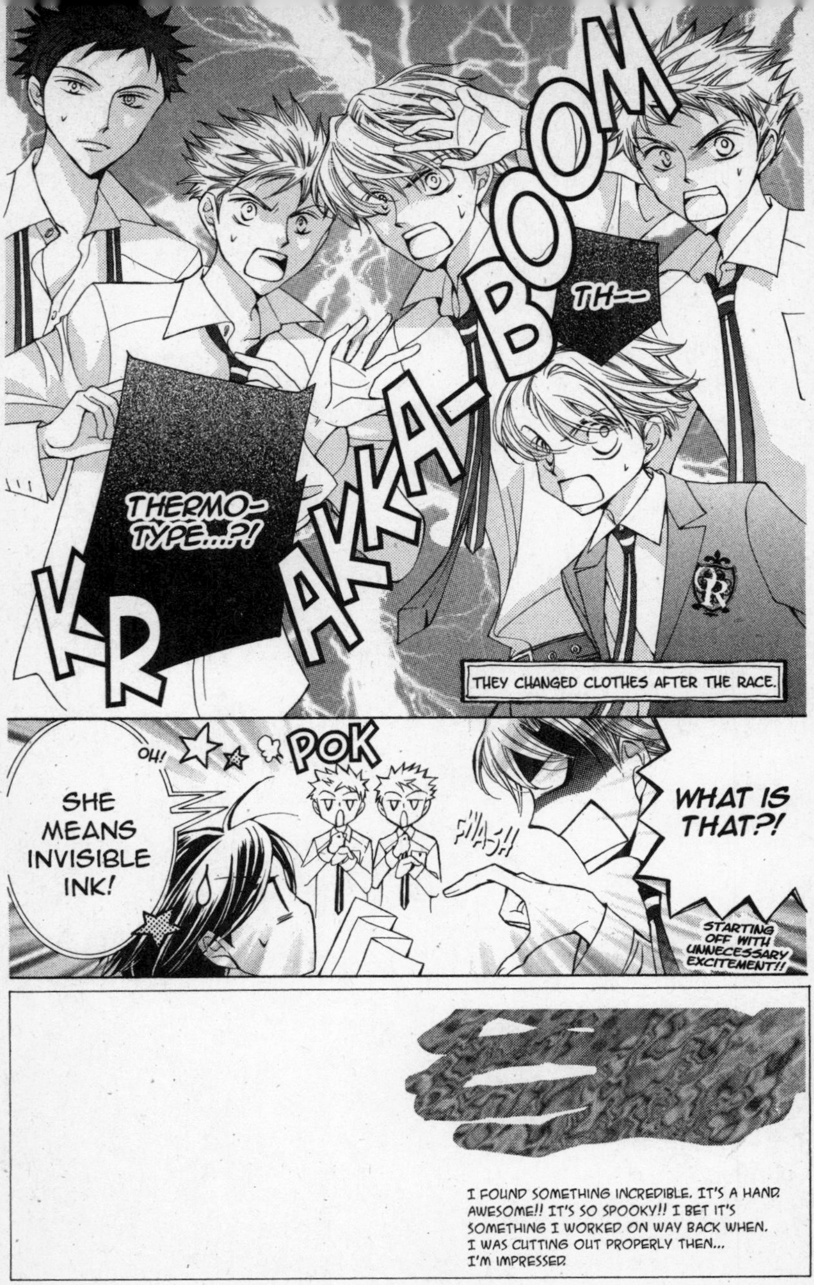
TH--
KR AKKA-BOOM
THERMO-TYPE...?!
THEY CHANGED CLOTHES AFTER THE RACE.
WHAT IS THAT?!
STARTING OFF WITH UNNECESSARY EXCITEMENT!!
FWASH
POK
OH!
SHE MEANS INVISIBLE INK!
I FOUND SOMETHING INCREDIBLE. IT'S A HAND. AWESOME!! IT'S SO SPOOKY!! I BET IT'S SOMETHING I WORKED ON WAY BACK WHEN. I WAS CUTTING OUT PROPERLY THEN... I'M IMPRESSED.

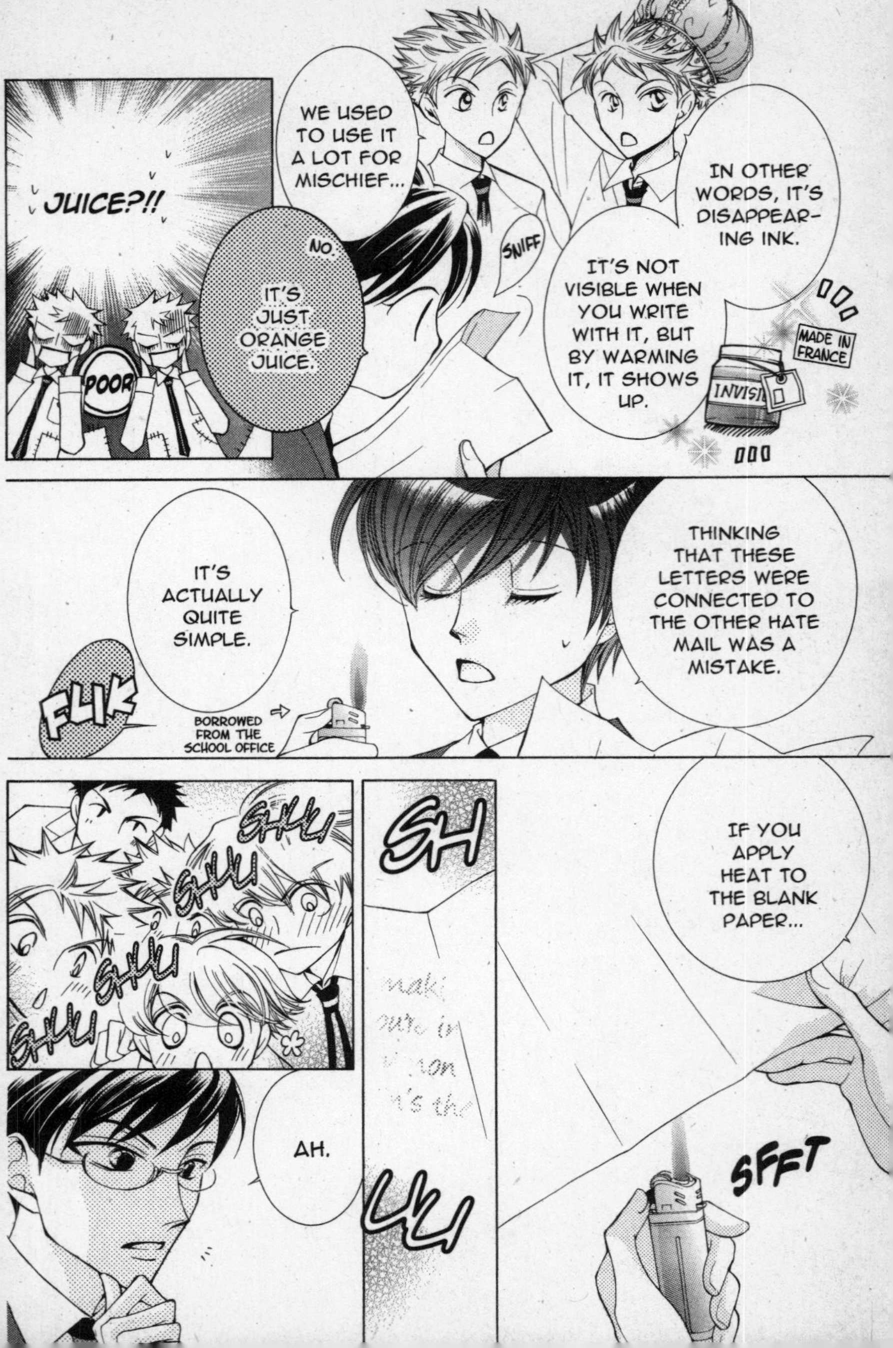
IN OTHER WORDS, IT'S DISAPPEARING INK.
IT'S NOT VISIBLE WHEN YOU WRITE WITH IT, BUT BY WARMING IT, IT SHOWS UP.
MADE IN FRANCE
INVISI
WE USED TO USE IT A LOT FOR MISCHIEF...
SNIFF
NO.
IT'S JUST ORANGE JUICE.
JUICE?!!
POOR
THINKING THAT THESE LETTERS WERE CONNECTED TO THE OTHER HATE MAIL WAS A MISTAKE.
IT'S ACTUALLY QUITE SIMPLE.
BORROWED FROM THE SCHOOL OFFICE
FLIK
IF YOU APPLY HEAT TO THE BLANK PAPER...
SFFT
SH
UU
SHU
SHU
SHU
SHU
AH.

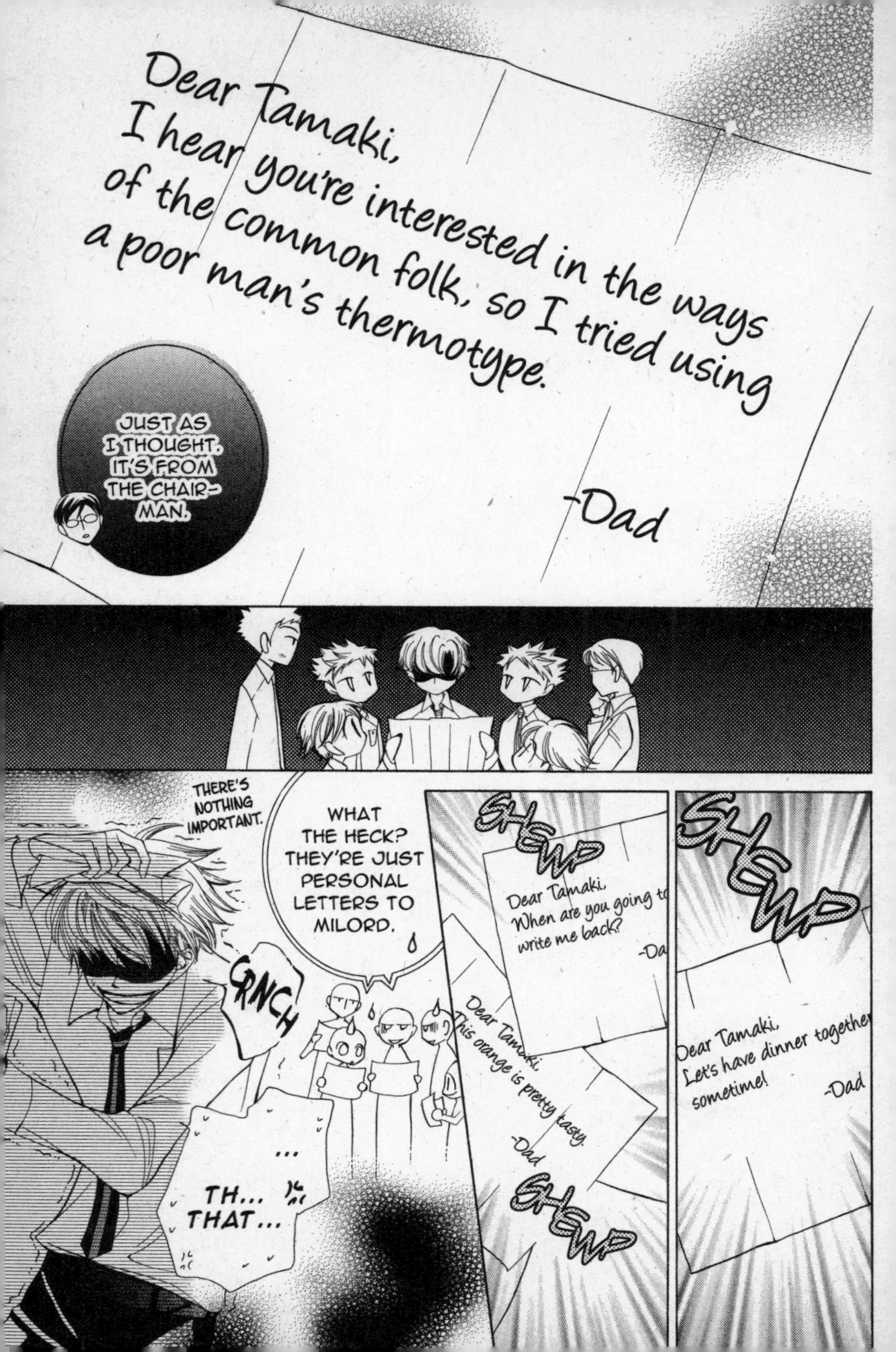
Dear Tamaki,
I hear you're interested in the ways of the common folk, so I tried using a poor man's thermotype.
-Dad
JUST AS I THOUGHT. IT'S FROM THE CHAIRMAN.
SHEWP
Dear Tamaki,
Let's have dinner together sometime!
-Dad
SHEWP
Dear Tamaki,
When are you going t
write me back?
-Da
Dear Tamaki,
This orange is pretty tasty.
-Dad
SHEWP
WHAT THE HECK? THEY'RE JUST PERSONAL LETTERS TO MILORD.
THERE'S NOTHING IMPORTANT.
CRNCH
...
TH... THAT...

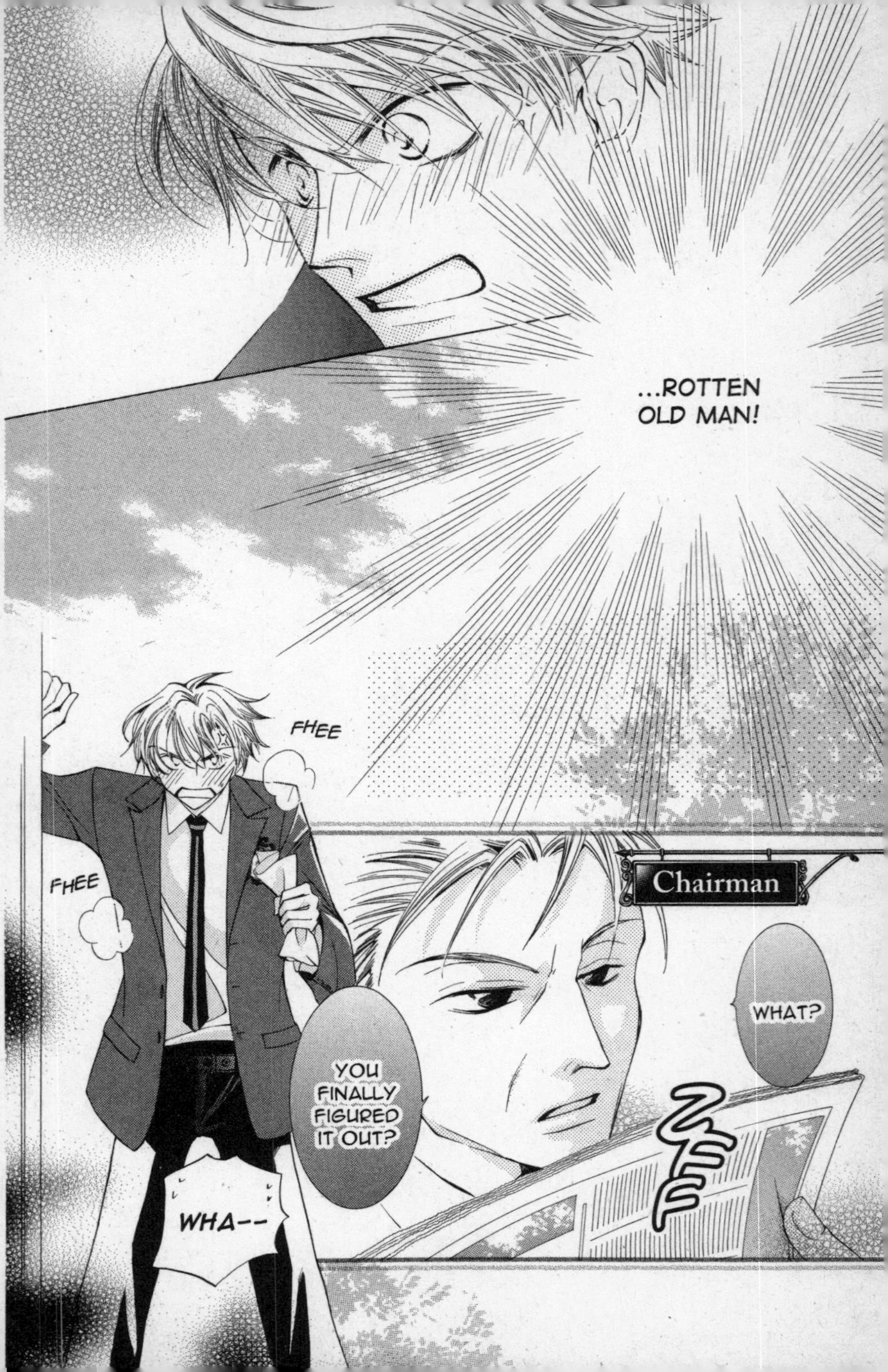
...ROTTEN OLD MAN!
Chairman
WHAT?
YOU FINALLY FIGURED IT OUT?
FHEE
FHEE
WHA--

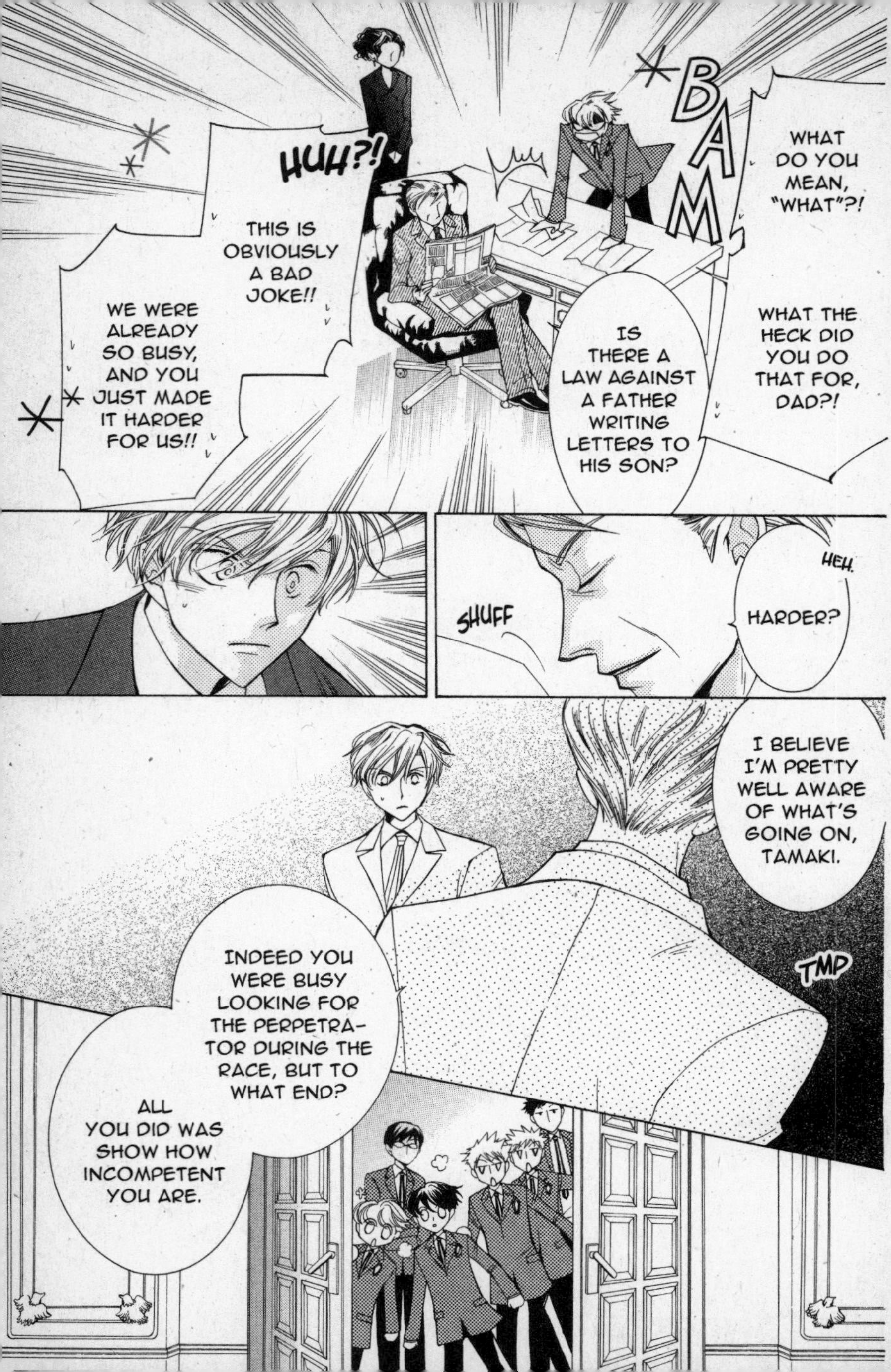
BAM
WHAT DO YOU MEAN, "WHAT"?!
WHAT THE HECK DID YOU DO THAT FOR, DAD?!
IS THERE A LAW AGAINST A FATHER WRITING LETTERS TO HIS SON?
HUH?!
THIS IS OBVIOUSLY A BAD JOKE!!
WE WERE ALREADY SO BUSY, AND YOU JUST MADE IT HARDER FOR US!!
HEH.
HARDER?
SHUFF
I BELIEVE I'M PRETTY WELL AWARE OF WHAT'S GOING ON, TAMAKI.
TMP
INDEED YOU WERE BUSY LOOKING FOR THE PERPETRATOR DURING THE RACE, BUT TO WHAT END?
ALL YOU DID WAS SHOW HOW INCOMPETENT YOU ARE.

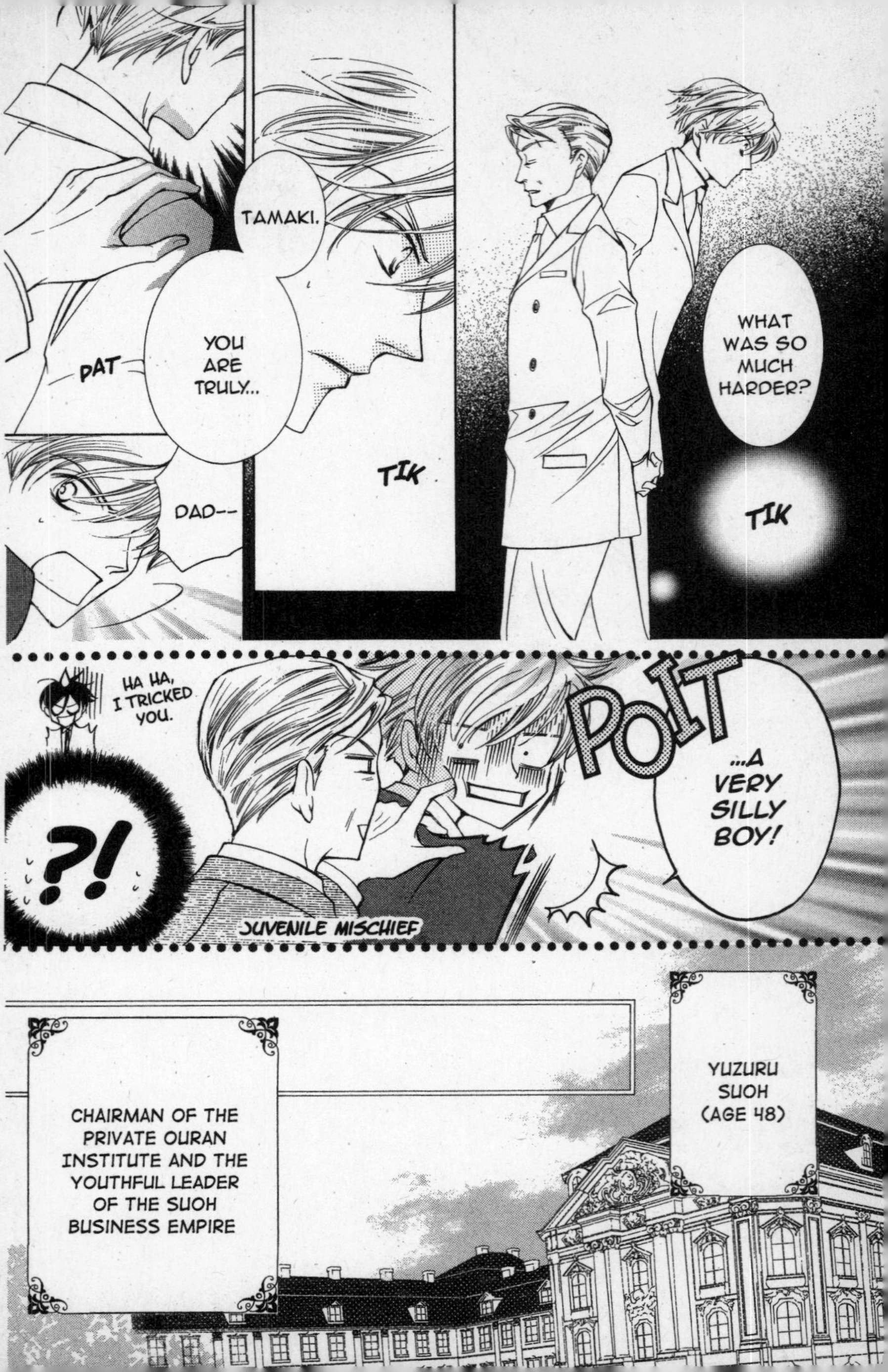
WHAT WAS SO MUCH HARDER?
TIK
TAMAKI.
YOU ARE TRULY...
TIK
PAT
DAD--
POIT
...A VERY SILLY BOY!
HA HA, I TRICKED YOU.
?!
JUVENILE MISCHIEF
YUZURU SUOH (AGE 48)
CHAIRMAN OF THE PRIVATE OURAN INSTITUTE AND THE YOUTHFUL LEADER OF THE SUOH BUSINESS EMPIRE

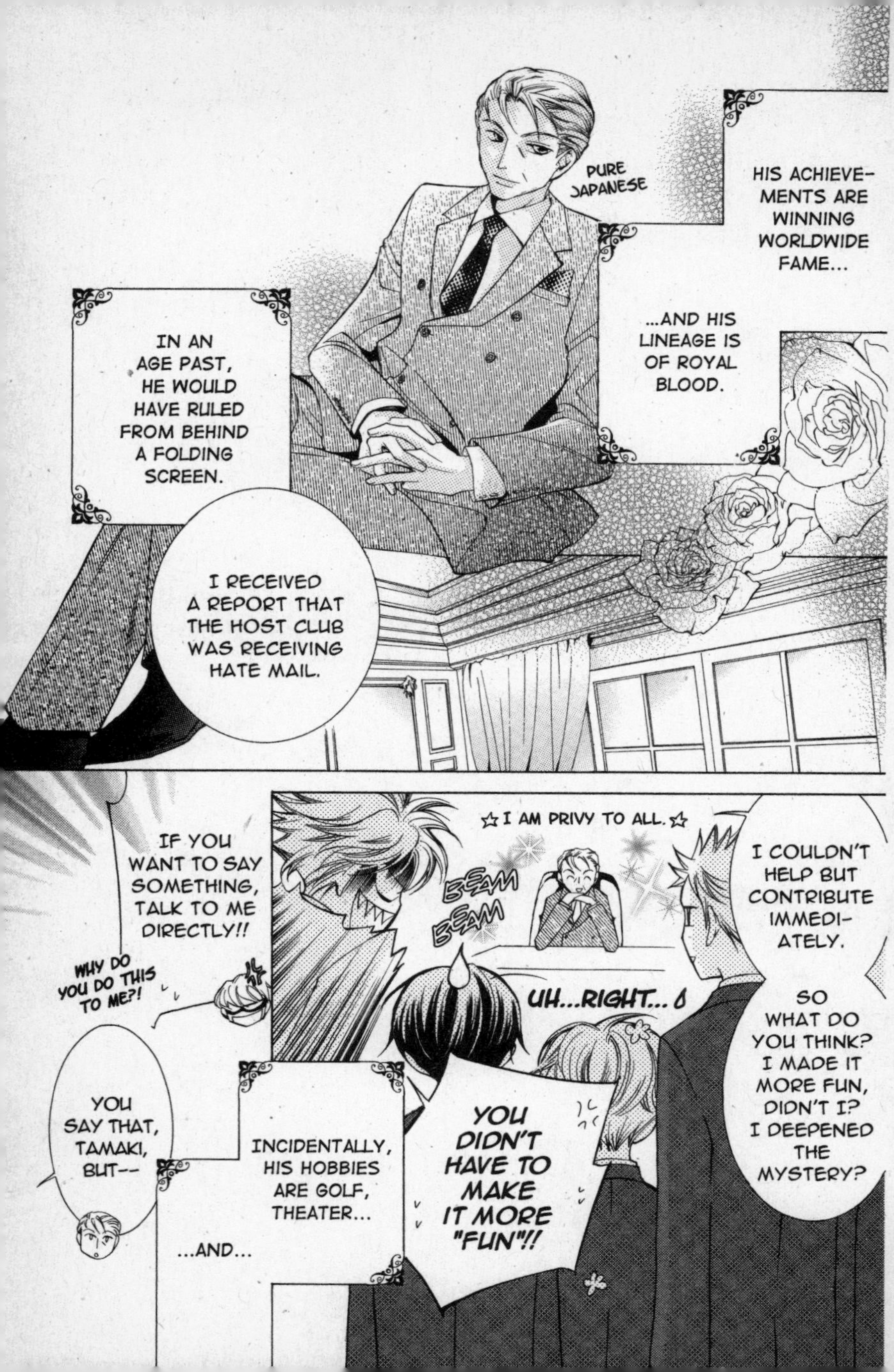
PURE JAPANESE
HIS ACHIEVEMENTS ARE WINNING WORLDWIDE FAME...
...AND HIS LINEAGE IS OF ROYAL BLOOD.
IN AN AGE PAST, HE WOULD HAVE RULED FROM BEHIND A FOLDING SCREEN.
I RECEIVED A REPORT THAT THE HOST CLUB WAS RECEIVING HATE MAIL.
☆ I AM PRIVY TO ALL. ☆
I COULDN'T HELP BUT CONTRIBUTE IMMEDIATELY.
BEAM BEAM
SO WHAT DO YOU THINK? I MADE IT MORE FUN, DIDN'T I? I DEEPENED THE MYSTERY?
UH...RIGHT...
YOU DIDN'T HAVE TO MAKE IT MORE "FUN"!!
IF YOU WANT TO SAY SOMETHING, TALK TO ME DIRECTLY!!
WHY DO YOU DO THIS TO ME?!
YOU SAY THAT, TAMAKI, BUT--
INCIDENTALLY, HIS HOBBIES ARE GOLF, THEATER...
...AND...

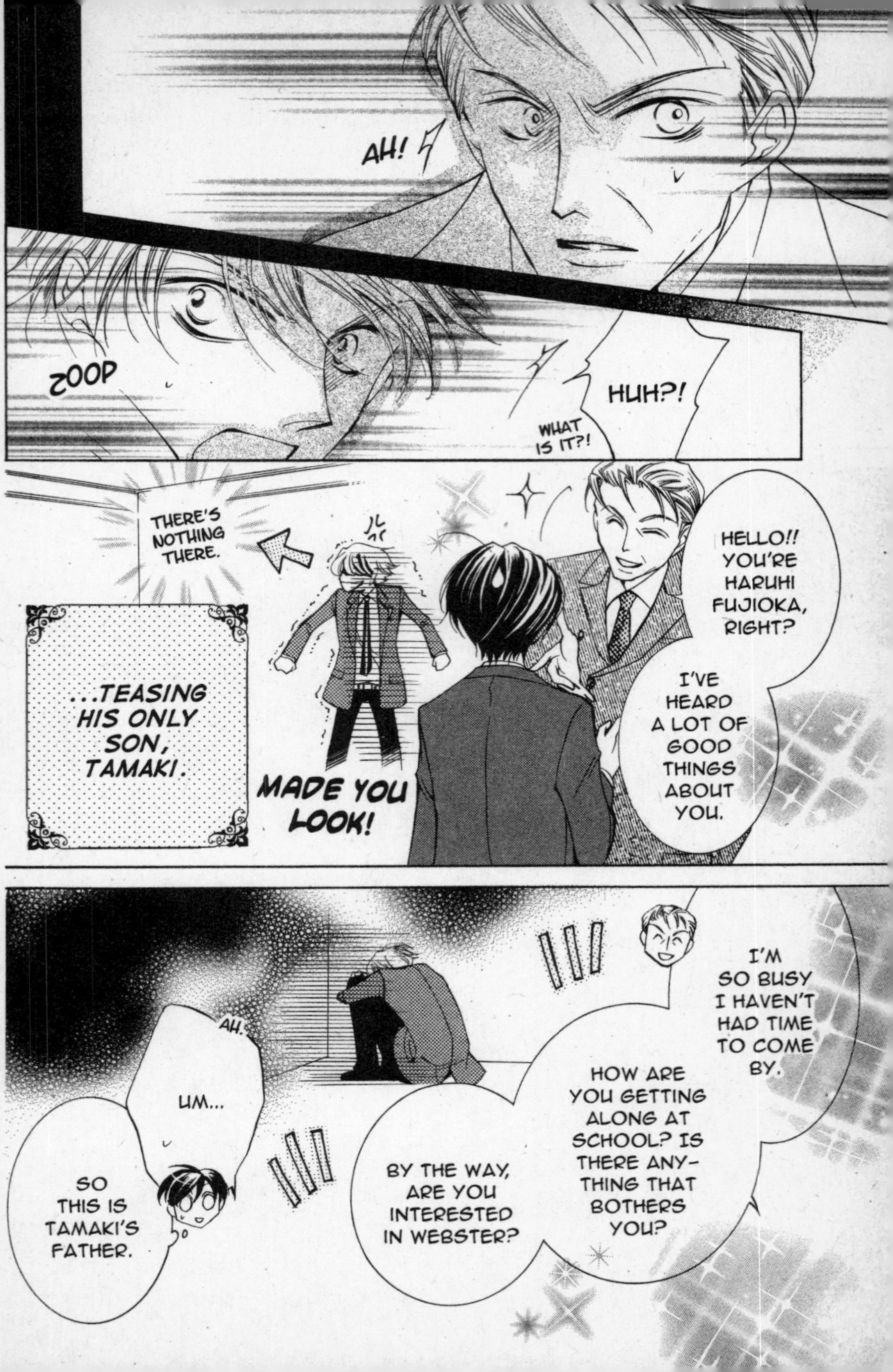
AH!
HUH?!
WHAT IS IT?!
ZOOP
HELLO!! YOU'RE HARUHI FUJIOKA, RIGHT?
I'VE HEARD A LOT OF GOOD THINGS ABOUT YOU.
THERE'S NOTHING THERE.
MADE YOU LOOK!
...TEASING HIS ONLY SON, TAMAKI.
I'M SO BUSY I HAVEN'T HAD TIME TO COME BY.
HOW ARE YOU GETTING ALONG AT SCHOOL? IS THERE ANY-THING THAT BOTHERS YOU?
BY THE WAY, ARE YOU INTERESTED IN WEBSTER?
AH.
UM...
SO THIS IS TAMAKI'S FATHER.

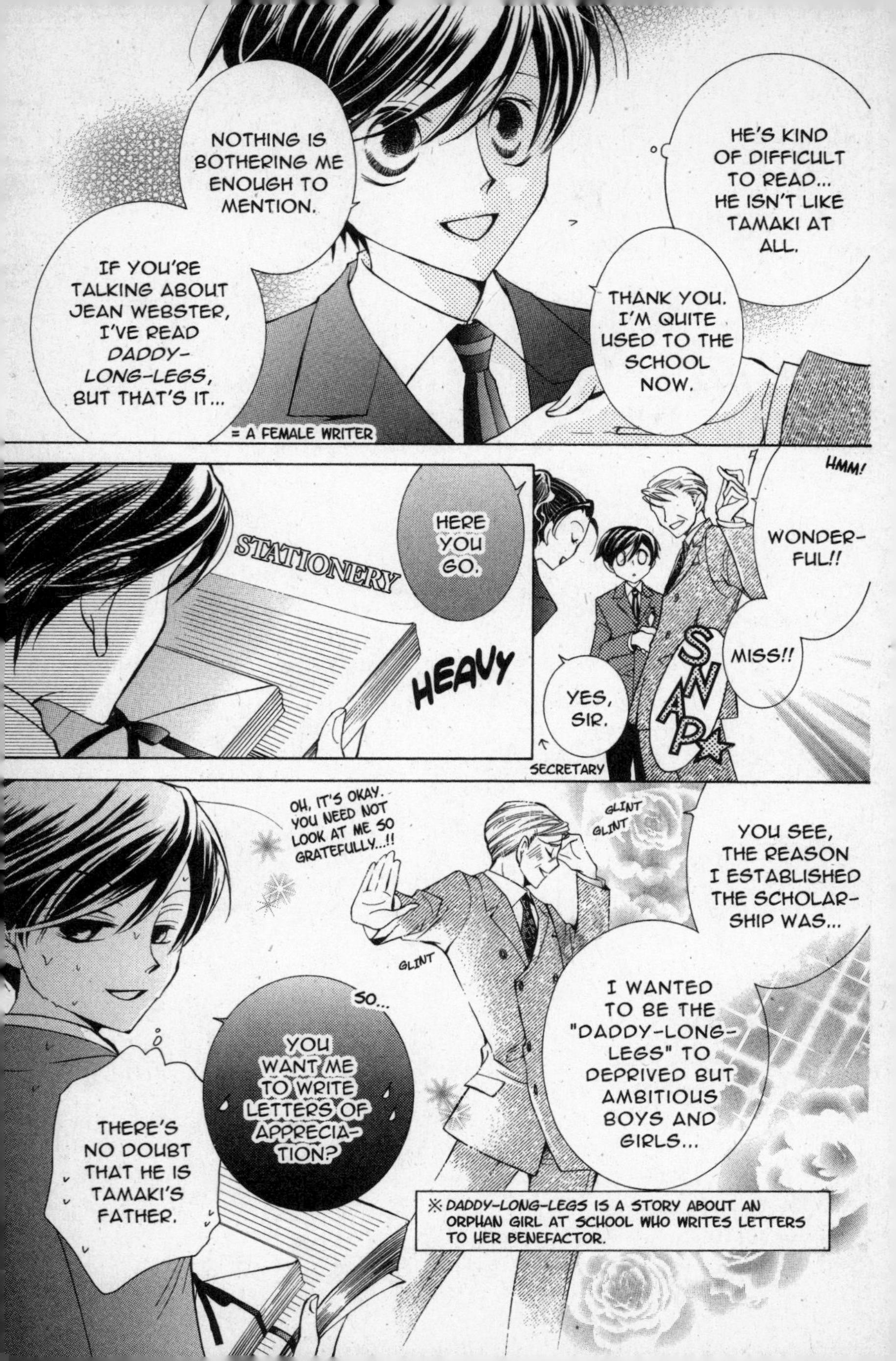
HE'S KIND OF DIFFICULT TO READ... HE ISN'T LIKE TAMAKI AT ALL.
THANK YOU. I'M QUITE USED TO THE SCHOOL NOW.
NOTHING IS BOTHERING ME ENOUGH TO MENTION.
IF YOU'RE TALKING ABOUT JEAN WEBSTER, I'VE READ *DADDY-LONG-LEGS*, BUT THAT'S IT...
= A FEMALE WRITER
HMM!
WONDERFUL!!
MISS!!
SNAP
YES, SIR.
SECRETARY
HERE YOU GO.
STATIONERY
HEAVY
YOU SEE, THE REASON I ESTABLISHED THE SCHOLARSHIP WAS...
I WANTED TO BE THE "DADDY-LONG-LEGS" TO DEPRIVED BUT AMBITIOUS BOYS AND GIRLS...
GLINT GLINT
OH, IT'S OKAY. YOU NEED NOT LOOK AT ME SO GRATEFULLY...!!
GLINT
※ *DADDY-LONG-LEGS* IS A STORY ABOUT AN ORPHAN GIRL AT SCHOOL WHO WRITES LETTERS TO HER BENEFACTOR.
SO...
YOU WANT ME TO WRITE LETTERS OF APPRECIATION?
THERE'S NO DOUBT THAT HE IS TAMAKI'S FATHER.

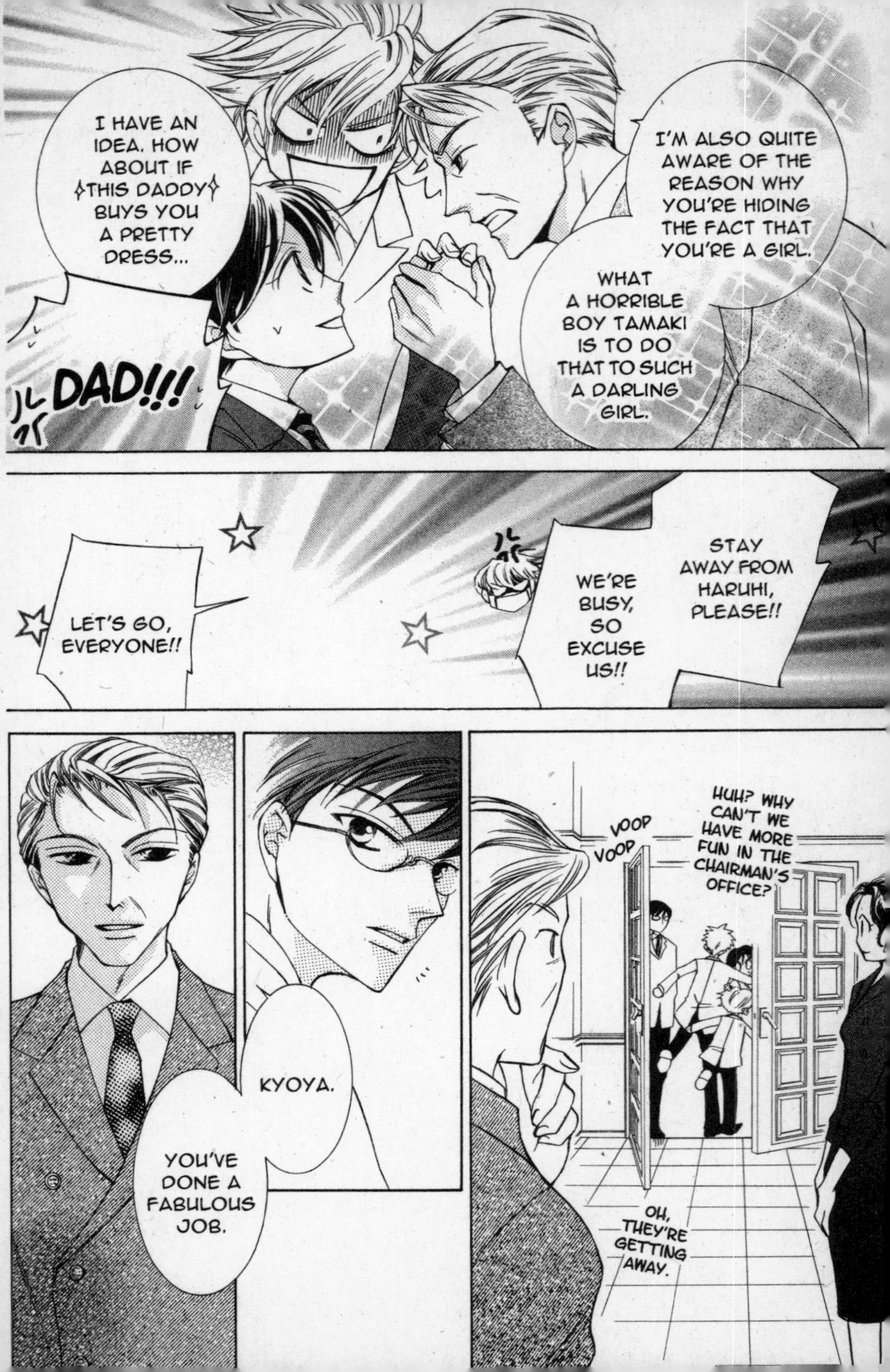
I'M ALSO QUITE AWARE OF THE REASON WHY YOU'RE HIDING THE FACT THAT YOU'RE A GIRL.
WHAT A HORRIBLE BOY TAMAKI IS TO DO THAT TO SUCH A DARLING GIRL.
I HAVE AN IDEA. HOW ABOUT IF ✧THIS DADDY✧ BUYS YOU A PRETTY DRESS...
DAD!!!
STAY AWAY FROM HARUHI, PLEASE!!
WE'RE BUSY, SO EXCUSE US!!
LET'S GO, EVERYONE!!
HUH? WHY CAN'T WE HAVE MORE FUN IN THE CHAIRMAN'S OFFICE?
VOOP VOOP
OH, THEY'RE GETTING AWAY.
KYOYA.
YOU'VE DONE A FABULOUS JOB.

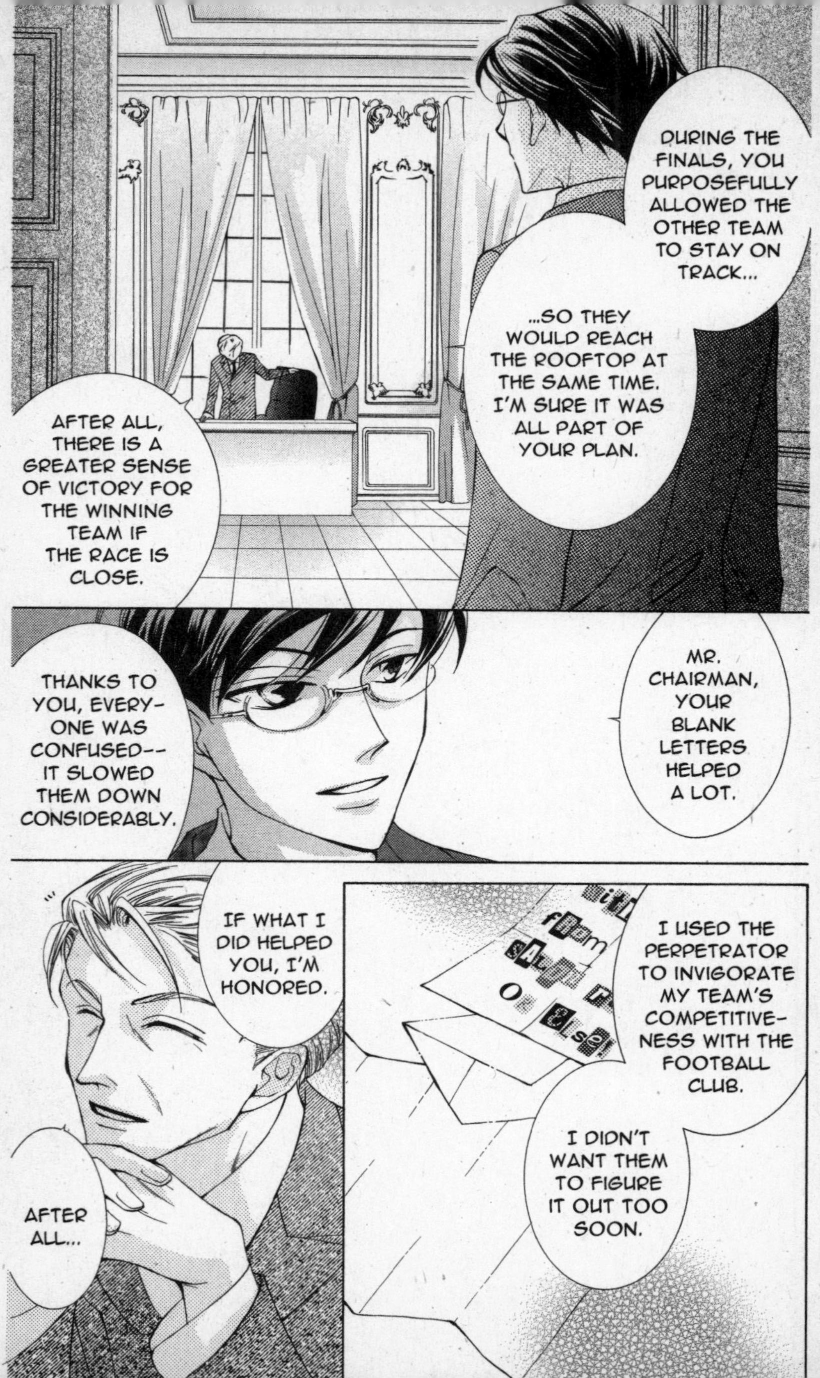

DURING THE FINALS, YOU PURPOSEFULLY ALLOWED THE OTHER TEAM TO STAY ON TRACK...
...SO THEY WOULD REACH THE ROOFTOP AT THE SAME TIME. I'M SURE IT WAS ALL PART OF YOUR PLAN.
AFTER ALL, THERE IS A GREATER SENSE OF VICTORY FOR THE WINNING TEAM IF THE RACE IS CLOSE.
MR. CHAIRMAN, YOUR BLANK LETTERS HELPED A LOT.
THANKS TO YOU, EVERY-ONE WAS CONFUSED--IT SLOWED THEM DOWN CONSIDERABLY.
I USED THE PERPETRATOR TO INVIGORATE MY TEAM'S COMPETITIVE-NESS WITH THE FOOTBALL CLUB.
I DIDN'T WANT THEM TO FIGURE IT OUT TOO SOON.
IF WHAT I DID HELPED YOU, I'M HONORED.
AFTER ALL...

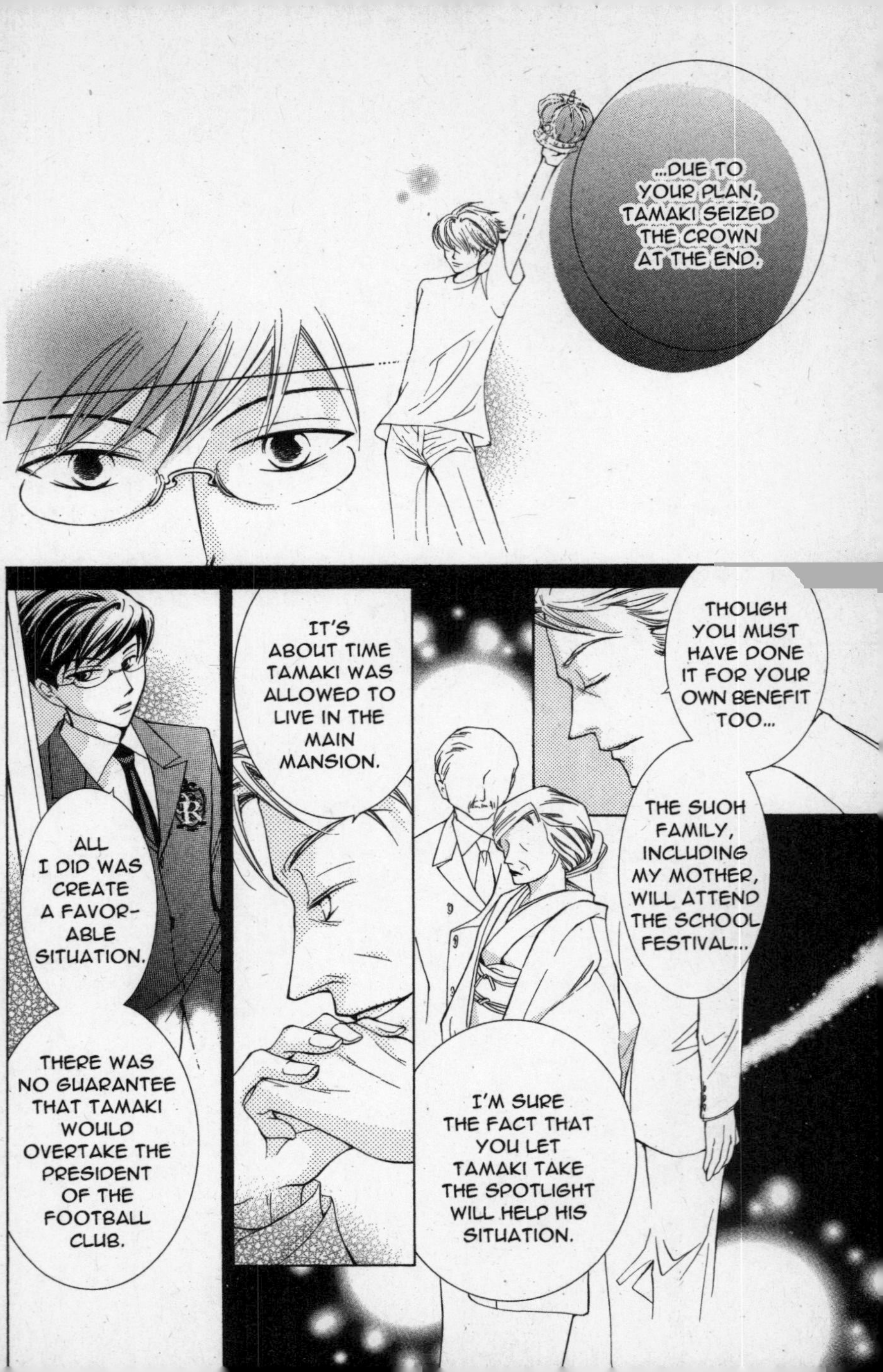
...DUE TO YOUR PLAN, TAMAKI SEIZED THE CROWN AT THE END.
THOUGH YOU MUST HAVE DONE IT FOR YOUR OWN BENEFIT TOO...
THE SUOH FAMILY, INCLUDING MY MOTHER, WILL ATTEND THE SCHOOL FESTIVAL...
I'M SURE THE FACT THAT YOU LET TAMAKI TAKE THE SPOTLIGHT WILL HELP HIS SITUATION.
IT'S ABOUT TIME TAMAKI WAS ALLOWED TO LIVE IN THE MAIN MANSION.
ALL I DID WAS CREATE A FAVOR-ABLE SITUATION.
THERE WAS NO GUARANTEE THAT TAMAKI WOULD OVERTAKE THE PRESIDENT OF THE FOOTBALL CLUB.

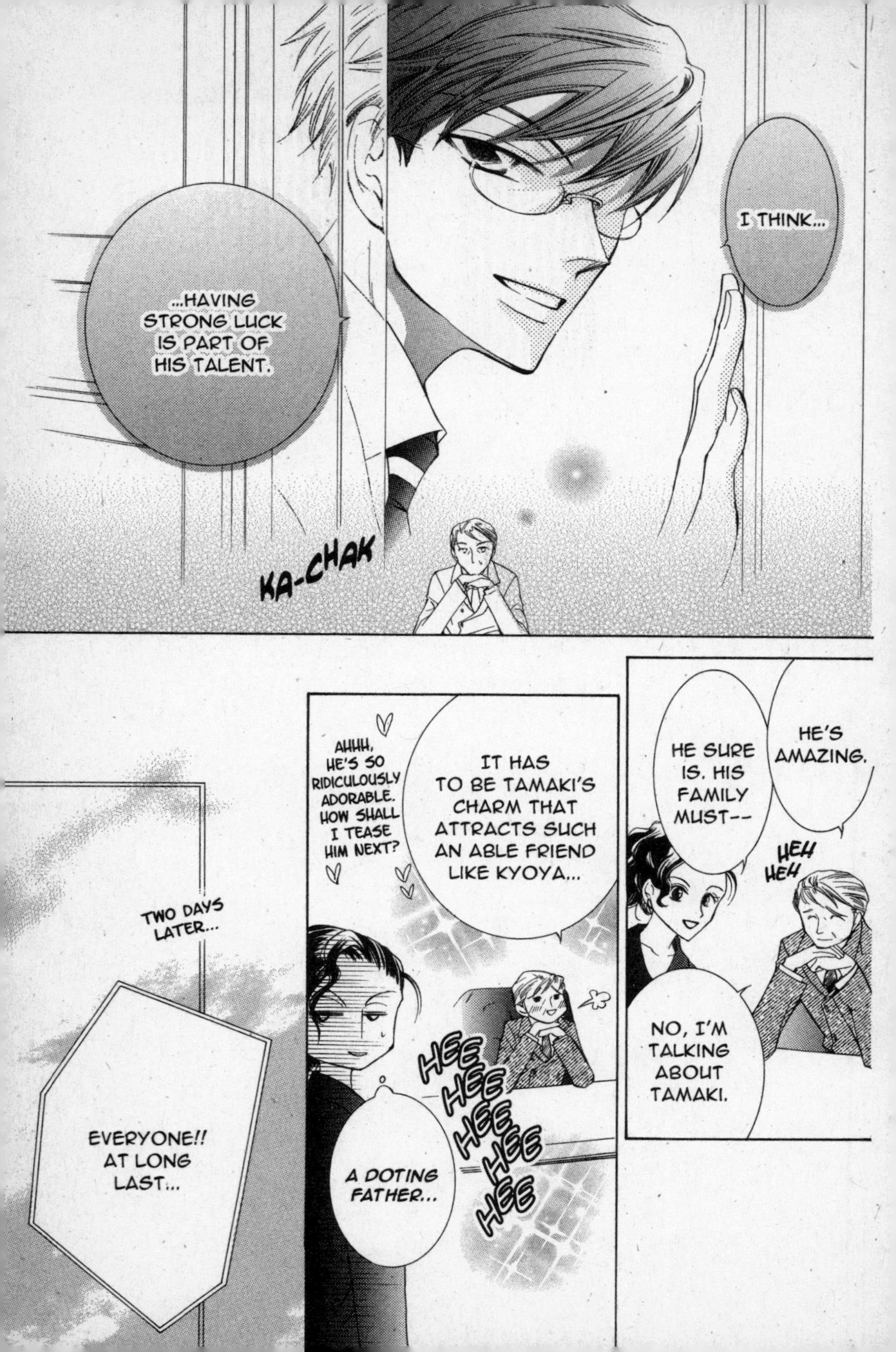
I THINK...
...HAVING STRONG LUCK IS PART OF HIS TALENT.
KA-CHAK
HE'S AMAZING.
HE SURE IS. HIS FAMILY MUST--
HEH HEH
NO, I'M TALKING ABOUT TAMAKI.
IT HAS TO BE TAMAKI'S CHARM THAT ATTRACTS SUCH AN ABLE FRIEND LIKE KYOYA...
AHHH, HE'S SO RIDICULOUSLY ADORABLE. HOW SHALL I TEASE HIM NEXT?
HEE HEE HEE HEE HEE
A DOTING FATHER...
TWO DAYS LATER...
EVERYONE!! AT LONG LAST...

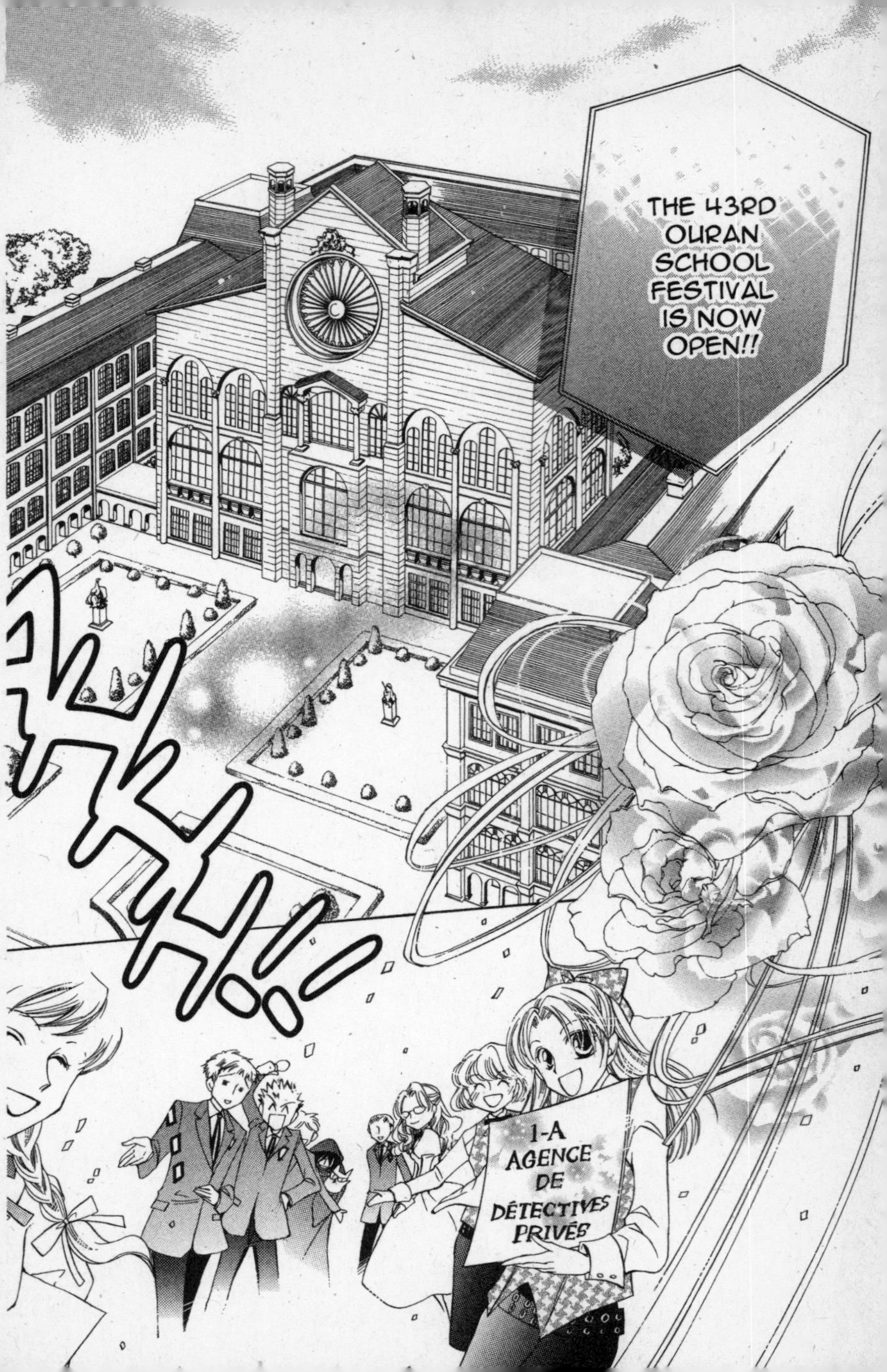
THE 43RD OURAN SCHOOL FESTIVAL IS NOW OPEN!!
1-A AGENCE DE DÉTECTIVES PRIVÉS

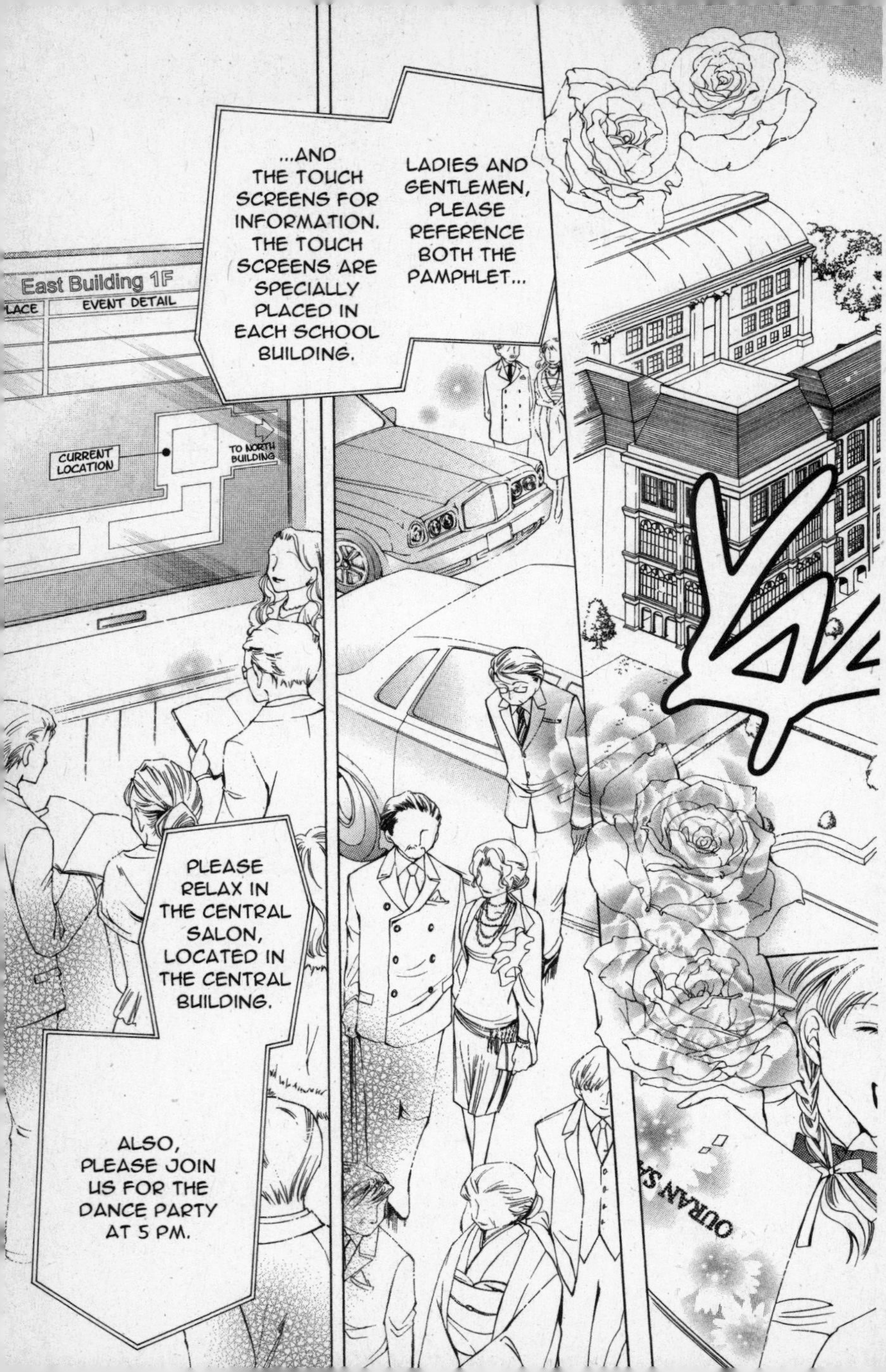

LADIES AND GENTLEMEN, PLEASE REFERENCE BOTH THE PAMPHLET...
...AND THE TOUCH SCREENS FOR INFORMATION. THE TOUCH SCREENS ARE SPECIALLY PLACED IN EACH SCHOOL BUILDING.
East Building 1F
EVENT DETAIL
CURRENT LOCATION
TO NORTH BUILDING
PLEASE RELAX IN THE CENTRAL SALON, LOCATED IN THE CENTRAL BUILDING.
ALSO, PLEASE JOIN US FOR THE DANCE PARTY AT 5 PM.

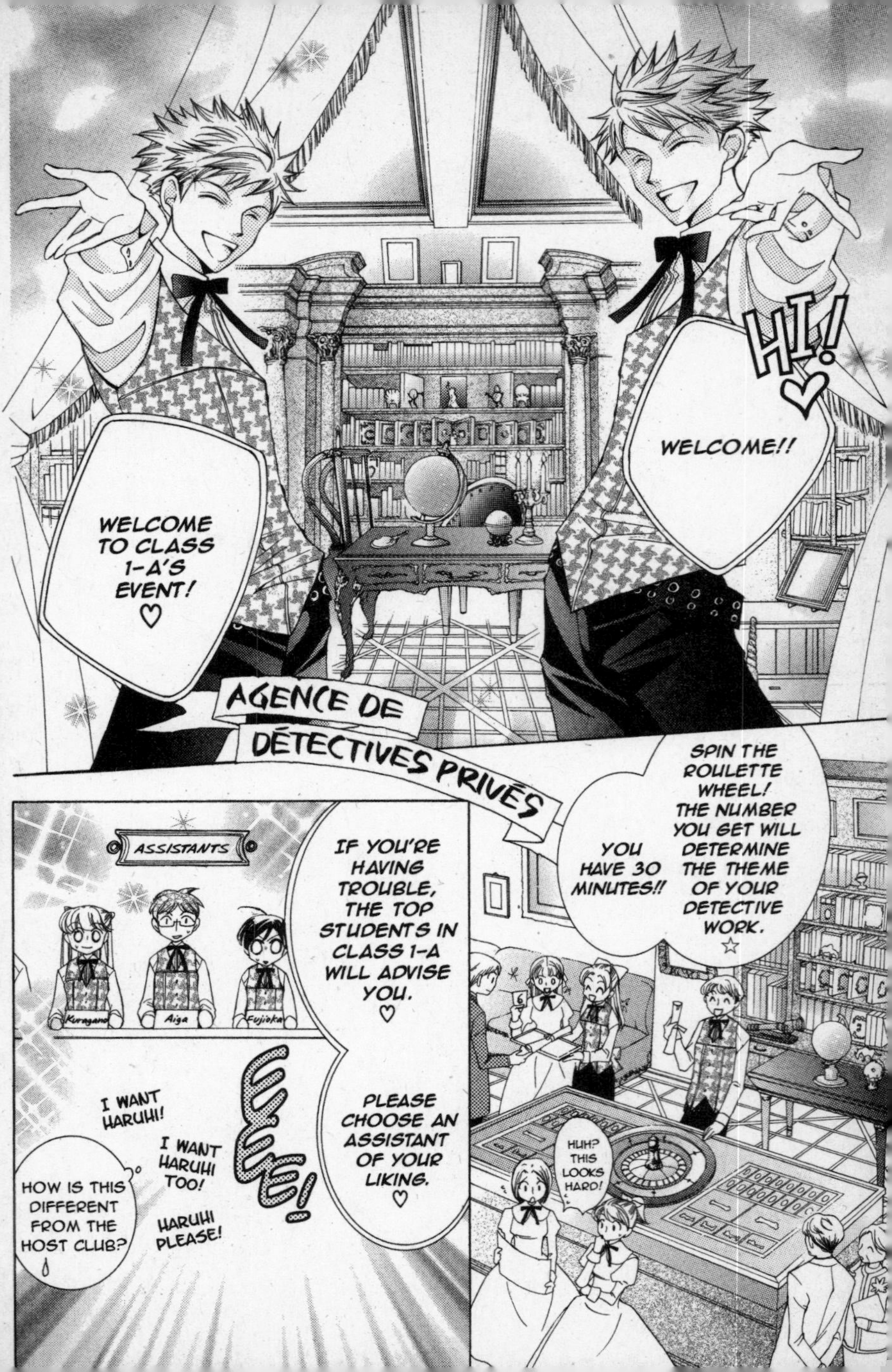
HI! ♡
WELCOME!!
WELCOME TO CLASS 1-A'S EVENT! ♡
AGENCE DE DÉTECTIVES PRIVÉS
SPIN THE ROULETTE WHEEL! THE NUMBER YOU GET WILL DETERMINE THE THEME OF YOUR DETECTIVE WORK. ☆
YOU HAVE 30 MINUTES!!
HUH? THIS LOOKS HARD!
ASSISTANTS
Kuragano
Aiga
Fujioka
IF YOU'RE HAVING TROUBLE, THE TOP STUDENTS IN CLASS 1-A WILL ADVISE YOU. ♡
PLEASE CHOOSE AN ASSISTANT OF YOUR LIKING. ♡
EEE!
I WANT HARUHI!
I WANT HARUHI TOO!
HARUHI PLEASE!
HOW IS THIS DIFFERENT FROM THE HOST CLUB?

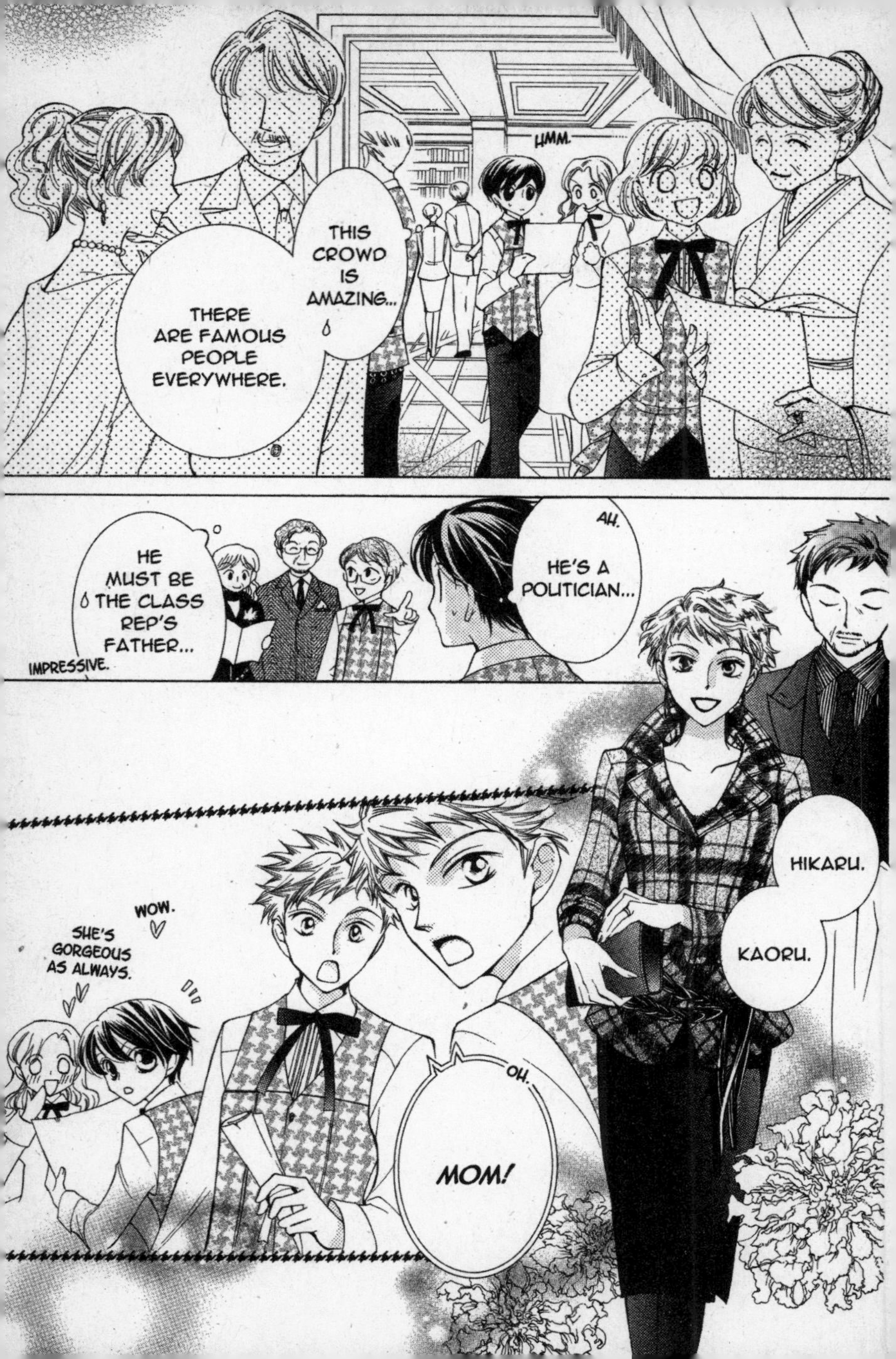
HMM.
THIS CROWD IS AMAZING...
THERE ARE FAMOUS PEOPLE EVERYWHERE.
AH. HE'S A POLITICIAN...
HE MUST BE THE CLASS REP'S FATHER...
IMPRESSIVE.
HIKARU.
KAORU.
OH.
MOM!
WOW.
SHE'S GORGEOUS AS ALWAYS.

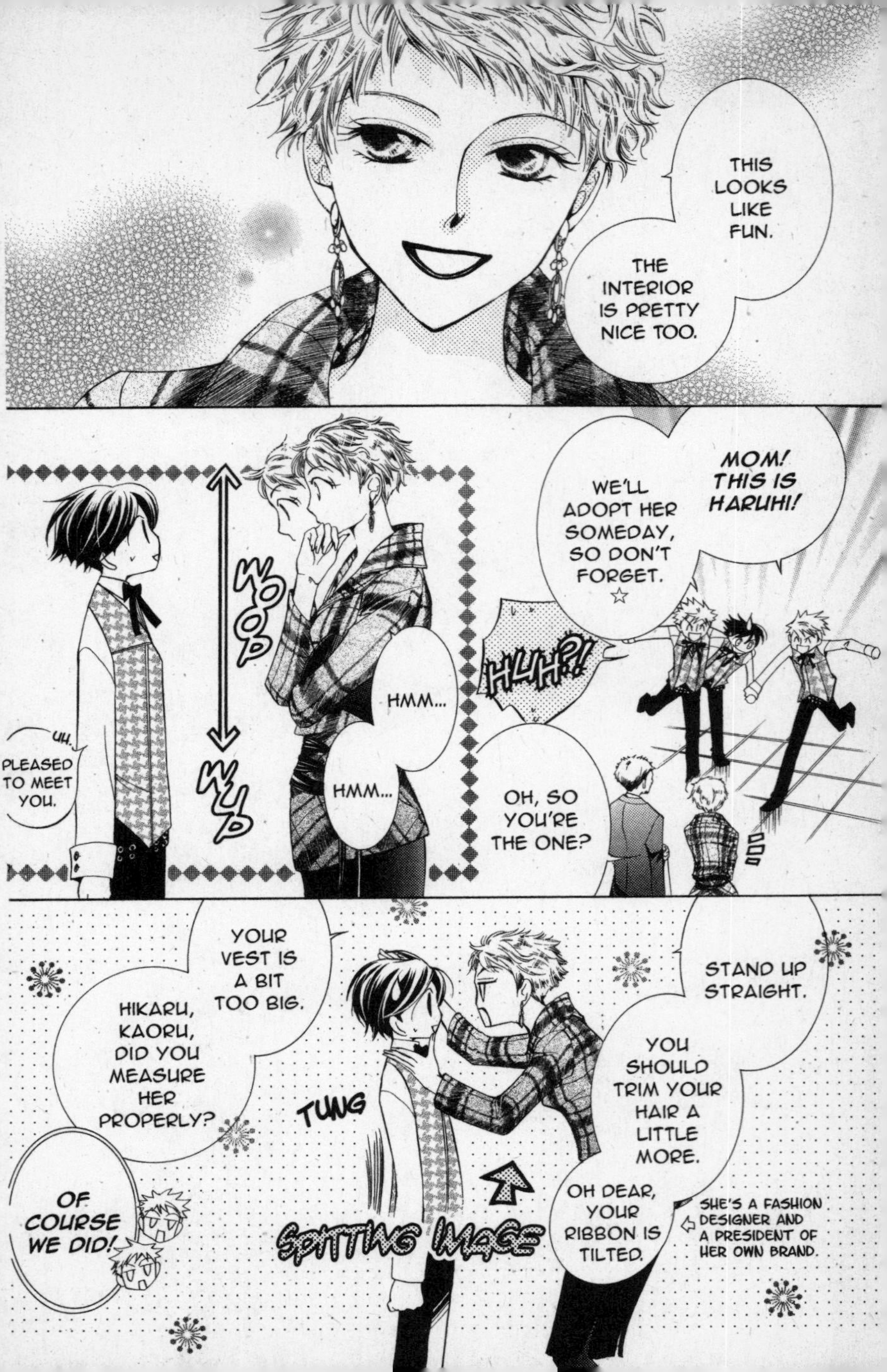
THIS LOOKS LIKE FUN.
THE INTERIOR IS PRETTY NICE TOO.
MOM! THIS IS HARUHI!
WE'LL ADOPT HER SOMEDAY, SO DON'T FORGET. ☆
HUH?!
OH, SO YOU'RE THE ONE?
HMM...
HMM...
WOOP
WUP
UH. PLEASED TO MEET YOU.
STAND UP STRAIGHT.
YOU SHOULD TRIM YOUR HAIR A LITTLE MORE.
OH DEAR, YOUR RIBBON IS TILTED.
SHE'S A FASHION DESIGNER AND A PRESIDENT OF HER OWN BRAND.
YOUR VEST IS A BIT TOO BIG.
HIKARU, KAORU, DID YOU MEASURE HER PROPERLY?
TUNG
SPITTING IMAGE
OF COURSE WE DID!

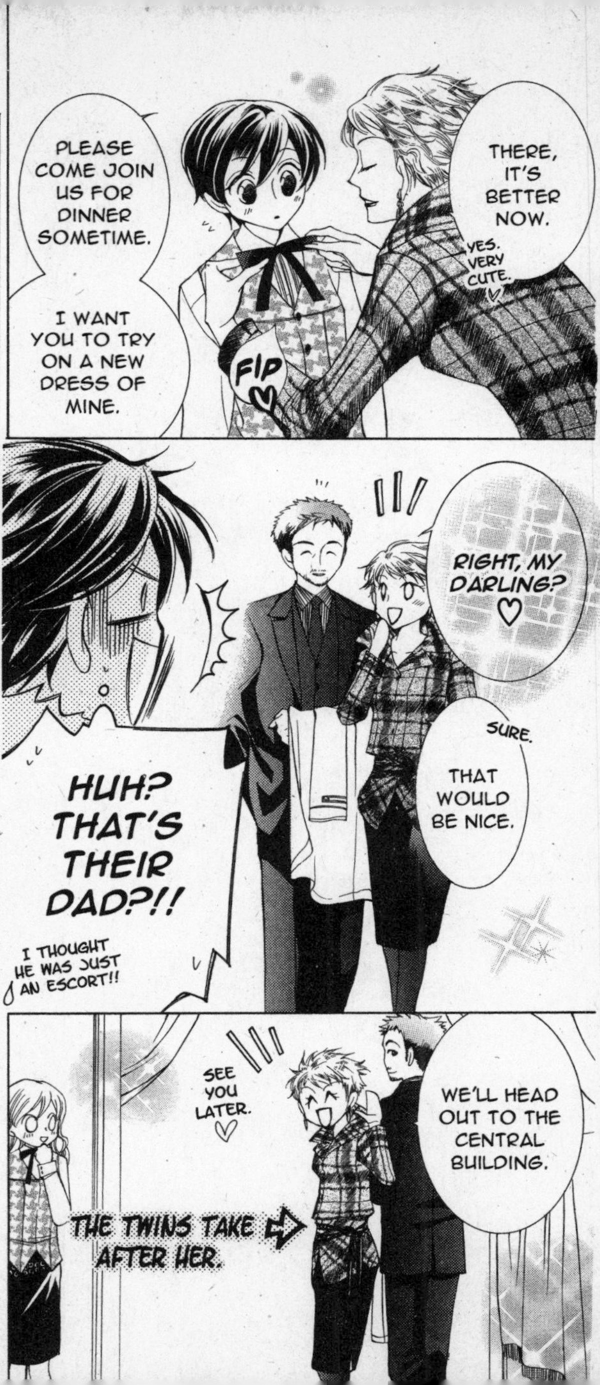
THERE, IT'S BETTER NOW.
YES. VERY CUTE.
FIP
PLEASE COME JOIN US FOR DINNER SOMETIME.
I WANT YOU TO TRY ON A NEW DRESS OF MINE.
RIGHT, MY DARLING?
SURE.
THAT WOULD BE NICE.
HUH? THAT'S THEIR DAD?!!
I THOUGHT HE WAS JUST AN ESCORT!!
WE'LL HEAD OUT TO THE CENTRAL BUILDING.
SEE YOU LATER.
THE TWINS TAKE AFTER HER.

Q2.

WHICH HOST CLUB CHARACTER DO YOU LIKE BEST?

A2. I'M ASKED THIS QUESTION A LOT. MY ORDER OF PREFERENCE IS BASED ON HOW EASY THEY ARE TO DRAW. SO...

1. BUN-BUN
2. BEARY
3. BEREZNOFF

...I THINK.

IF WE'RE TALKING ABOUT ACTUAL PEOPLE, THEN I SAY MISUZU, SUZUSHIMA, AND THE MEMBERS OF THE FOOTBALL CLUB.

WHAT I LIKE IS THAT NONE OF THEM ARE "HANDSOME." I HAVE A HARD TIME DRAWING HANDSOME CHARACTERS--I GET NERVOUS THAT I'LL MESS UP THEIR FACES.

I'M SO SORRY...

I'LL DO MY BEST!!

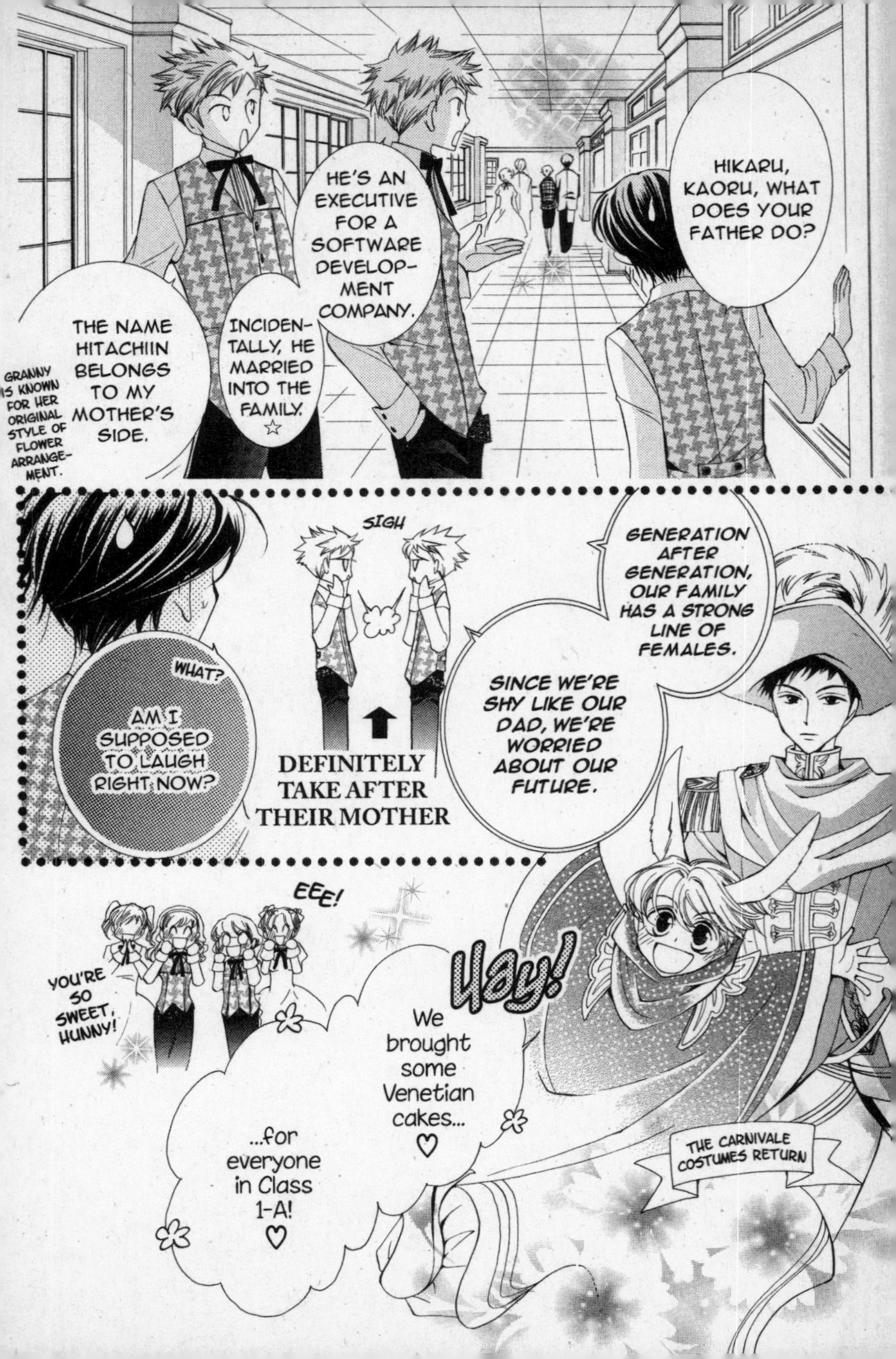
HIKARU, KAORU, WHAT DOES YOUR FATHER DO?
HE'S AN EXECUTIVE FOR A SOFTWARE DEVELOPMENT COMPANY.
INCIDENTALLY, HE MARRIED INTO THE FAMILY. ☆
THE NAME HITACHIIN BELONGS TO MY MOTHER'S SIDE.
GRANNY IS KNOWN FOR HER ORIGINAL STYLE OF FLOWER ARRANGEMENT.
GENERATION AFTER GENERATION, OUR FAMILY HAS A STRONG LINE OF FEMALES.
SINCE WE'RE SHY LIKE OUR DAD, WE'RE WORRIED ABOUT OUR FUTURE.
SIGH
DEFINITELY TAKE AFTER THEIR MOTHER
WHAT?
AM I SUPPOSED TO LAUGH RIGHT NOW?
THE CARNIVALE COSTUMES RETURN
YAY!
We brought some Venetian cakes... ♡
...for everyone in Class 1-A! ♡
EEE!
YOU'RE SO SWEET, HUNNY!

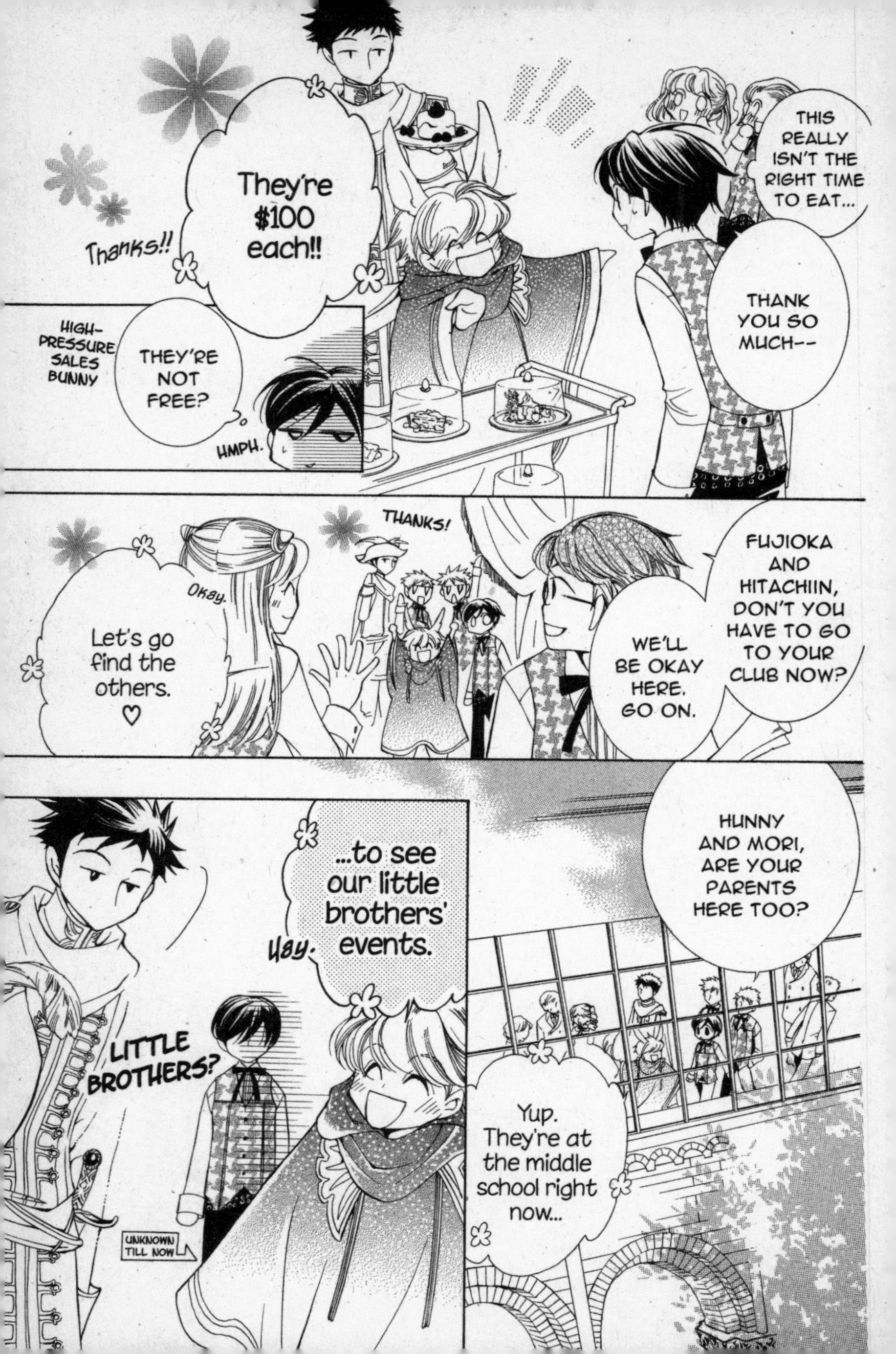
THIS REALLY ISN'T THE RIGHT TIME TO EAT...
THANK YOU SO MUCH--
They're $100 each!!
Thanks!!
THEY'RE NOT FREE?
HMPH.
HIGH-PRESSURE SALES BUNNY
FUJIOKA AND HITACHIIN, DON'T YOU HAVE TO GO TO YOUR CLUB NOW?
WE'LL BE OKAY HERE. GO ON.
THANKS!
Okay.
Let's go find the others. ♡
HUNNY AND MORI, ARE YOUR PARENTS HERE TOO?
Yup. They're at the middle school right now...
...to see our little brothers' events.
Yay.
LITTLE BROTHERS?
UNKNOWN TILL NOW

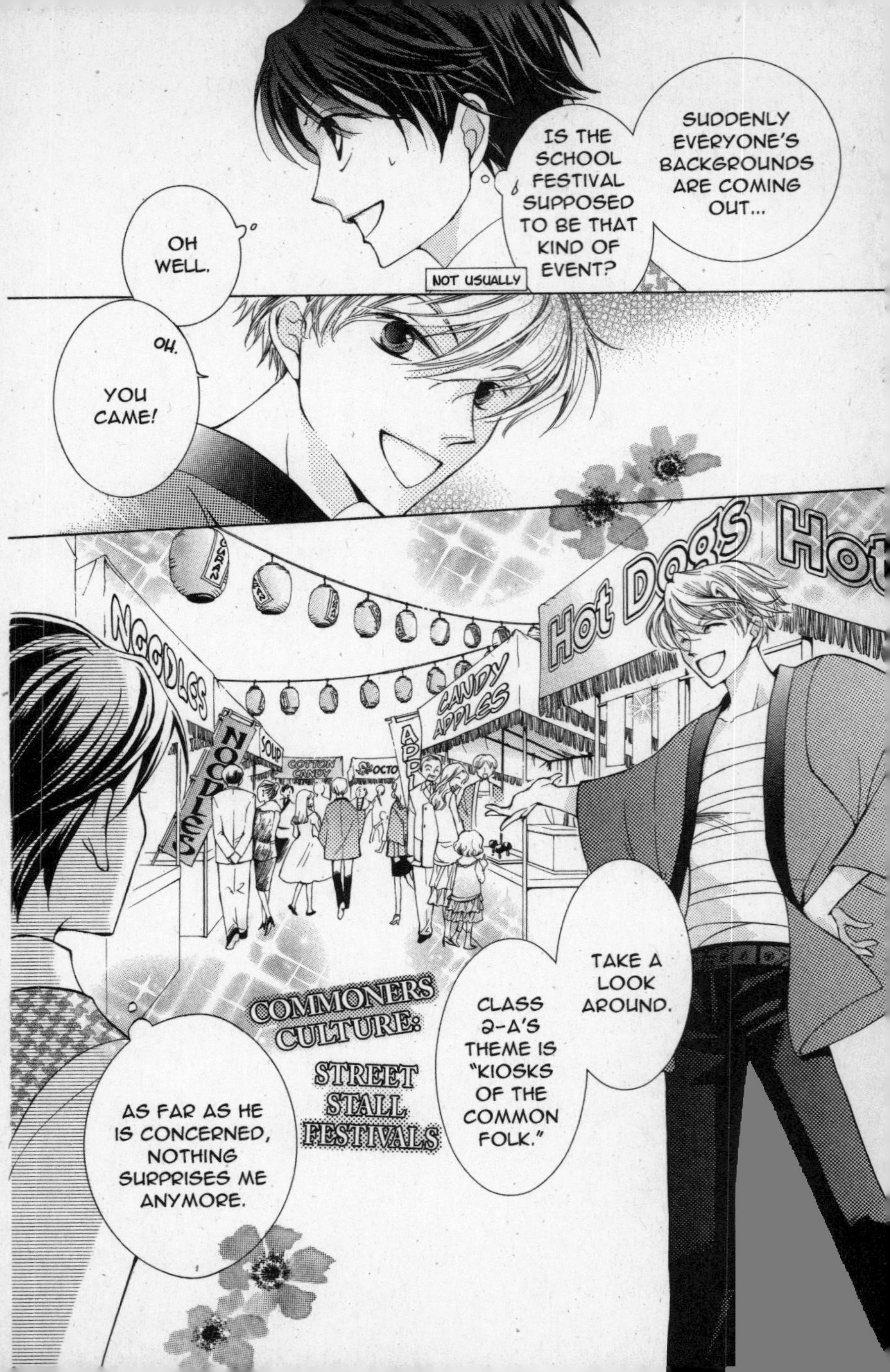

SUDDENLY EVERYONE'S BACKGROUNDS ARE COMING OUT...
IS THE SCHOOL FESTIVAL SUPPOSED TO BE THAT KIND OF EVENT?
NOT USUALLY
OH WELL.
OH.
YOU CAME!
Hot Dogs
CANDY APPLES
NOODLES
NOODLES
SOUP
COTTON CANDY
TAKE A LOOK AROUND.
CLASS 2-A'S THEME IS "KIOSKS OF THE COMMON FOLK."
COMMONERS CULTURE:
STREET STALL FESTIVALS
AS FAR AS HE IS CONCERNED, NOTHING SURPRISES ME ANYMORE.

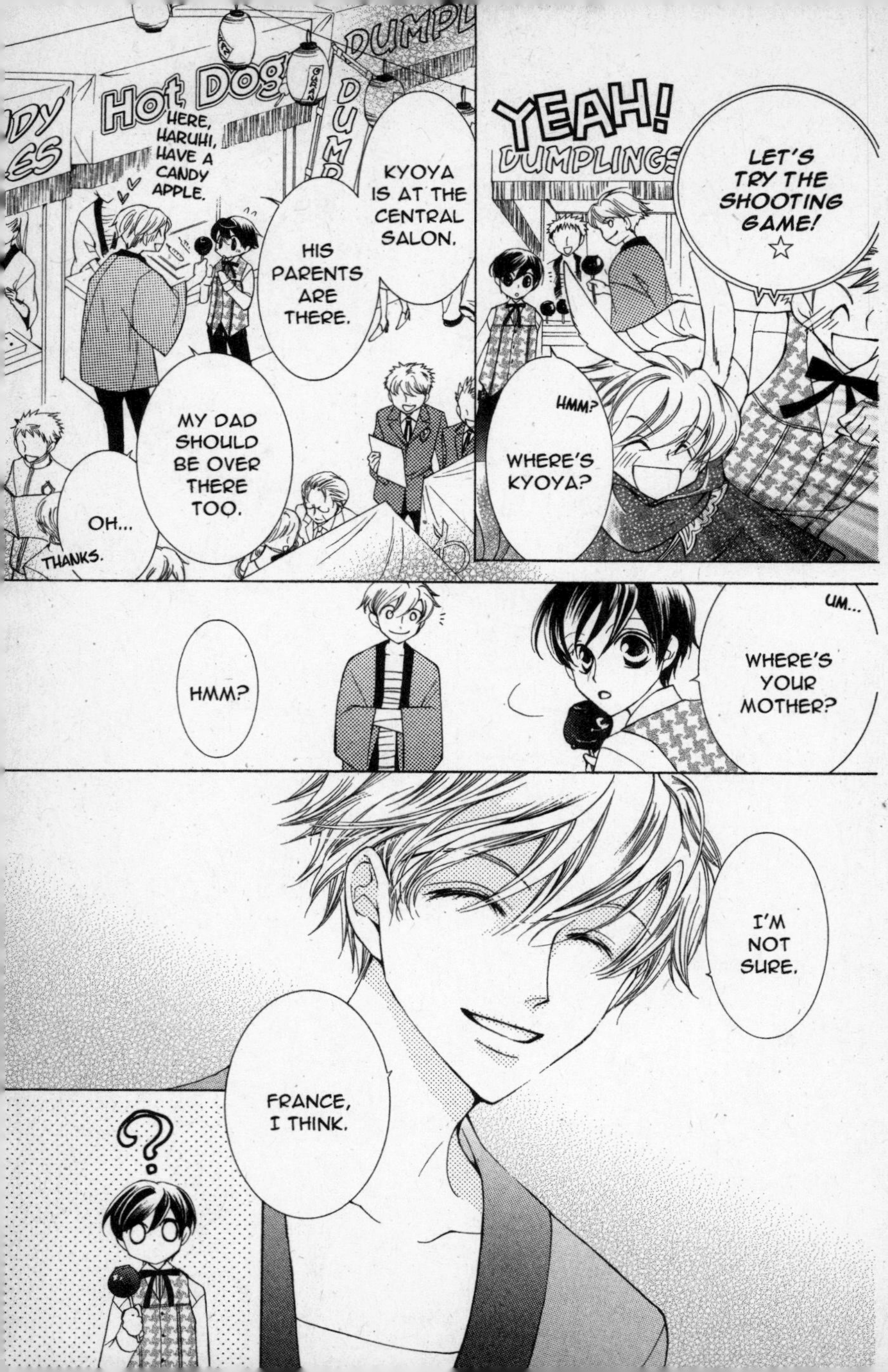
YEAH!
DUMPLINGS
LET'S TRY THE SHOOTING GAME! ☆
HMM?
WHERE'S KYOYA?
Hot Dog
DUMPL
KYOYA IS AT THE CENTRAL SALON.
HIS PARENTS ARE THERE.
MY DAD SHOULD BE OVER THERE TOO.
HERE, HARUHI, HAVE A CANDY APPLE.
OH...
THANKS.
UM...
WHERE'S YOUR MOTHER?
HMM?
I'M NOT SURE.
FRANCE, I THINK.

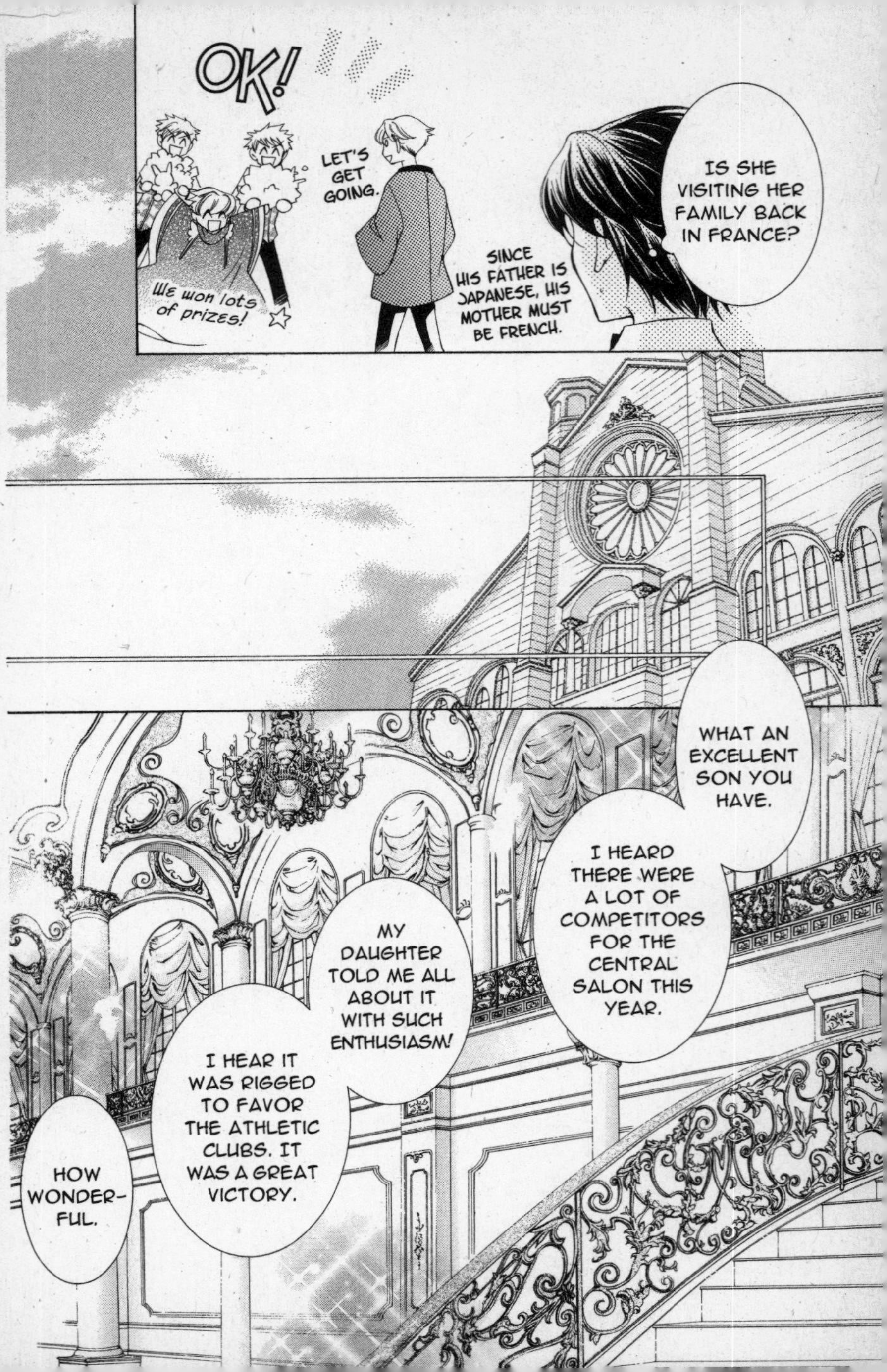
IS SHE VISITING HER FAMILY BACK IN FRANCE?
SINCE HIS FATHER IS JAPANESE, HIS MOTHER MUST BE FRENCH.
LET'S GET GOING.
OK!
We won lots of prizes!
WHAT AN EXCELLENT SON YOU HAVE.
I HEARD THERE WERE A LOT OF COMPETITORS FOR THE CENTRAL SALON THIS YEAR.
MY DAUGHTER TOLD ME ALL ABOUT IT WITH SUCH ENTHUSIASM!
I HEAR IT WAS RIGGED TO FAVOR THE ATHLETIC CLUBS. IT WAS A GREAT VICTORY.
HOW WONDERFUL.

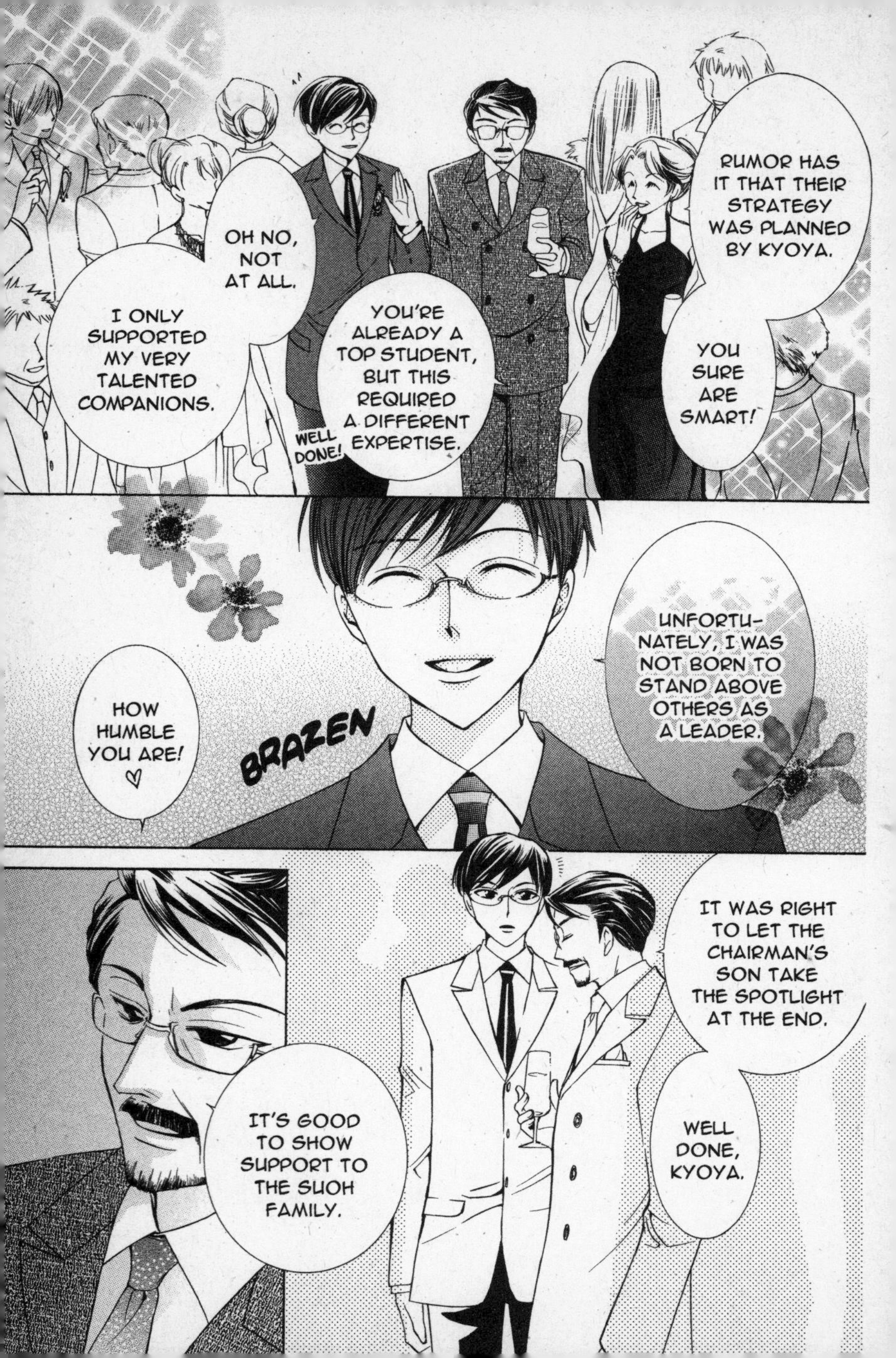
RUMOR HAS IT THAT THEIR STRATEGY WAS PLANNED BY KYOYA.
YOU SURE ARE SMART!
YOU'RE ALREADY A TOP STUDENT, BUT THIS REQUIRED A DIFFERENT EXPERTISE.
WELL DONE!
OH NO, NOT AT ALL.
I ONLY SUPPORTED MY VERY TALENTED COMPANIONS.
UNFORTUNATELY, I WAS NOT BORN TO STAND ABOVE OTHERS AS A LEADER.
BRAZEN
HOW HUMBLE YOU ARE! ♡
IT WAS RIGHT TO LET THE CHAIRMAN'S SON TAKE THE SPOTLIGHT AT THE END.
WELL DONE, KYOYA.
IT'S GOOD TO SHOW SUPPORT TO THE SUOH FAMILY.

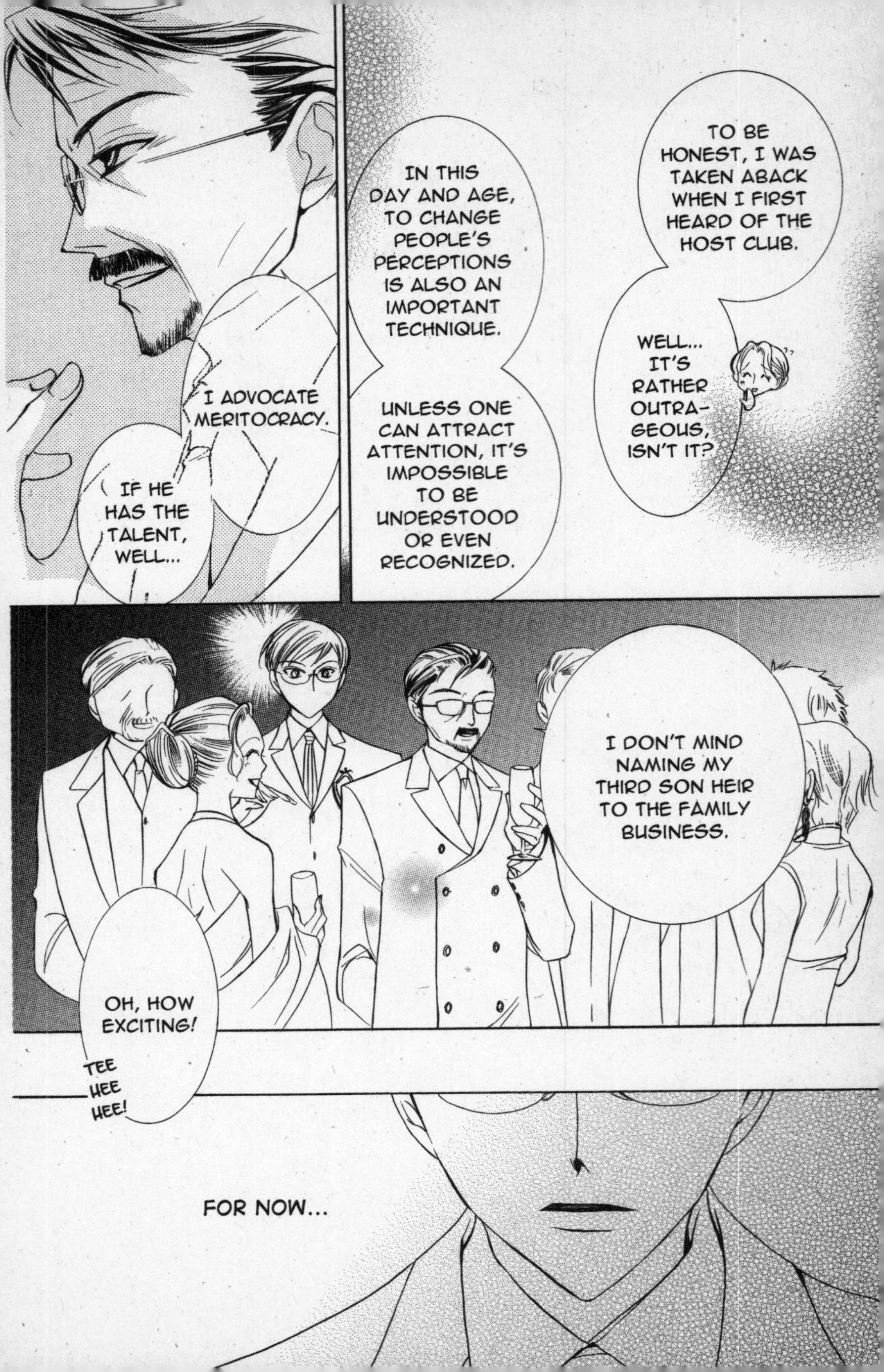
TO BE HONEST, I WAS TAKEN ABACK WHEN I FIRST HEARD OF THE HOST CLUB.
WELL... IT'S RATHER OUTRA-GEOUS, ISN'T IT?
IN THIS DAY AND AGE, TO CHANGE PEOPLE'S PERCEPTIONS IS ALSO AN IMPORTANT TECHNIQUE.
UNLESS ONE CAN ATTRACT ATTENTION, IT'S IMPOSSIBLE TO BE UNDERSTOOD OR EVEN RECOGNIZED.
I ADVOCATE MERITOCRACY.
IF HE HAS THE TALENT, WELL...
I DON'T MIND NAMING MY THIRD SON HEIR TO THE FAMILY BUSINESS.
OH, HOW EXCITING!
TEE HEE HEE!
FOR NOW...

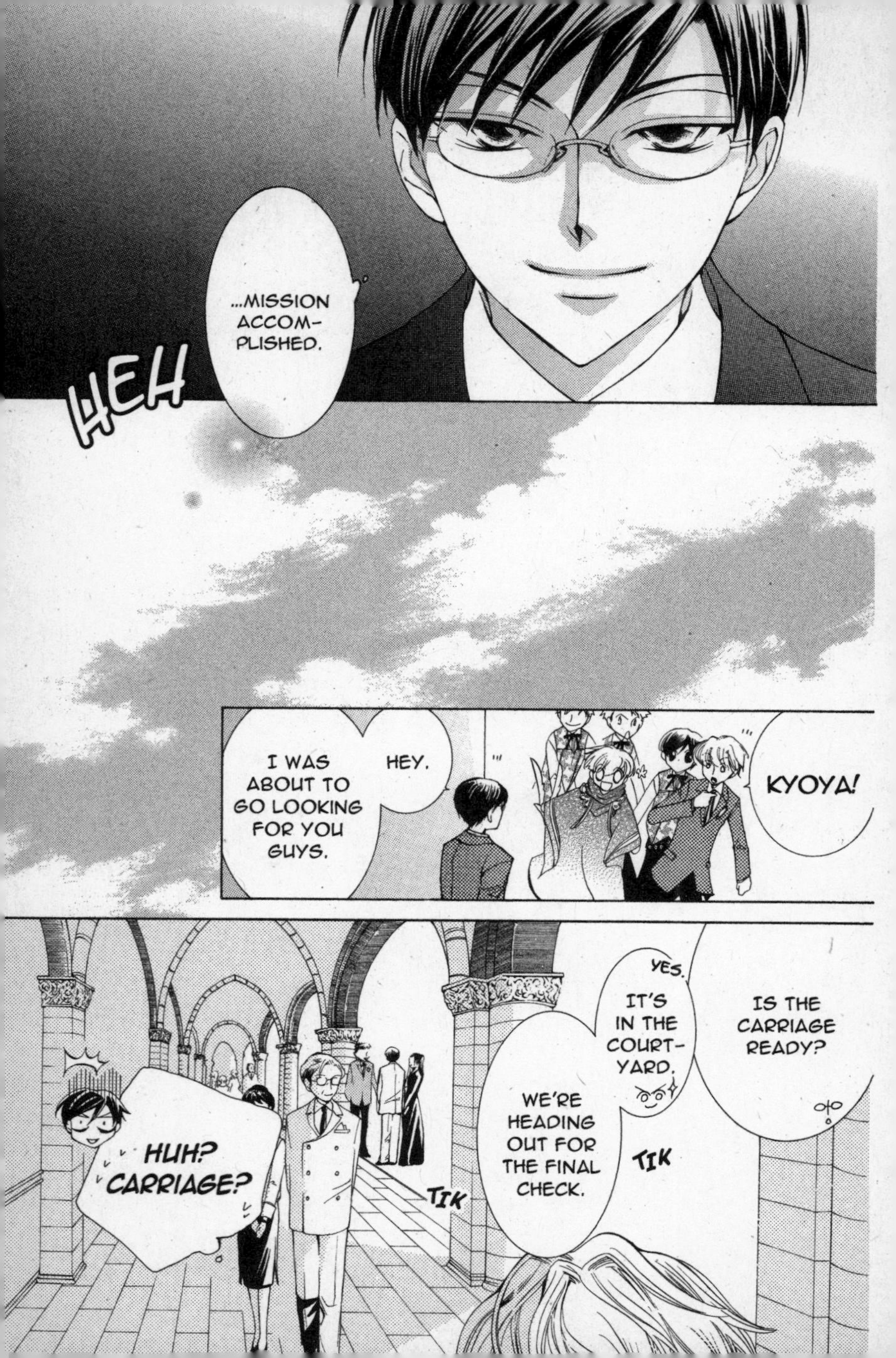
...MISSION ACCOM-PLISHED.
HEH
KYOYA!
HEY.
I WAS ABOUT TO GO LOOKING FOR YOU GUYS.
IS THE CARRIAGE READY?
YES.
IT'S IN THE COURT-YARD.
WE'RE HEADING OUT FOR THE FINAL CHECK.
TIK
TIK
HUH? CARRIAGE?

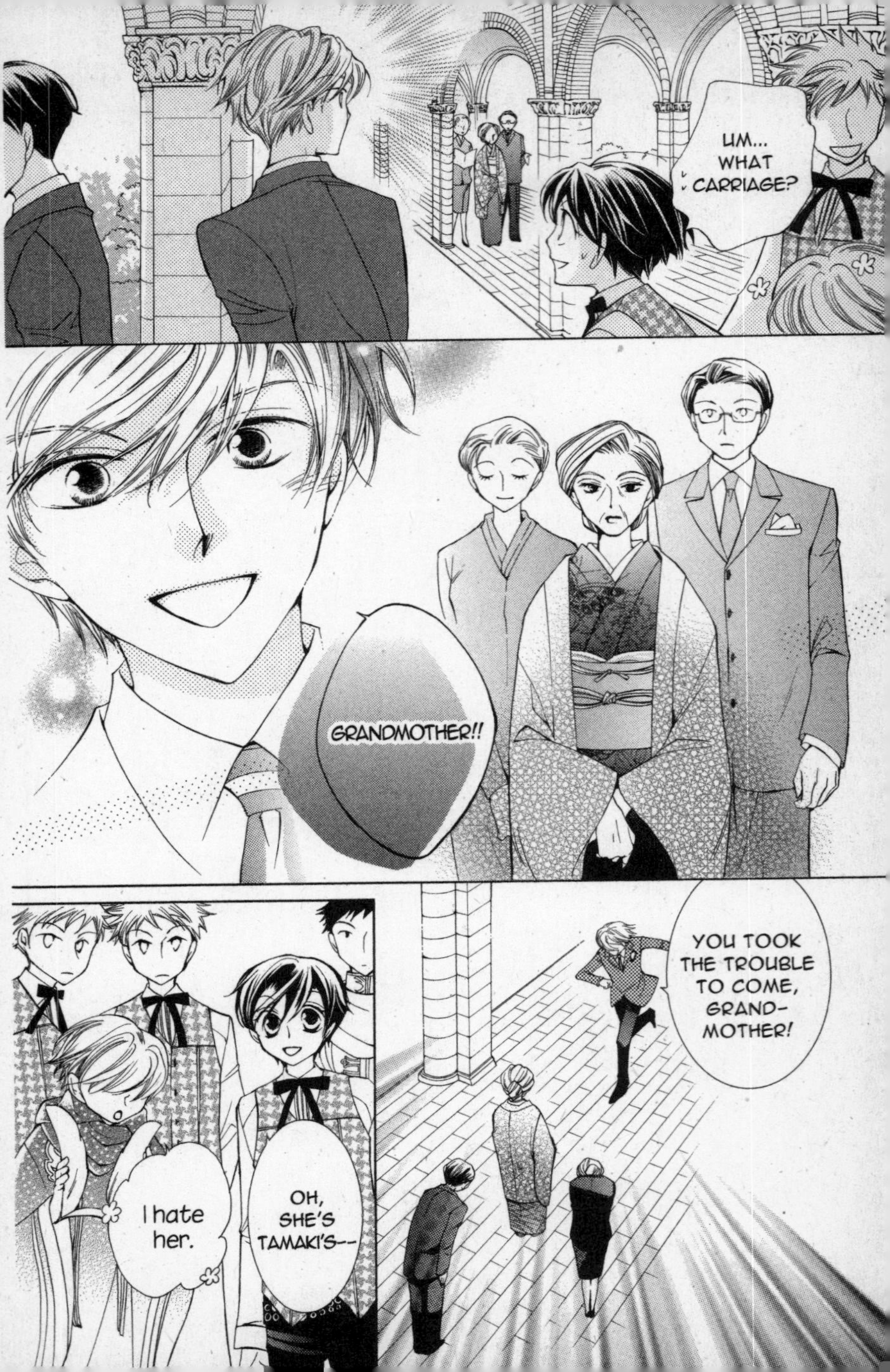
UM... WHAT CARRIAGE?
GRANDMOTHER!!
YOU TOOK THE TROUBLE TO COME, GRAND-MOTHER!
OH, SHE'S TAMAKI'S--
I hate her.

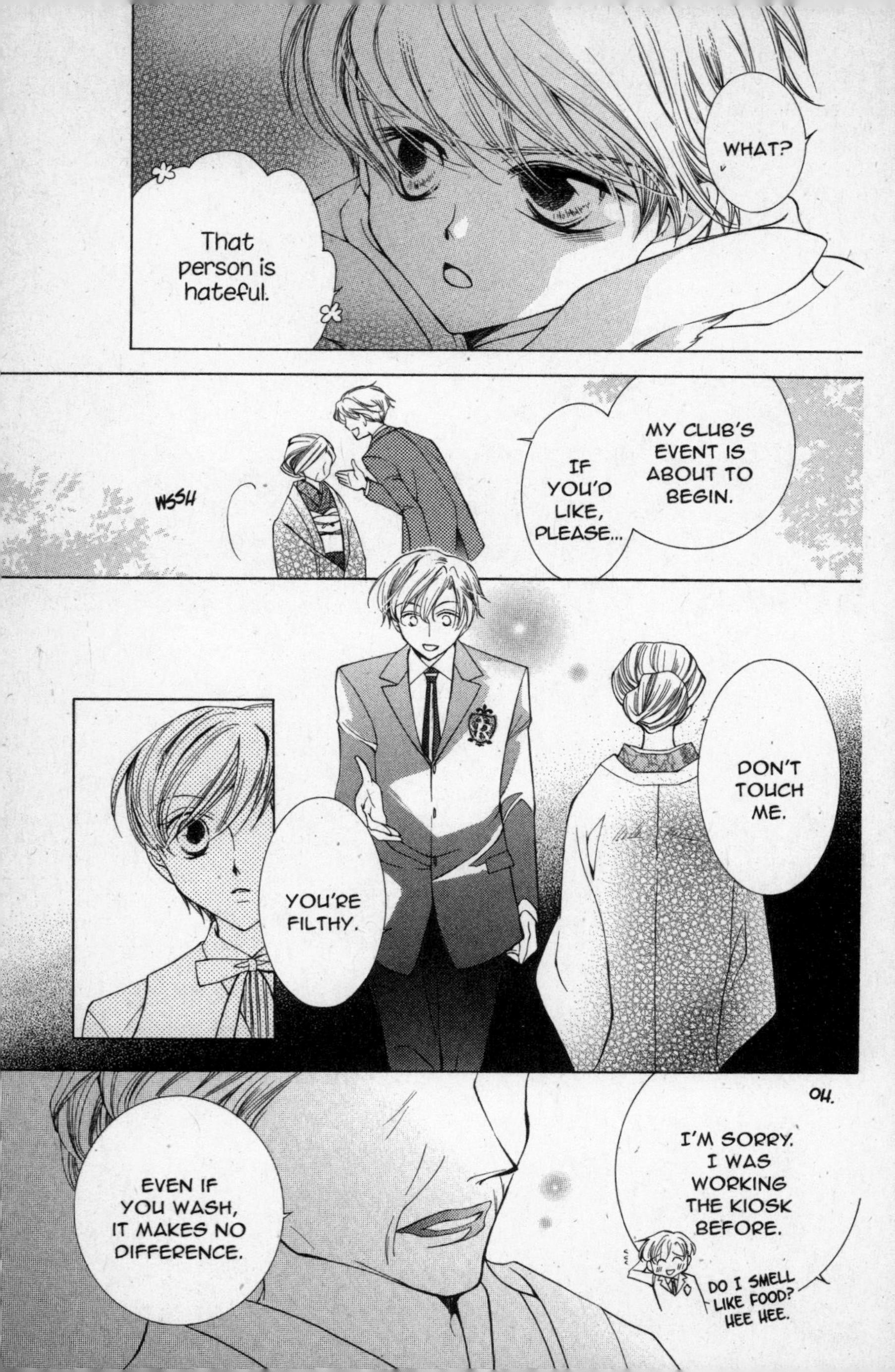
WHAT?
That person is hateful.
MY CLUB'S EVENT IS ABOUT TO BEGIN.
IF YOU'D LIKE, PLEASE...
WSSH
DON'T TOUCH ME.
YOU'RE FILTHY.
OH.
I'M SORRY. I WAS WORKING THE KIOSK BEFORE.
DO I SMELL LIKE FOOD? HEE HEE.
EVEN IF YOU WASH, IT MAKES NO DIFFERENCE.

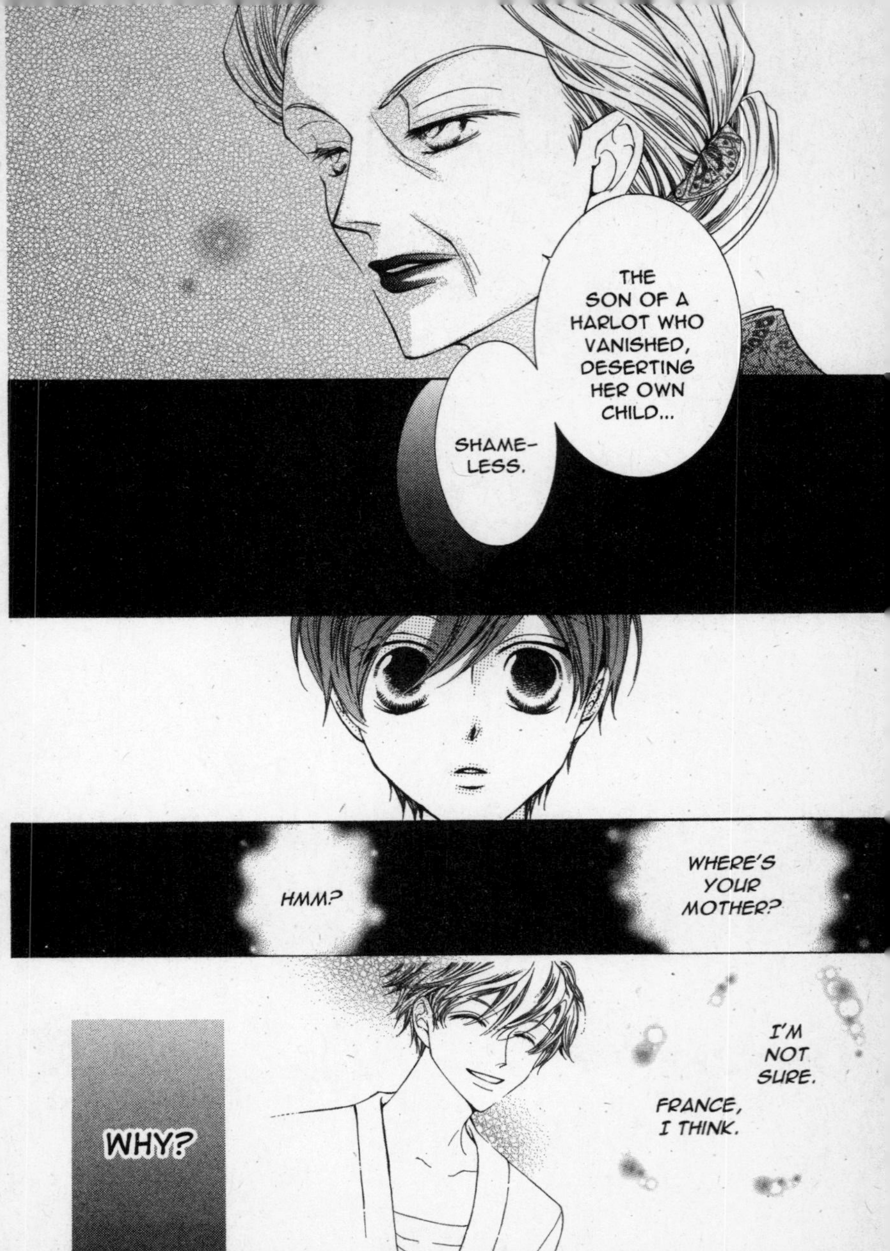
THE SON OF A HARLOT WHO VANISHED, DESERTING HER OWN CHILD...
SHAME-LESS.
WHERE'S YOUR MOTHER?
HMM?
I'M NOT SURE.
FRANCE, I THINK.
WHY?

DON'T TOUCH ME.

THE SON OF A HARLOT WHO VANISHED, DESERTING HER OWN CHILD...

WHY?

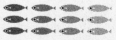

I RAN OUT OF IDEAS FOR THIS SPACE. I THOUGHT I HAD A LOT MORE.

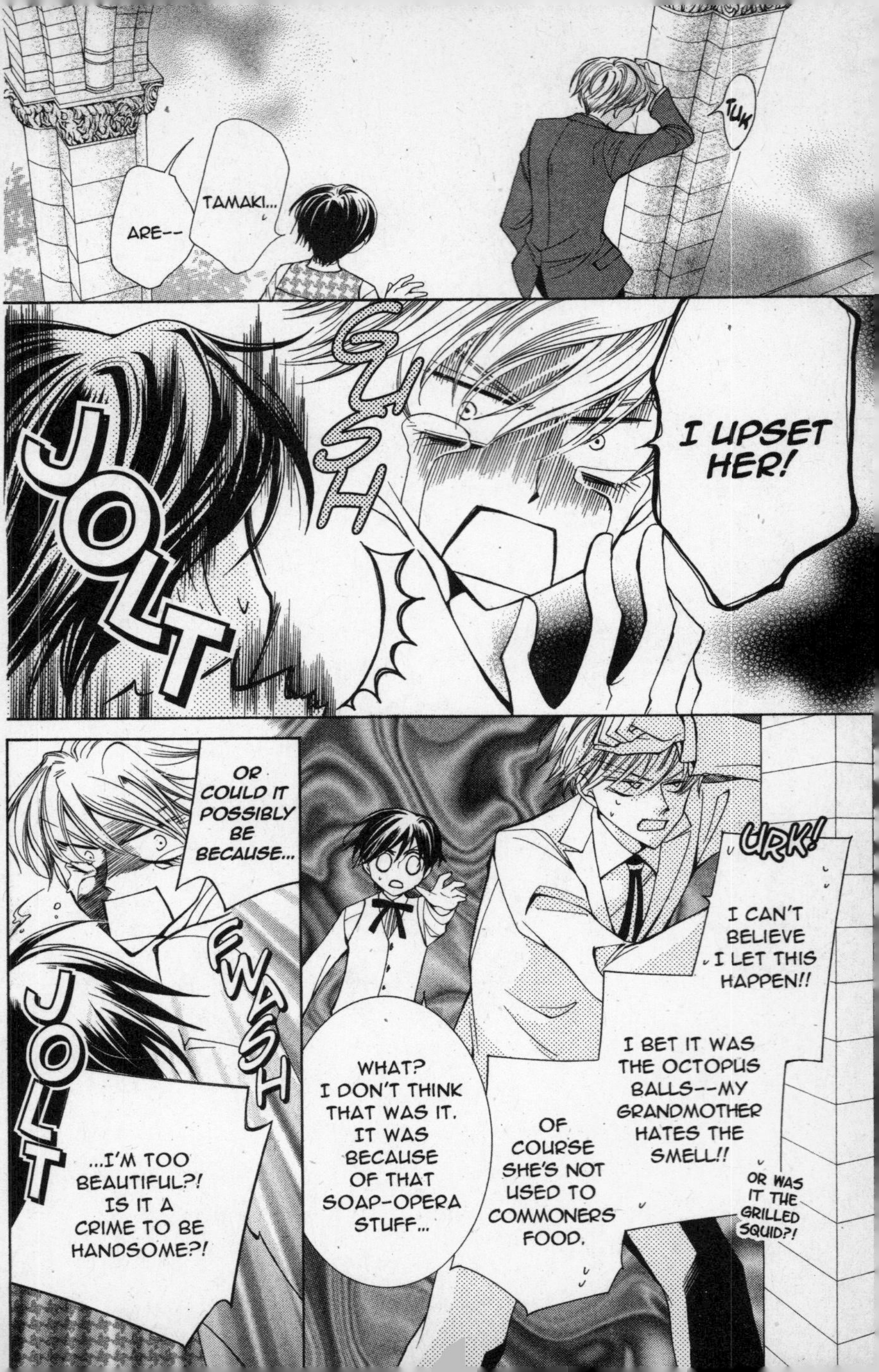
TUK
TAMAKI...
ARE--
I UPSET HER!
GUSH
JOLT
URK!
I CAN'T BELIEVE I LET THIS HAPPEN!!
I BET IT WAS THE OCTOPUS BALLS--MY GRANDMOTHER HATES THE SMELL!!
OR WAS IT THE GRILLED SQUID?!
OF COURSE SHE'S NOT USED TO COMMONERS FOOD.
WHAT? I DON'T THINK THAT WAS IT. IT WAS BECAUSE OF THAT SOAP-OPERA STUFF...
OR COULD IT POSSIBLY BE BECAUSE...
FWASH
JOLT
...I'M TOO BEAUTIFUL?! IS IT A CRIME TO BE HANDSOME?!

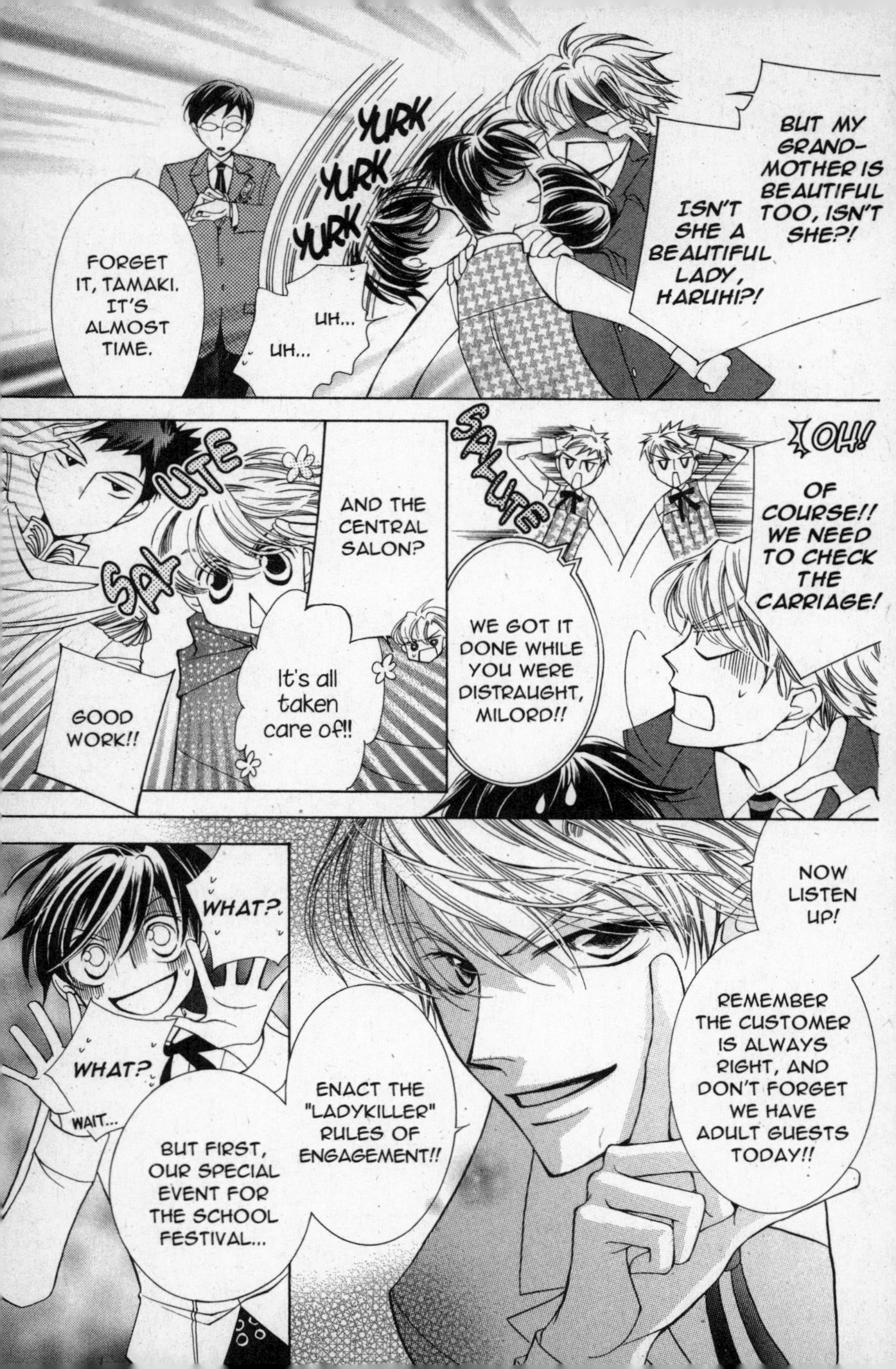
BUT MY GRANDMOTHER IS BEAUTIFUL TOO, ISN'T SHE?!
ISN'T SHE A BEAUTIFUL LADY, HARUHI?!
YURK
YURK
YURK
UH...
UH...
FORGET IT, TAMAKI. IT'S ALMOST TIME.
OH!
OF COURSE!! WE NEED TO CHECK THE CARRIAGE!
SALUTE
WE GOT IT DONE WHILE YOU WERE DISTRAUGHT, MILORD!!
AND THE CENTRAL SALON?
SALUTE
It's all taken care of!!
GOOD WORK!!
NOW LISTEN UP!
REMEMBER THE CUSTOMER IS ALWAYS RIGHT, AND DON'T FORGET WE HAVE ADULT GUESTS TODAY!!
ENACT THE "LADYKILLER" RULES OF ENGAGEMENT!!
BUT FIRST, OUR SPECIAL EVENT FOR THE SCHOOL FESTIVAL...
WHAT?
WHAT?
WAIT...

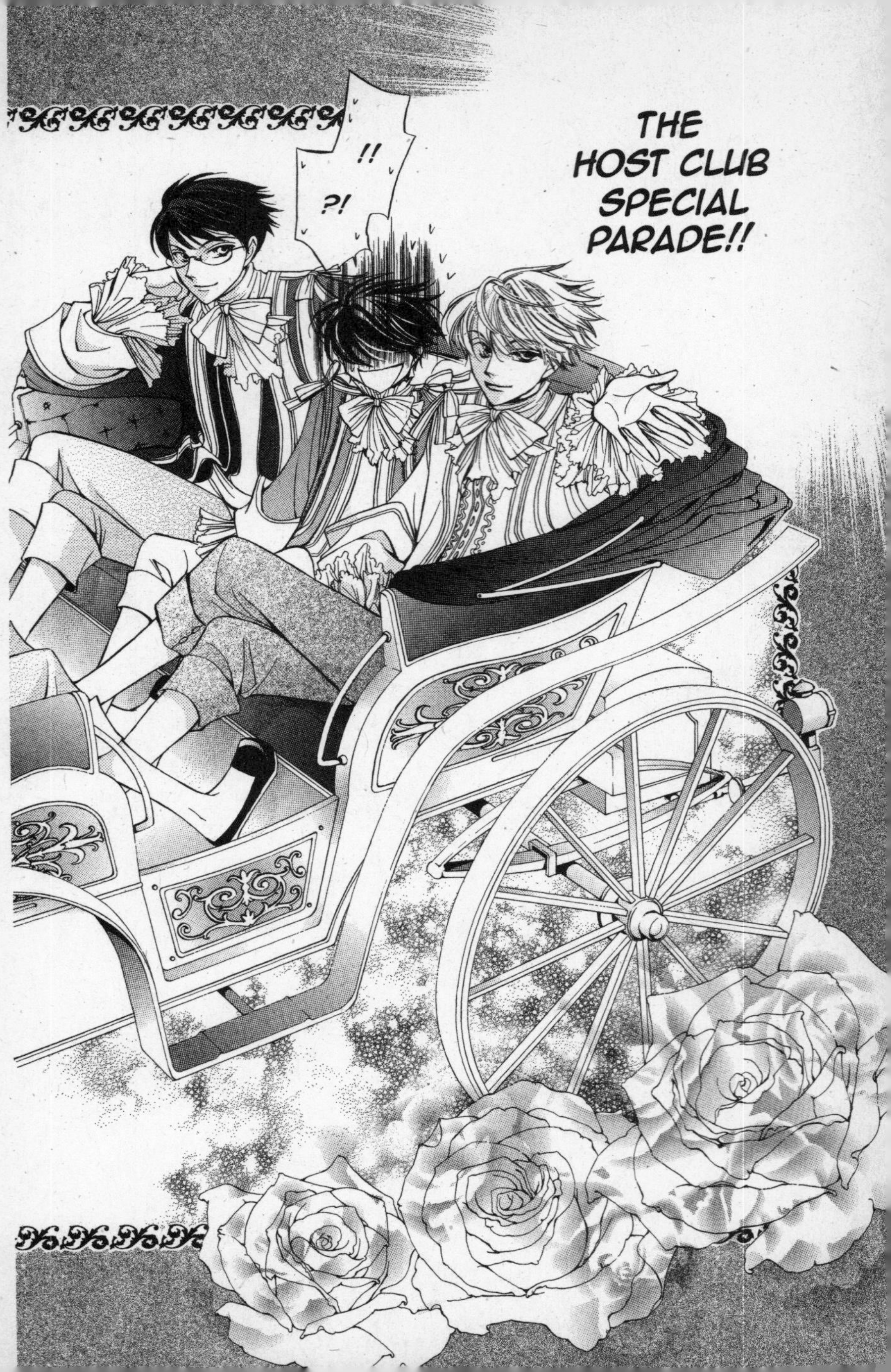
THE HOST CLUB SPECIAL PARADE!!
!!
?!

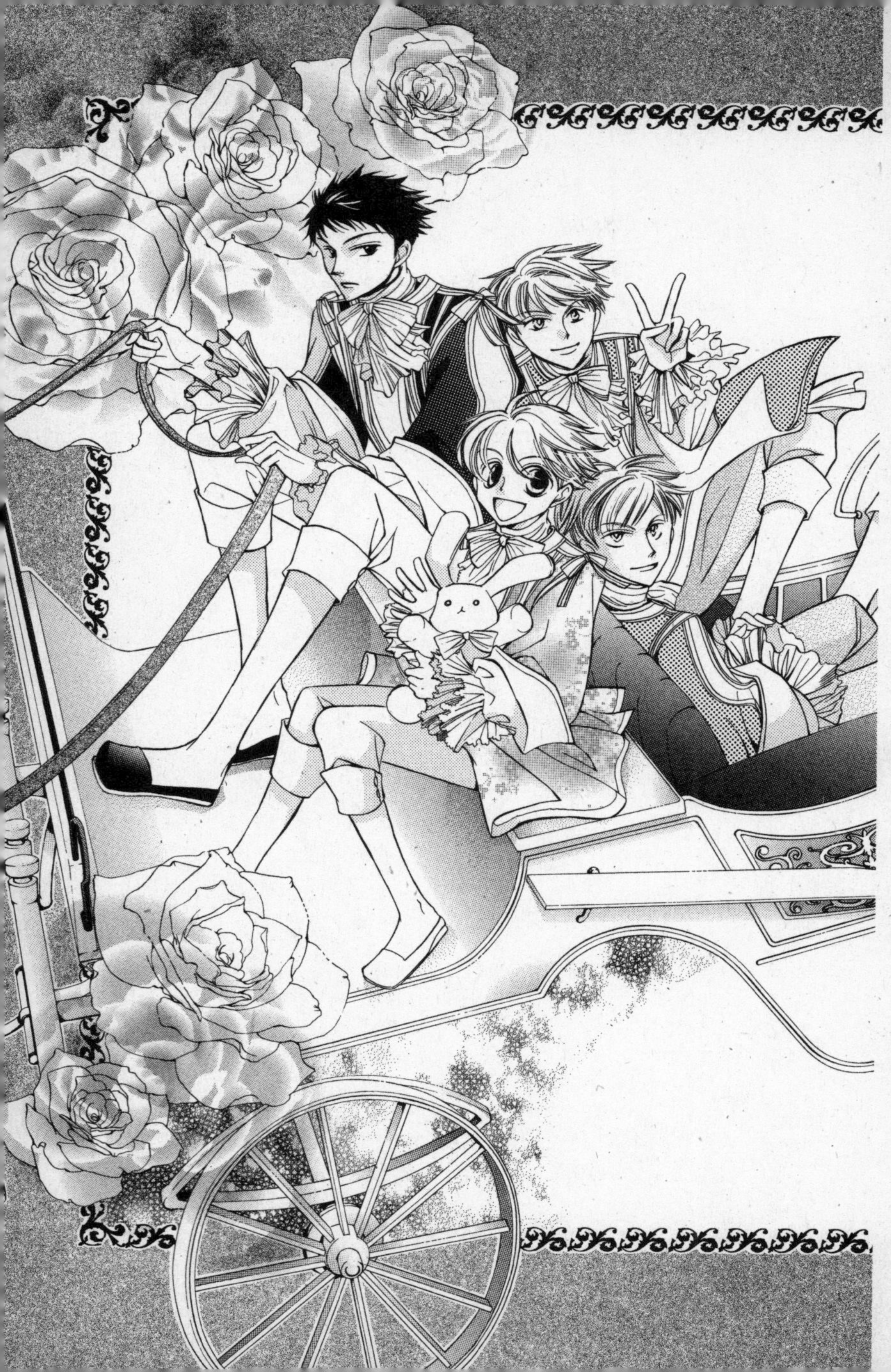

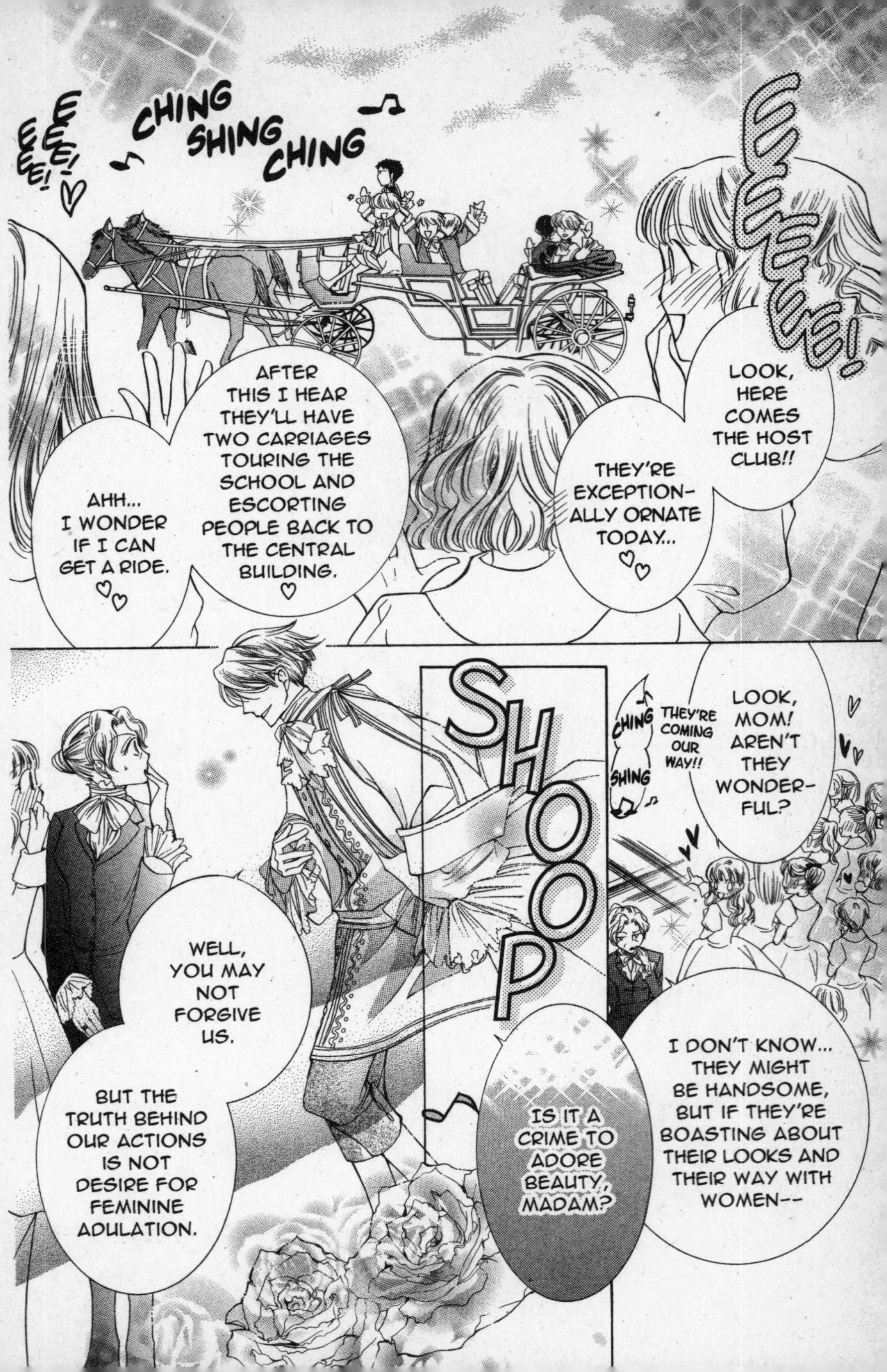

EEEEEE!
LOOK, HERE COMES THE HOST CLUB!!
THEY'RE EXCEPTION-ALLY ORNATE TODAY...
CHING SHING CHING
EEEEEE!
AFTER THIS I HEAR THEY'LL HAVE TWO CARRIAGES TOURING THE SCHOOL AND ESCORTING PEOPLE BACK TO THE CENTRAL BUILDING.
AHH... I WONDER IF I CAN GET A RIDE.
LOOK, MOM! AREN'T THEY WONDER-FUL?
THEY'RE COMING OUR WAY!!
CHING SHING
SHOOP
I DON'T KNOW... THEY MIGHT BE HANDSOME, BUT IF THEY'RE BOASTING ABOUT THEIR LOOKS AND THEIR WAY WITH WOMEN--
IS IT A CRIME TO ADORE BEAUTY, MADAM?
WELL, YOU MAY NOT FORGIVE US.
BUT THE TRUTH BEHIND OUR ACTIONS IS NOT DESIRE FOR FEMININE ADULATION.

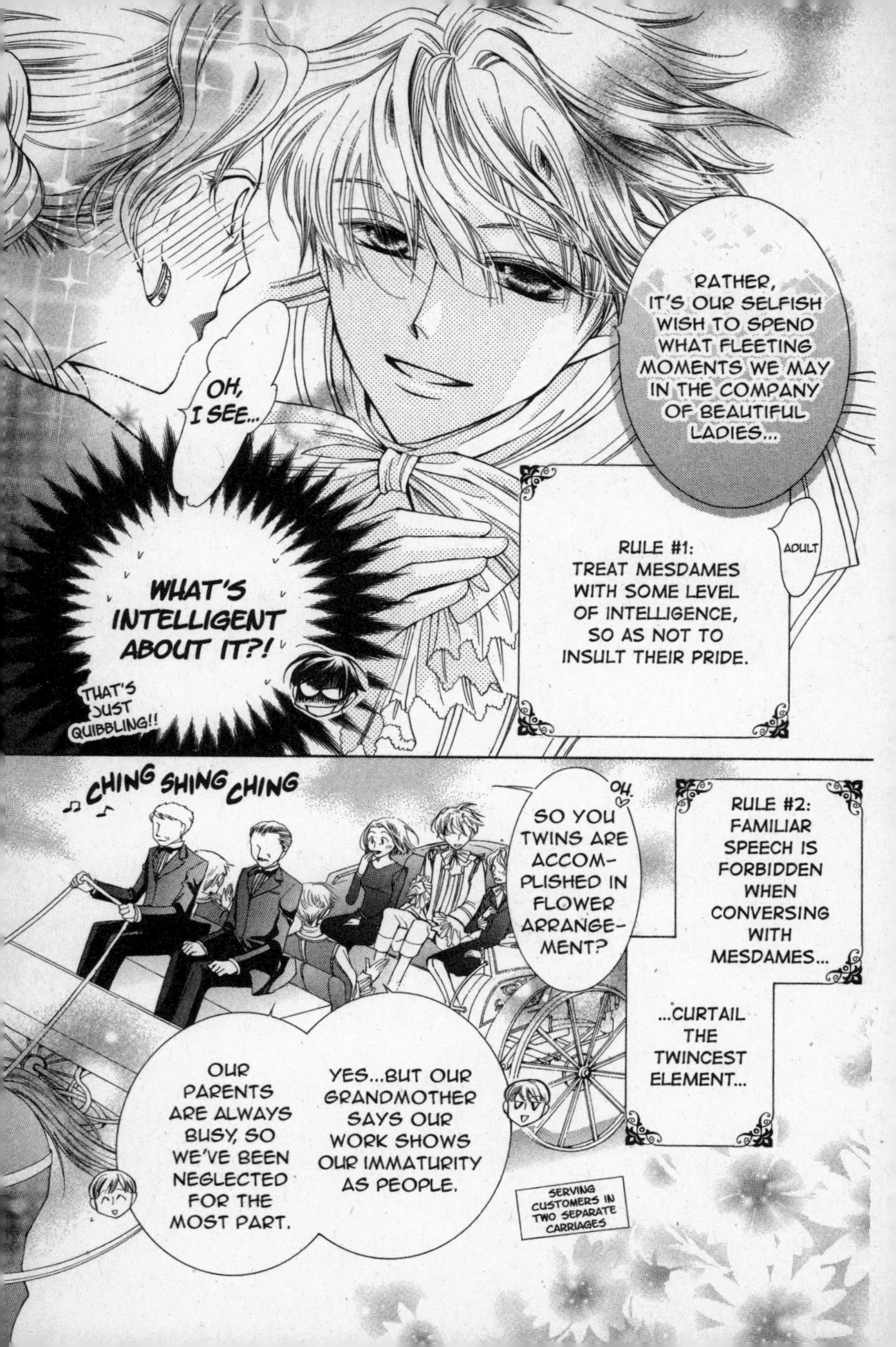
RATHER, IT'S OUR SELFISH WISH TO SPEND WHAT FLEETING MOMENTS WE MAY IN THE COMPANY OF BEAUTIFUL LADIES...
ADULT
RULE #1: TREAT MESDAMES WITH SOME LEVEL OF INTELLIGENCE, SO AS NOT TO INSULT THEIR PRIDE.
OH, I SEE...
WHAT'S INTELLIGENT ABOUT IT?!
THAT'S JUST QUIBBLING!!
RULE #2: FAMILIAR SPEECH IS FORBIDDEN WHEN CONVERSING WITH MESDAMES...
...CURTAIL THE TWINCEST ELEMENT...
OH.
SO YOU TWINS ARE ACCOM-PLISHED IN FLOWER ARRANGE-MENT?
CHING SHING CHING
YES...BUT OUR GRANDMOTHER SAYS OUR WORK SHOWS OUR IMMATURITY AS PEOPLE.
OUR PARENTS ARE ALWAYS BUSY, SO WE'VE BEEN NEGLECTED FOR THE MOST PART.
SERVING CUSTOMERS IN TWO SEPARATE CARRIAGES

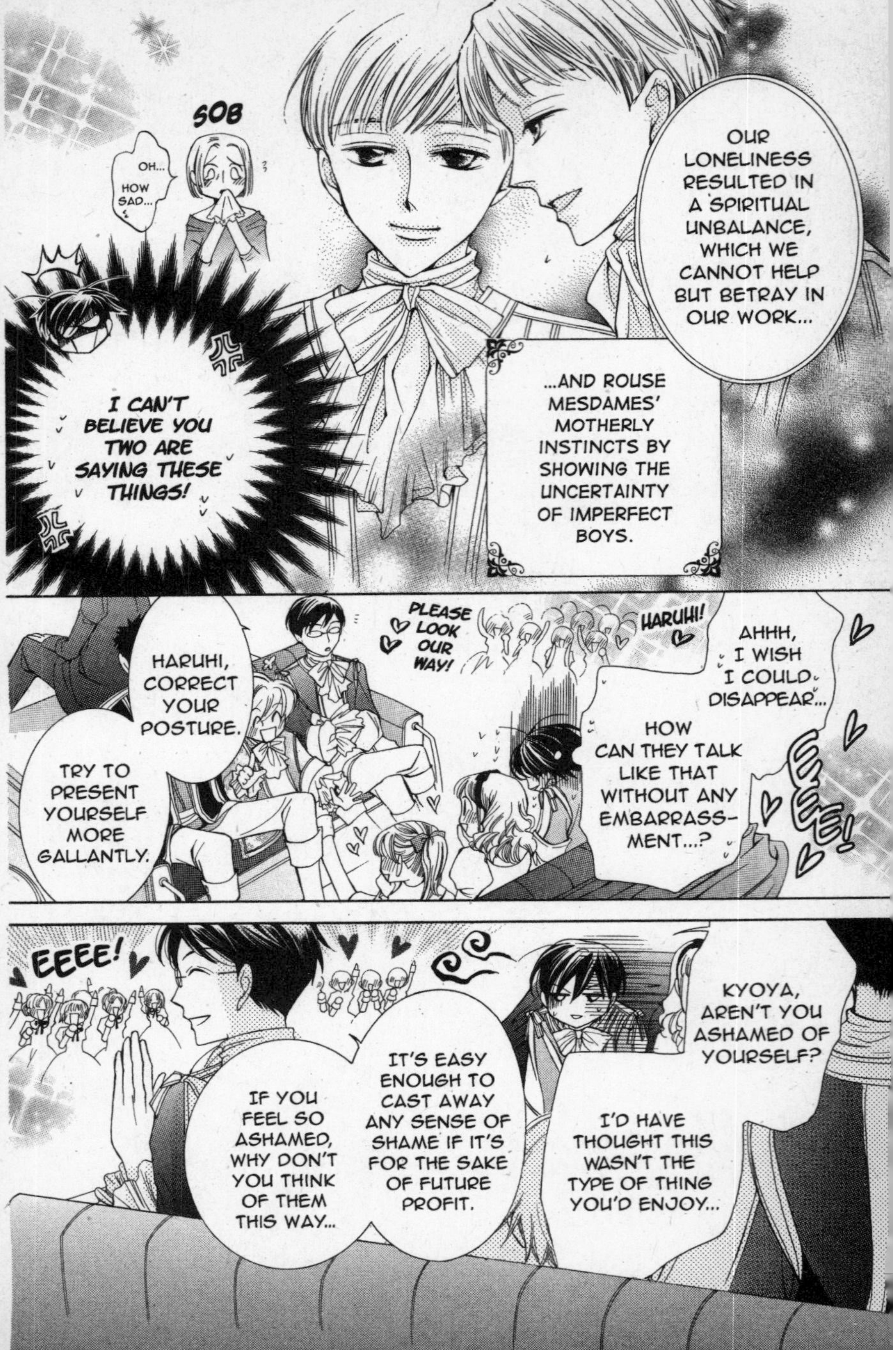
OUR LONELINESS RESULTED IN A SPIRITUAL UNBALANCE, WHICH WE CANNOT HELP BUT BETRAY IN OUR WORK...
...AND ROUSE MESDAMES' MOTHERLY INSTINCTS BY SHOWING THE UNCERTAINTY OF IMPERFECT BOYS.
SOB
OH... HOW SAD...
I CAN'T BELIEVE YOU TWO ARE SAYING THESE THINGS!
AHHH, I WISH I COULD DISAPPEAR...
HOW CAN THEY TALK LIKE THAT WITHOUT ANY EMBARRASS-MENT...?
EEEE!
HARUHI!
PLEASE LOOK OUR WAY!
HARUHI, CORRECT YOUR POSTURE.
TRY TO PRESENT YOURSELF MORE GALLANTLY.
KYOYA, AREN'T YOU ASHAMED OF YOURSELF?
I'D HAVE THOUGHT THIS WASN'T THE TYPE OF THING YOU'D ENJOY...
IT'S EASY ENOUGH TO CAST AWAY ANY SENSE OF SHAME IF IT'S FOR THE SAKE OF FUTURE PROFIT.
IF YOU FEEL SO ASHAMED, WHY DON'T YOU THINK OF THEM THIS WAY...
EEEE!

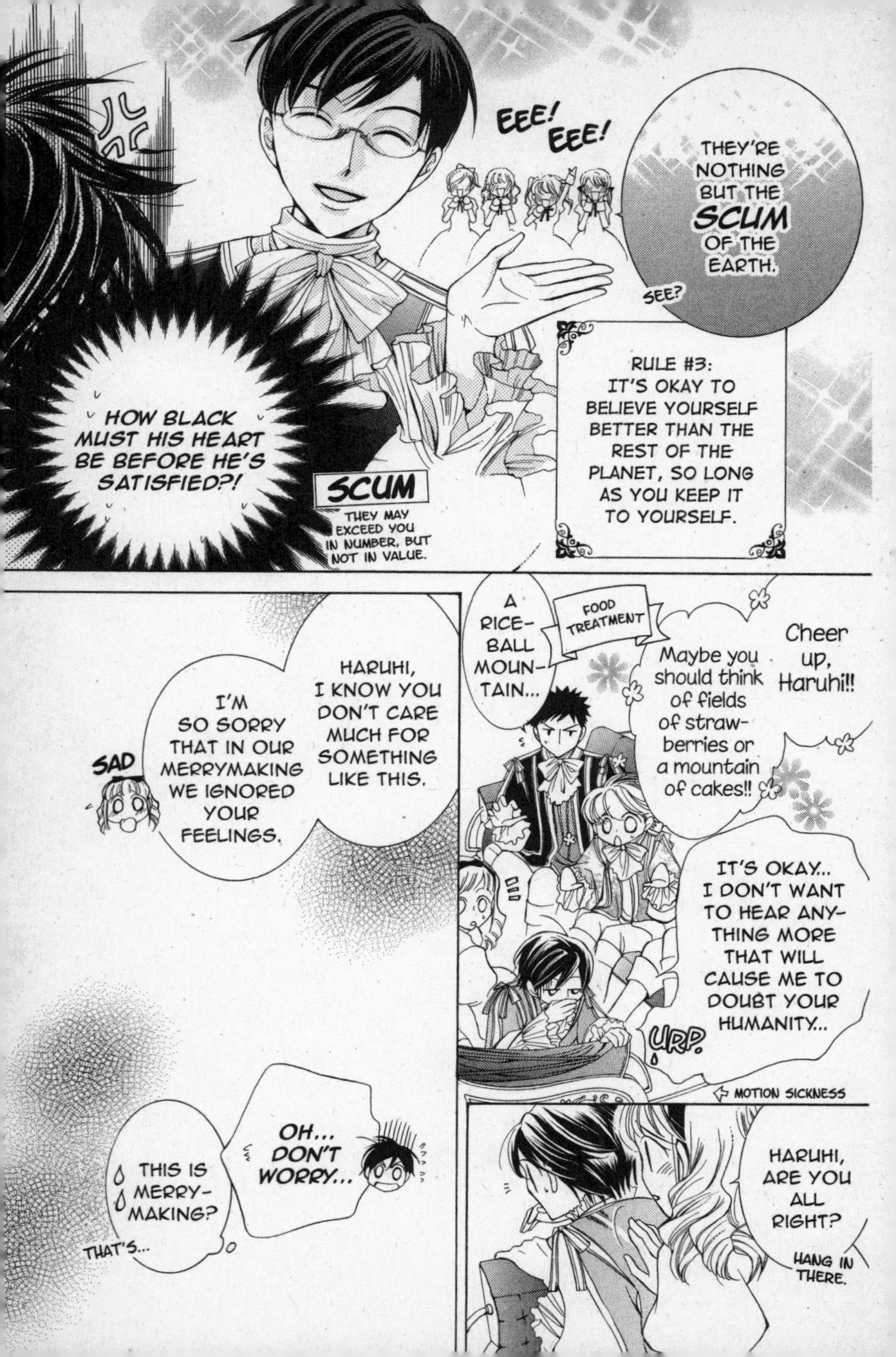
THEY'RE NOTHING BUT THE SCUM OF THE EARTH.
SEE?
EEE! EEE!
RULE #3: IT'S OKAY TO BELIEVE YOURSELF BETTER THAN THE REST OF THE PLANET, SO LONG AS YOU KEEP IT TO YOURSELF.
HOW BLACK MUST HIS HEART BE BEFORE HE'S SATISFIED?!
SCUM
THEY MAY EXCEED YOU IN NUMBER, BUT NOT IN VALUE.
Cheer up, Haruhi!!
Maybe you should think of fields of straw-berries or a mountain of cakes!!
FOOD TREATMENT
A RICE-BALL MOUN-TAIN...
IT'S OKAY... I DON'T WANT TO HEAR ANY-THING MORE THAT WILL CAUSE ME TO DOUBT YOUR HUMANITY...
URP.
MOTION SICKNESS
HARUHI, ARE YOU ALL RIGHT?
HANG IN THERE.
HARUHI, I KNOW YOU DON'T CARE MUCH FOR SOMETHING LIKE THIS.
I'M SO SORRY THAT IN OUR MERRYMAKING WE IGNORED YOUR FEELINGS.
SAD
OH... DON'T WORRY...
THIS IS MERRY-MAKING?
THAT'S...

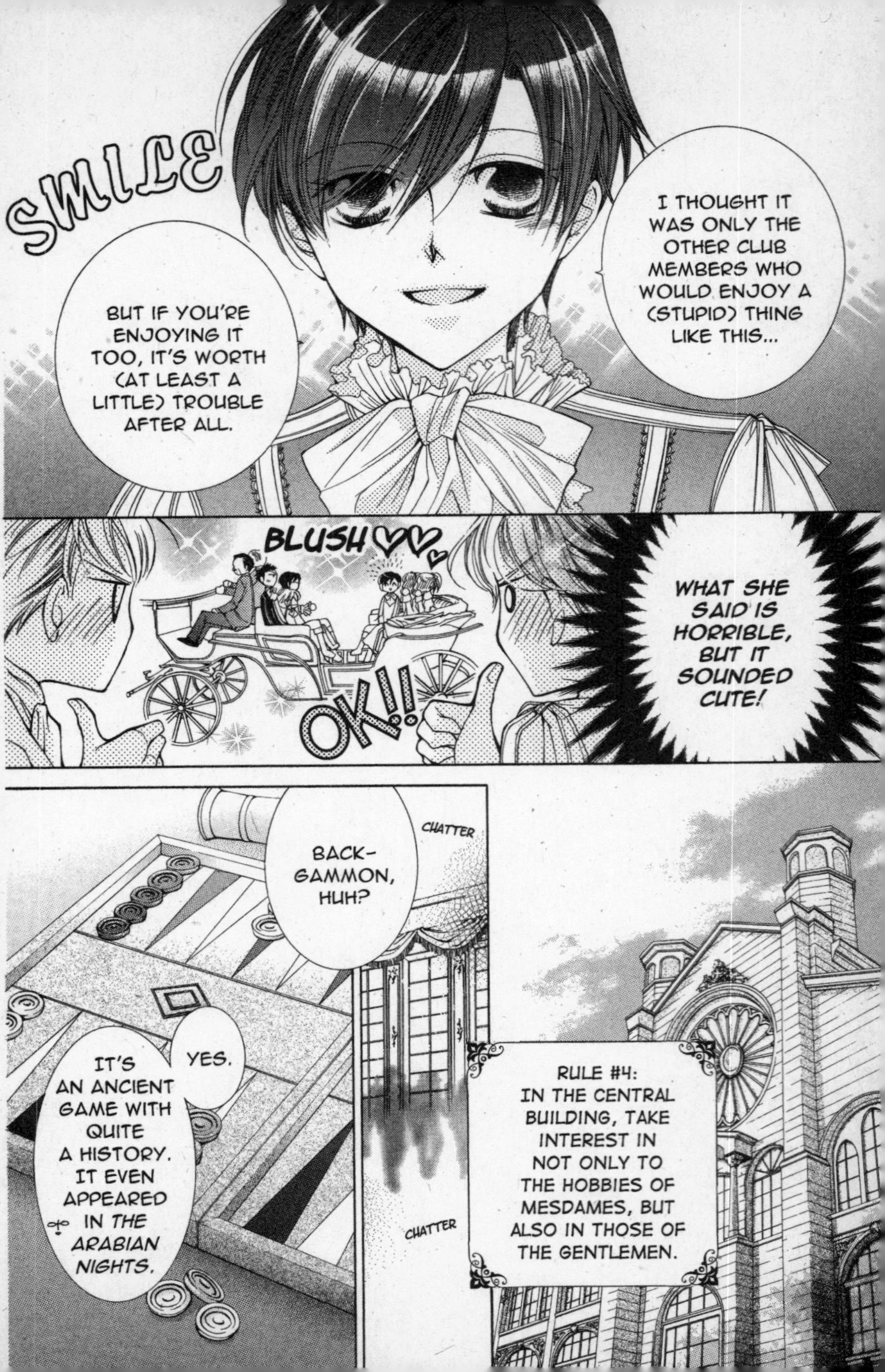
I THOUGHT IT WAS ONLY THE OTHER CLUB MEMBERS WHO WOULD ENJOY A (STUPID) THING LIKE THIS...
SMILE
BUT IF YOU'RE ENJOYING IT TOO, IT'S WORTH (AT LEAST A LITTLE) TROUBLE AFTER ALL.
WHAT SHE SAID IS HORRIBLE, BUT IT SOUNDED CUTE!
BLUSH
OK!!
RULE #4: IN THE CENTRAL BUILDING, TAKE INTEREST IN NOT ONLY TO THE HOBBIES OF MESDAMES, BUT ALSO IN THOSE OF THE GENTLEMEN.
CHATTER
BACK-GAMMON, HUH?
CHATTER
YES.
IT'S AN ANCIENT GAME WITH QUITE A HISTORY. IT EVEN APPEARED IN *THE ARABIAN NIGHTS*.

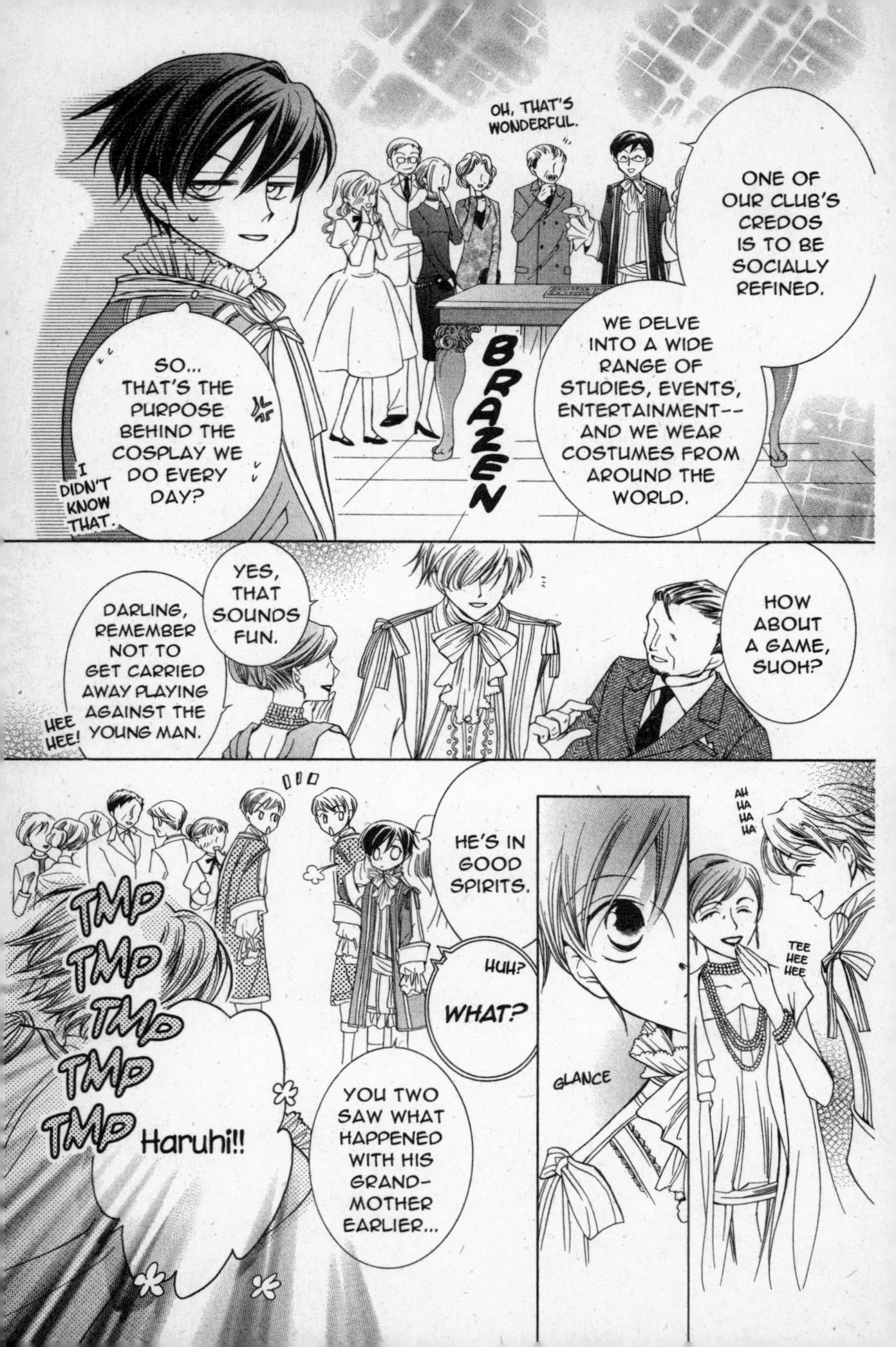
ONE OF OUR CLUB'S CREDOS IS TO BE SOCIALLY REFINED.
WE DELVE INTO A WIDE RANGE OF STUDIES, EVENTS, ENTERTAINMENT-- AND WE WEAR COSTUMES FROM AROUND THE WORLD.
BRAZEN
OH, THAT'S WONDERFUL.
SO... THAT'S THE PURPOSE BEHIND THE COSPLAY WE DO EVERY DAY?
I DIDN'T KNOW THAT.
HOW ABOUT A GAME, SUOH?
YES, THAT SOUNDS FUN.
DARLING, REMEMBER NOT TO GET CARRIED AWAY PLAYING AGAINST THE YOUNG MAN.
HEE HEE!
AH HA HA HA
TEE HEE HEE
GLANCE
HE'S IN GOOD SPIRITS.
HUH?
WHAT?
YOU TWO SAW WHAT HAPPENED WITH HIS GRAND-MOTHER EARLIER...
TMP TMP TMP TMP TMP
Haruhi!!

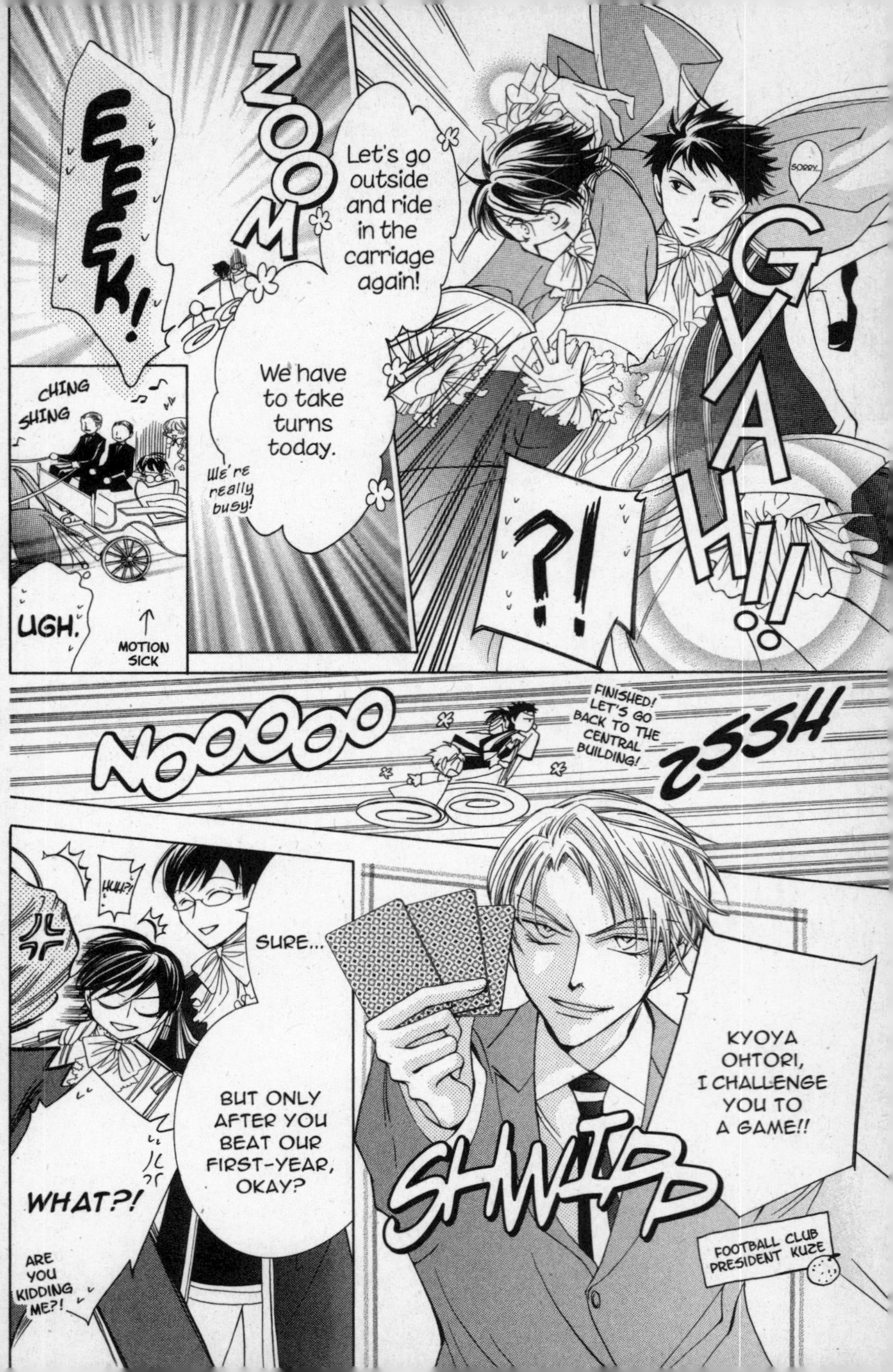
SORRY...
GYAH!!
?!
ZOOM
Let's go outside and ride in the carriage again!
We have to take turns today.
We're really busy!
EEEEK!
CHING SHING
UGH.
MOTION SICK
FINISHED! LET'S GO BACK TO THE CENTRAL BUILDING!
ZSSH
NOOOOO
KYOYA OHTORI, I CHALLENGE YOU TO A GAME!!
SHWIP
FOOTBALL CLUB PRESIDENT KUZE
HUH?!
SURE...
BUT ONLY AFTER YOU BEAT OUR FIRST-YEAR, OKAY?
WHAT?!
ARE YOU KIDDING ME?!

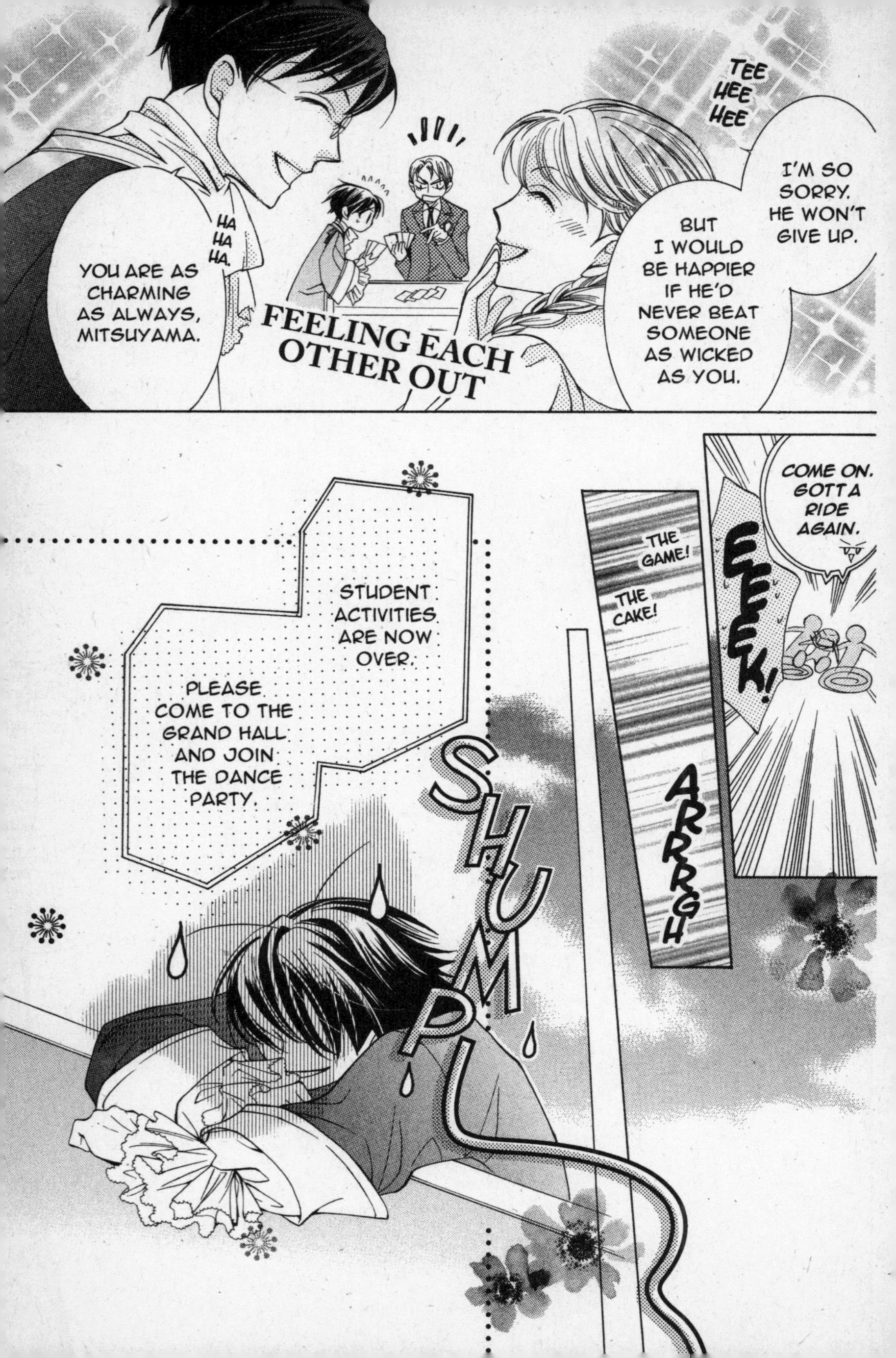
TEE HEE HEE
I'M SO SORRY. HE WON'T GIVE UP.
BUT I WOULD BE HAPPIER IF HE'D NEVER BEAT SOMEONE AS WICKED AS YOU.
FEELING EACH OTHER OUT
HA HA HA.
YOU ARE AS CHARMING AS ALWAYS, MITSUYAMA.
COME ON. GOTTA RIDE AGAIN.
EEEEK!
THE GAME!
THE CAKE!
ARRRGH
STUDENT ACTIVITIES ARE NOW OVER.
PLEASE COME TO THE GRAND HALL AND JOIN THE DANCE PARTY.
SHUMP

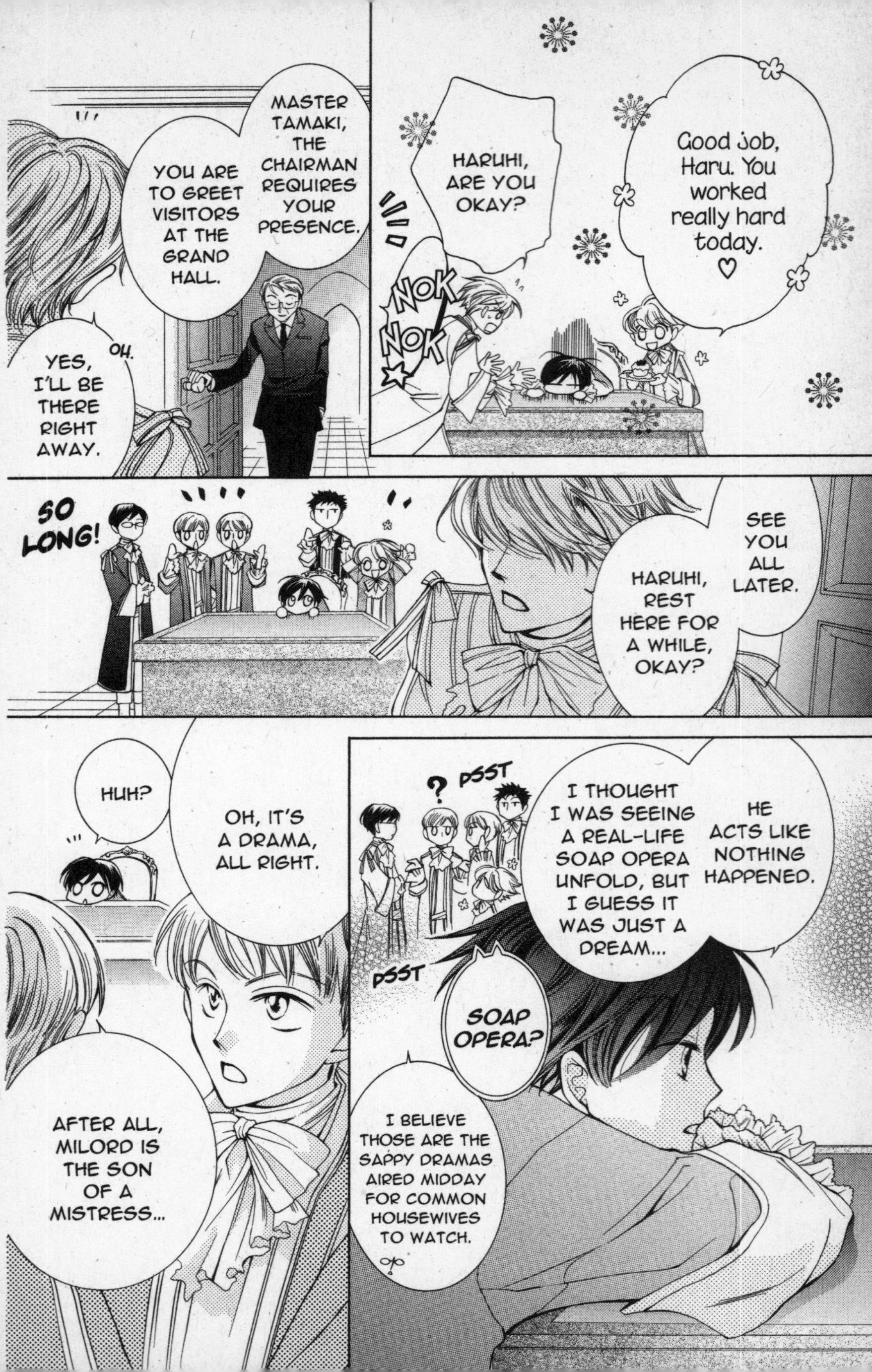
Good job, Haru. You worked really hard today. ♡
HARUHI, ARE YOU OKAY?
NOK NOK
MASTER TAMAKI, THE CHAIRMAN REQUIRES YOUR PRESENCE.
YOU ARE TO GREET VISITORS AT THE GRAND HALL.
OH.
YES, I'LL BE THERE RIGHT AWAY.
SEE YOU ALL LATER.
HARUHI, REST HERE FOR A WHILE, OKAY?
SO LONG!
HE ACTS LIKE NOTHING HAPPENED.
I THOUGHT I WAS SEEING A REAL-LIFE SOAP OPERA UNFOLD, BUT I GUESS IT WAS JUST A DREAM...
?
PSST
PSST
SOAP OPERA?
I BELIEVE THOSE ARE THE SAPPY DRAMAS AIRED MIDDAY FOR COMMON HOUSEWIVES TO WATCH.
HUH?
OH, IT'S A DRAMA, ALL RIGHT.
AFTER ALL, MILORD IS THE SON OF A MISTRESS...

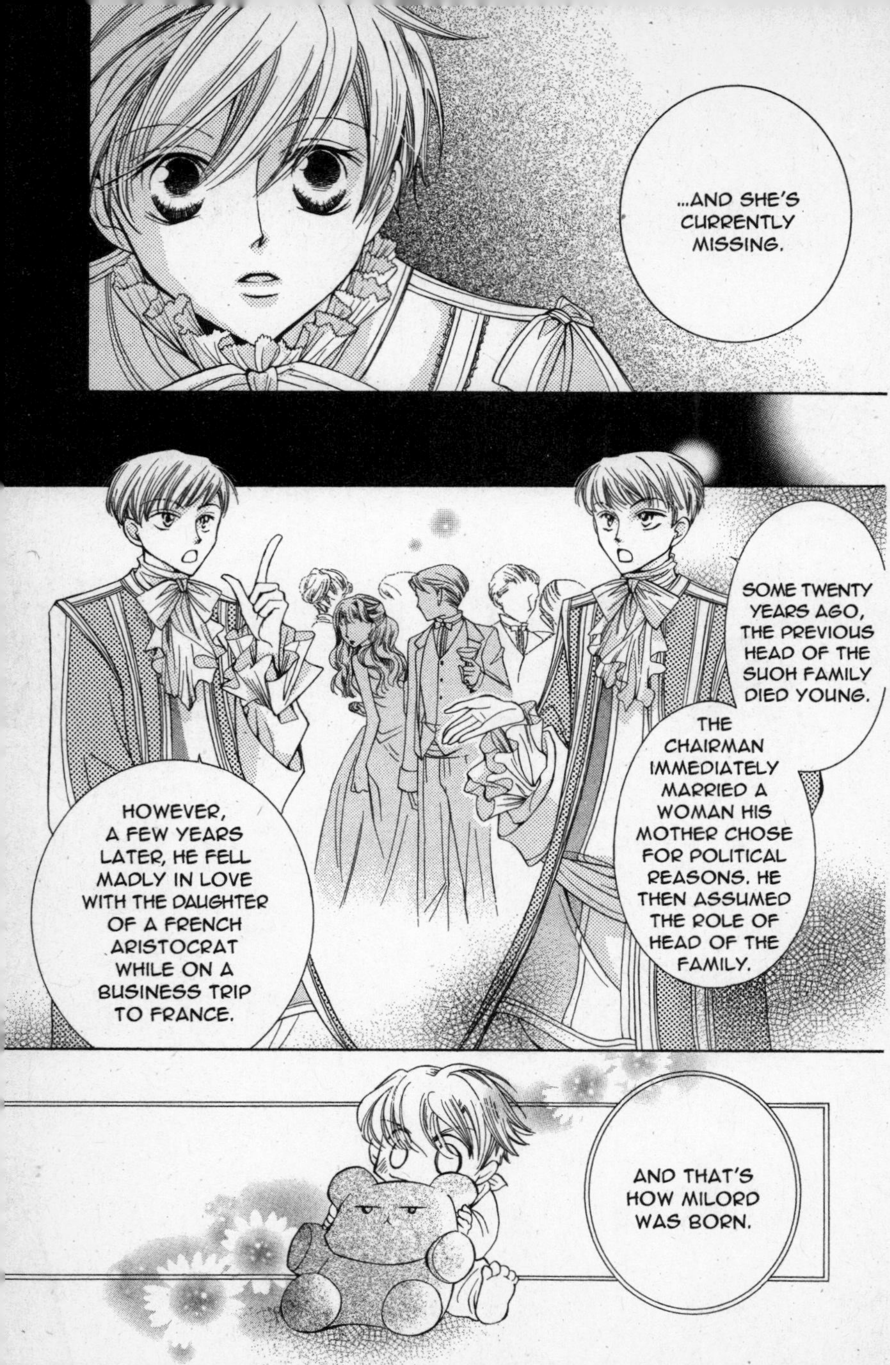
...AND SHE'S CURRENTLY MISSING.
SOME TWENTY YEARS AGO, THE PREVIOUS HEAD OF THE SUOH FAMILY DIED YOUNG.
THE CHAIRMAN IMMEDIATELY MARRIED A WOMAN HIS MOTHER CHOSE FOR POLITICAL REASONS. HE THEN ASSUMED THE ROLE OF HEAD OF THE FAMILY.
HOWEVER, A FEW YEARS LATER, HE FELL MADLY IN LOVE WITH THE DAUGHTER OF A FRENCH ARISTOCRAT WHILE ON A BUSINESS TRIP TO FRANCE.
AND THAT'S HOW MILORD WAS BORN.

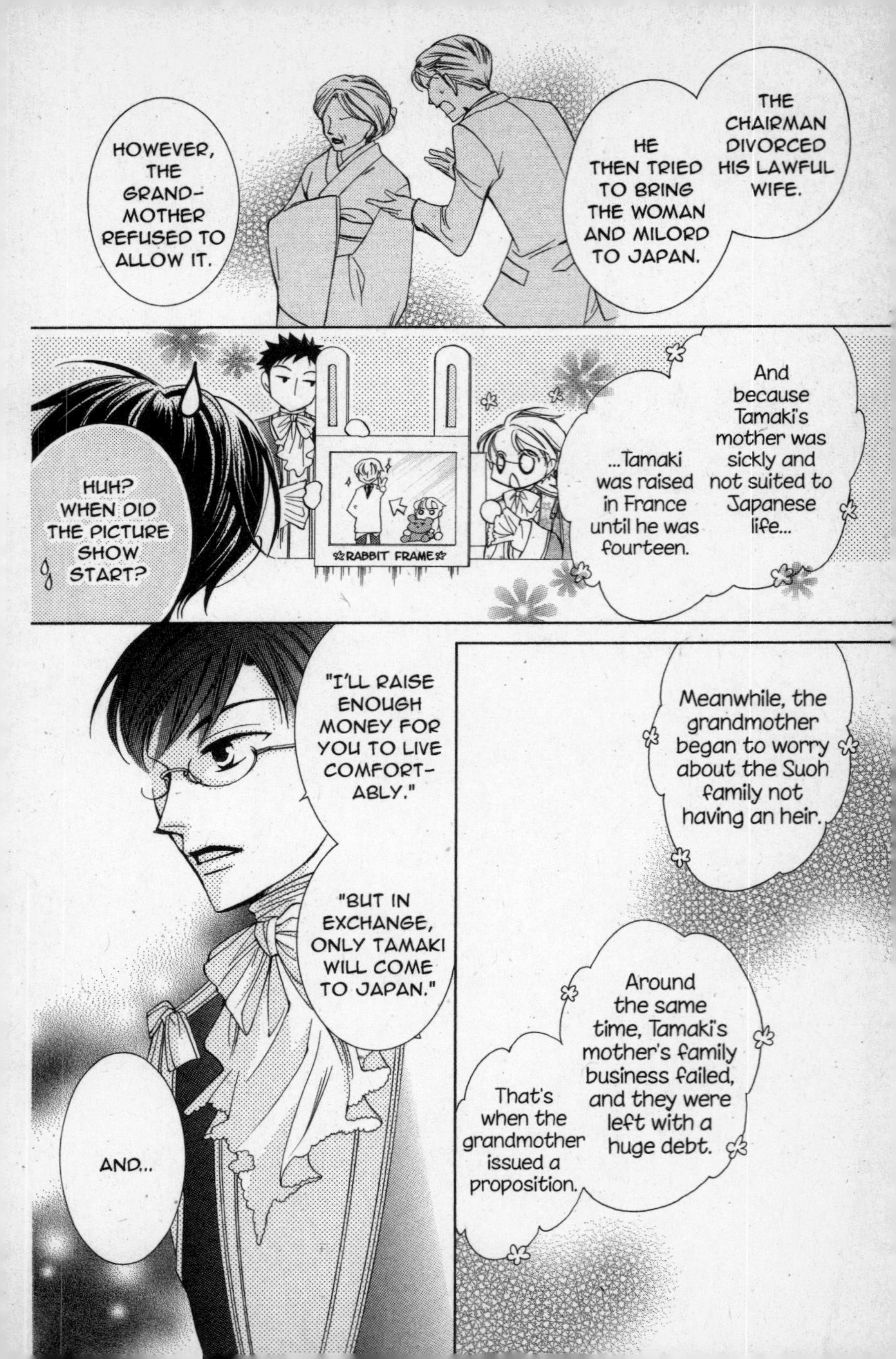
THE CHAIRMAN DIVORCED HIS LAWFUL WIFE.
HE THEN TRIED TO BRING THE WOMAN AND MILORD TO JAPAN.
HOWEVER, THE GRAND-MOTHER REFUSED TO ALLOW IT.
And because Tamaki's mother was sickly and not suited to Japanese life...
...Tamaki was raised in France until he was fourteen.
☆RABBIT FRAME☆
HUH? WHEN DID THE PICTURE SHOW START?
Meanwhile, the grandmother began to worry about the Suoh family not having an heir.
Around the same time, Tamaki's mother's family business failed, and they were left with a huge debt.
That's when the grandmother issued a proposition.
"I'LL RAISE ENOUGH MONEY FOR YOU TO LIVE COMFORT-ABLY."
"BUT IN EXCHANGE, ONLY TAMAKI WILL COME TO JAPAN."
AND...

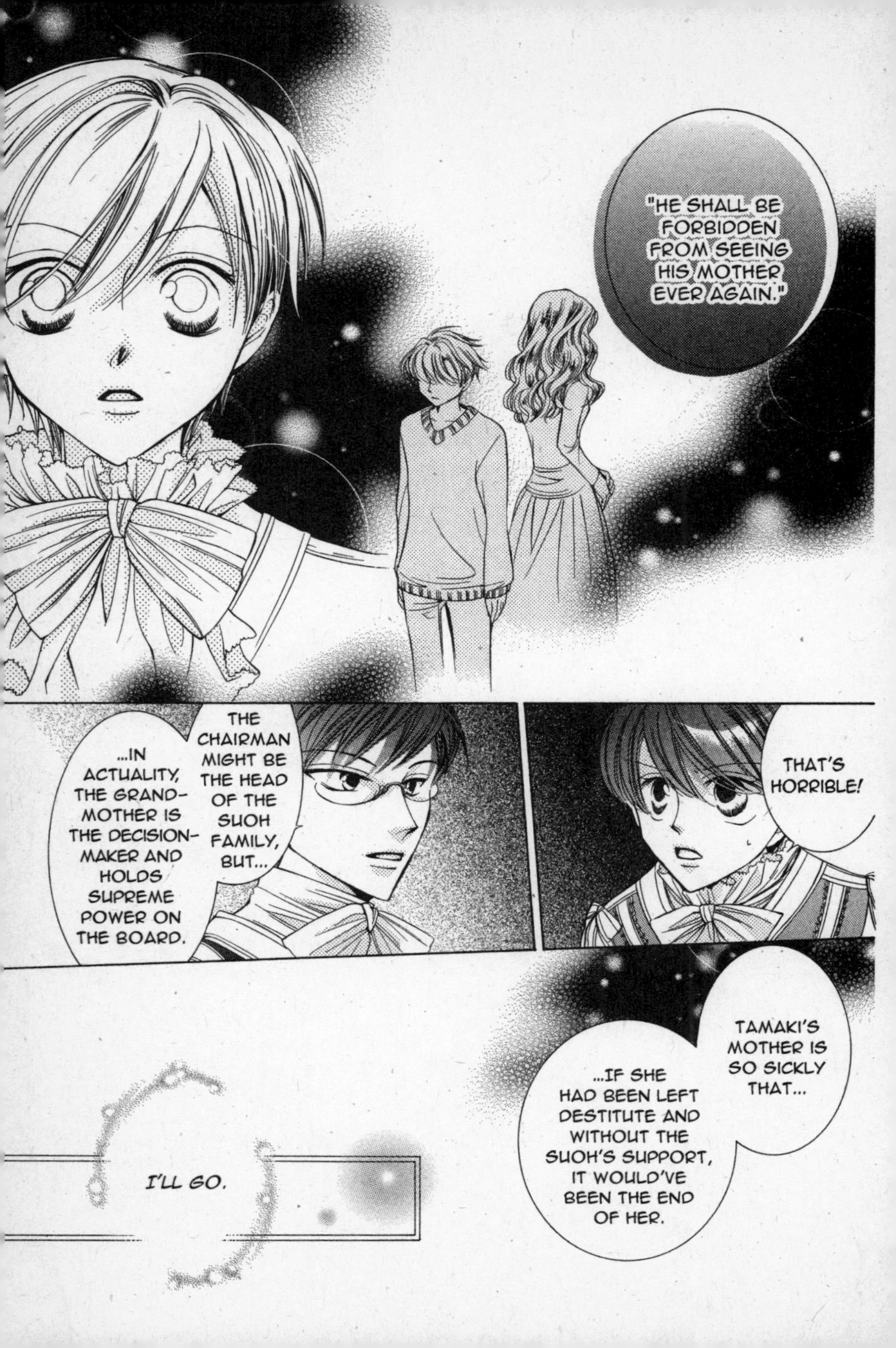
"HE SHALL BE FORBIDDEN FROM SEEING HIS MOTHER EVER AGAIN."
THAT'S HORRIBLE!
THE CHAIRMAN MIGHT BE THE HEAD OF THE SUOH FAMILY, BUT...
...IN ACTUALITY, THE GRAND-MOTHER IS THE DECISION-MAKER AND HOLDS SUPREME POWER ON THE BOARD.
TAMAKI'S MOTHER IS SO SICKLY THAT...
...IF SHE HAD BEEN LEFT DESTITUTE AND WITHOUT THE SUOH'S SUPPORT, IT WOULD'VE BEEN THE END OF HER.
I'LL GO.

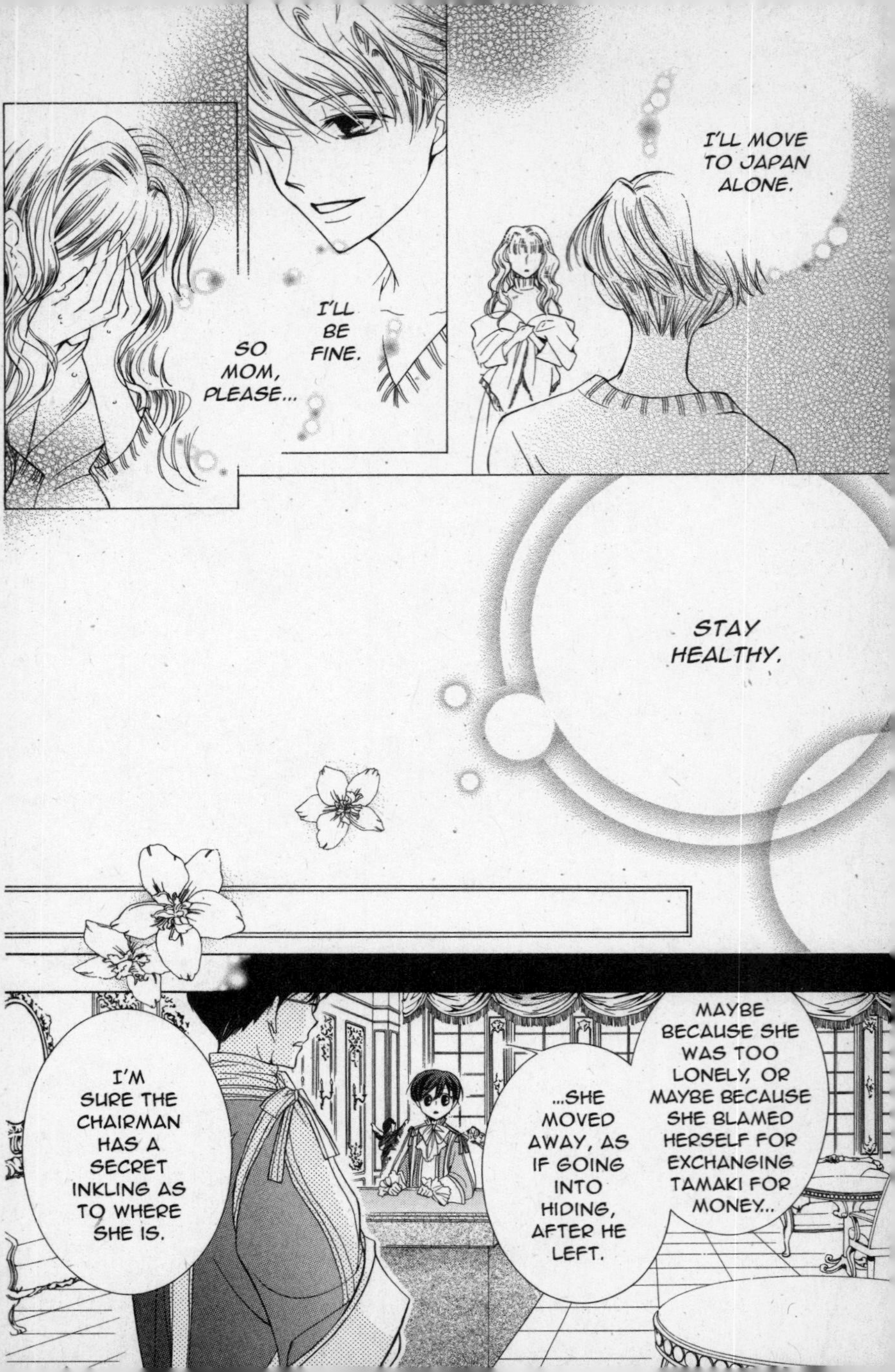
I'LL MOVE TO JAPAN ALONE.
I'LL BE FINE.
SO MOM, PLEASE...
STAY HEALTHY.
MAYBE BECAUSE SHE WAS TOO LONELY, OR MAYBE BECAUSE SHE BLAMED HERSELF FOR EXCHANGING TAMAKI FOR MONEY...
...SHE MOVED AWAY, AS IF GOING INTO HIDING, AFTER HE LEFT.
I'M SURE THE CHAIRMAN HAS A SECRET INKLING AS TO WHERE SHE IS.

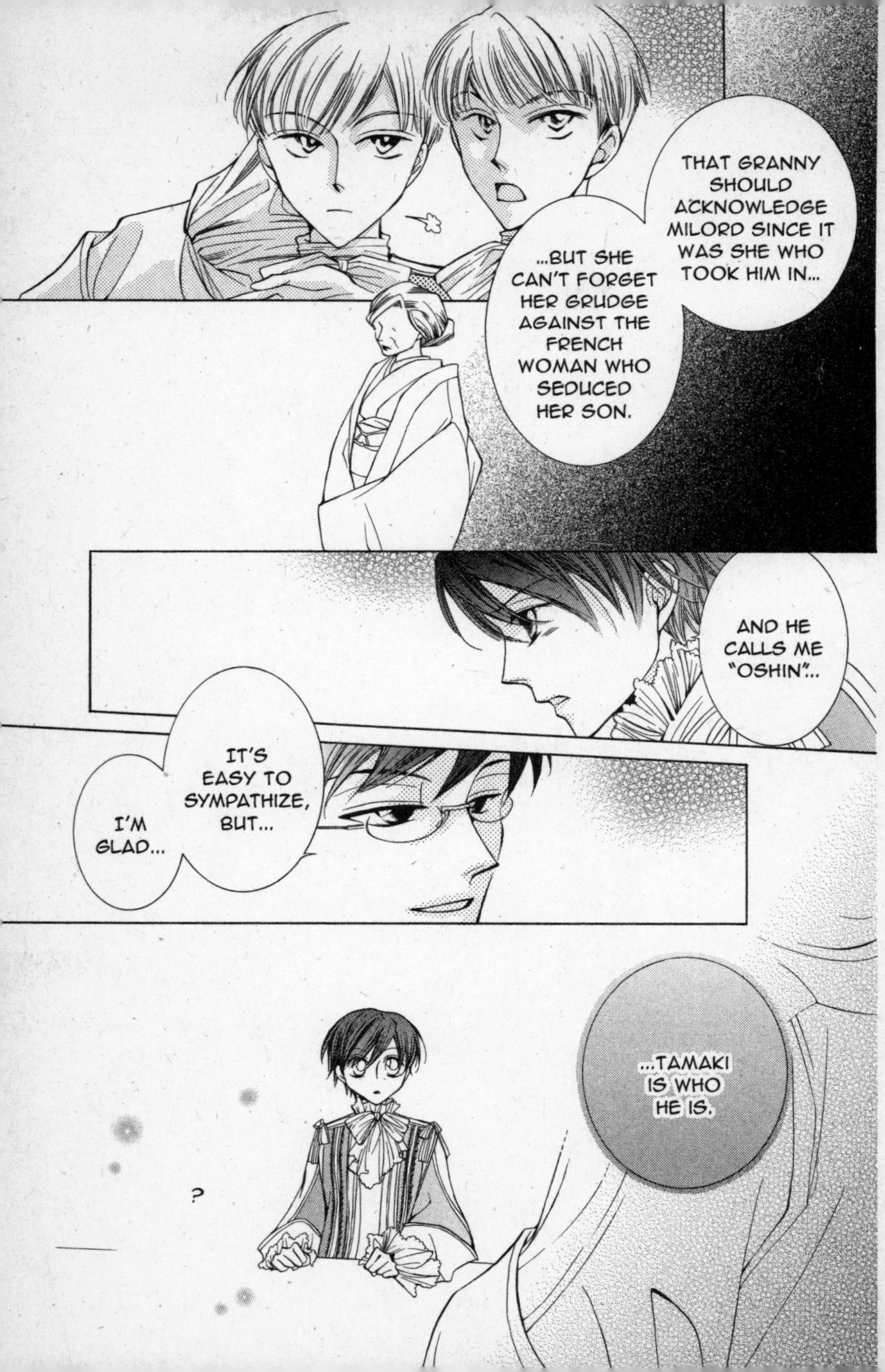
THAT GRANNY SHOULD ACKNOWLEDGE MILORD SINCE IT WAS SHE WHO TOOK HIM IN...
...BUT SHE CAN'T FORGET HER GRUDGE AGAINST THE FRENCH WOMAN WHO SEDUCED HER SON.
AND HE CALLS ME "OSHIN"...
IT'S EASY TO SYMPATHIZE, BUT...
I'M GLAD...
...TAMAKI IS WHO HE IS.
?

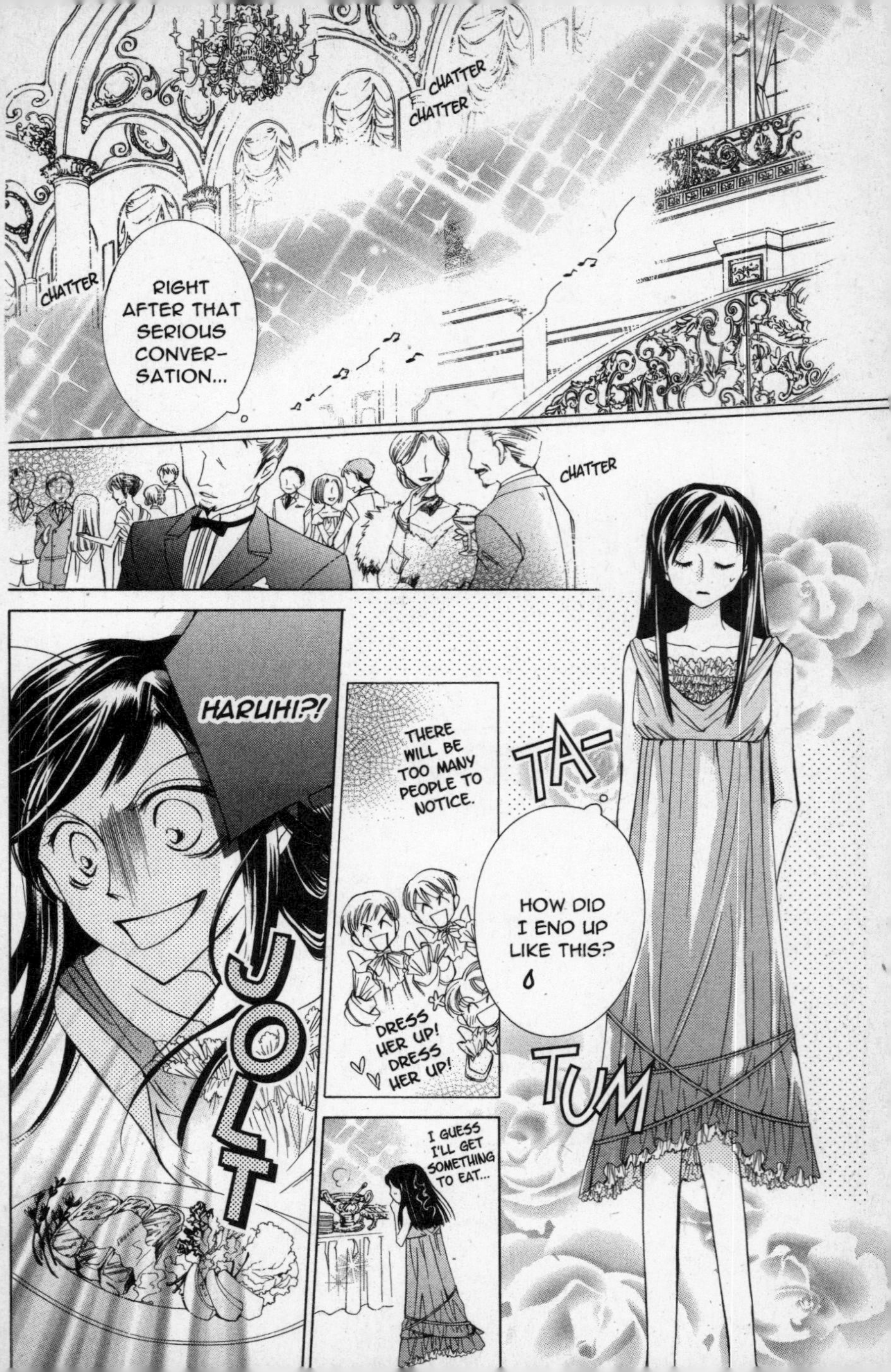
CHATTER
CHATTER
RIGHT AFTER THAT SERIOUS CONVER-SATION...
CHATTER
CHATTER
TA-
TUM
HOW DID I END UP LIKE THIS?
THERE WILL BE TOO MANY PEOPLE TO NOTICE.
DRESS HER UP! DRESS HER UP!
I GUESS I'LL GET SOMETHING TO EAT...
HARUHI?!
JOLT

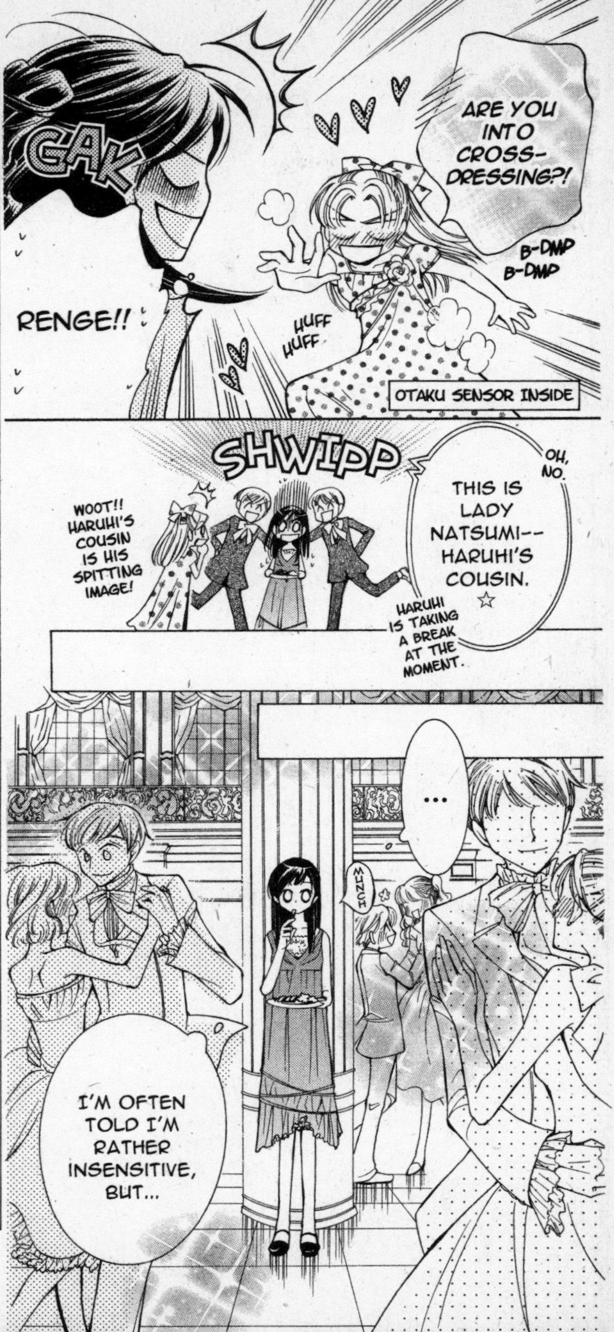
ARE YOU INTO CROSS-DRESSING?!
B-DMP B-DMP
HUFF HUFF
OTAKU SENSOR INSIDE
GAK
RENGE!!
SHWIPP
OH, NO.
THIS IS LADY NATSUMI-- HARUHI'S COUSIN. ☆
HARUHI IS TAKING A BREAK AT THE MOMENT.
WOOT!! HARUHI'S COUSIN IS HIS SPITTING IMAGE!
...
MUNCH
I'M OFTEN TOLD I'M RATHER INSENSITIVE, BUT...

Q3.

DOES KYOYA EVER WEAR CONTACT LENSES?

A. NO, BECAUSE HE'S A MEGANE CHARACTER.

ALTHOUGH IT'S IRRELEVANT, I WAS WONDERING THE OTHER DAY WHY HE'S BEEN NAMED KYOYA.
I THOUGHT I CAME UP WITH IT RANDOMLY, BUT WHEN I MULLED IT OVER, I REALIZED THE AWFUL FACT. BASICALLY, KYOYA'S NAME AROSE WHEN I WAS TRYING TO COME UP WITH A MEGANE CHARACTER. AND YES, IT MEANS "SPECTACLES":

MEGANE = GANKYO → KYOYA

CONCLUSION

I THINK **KYOYA'S "KYO" COMES FROM "GANKYO" (SPECTACLES).**

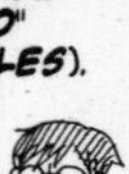
YOU SERIOUS?

YEAH. SORRY.

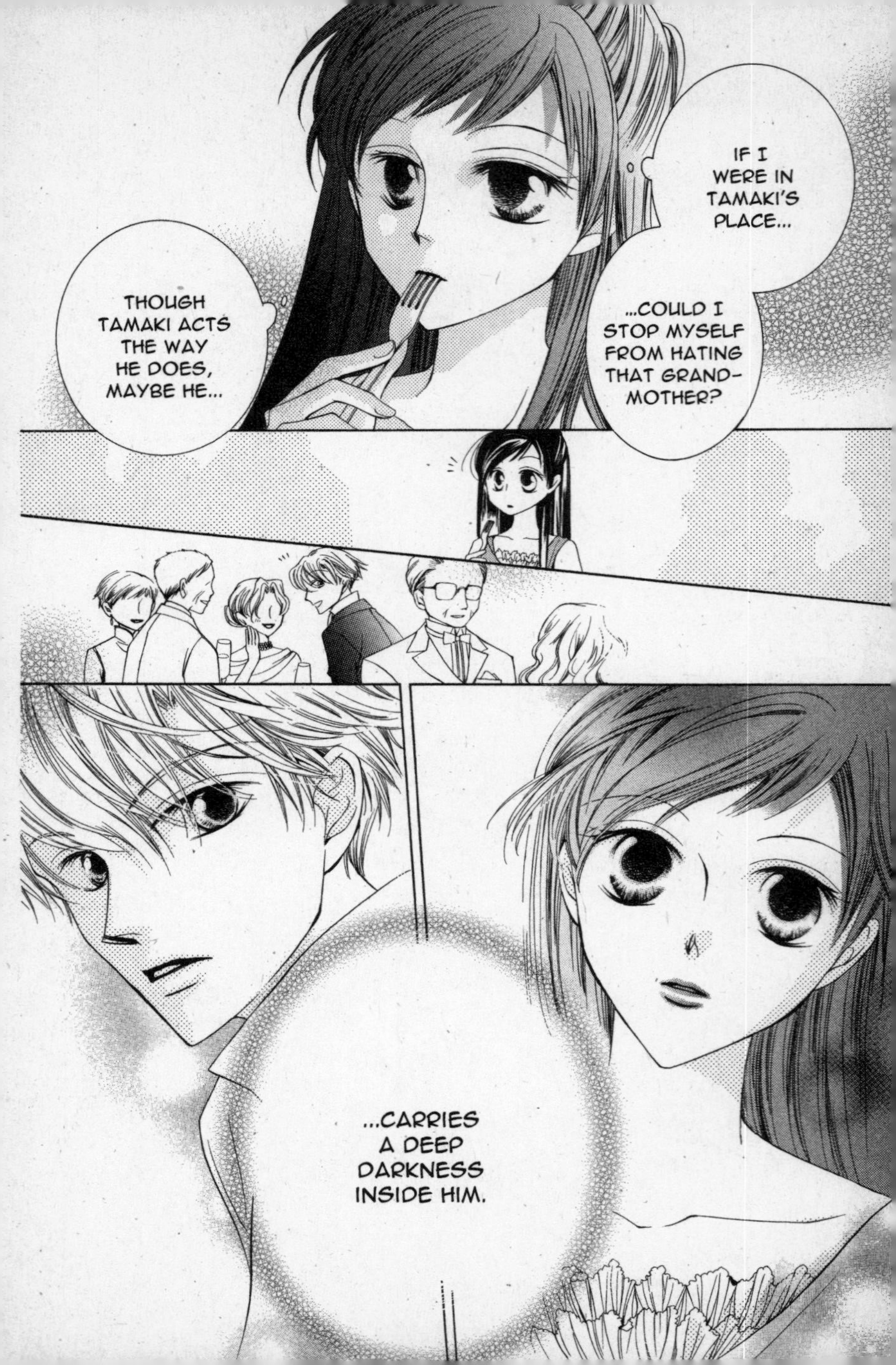
IF I WERE IN TAMAKI'S PLACE...
...COULD I STOP MYSELF FROM HATING THAT GRAND-MOTHER?
THOUGH TAMAKI ACTS THE WAY HE DOES, MAYBE HE...
...CARRIES A DEEP DARKNESS INSIDE HIM.

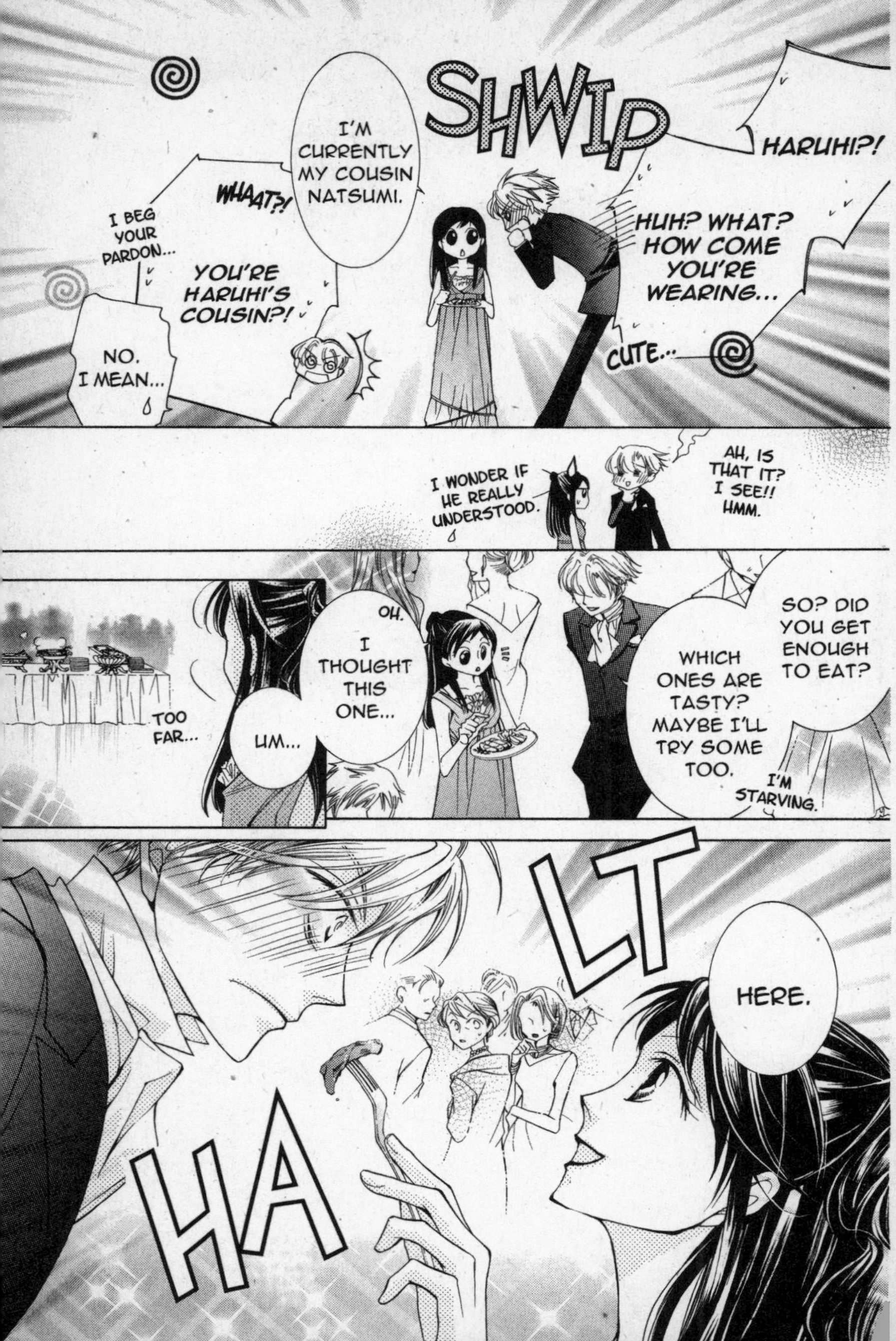
HARUHI?!
SHWIP
HUH? WHAT? HOW COME YOU'RE WEARING...
CUTE...
I'M CURRENTLY MY COUSIN NATSUMI.
WHAAT?!
YOU'RE HARUHI'S COUSIN?!
I BEG YOUR PARDON...
NO. I MEAN...
AH, IS THAT IT? I SEE!! HMM.
I WONDER IF HE REALLY UNDERSTOOD.
SO? DID YOU GET ENOUGH TO EAT?
I'M STARVING.
WHICH ONES ARE TASTY? MAYBE I'LL TRY SOME TOO.
OH.
I THOUGHT THIS ONE...
UM...
TOO FAR...
HERE.
HALT

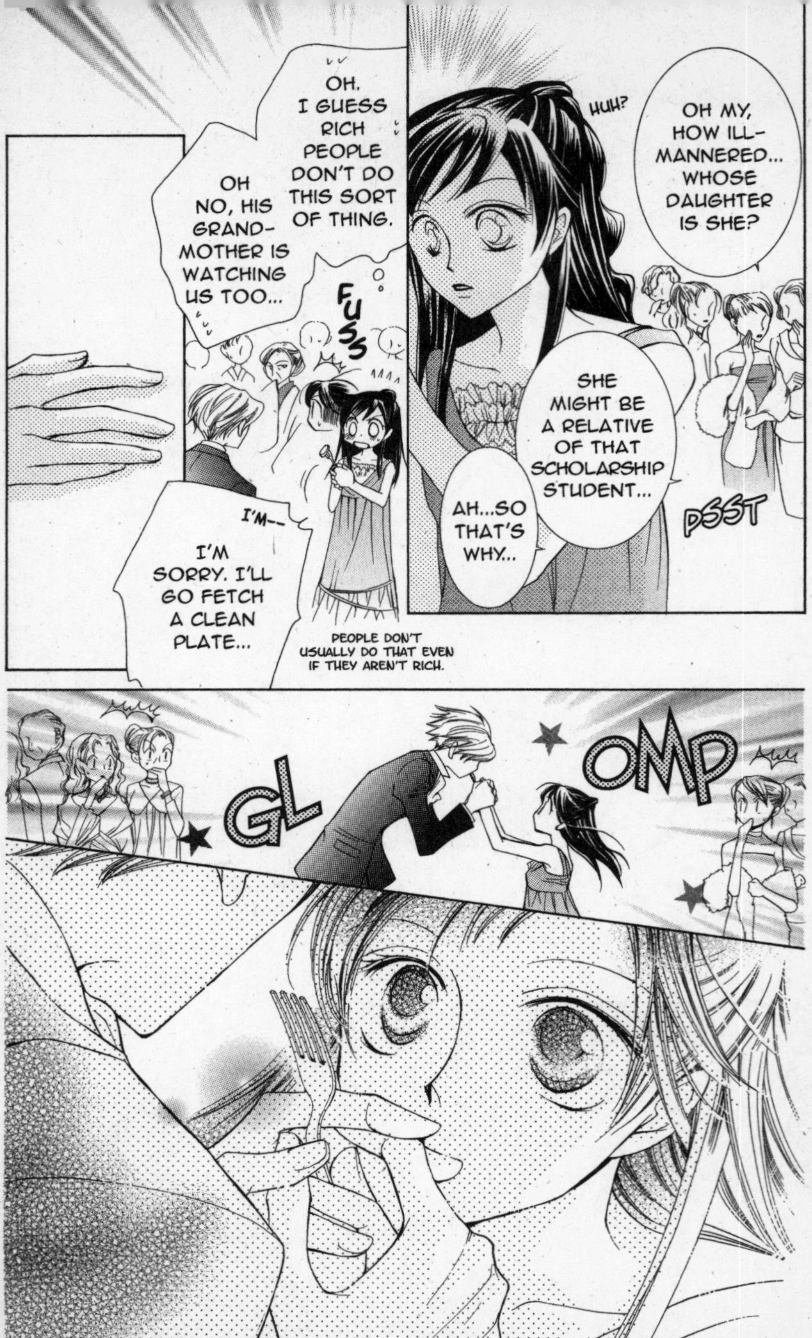
OH MY, HOW ILL-MANNERED... WHOSE DAUGHTER IS SHE?
HUH?
SHE MIGHT BE A RELATIVE OF THAT SCHOLARSHIP STUDENT...
AH...SO THAT'S WHY...
PSST
OH. I GUESS RICH PEOPLE DON'T DO THIS SORT OF THING.
OH NO, HIS GRANDMOTHER IS WATCHING US TOO...
FUSS
I'M--
I'M SORRY. I'LL GO FETCH A CLEAN PLATE...
PEOPLE DON'T USUALLY DO THAT EVEN IF THEY AREN'T RICH.
GL
OMP

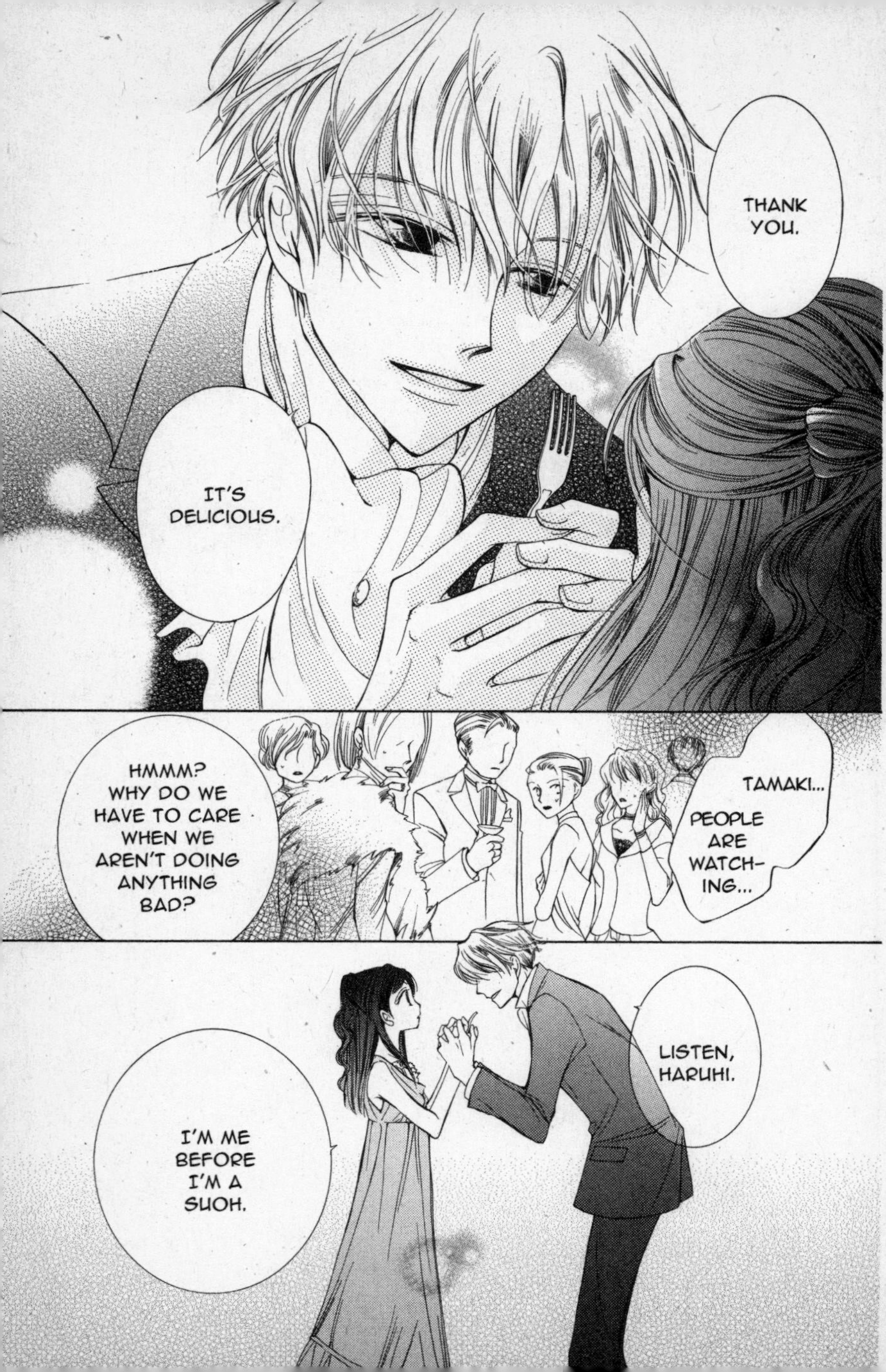
THANK YOU.
IT'S DELICIOUS.
TAMAKI... PEOPLE ARE WATCH-ING...
HMMM? WHY DO WE HAVE TO CARE WHEN WE AREN'T DOING ANYTHING BAD?
LISTEN, HARUHI.
I'M ME BEFORE I'M A SUOH.

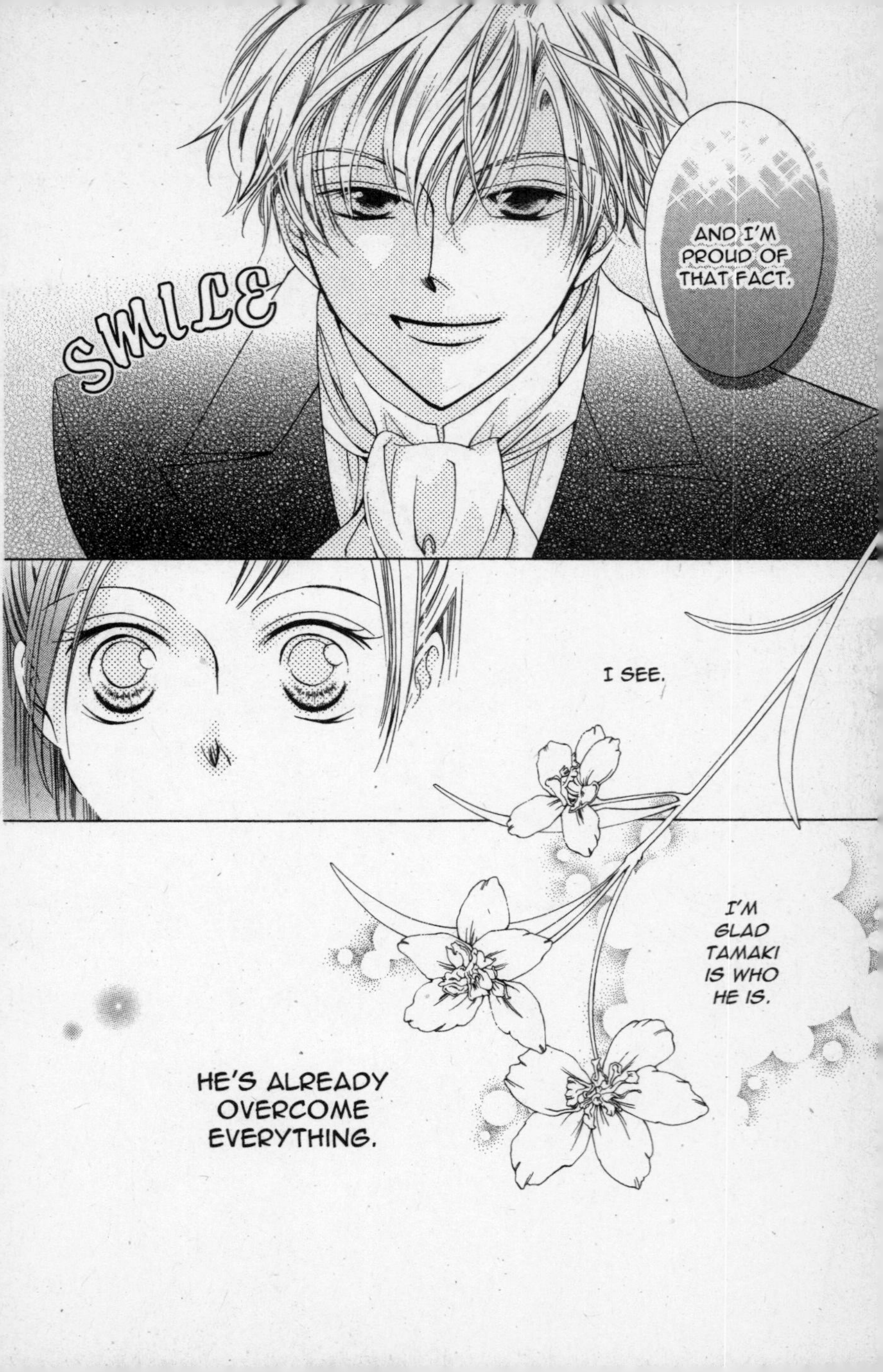
AND I'M PROUD OF THAT FACT.
SMILE
I SEE.
I'M GLAD TAMAKI IS WHO HE IS.
HE'S ALREADY OVERCOME EVERYTHING.

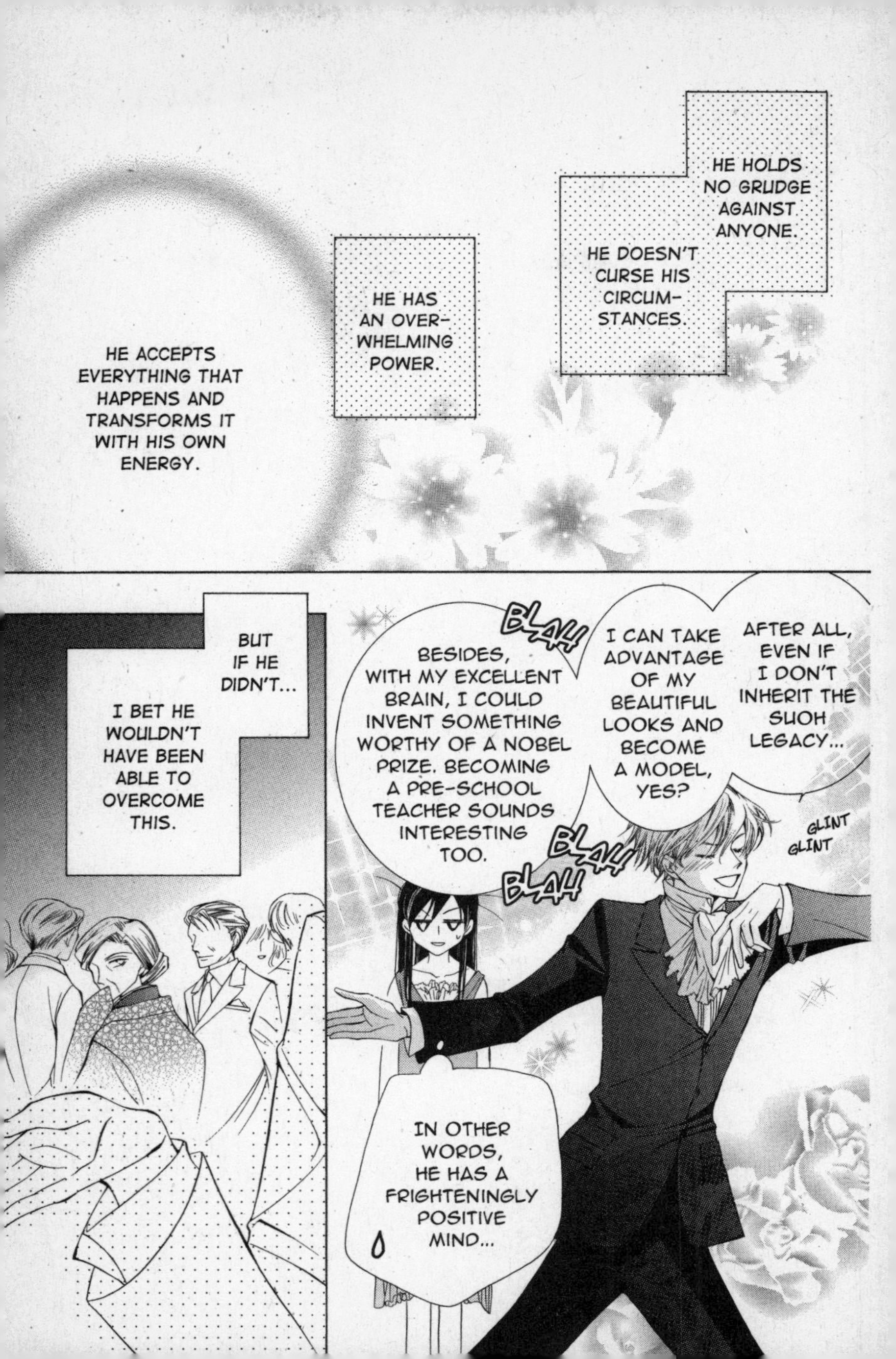
HE HOLDS NO GRUDGE AGAINST ANYONE.
HE DOESN'T CURSE HIS CIRCUM-STANCES.
HE HAS AN OVER-WHELMING POWER.
HE ACCEPTS EVERYTHING THAT HAPPENS AND TRANSFORMS IT WITH HIS OWN ENERGY.
AFTER ALL, EVEN IF I DON'T INHERIT THE SUOH LEGACY...
I CAN TAKE ADVANTAGE OF MY BEAUTIFUL LOOKS AND BECOME A MODEL, YES?
BLAH
BESIDES, WITH MY EXCELLENT BRAIN, I COULD INVENT SOMETHING WORTHY OF A NOBEL PRIZE. BECOMING A PRE-SCHOOL TEACHER SOUNDS INTERESTING TOO.
BLAH
BLAH
GLINT GLINT
IN OTHER WORDS, HE HAS A FRIGHTENINGLY POSITIVE MIND...
BUT IF HE DIDN'T...
I BET HE WOULDN'T HAVE BEEN ABLE TO OVERCOME THIS.

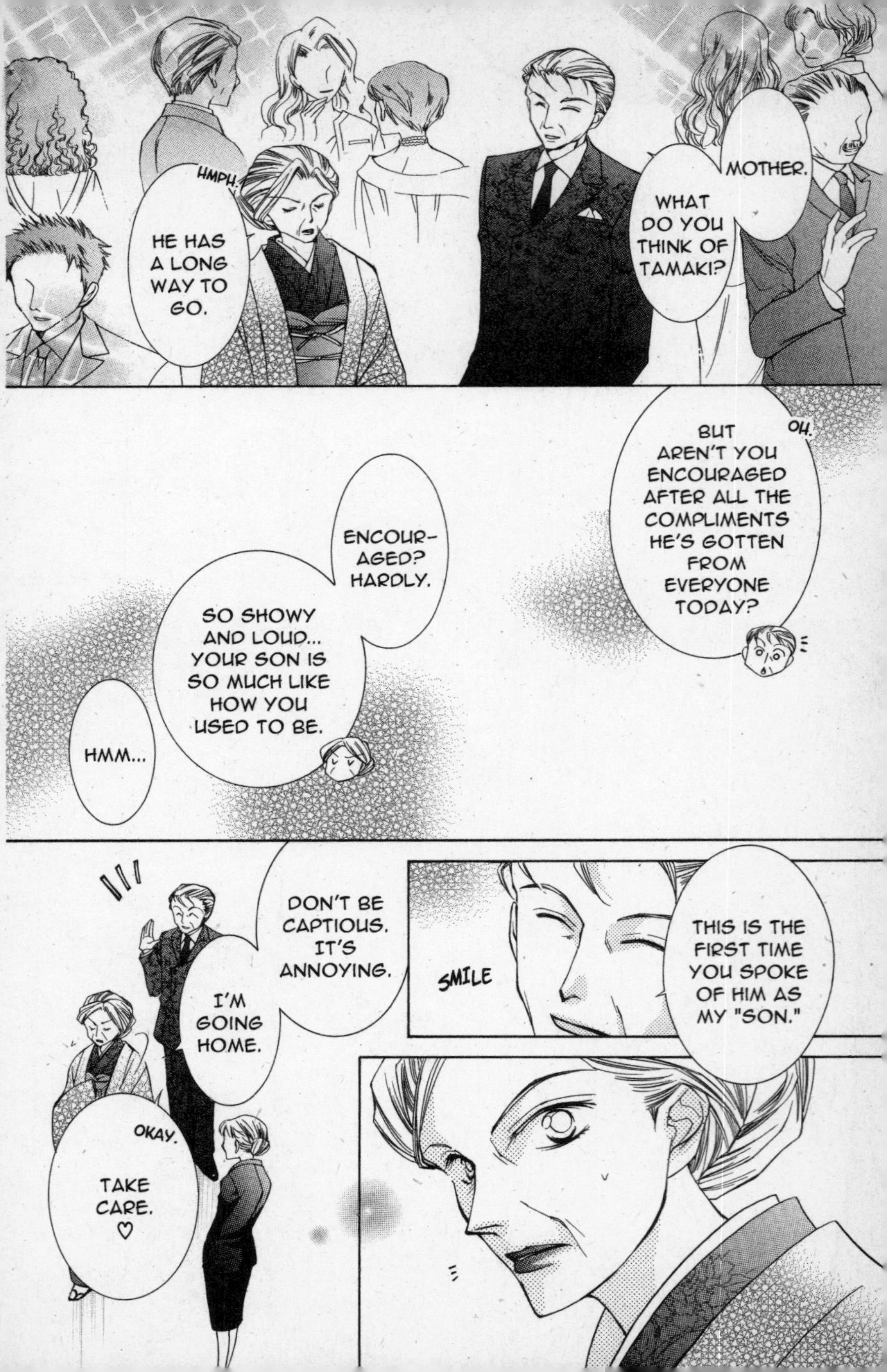
MOTHER.
WHAT DO YOU THINK OF TAMAKI?
HMPH.
HE HAS A LONG WAY TO GO.
OH.
BUT AREN'T YOU ENCOURAGED AFTER ALL THE COMPLIMENTS HE'S GOTTEN FROM EVERYONE TODAY?
ENCOUR-AGED? HARDLY.
SO SHOWY AND LOUD... YOUR SON IS SO MUCH LIKE HOW YOU USED TO BE.
HMM...
THIS IS THE FIRST TIME YOU SPOKE OF HIM AS MY "SON."
SMILE
DON'T BE CAPTIOUS. IT'S ANNOYING.
I'M GOING HOME.
OKAY.
TAKE CARE. ♡

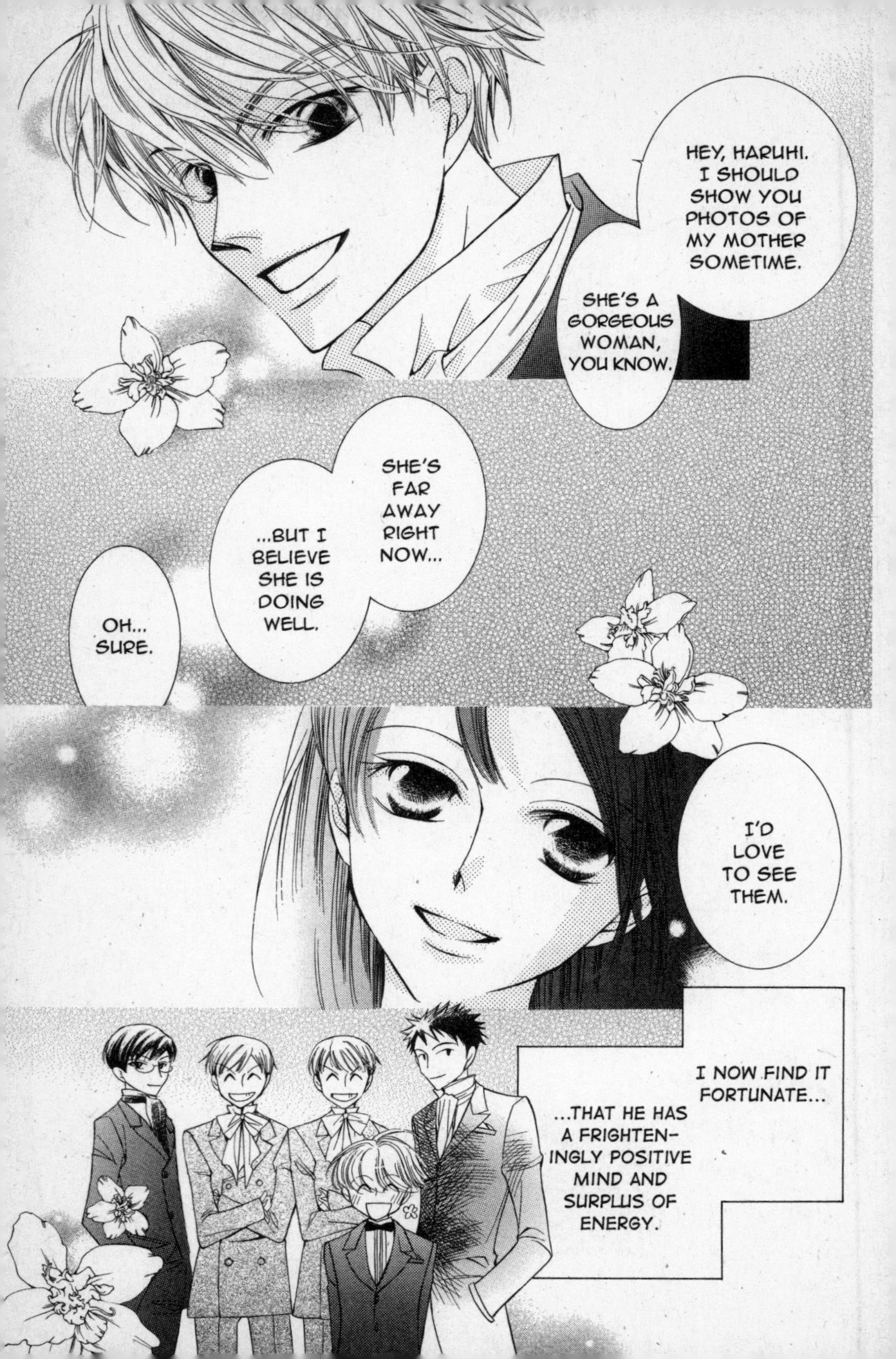
HEY, HARUHI. I SHOULD SHOW YOU PHOTOS OF MY MOTHER SOMETIME.
SHE'S A GORGEOUS WOMAN, YOU KNOW.
SHE'S FAR AWAY RIGHT NOW...
...BUT I BELIEVE SHE IS DOING WELL.
OH... SURE.
I'D LOVE TO SEE THEM.
I NOW FIND IT FORTUNATE...
...THAT HE HAS A FRIGHTEN-INGLY POSITIVE MIND AND SURPLUS OF ENERGY.

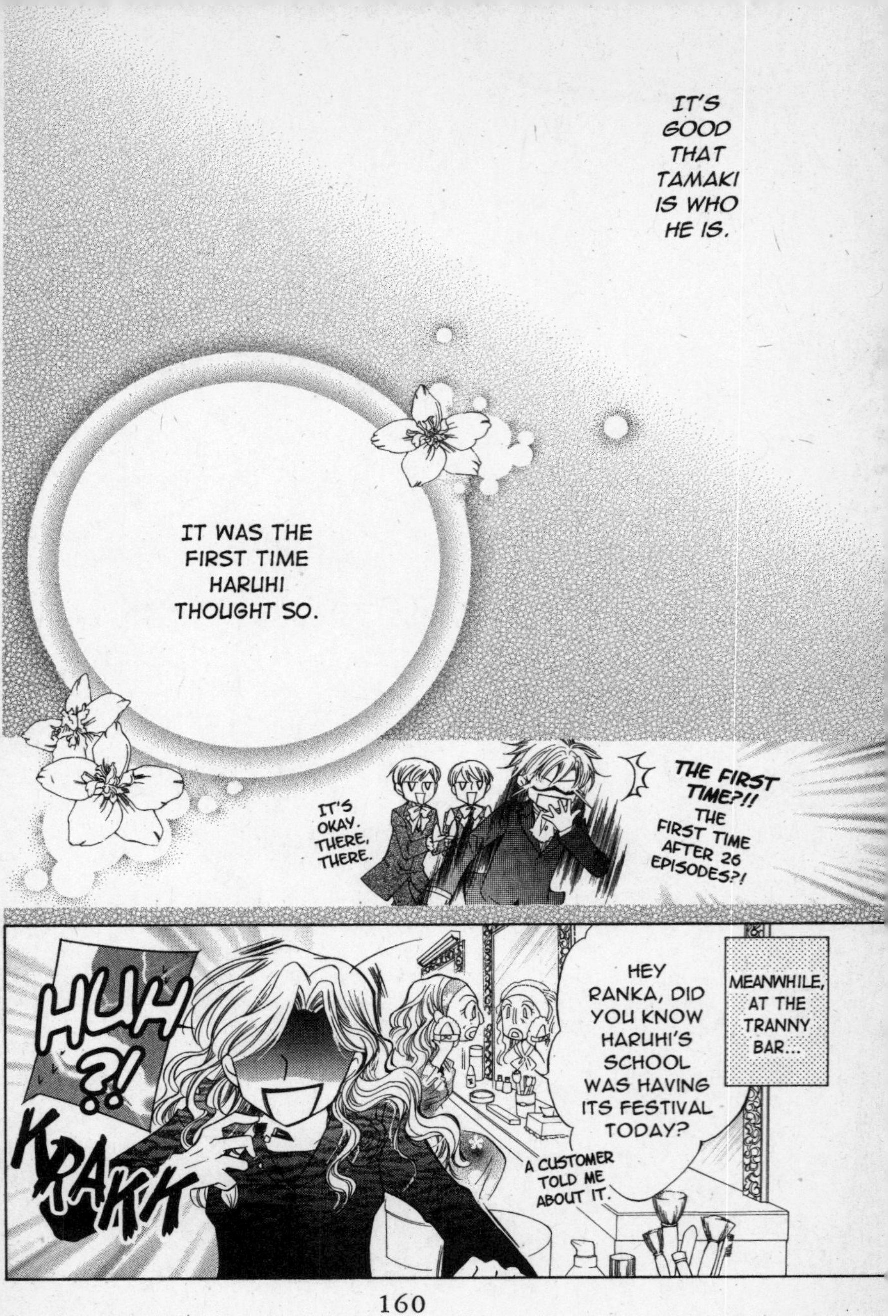
IT'S GOOD THAT TAMAKI IS WHO HE IS.
IT WAS THE FIRST TIME HARUHI THOUGHT SO.
THE FIRST TIME?!! THE FIRST TIME AFTER 26 EPISODES?!
IT'S OKAY. THERE, THERE.
MEANWHILE, AT THE TRANNY BAR...
HEY RANKA, DID YOU KNOW HARUHI'S SCHOOL WAS HAVING ITS FESTIVAL TODAY?
A CUSTOMER TOLD ME ABOUT IT.
HUH ?!
KRAKK

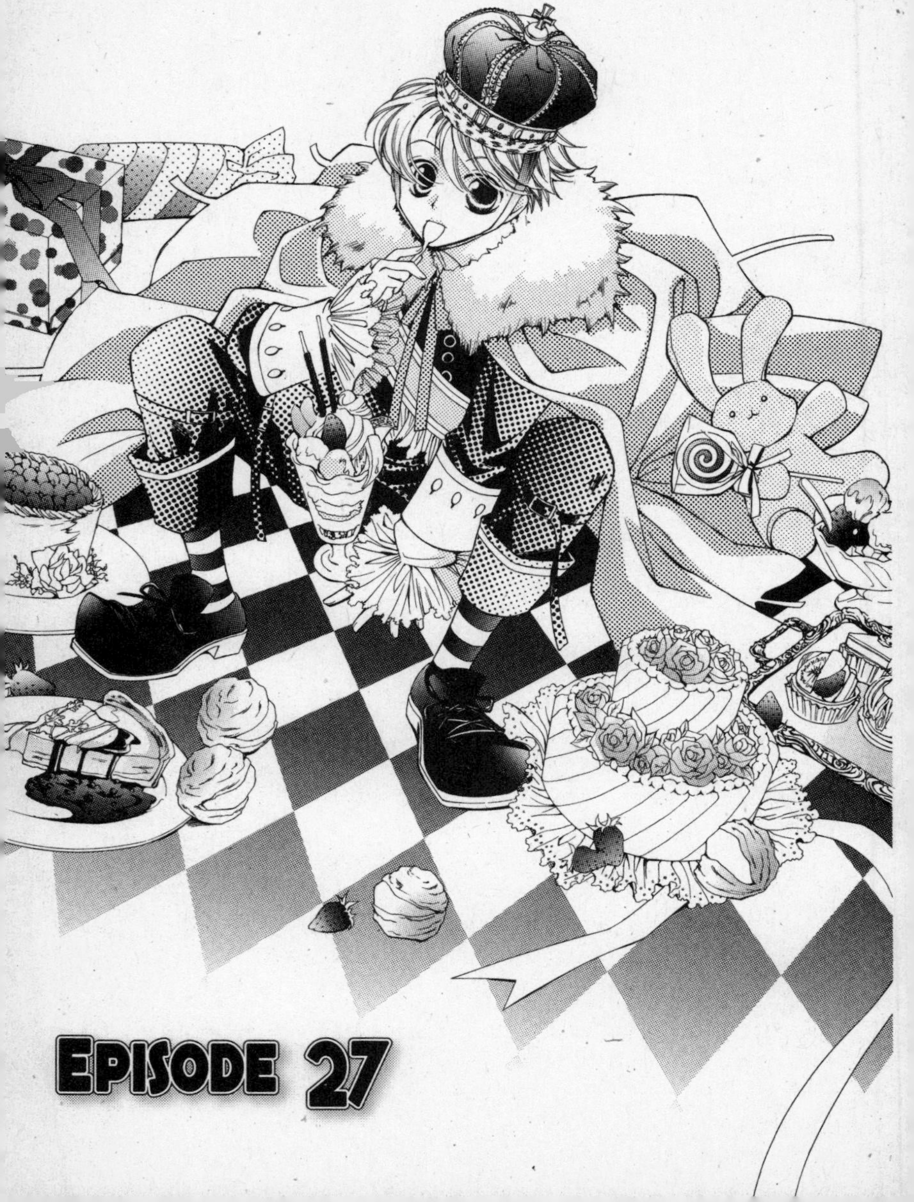
Episode 27

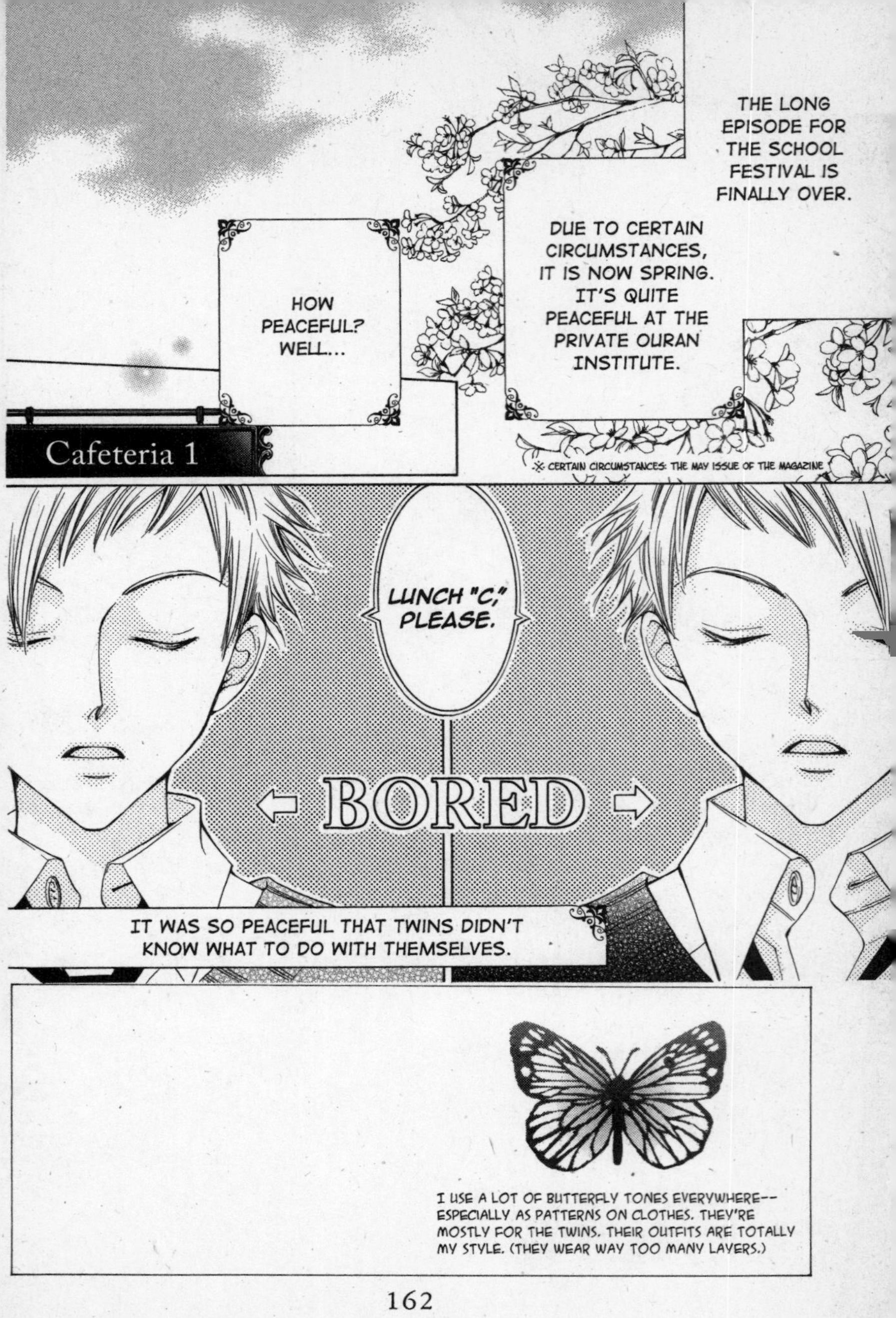
THE LONG EPISODE FOR THE SCHOOL FESTIVAL IS FINALLY OVER.
DUE TO CERTAIN CIRCUMSTANCES, IT IS NOW SPRING. IT'S QUITE PEACEFUL AT THE PRIVATE OURAN INSTITUTE.
※ CERTAIN CIRCUMSTANCES: THE MAY ISSUE OF THE MAGAZINE
HOW PEACEFUL? WELL...
Cafeteria 1
LUNCH "C," PLEASE.
BORED
IT WAS SO PEACEFUL THAT TWINS DIDN'T KNOW WHAT TO DO WITH THEMSELVES.
I USE A LOT OF BUTTERFLY TONES EVERYWHERE--ESPECIALLY AS PATTERNS ON CLOTHES. THEY'RE MOSTLY FOR THE TWINS. THEIR OUTFITS ARE TOTALLY MY STYLE. (THEY WEAR WAY TOO MANY LAYERS.)

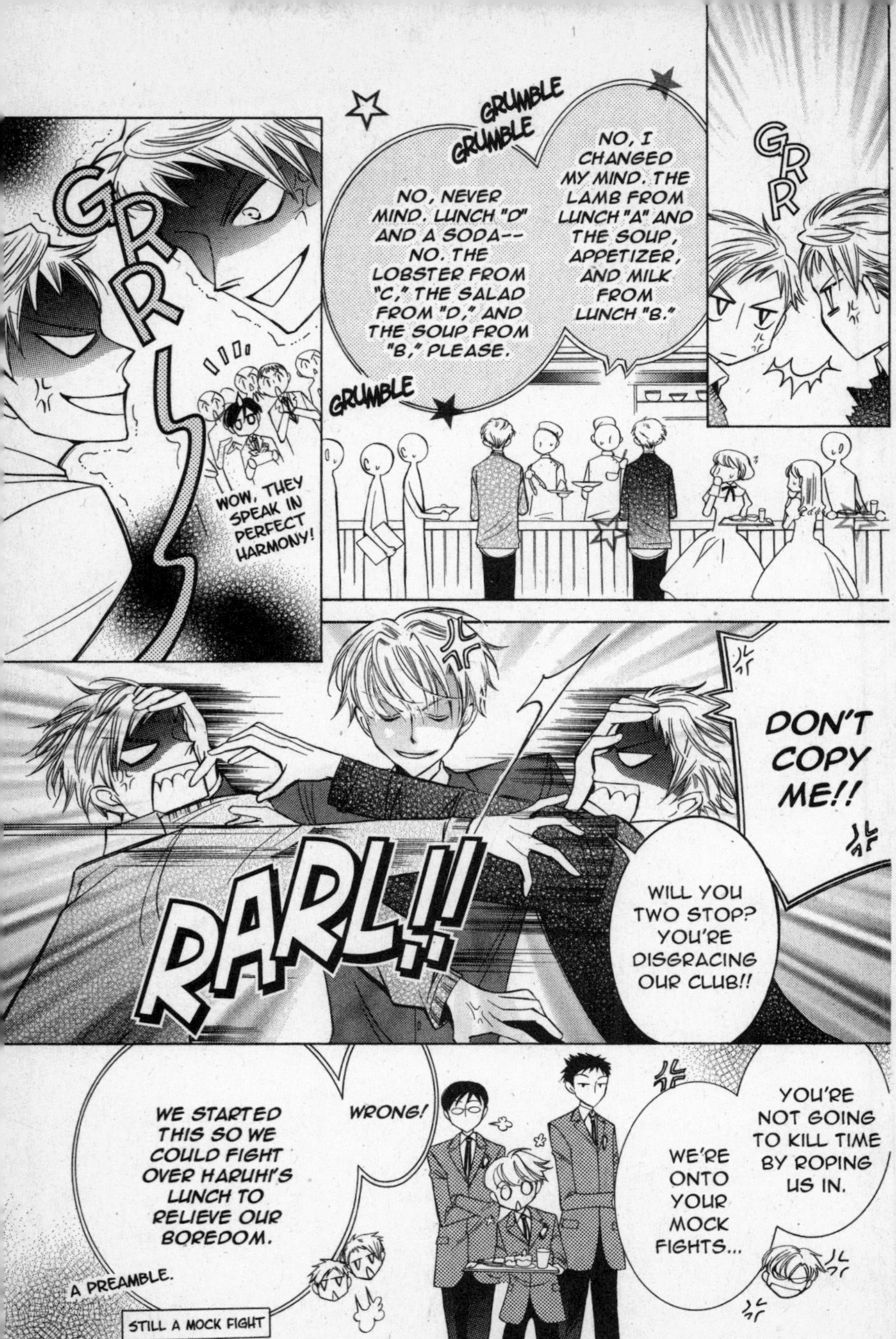
GRR
GRUMBLE GRUMBLE
NO, I CHANGED MY MIND. THE LAMB FROM LUNCH "A" AND THE SOUP, APPETIZER, AND MILK FROM LUNCH "B."
NO, NEVER MIND. LUNCH "D" AND A SODA-- NO. THE LOBSTER FROM "C," THE SALAD FROM "D," AND THE SOUP FROM "B," PLEASE.
GRUMBLE
GRRRLS
WOW, THEY SPEAK IN PERFECT HARMONY!
DON'T COPY ME!!
RARL!!
WILL YOU TWO STOP? YOU'RE DISGRACING OUR CLUB!!
YOU'RE NOT GOING TO KILL TIME BY ROPING US IN.
WE'RE ONTO YOUR MOCK FIGHTS...
WRONG!
WE STARTED THIS SO WE COULD FIGHT OVER HARUHI'S LUNCH TO RELIEVE OUR BOREDOM.
A PREAMBLE.
STILL A MOCK FIGHT

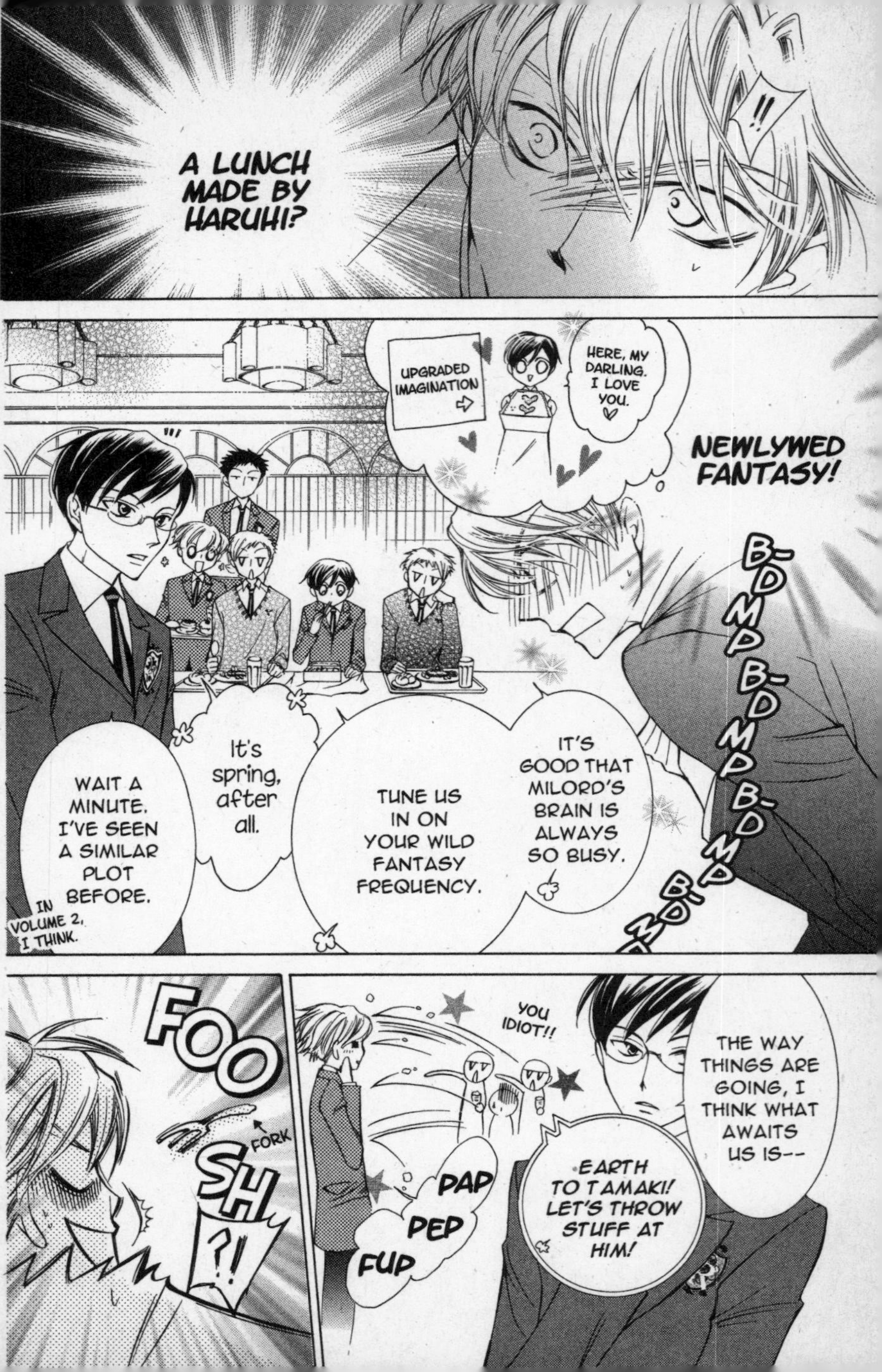
!!
A LUNCH MADE BY HARUHI?
NEWLYWED FANTASY!
HERE, MY DARLING. I LOVE YOU.
UPGRADED IMAGINATION
B-DMP B-DMP B-DMP B-DMP B-DM
IT'S GOOD THAT MILORD'S BRAIN IS ALWAYS SO BUSY.
TUNE US IN ON YOUR WILD FANTASY FREQUENCY.
It's spring, after all.
WAIT A MINUTE. I'VE SEEN A SIMILAR PLOT BEFORE.
IN VOLUME 2, I THINK.
THE WAY THINGS ARE GOING, I THINK WHAT AWAITS US IS--
YOU IDIOT!!
EARTH TO TAMAKI! LET'S THROW STUFF AT HIM!
PAP
PEP
FUP
FOO
FORK
SH
?!

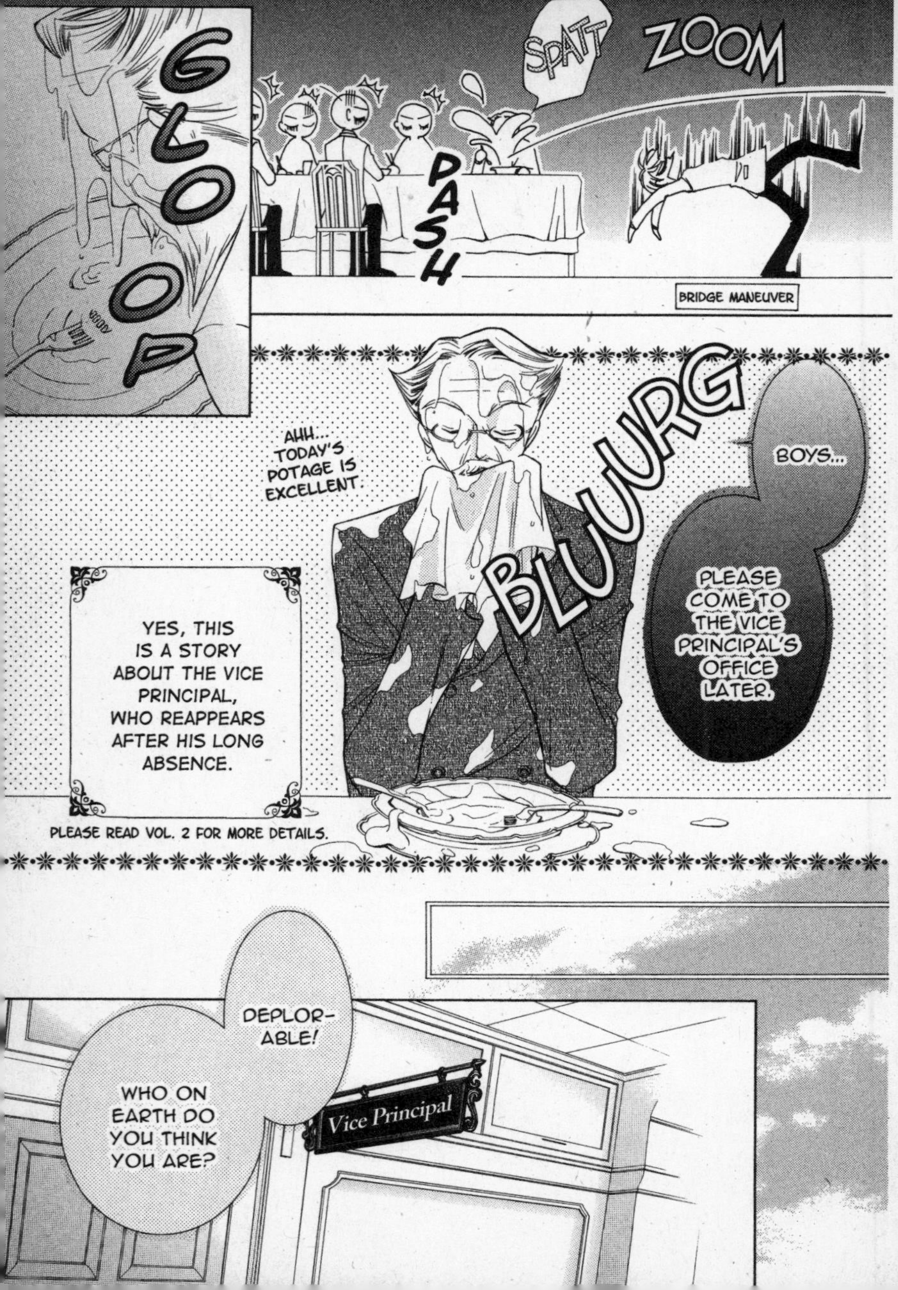
ZOOM
SPATT
PASH
BRIDGE MANEUVER
GLOOP
BLUUURG
BOYS...
PLEASE COME TO THE VICE PRINCIPAL'S OFFICE LATER.
AHH... TODAY'S POTAGE IS EXCELLENT.
YES, THIS IS A STORY ABOUT THE VICE PRINCIPAL, WHO REAPPEARS AFTER HIS LONG ABSENCE.
PLEASE READ VOL. 2 FOR MORE DETAILS.
DEPLOR-ABLE!
WHO ON EARTH DO YOU THINK YOU ARE?
Vice Principal

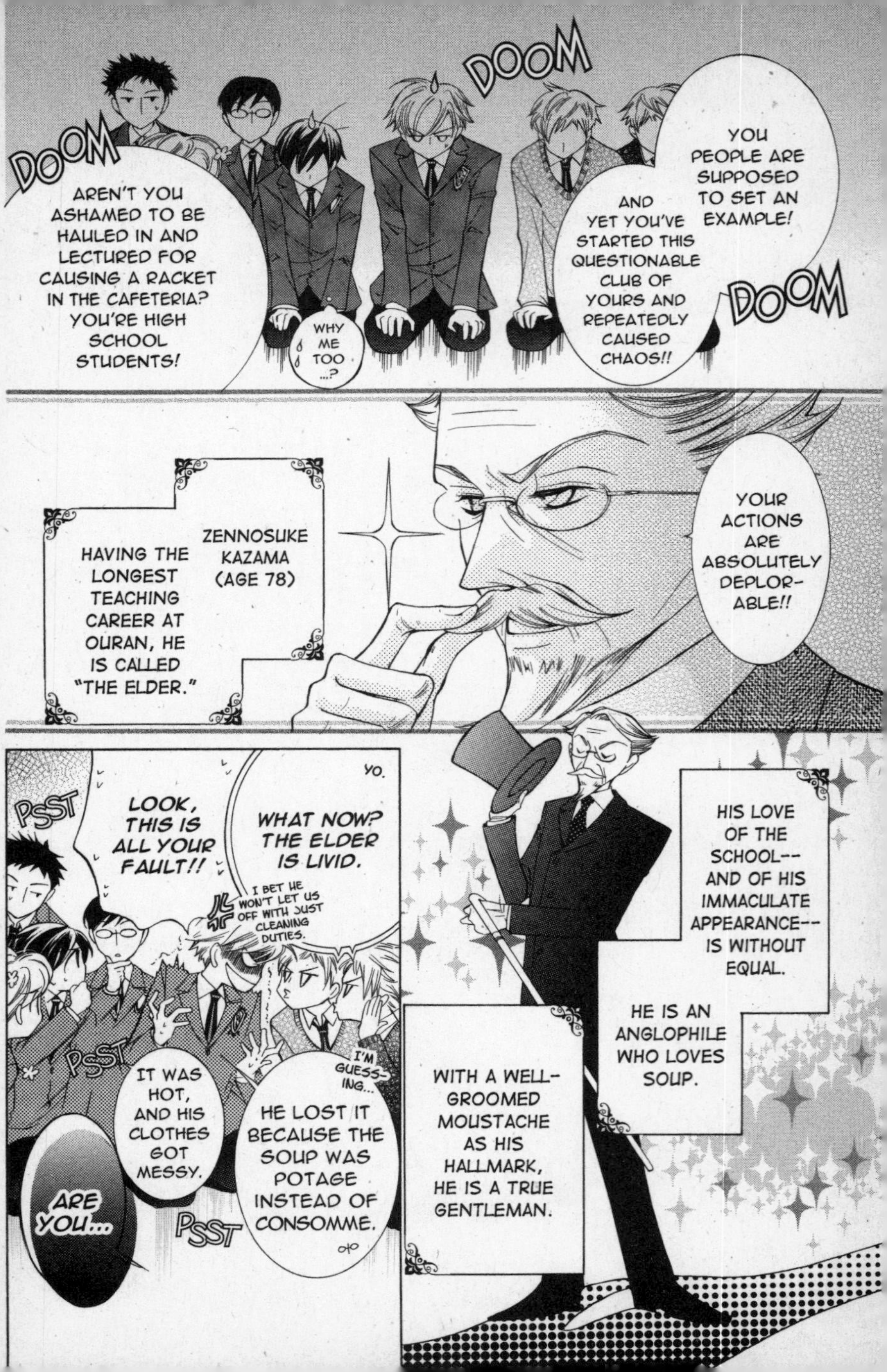
DOOM
YOU PEOPLE ARE SUPPOSED TO SET AN EXAMPLE!
AND YET YOU'VE STARTED THIS QUESTIONABLE CLUB OF YOURS AND REPEATEDLY CAUSED CHAOS!!
DOOM
WHY ME TOO ...?
DOOM
AREN'T YOU ASHAMED TO BE HAULED IN AND LECTURED FOR CAUSING A RACKET IN THE CAFETERIA? YOU'RE HIGH SCHOOL STUDENTS!
YOUR ACTIONS ARE ABSOLUTELY DEPLOR-ABLE!!
ZENNOSUKE KAZAMA (AGE 78)
HAVING THE LONGEST TEACHING CAREER AT OURAN, HE IS CALLED "THE ELDER."
HIS LOVE OF THE SCHOOL-- AND OF HIS IMMACULATE APPEARANCE-- IS WITHOUT EQUAL.
HE IS AN ANGLOPHILE WHO LOVES SOUP.
WITH A WELL-GROOMED MOUSTACHE AS HIS HALLMARK, HE IS A TRUE GENTLEMAN.
YO.
WHAT NOW? THE ELDER IS LIVID.
I BET HE WON'T LET US OFF WITH JUST CLEANING DUTIES.
LOOK, THIS IS ALL YOUR FAULT!!
PSST
I'M GUESS-ING...
HE LOST IT BECAUSE THE SOUP WAS POTAGE INSTEAD OF CONSOMME.
IT WAS HOT, AND HIS CLOTHES GOT MESSY.
PSST
ARE YOU...
PSST

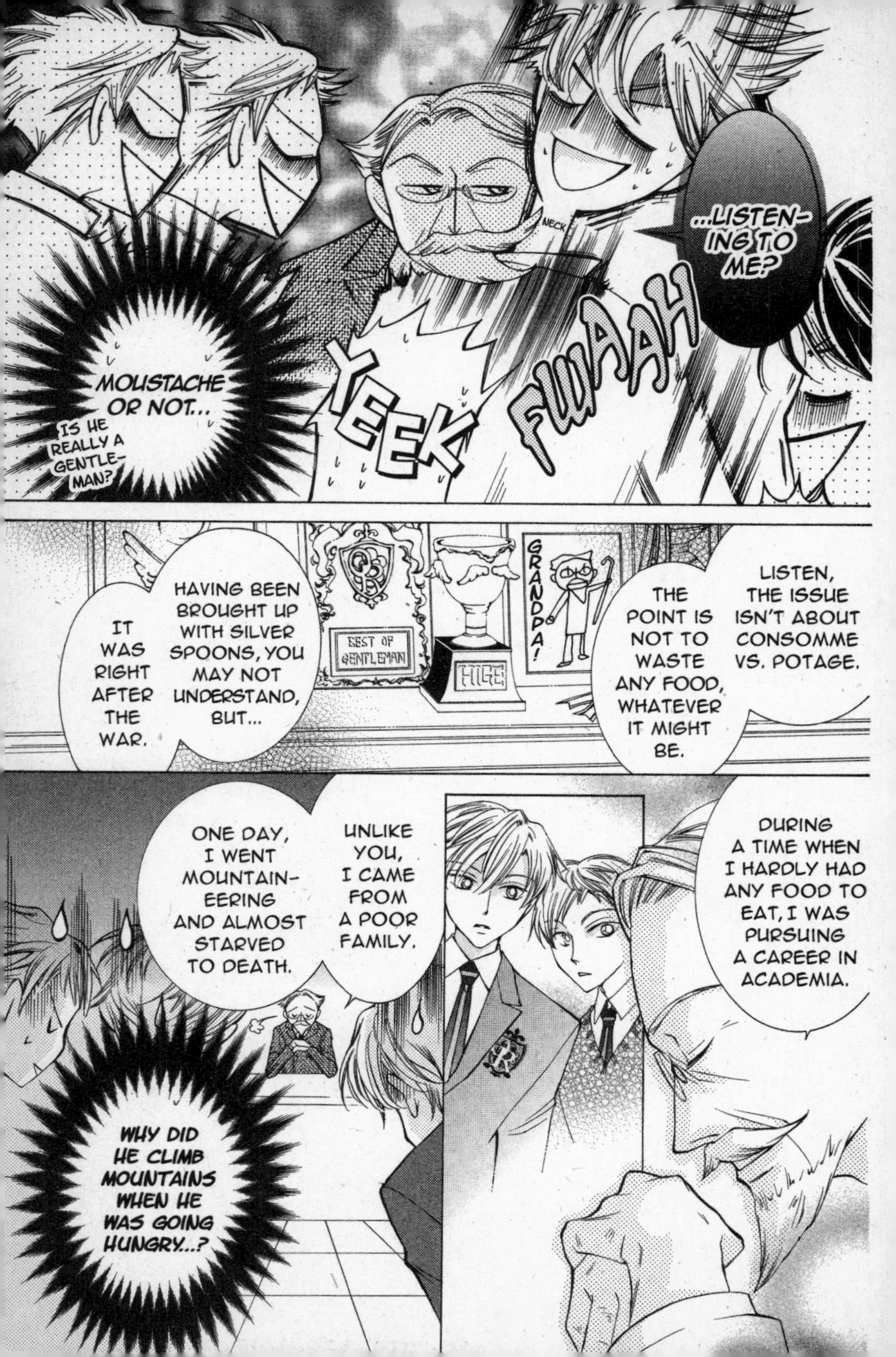
...LISTENING TO ME?
NECK
FWAAH
YEEK
MOUSTACHE OR NOT...
IS HE REALLY A GENTLEMAN?
LISTEN, THE ISSUE ISN'T ABOUT CONSOMME VS. POTAGE.
THE POINT IS NOT TO WASTE ANY FOOD, WHATEVER IT MIGHT BE.
GRANDPA!
HIGE
BEST OF GENTLEMAN
HAVING BEEN BROUGHT UP WITH SILVER SPOONS, YOU MAY NOT UNDERSTAND, BUT...
IT WAS RIGHT AFTER THE WAR.
DURING A TIME WHEN I HARDLY HAD ANY FOOD TO EAT, I WAS PURSUING A CAREER IN ACADEMIA.
UNLIKE YOU, I CAME FROM A POOR FAMILY.
ONE DAY, I WENT MOUNTAINEERING AND ALMOST STARVED TO DEATH.
WHY DID HE CLIMB MOUNTAINS WHEN HE WAS GOING HUNGRY...?

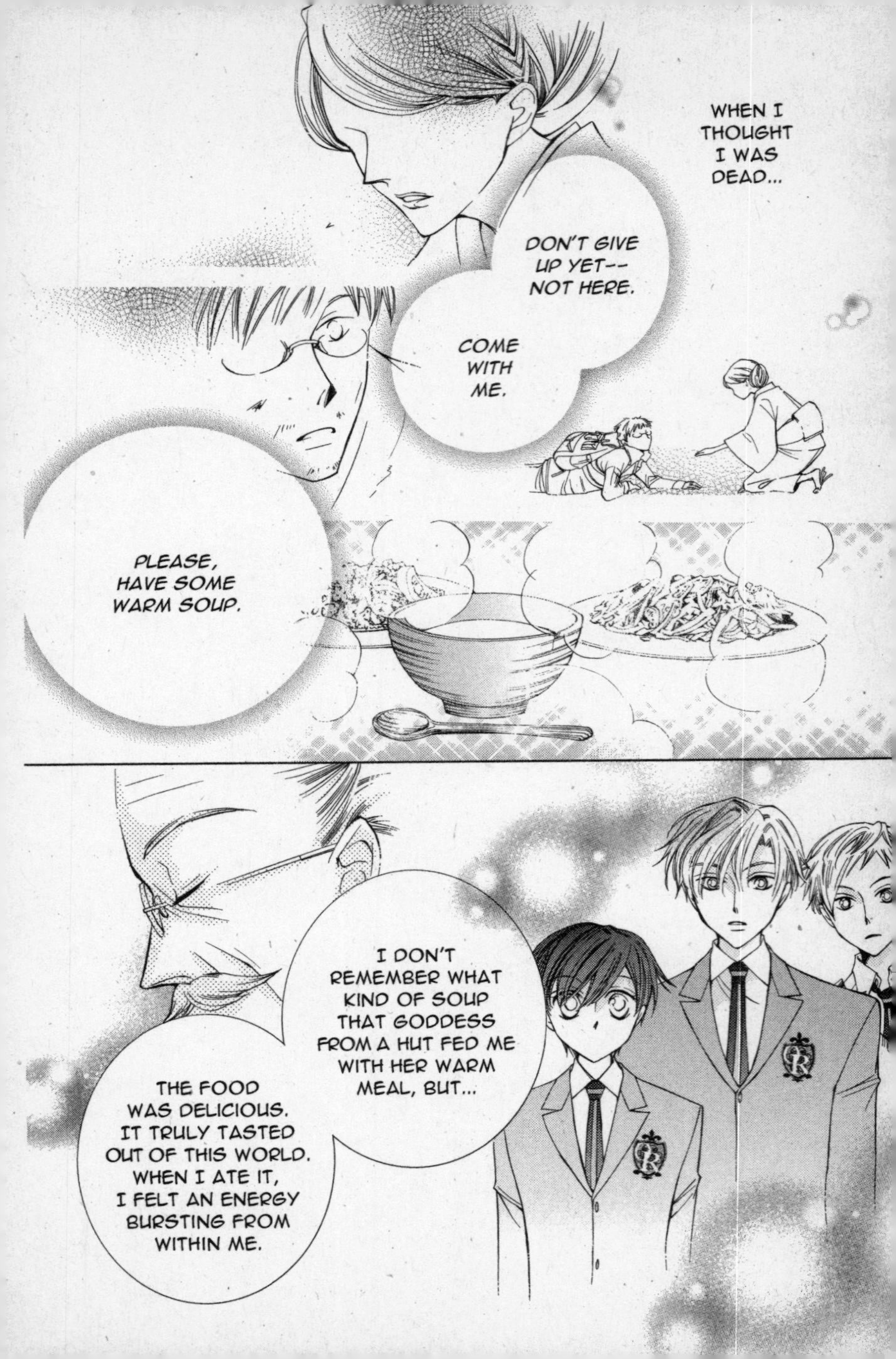
WHEN I THOUGHT I WAS DEAD...
DON'T GIVE UP YET-- NOT HERE.
COME WITH ME.
PLEASE, HAVE SOME WARM SOUP.
I DON'T REMEMBER WHAT KIND OF SOUP THAT GODDESS FROM A HUT FED ME WITH HER WARM MEAL, BUT...
THE FOOD WAS DELICIOUS. IT TRULY TASTED OUT OF THIS WORLD. WHEN I ATE IT, I FELT AN ENERGY BURSTING FROM WITHIN ME.

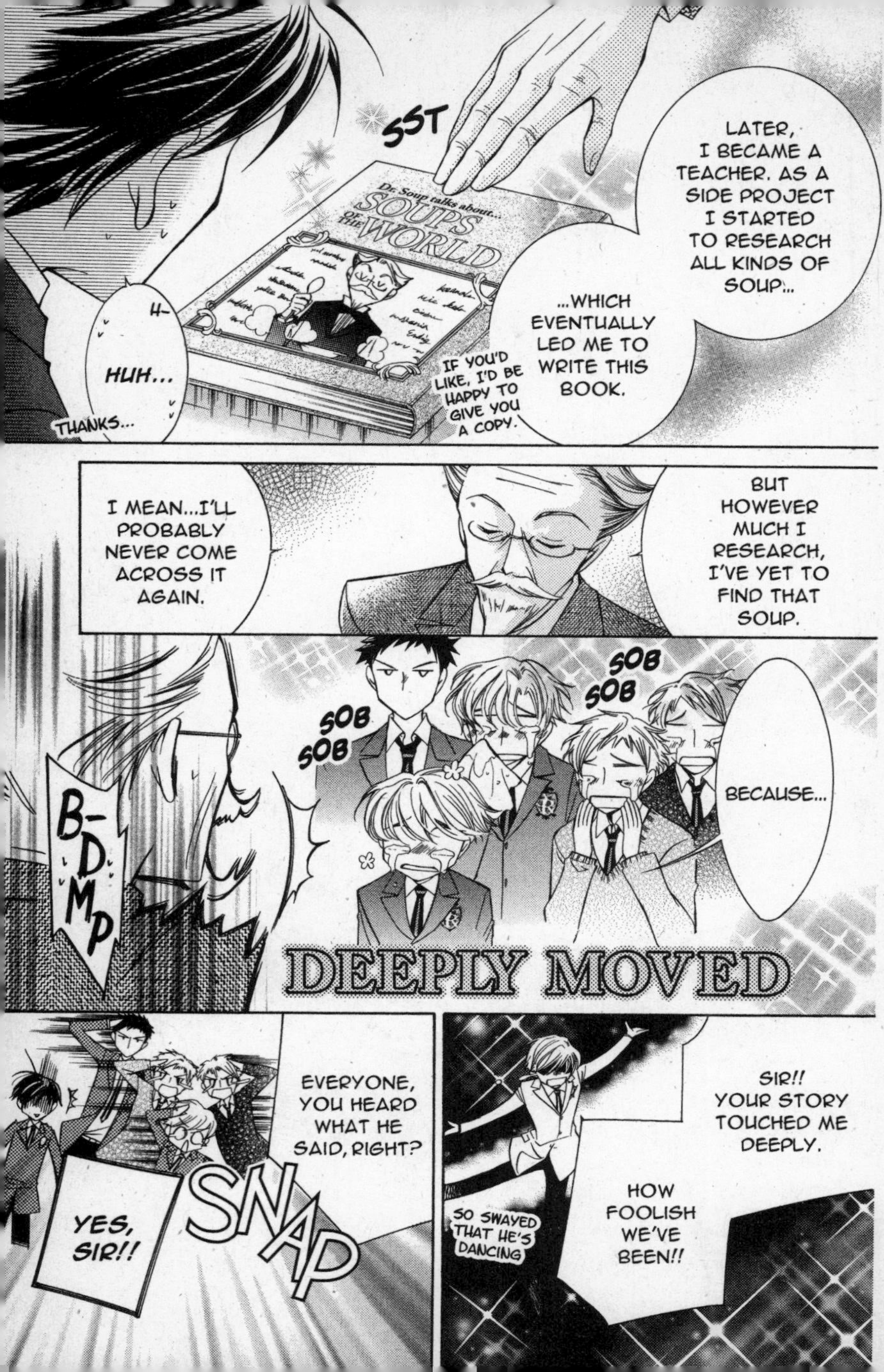

LATER, I BECAME A TEACHER. AS A SIDE PROJECT I STARTED TO RESEARCH ALL KINDS OF SOUP...
SST
Dr. Soup talks about... SOUPS OF THE WORLD
...WHICH EVENTUALLY LED ME TO WRITE THIS BOOK.
IF YOU'D LIKE, I'D BE HAPPY TO GIVE YOU A COPY.
H-HUH...
THANKS...
BUT HOWEVER MUCH I RESEARCH, I'VE YET TO FIND THAT SOUP.
I MEAN...I'LL PROBABLY NEVER COME ACROSS IT AGAIN.
BECAUSE...
SOB SOB
SOB SOB
B-DMP
DEEPLY MOVED
SIR!! YOUR STORY TOUCHED ME DEEPLY.
HOW FOOLISH WE'VE BEEN!!
SO SWAYED THAT HE'S DANCING
EVERYONE, YOU HEARD WHAT HE SAID, RIGHT?
SNAP
YES, SIR!!

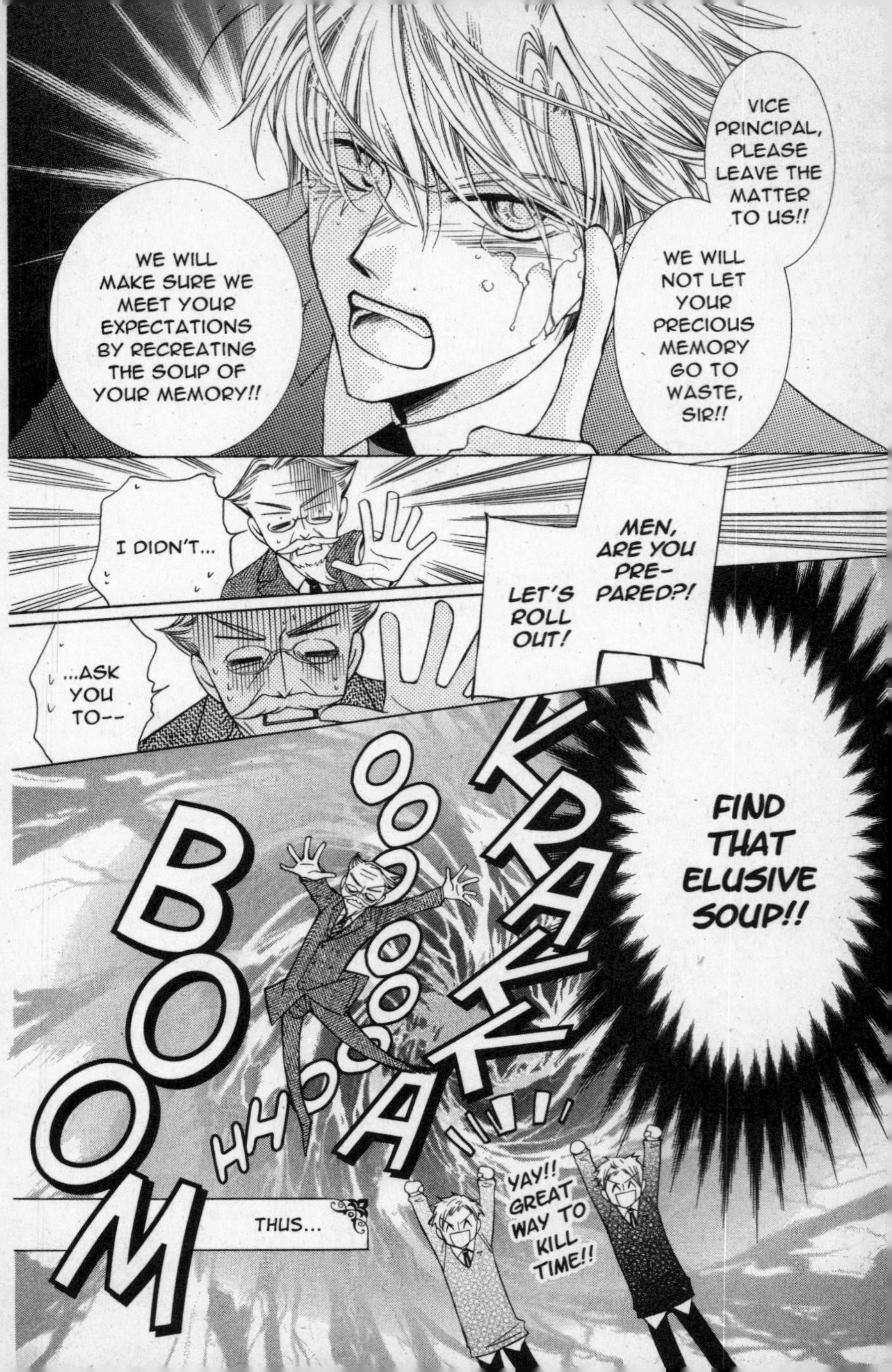
VICE PRINCIPAL, PLEASE LEAVE THE MATTER TO US!!
WE WILL NOT LET YOUR PRECIOUS MEMORY GO TO WASTE, SIR!!
WE WILL MAKE SURE WE MEET YOUR EXPECTATIONS BY RECREATING THE SOUP OF YOUR MEMORY!!
MEN, ARE YOU PRE-PARED?!
LET'S ROLL OUT!
I DIDN'T...
...ASK YOU TO--
FIND THAT ELUSIVE SOUP!!
KRAKA!!!
OOOOOHH
BOOOM
YAY!! GREAT WAY TO KILL TIME!!
THUS...

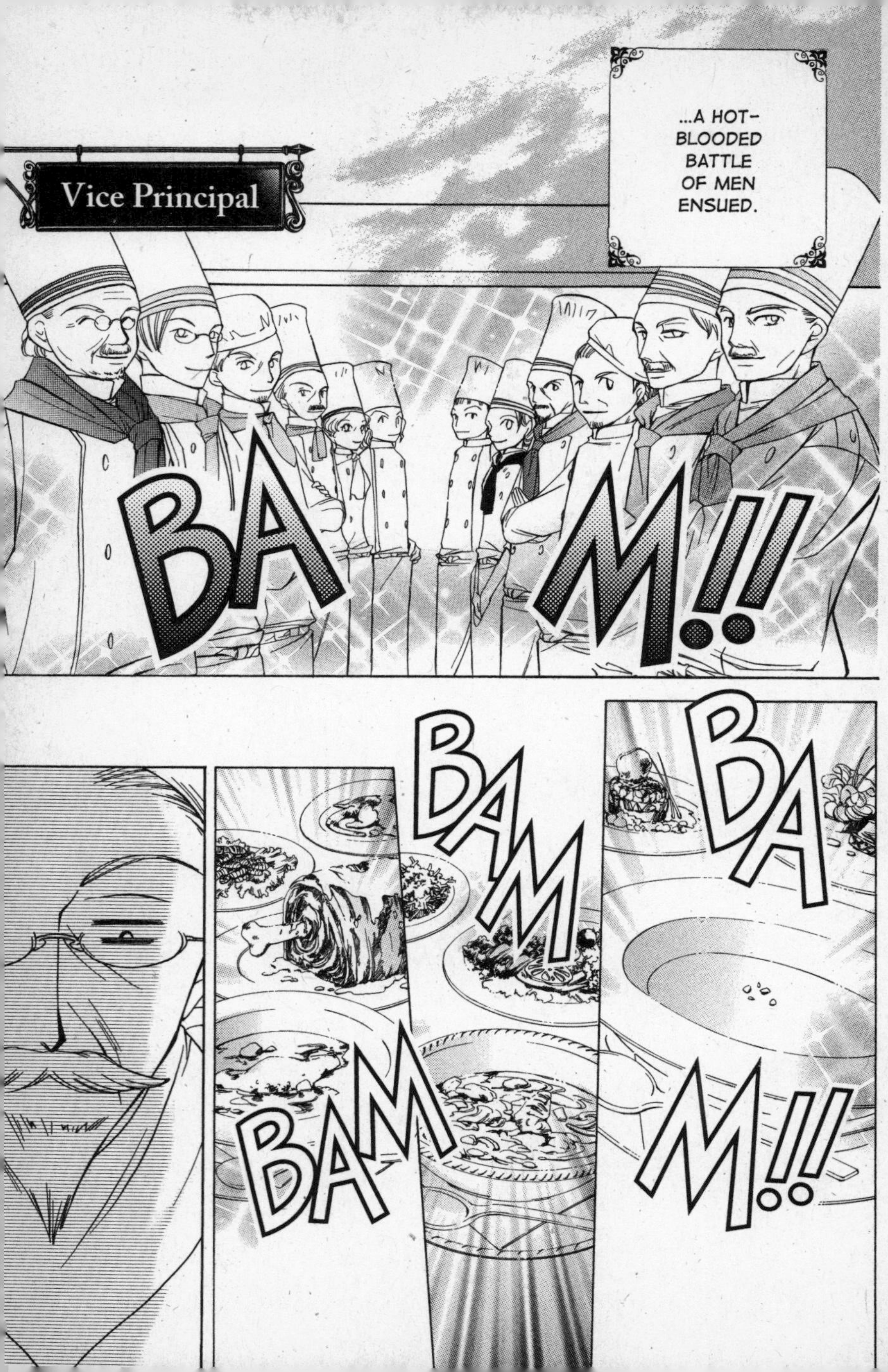
...A HOT-BLOODED BATTLE OF MEN ENSUED.
Vice Principal
BAM!!
BAM!!
BAM
BAM

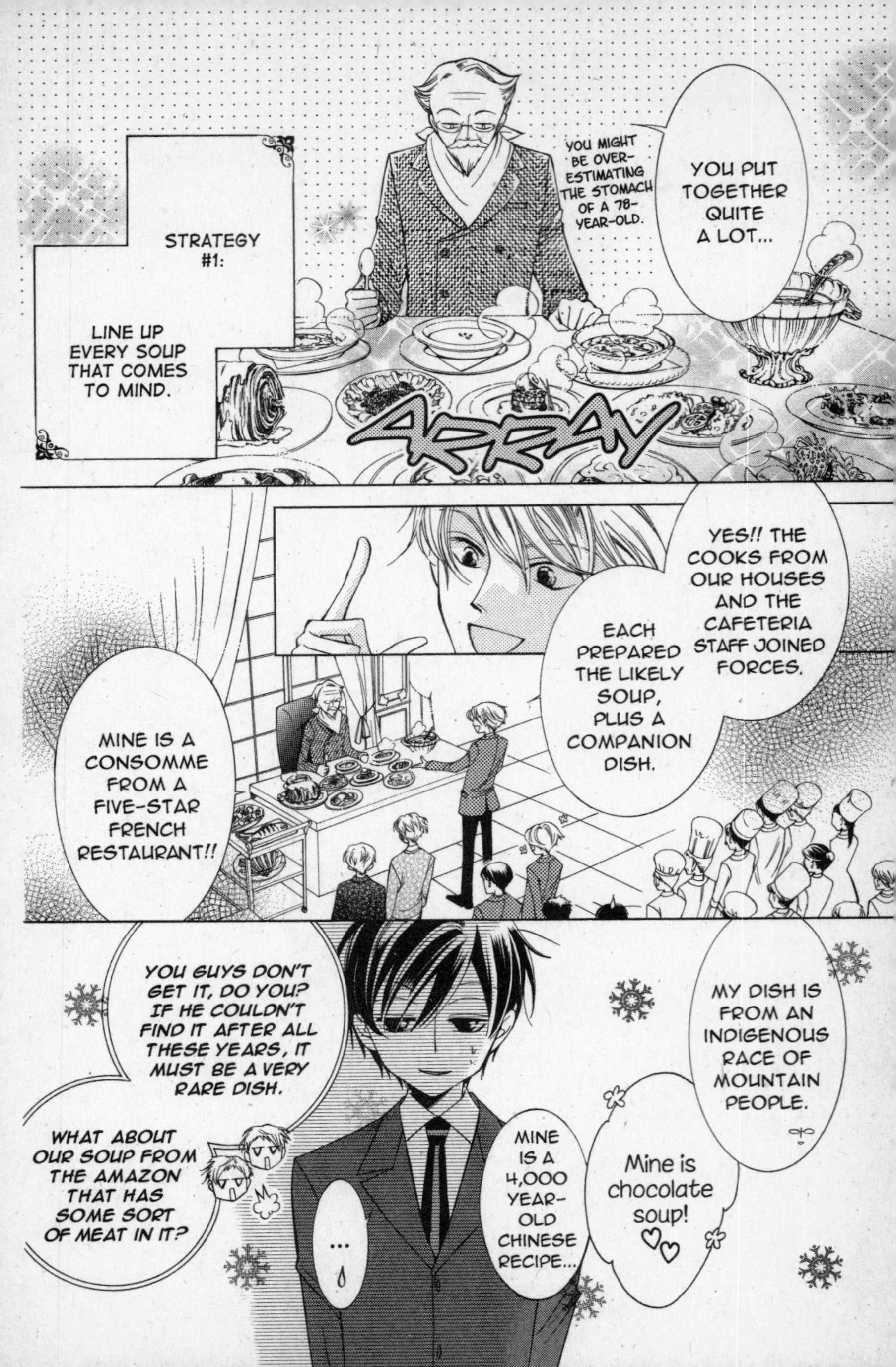
YOU PUT TOGETHER QUITE A LOT...
YOU MIGHT BE OVER-ESTIMATING THE STOMACH OF A 78-YEAR-OLD.
STRATEGY #1:
LINE UP EVERY SOUP THAT COMES TO MIND.
ARRAY
YES!! THE COOKS FROM OUR HOUSES AND THE CAFETERIA STAFF JOINED FORCES.
EACH PREPARED THE LIKELY SOUP, PLUS A COMPANION DISH.
MINE IS A CONSOMME FROM A FIVE-STAR FRENCH RESTAURANT!!
MY DISH IS FROM AN INDIGENOUS RACE OF MOUNTAIN PEOPLE.
Mine is chocolate soup!
MINE IS A 4,000 YEAR-OLD CHINESE RECIPE...
...
YOU GUYS DON'T GET IT, DO YOU? IF HE COULDN'T FIND IT AFTER ALL THESE YEARS, IT MUST BE A VERY RARE DISH.
WHAT ABOUT OUR SOUP FROM THE AMAZON THAT HAS SOME SORT OF MEAT IN IT?

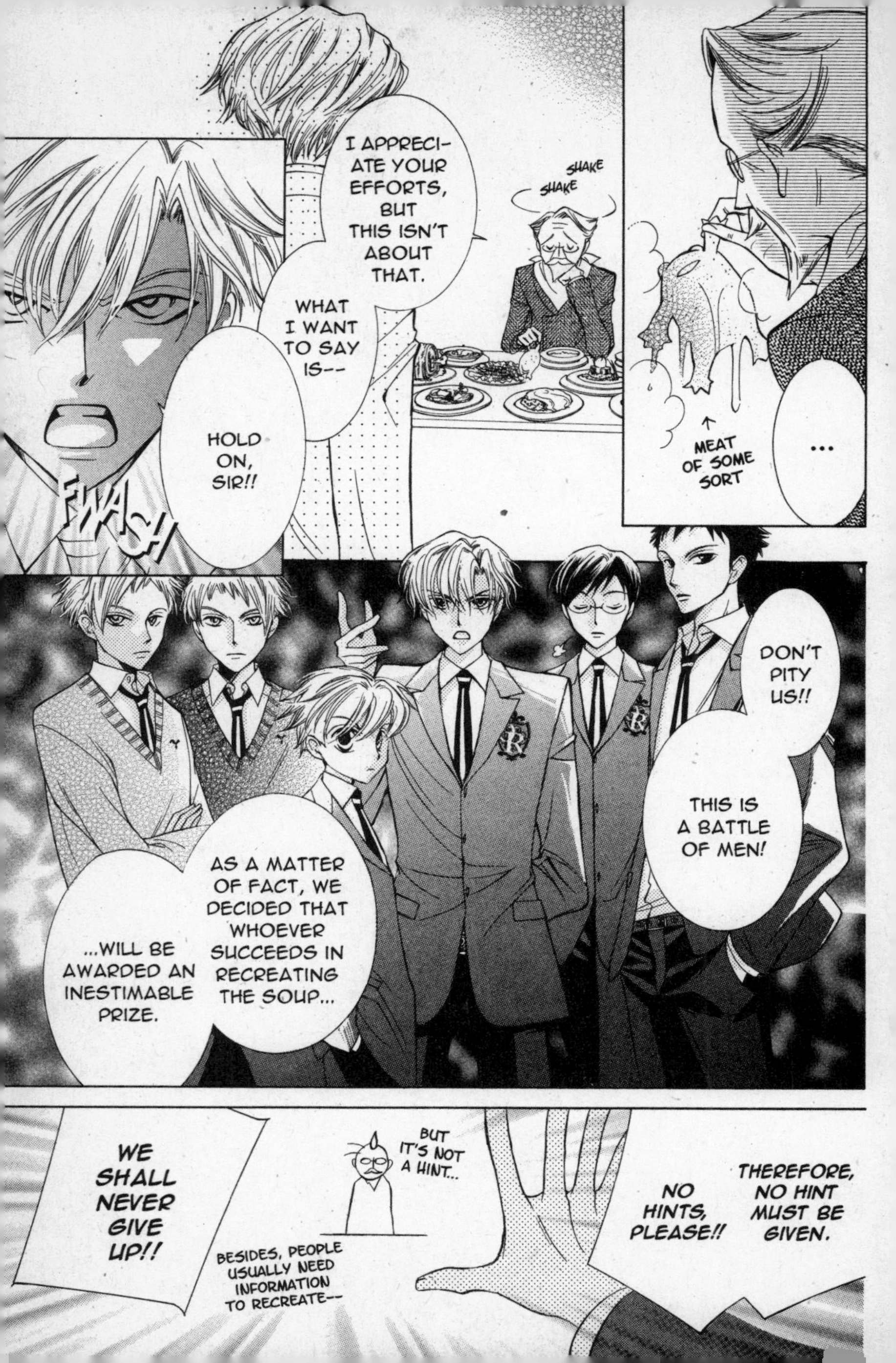
...
MEAT OF SOME SORT
SHAKE SHAKE
I APPRECIATE YOUR EFFORTS, BUT THIS ISN'T ABOUT THAT.
WHAT I WANT TO SAY IS--
HOLD ON, SIR!!
FWASH
DON'T PITY US!!
THIS IS A BATTLE OF MEN!
AS A MATTER OF FACT, WE DECIDED THAT WHOEVER SUCCEEDS IN RECREATING THE SOUP...
...WILL BE AWARDED AN INESTIMABLE PRIZE.
THEREFORE, NO HINT MUST BE GIVEN.
NO HINTS, PLEASE!!
BUT IT'S NOT A HINT...
BESIDES, PEOPLE USUALLY NEED INFORMATION TO RECREATE--
WE SHALL NEVER GIVE UP!!

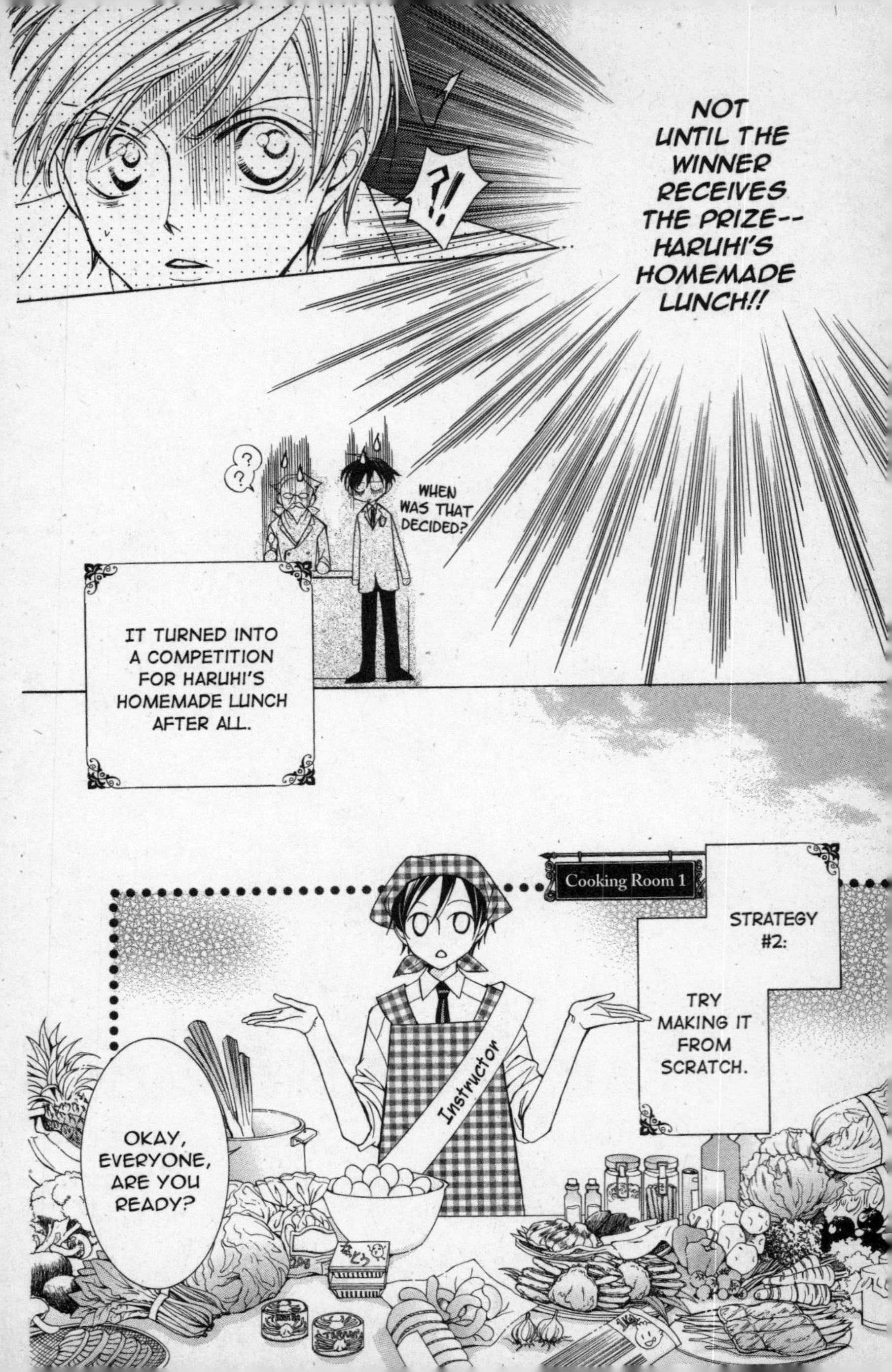
NOT UNTIL THE WINNER RECEIVES THE PRIZE-- HARUHI'S HOMEMADE LUNCH!!
?!
WHEN WAS THAT DECIDED?
IT TURNED INTO A COMPETITION FOR HARUHI'S HOMEMADE LUNCH AFTER ALL.
Cooking Room 1
STRATEGY #2:
TRY MAKING IT FROM SCRATCH.
Instructor
OKAY, EVERYONE, ARE YOU READY?

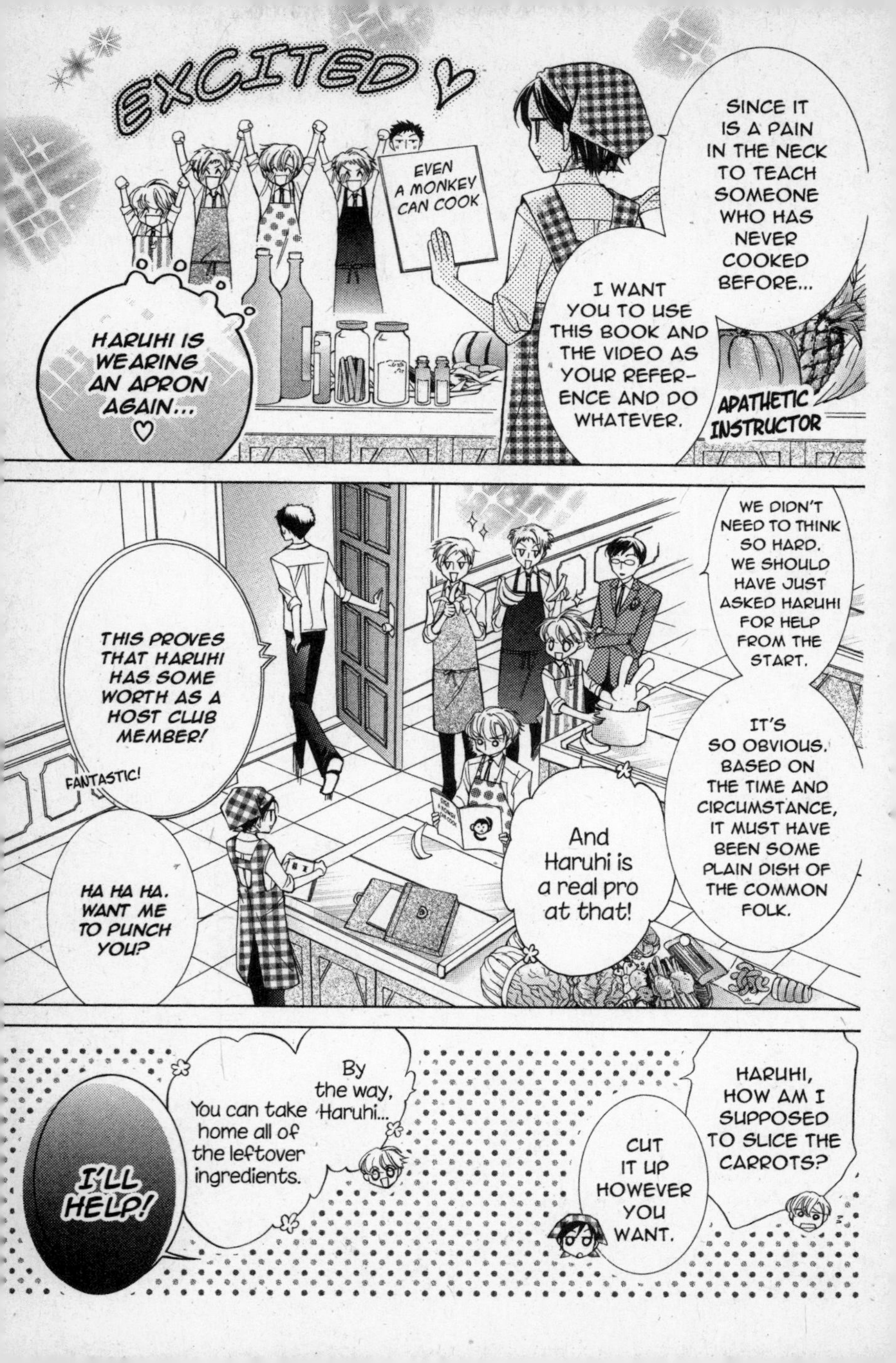
SINCE IT IS A PAIN IN THE NECK TO TEACH SOMEONE WHO HAS NEVER COOKED BEFORE...
I WANT YOU TO USE THIS BOOK AND THE VIDEO AS YOUR REFERENCE AND DO WHATEVER.
APATHETIC INSTRUCTOR
EVEN A MONKEY CAN COOK
EXCITED ♡
HARUHI IS WEARING AN APRON AGAIN... ♡
WE DIDN'T NEED TO THINK SO HARD. WE SHOULD HAVE JUST ASKED HARUHI FOR HELP FROM THE START.
IT'S SO OBVIOUS. BASED ON THE TIME AND CIRCUMSTANCE, IT MUST HAVE BEEN SOME PLAIN DISH OF THE COMMON FOLK.
And Haruhi is a real pro at that!
THIS PROVES THAT HARUHI HAS SOME WORTH AS A HOST CLUB MEMBER!
FANTASTIC!
HA HA HA. WANT ME TO PUNCH YOU?
HARUHI, HOW AM I SUPPOSED TO SLICE THE CARROTS?
CUT IT UP HOWEVER YOU WANT.
By the way, Haruhi...
You can take home all of the leftover ingredients.
I'LL HELP!

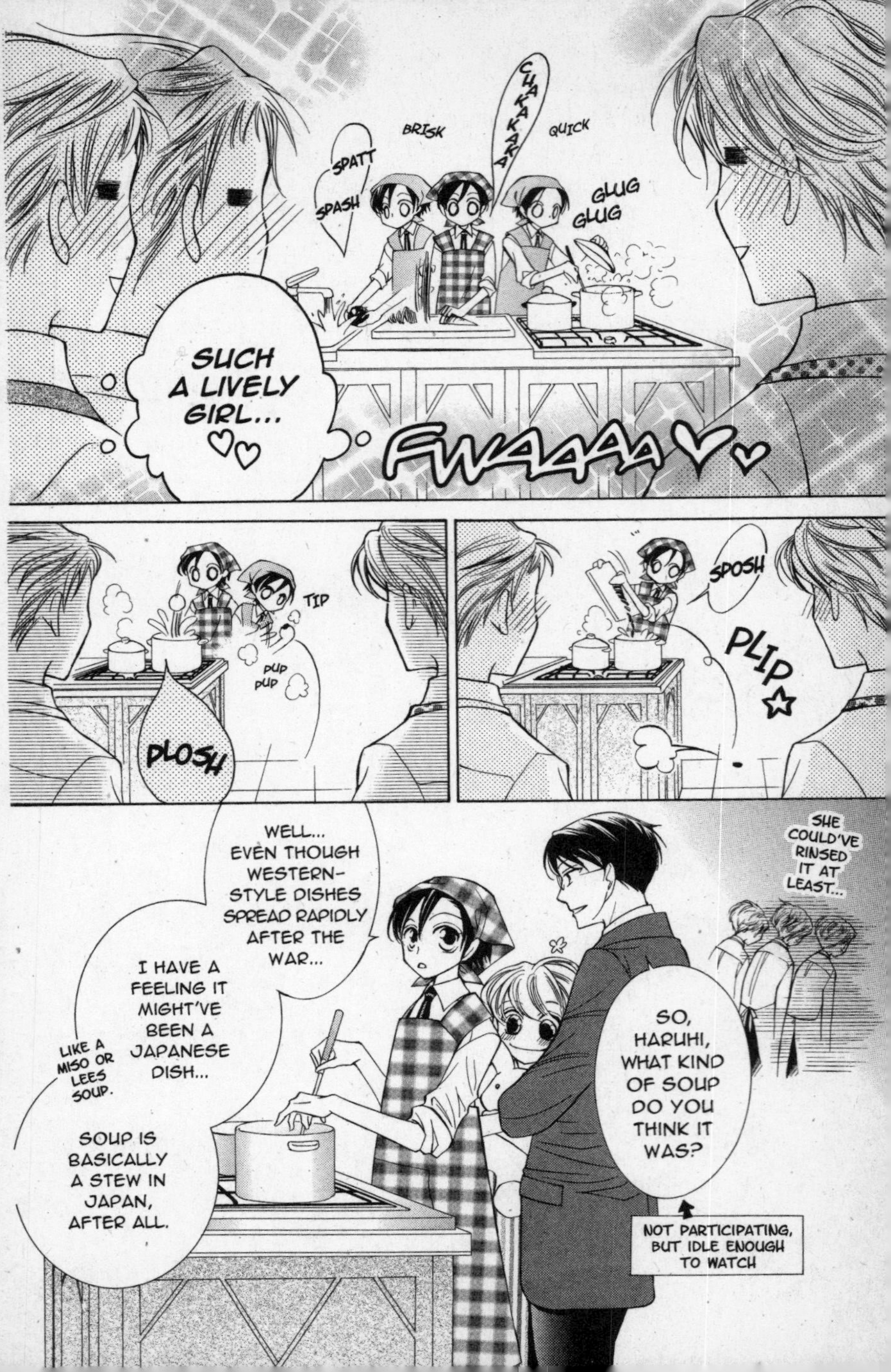
QUICK
GLUG GLUG
CHAKAKAKAKA
BRISK
SPATT SPASH
FWAAAA
SUCH A LIVELY GIRL...
SPOSH
PLIP
TIP
PUP PUP
PLOSH
SHE COULD'VE RINSED IT AT LEAST...
SO, HARUHI, WHAT KIND OF SOUP DO YOU THINK IT WAS?
NOT PARTICIPATING, BUT IDLE ENOUGH TO WATCH
WELL... EVEN THOUGH WESTERN-STYLE DISHES SPREAD RAPIDLY AFTER THE WAR...
I HAVE A FEELING IT MIGHT'VE BEEN A JAPANESE DISH...
LIKE A MISO OR LEES SOUP.
SOUP IS BASICALLY A STEW IN JAPAN, AFTER ALL.

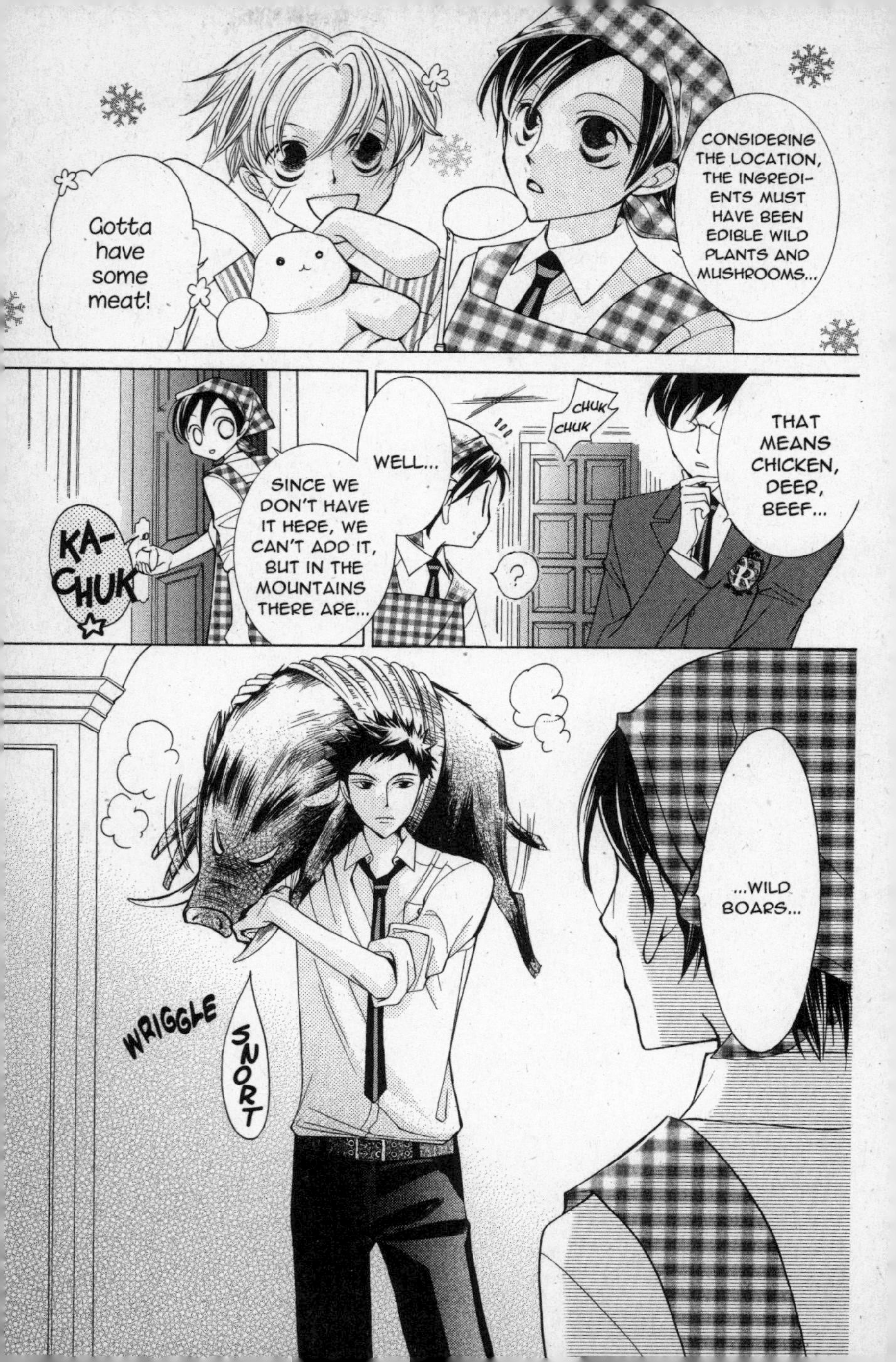
CONSIDERING THE LOCATION, THE INGREDI- ENTS MUST HAVE BEEN EDIBLE WILD PLANTS AND MUSHROOMS...
Gotta have some meat!
THAT MEANS CHICKEN, DEER, BEEF...
CHUK CHUK
?
WELL...
SINCE WE DON'T HAVE IT HERE, WE CAN'T ADD IT, BUT IN THE MOUNTAINS THERE ARE...
KA- CHUK
...WILD BOARS...
SNORT
WRIGGLE

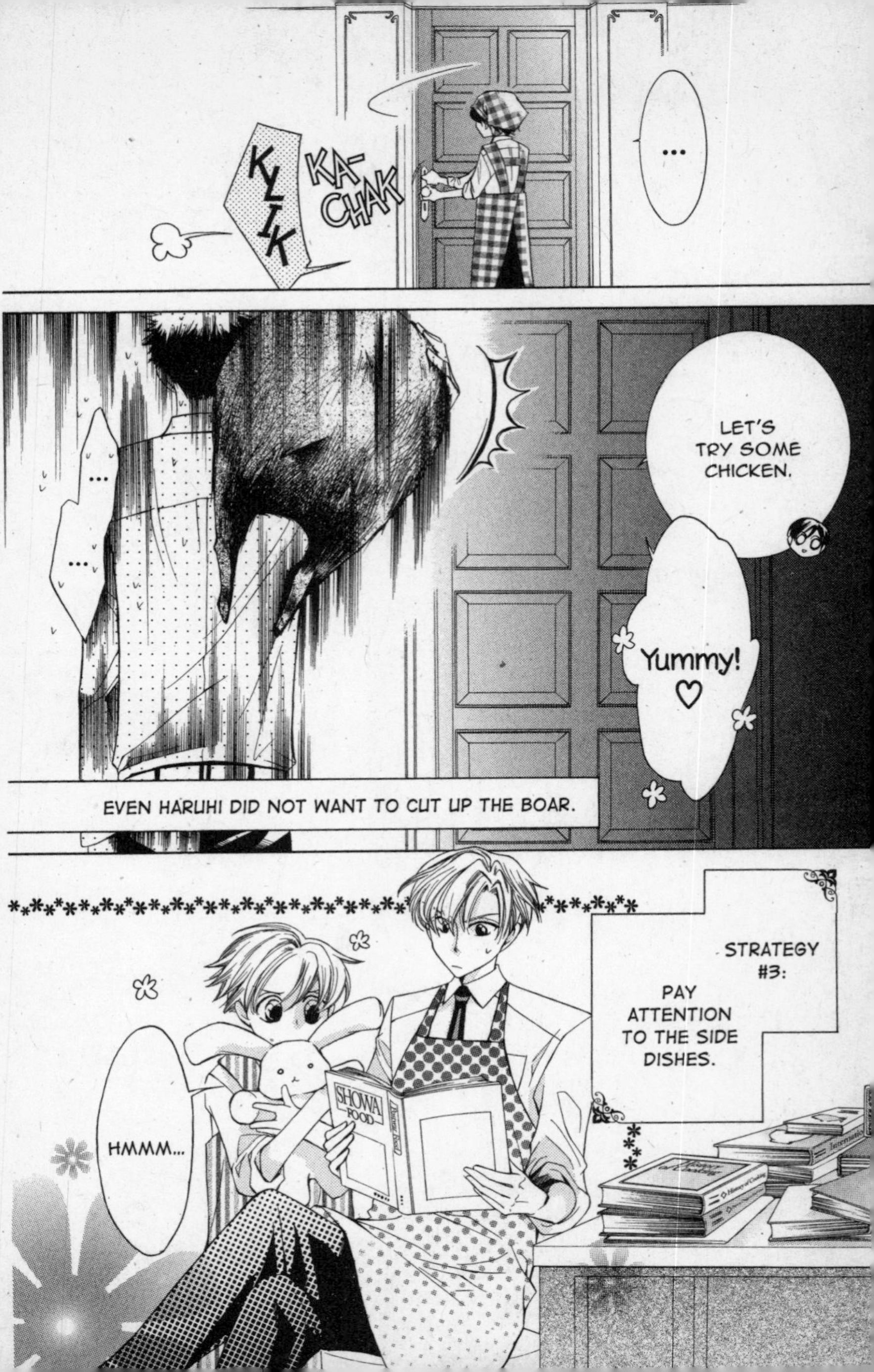
...
KA-CHAK
KLIK
LET'S TRY SOME CHICKEN.
Yummy! ♡
...
...
EVEN HARUHI DID NOT WANT TO CUT UP THE BOAR.
STRATEGY #3: PAY ATTENTION TO THE SIDE DISHES.
SHOWA FOOD
HMMM...

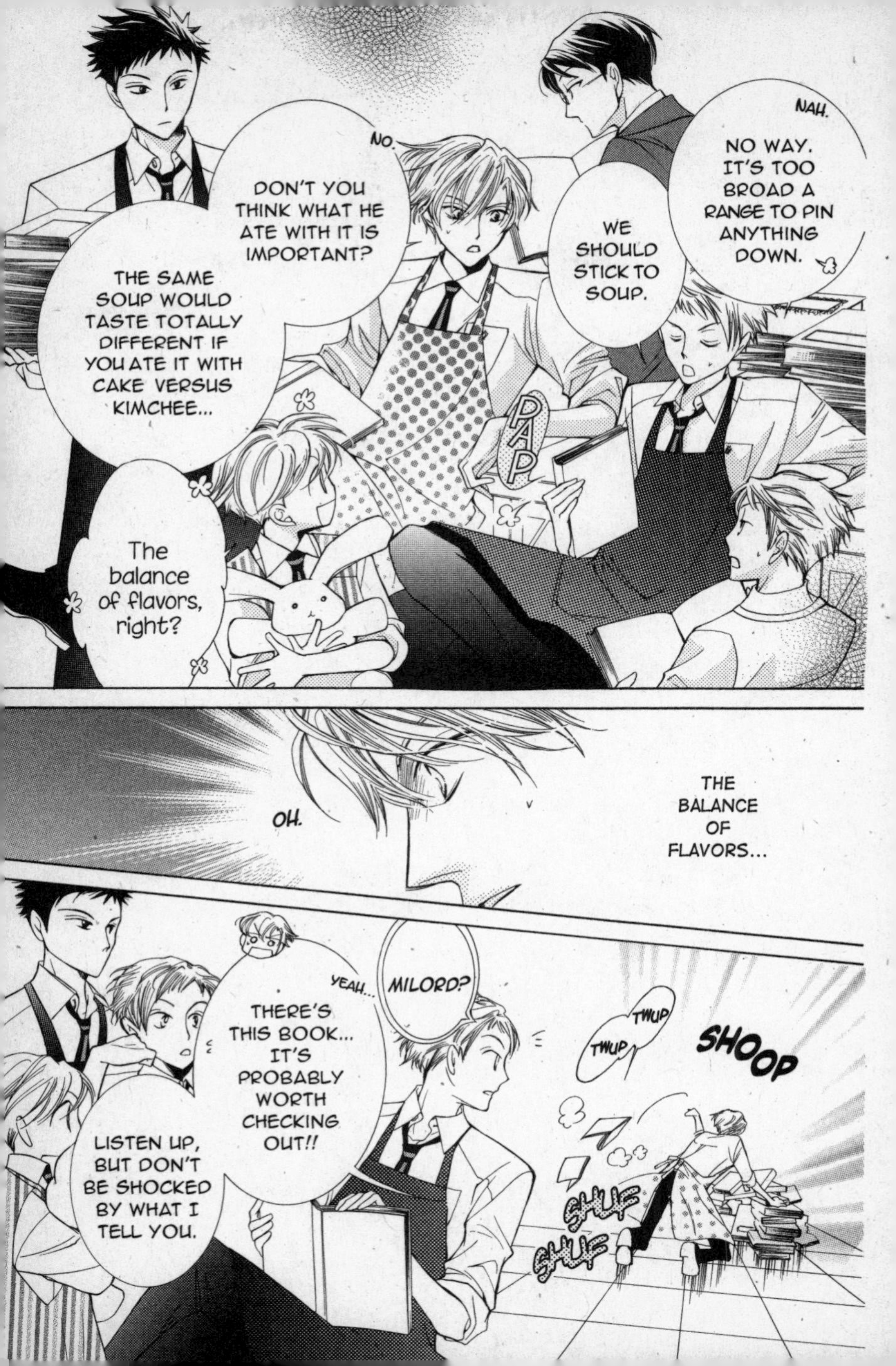
NAH.
NO WAY. IT'S TOO BROAD A RANGE TO PIN ANYTHING DOWN.
WE SHOULD STICK TO SOUP.
NO.
DON'T YOU THINK WHAT HE ATE WITH IT IS IMPORTANT?
THE SAME SOUP WOULD TASTE TOTALLY DIFFERENT IF YOU ATE IT WITH CAKE VERSUS KIMCHEE...
PAP
The balance of flavors, right?
THE BALANCE OF FLAVORS...
OH.
SHOOP
TWUP
TWUP
SHUF
SHUF
MILORD?
YEAH...
THERE'S THIS BOOK... IT'S PROBABLY WORTH CHECKING OUT!!
LISTEN UP, BUT DON'T BE SHOCKED BY WHAT I TELL YOU.

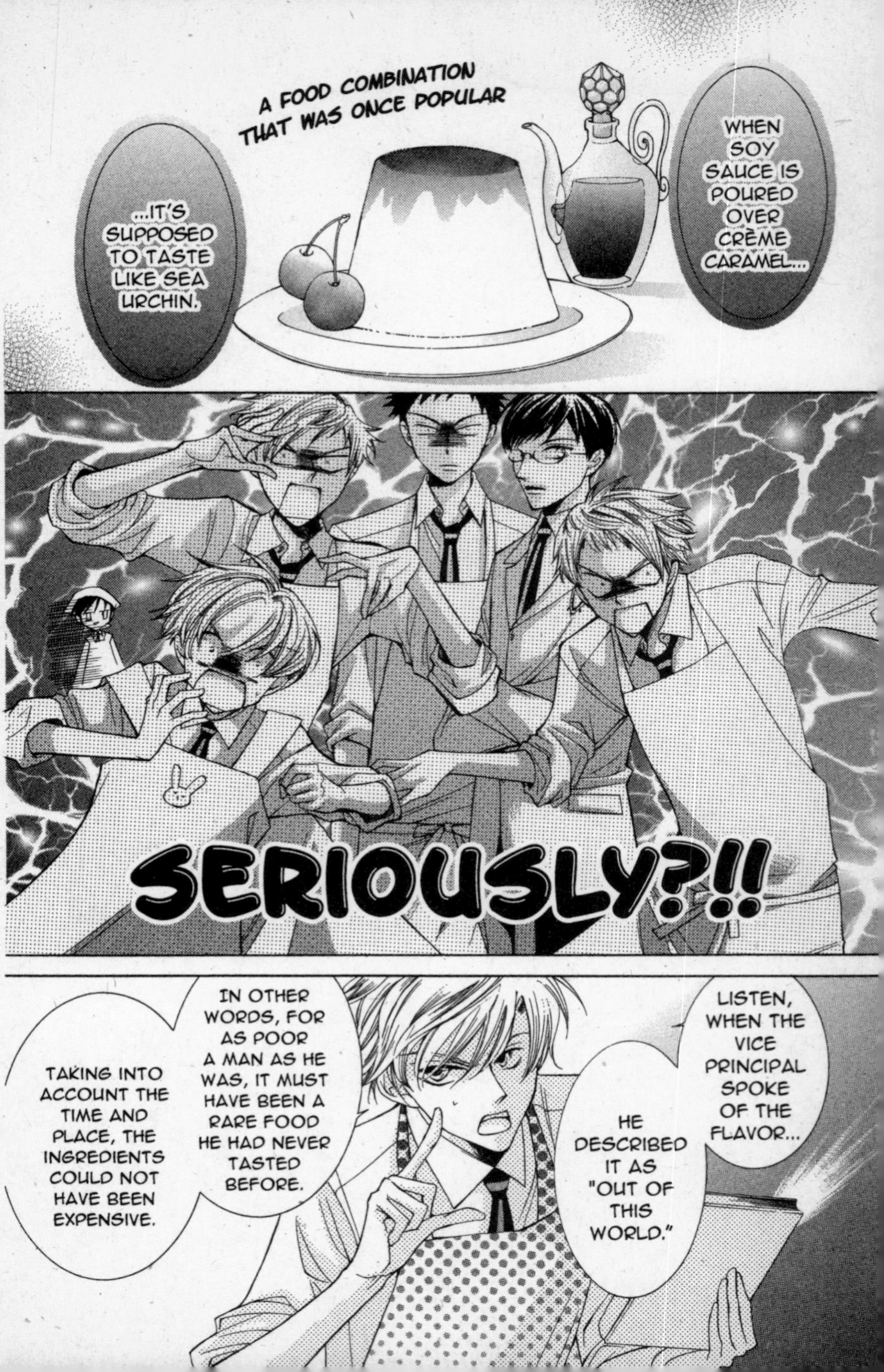
A FOOD COMBINATION THAT WAS ONCE POPULAR
WHEN SOY SAUCE IS POURED OVER CRÈME CARAMEL...
...IT'S SUPPOSED TO TASTE LIKE SEA URCHIN.
SERIOUSLY?!!
LISTEN, WHEN THE VICE PRINCIPAL SPOKE OF THE FLAVOR...
HE DESCRIBED IT AS "OUT OF THIS WORLD."
IN OTHER WORDS, FOR AS POOR A MAN AS HE WAS, IT MUST HAVE BEEN A RARE FOOD HE HAD NEVER TASTED BEFORE.
TAKING INTO ACCOUNT THE TIME AND PLACE, THE INGREDIENTS COULD NOT HAVE BEEN EXPENSIVE.

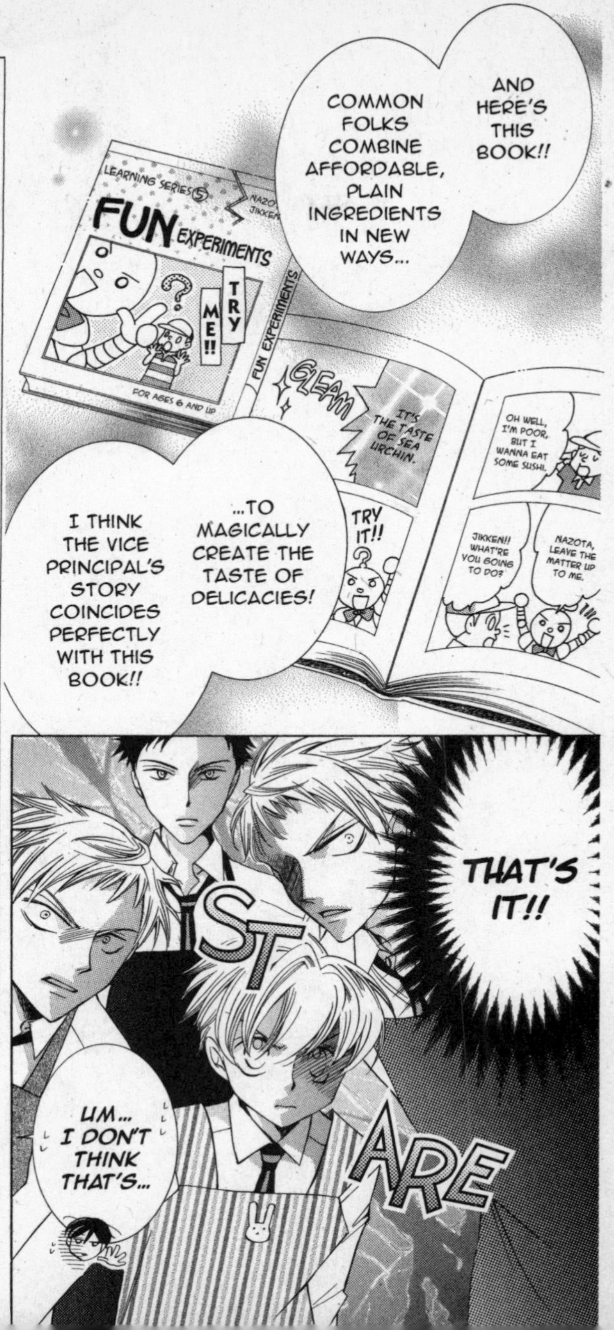
AND HERE'S THIS BOOK!!
COMMON FOLKS COMBINE AFFORDABLE, PLAIN INGREDIENTS IN NEW WAYS...
LEARNING SERIES 5
FUN EXPERIMENTS
TRY ME!!
FOR AGES 6 AND UP
FUN EXPERIMENTS
OH WELL, I'M POOR, BUT I WANNA EAT SOME SUSHI.
NAZOTA, LEAVE THE MATTER UP TO ME.
JIKKEN!! WHAT'RE YOU GOING TO DO?
GLEAM
IT'S THE TASTE OF SEA URCHIN.
TRY IT!!
...TO MAGICALLY CREATE THE TASTE OF DELICACIES!
I THINK THE VICE PRINCIPAL'S STORY COINCIDES PERFECTLY WITH THIS BOOK!!
THAT'S IT!!
STARE
UM... I DON'T THINK THAT'S...

✿COME TO THINK OF IT, WHILE I AM WORKING ON THIS EPISODE, THE THIRD DRAMA CD FROM *LALA* IS IN PRODUCTION.

THIS ONE... I MEAN, WE DID WORK HARD ON THE FIRST AND THE SECOND DISCS, BUT THIS ONE BEATS BOTH.

YAMASHII AND I ARE TOTALLY WORN OUT, BUT I THINK DOI-SAN, THE WRITER, IS HIT THE HARDEST. THANKS FOR ALWAYS GIVING US SUCH FUN SCRIPTS TO WORK WITH!

WE ALSO ACCEPTED SCRIPTS FROM OUR READERS. THEY WERE ALL GREAT! SO AWESOME!! THE HOST CLUB DOESN'T NEED ME ANYMORE--AND THAT MADE ME FEEL A BIT UNCOMFORTABLE. BUT I ENJOYED READING THEM ALL ANYWAY. THANK YOU SO MUCH FOR SENDING IN SCRIPTS WITH LOVE!!

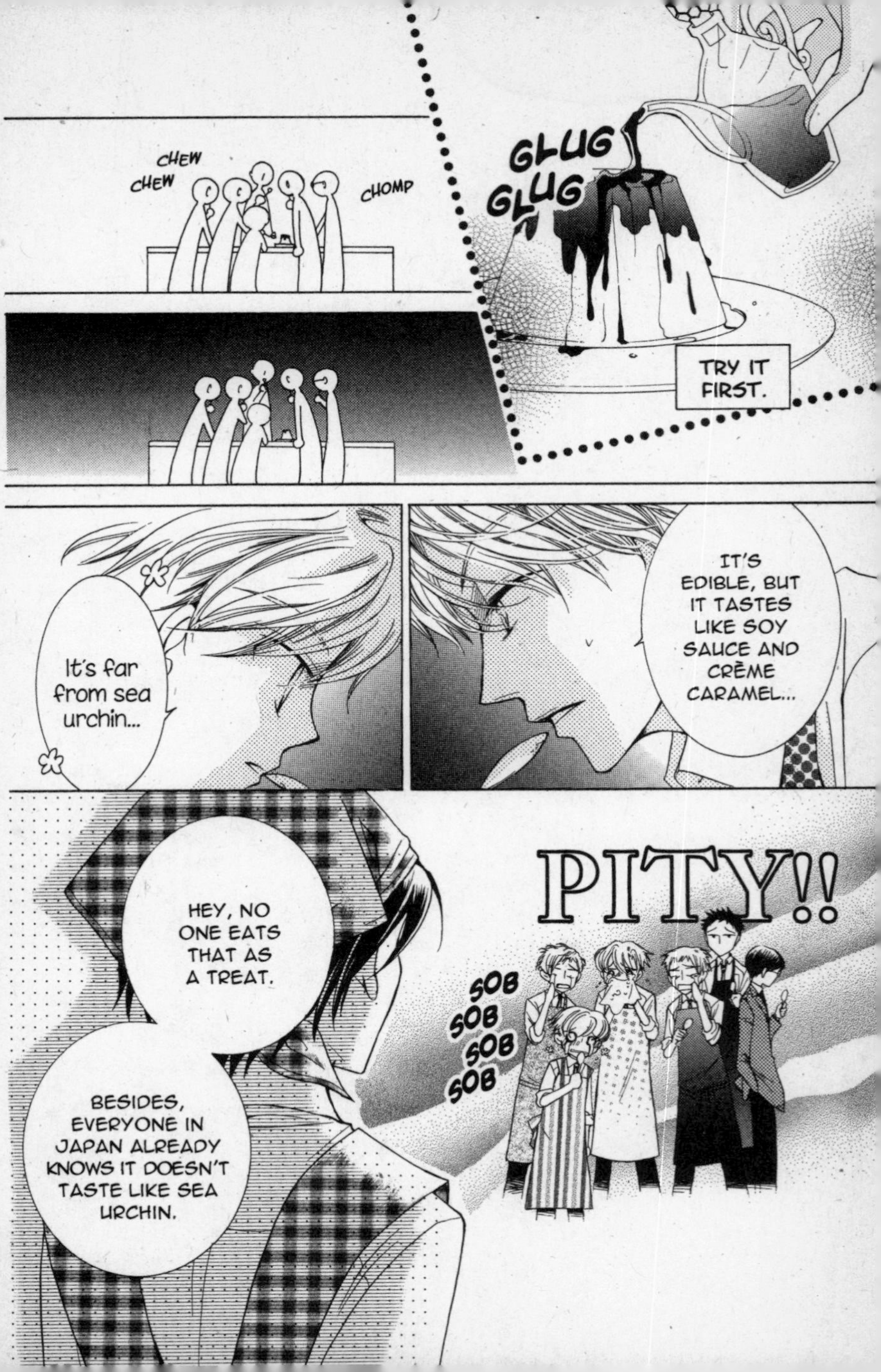
GLUG GLUG
TRY IT FIRST.
CHEW CHEW
CHOMP
IT'S EDIBLE, BUT IT TASTES LIKE SOY SAUCE AND CRÈME CARAMEL...
It's far from sea urchin...
PITY!!
HEY, NO ONE EATS THAT AS A TREAT.
SOB SOB SOB SOB
BESIDES, EVERYONE IN JAPAN ALREADY KNOWS IT DOESN'T TASTE LIKE SEA URCHIN.

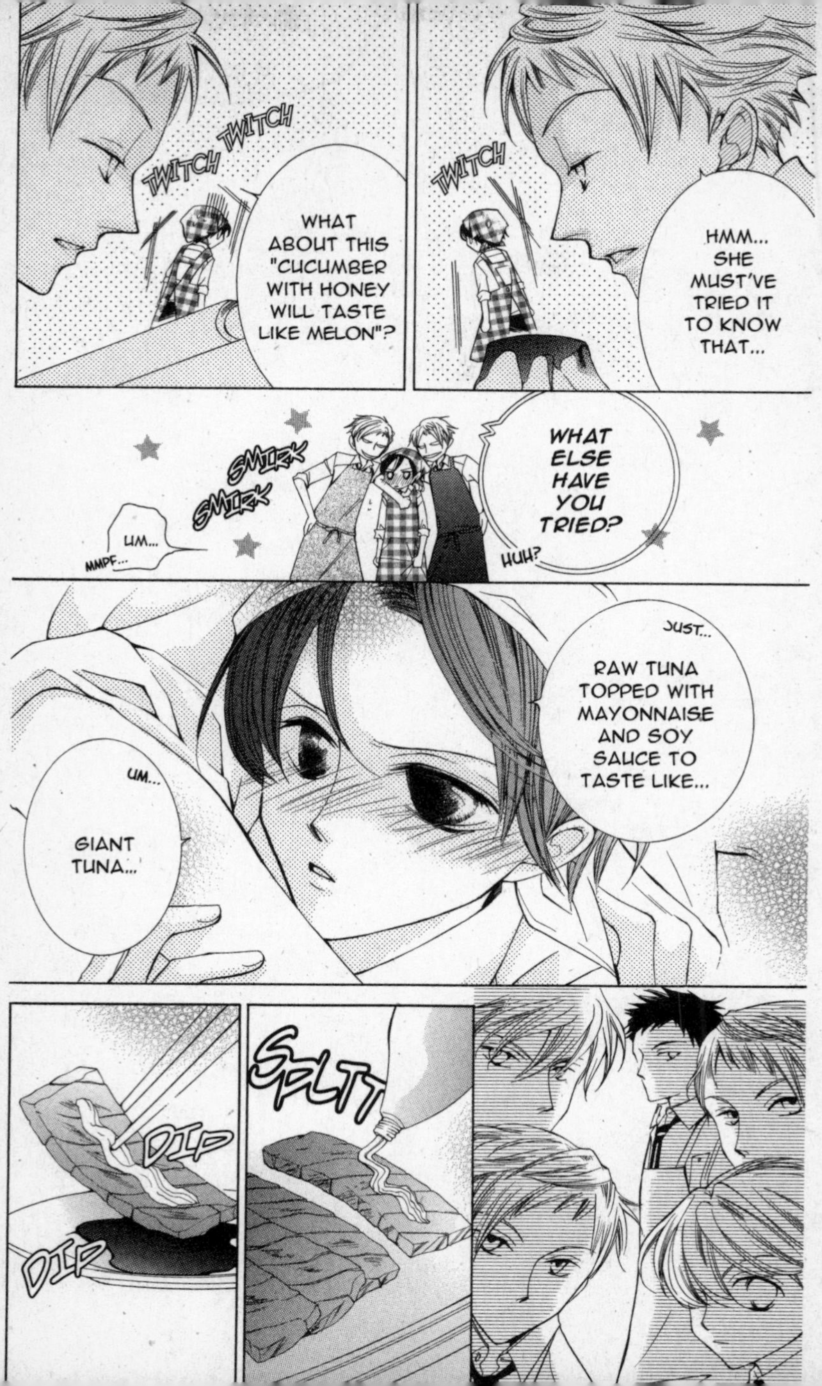
TWITCH
HMM... SHE MUST'VE TRIED IT TO KNOW THAT...
TWITCH TWITCH
WHAT ABOUT THIS "CUCUMBER WITH HONEY WILL TASTE LIKE MELON"?
WHAT ELSE HAVE YOU TRIED?
HUH?
SMIRK SMIRK
UM... MMPF...
JUST...
RAW TUNA TOPPED WITH MAYONNAISE AND SOY SAUCE TO TASTE LIKE...
UM...
GIANT TUNA...
SPLTT
DIP
DIP

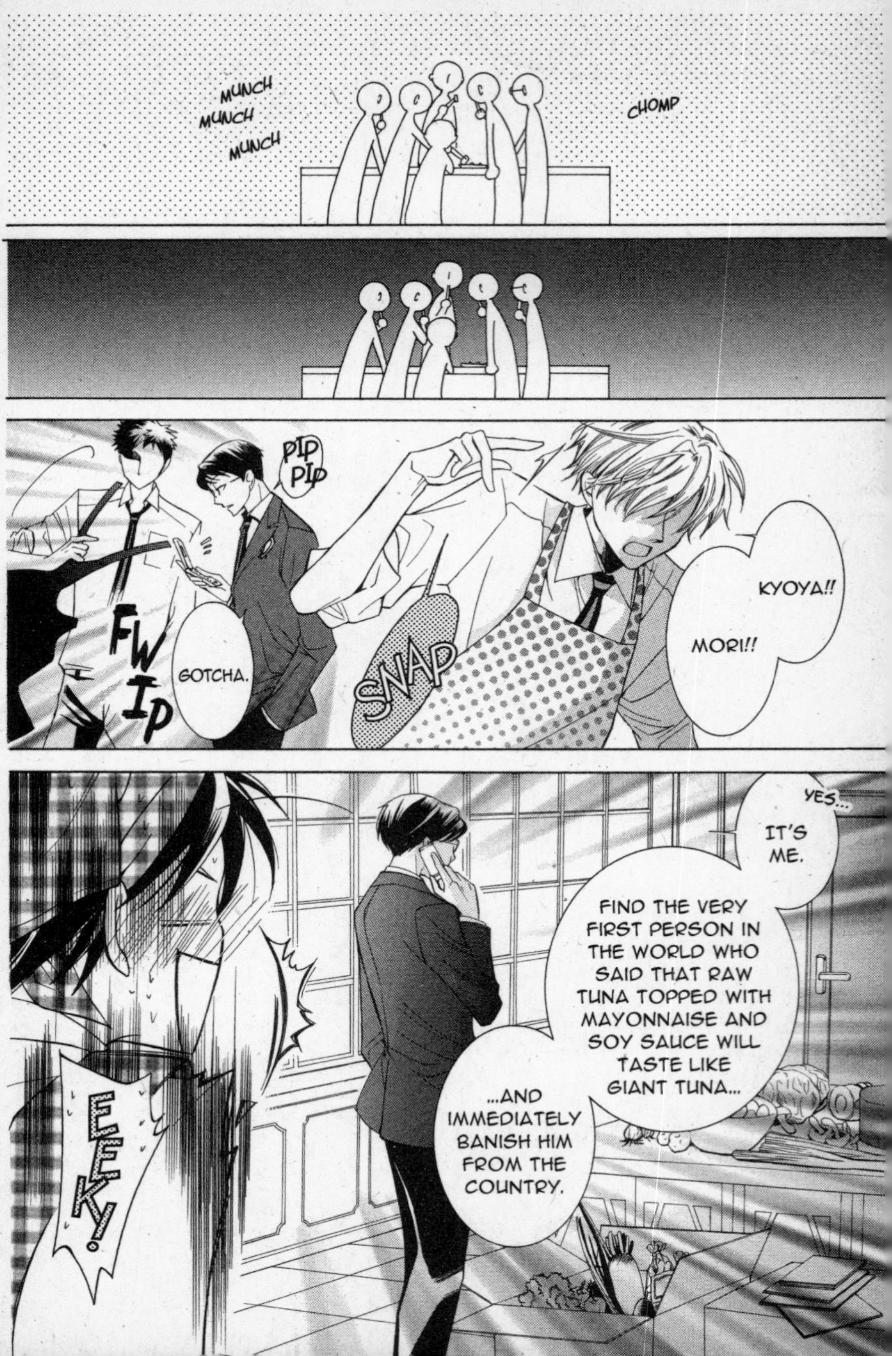
CHOMP
MUNCH MUNCH MUNCH
KYOYA!!
MORI!!
SNAP
PIP PIP
GOTCHA.
FWIP
YES...
IT'S ME.
FIND THE VERY FIRST PERSON IN THE WORLD WHO SAID THAT RAW TUNA TOPPED WITH MAYONNAISE AND SOY SAUCE WILL TASTE LIKE GIANT TUNA...
...AND IMMEDIATELY BANISH HIM FROM THE COUNTRY.
EEK!

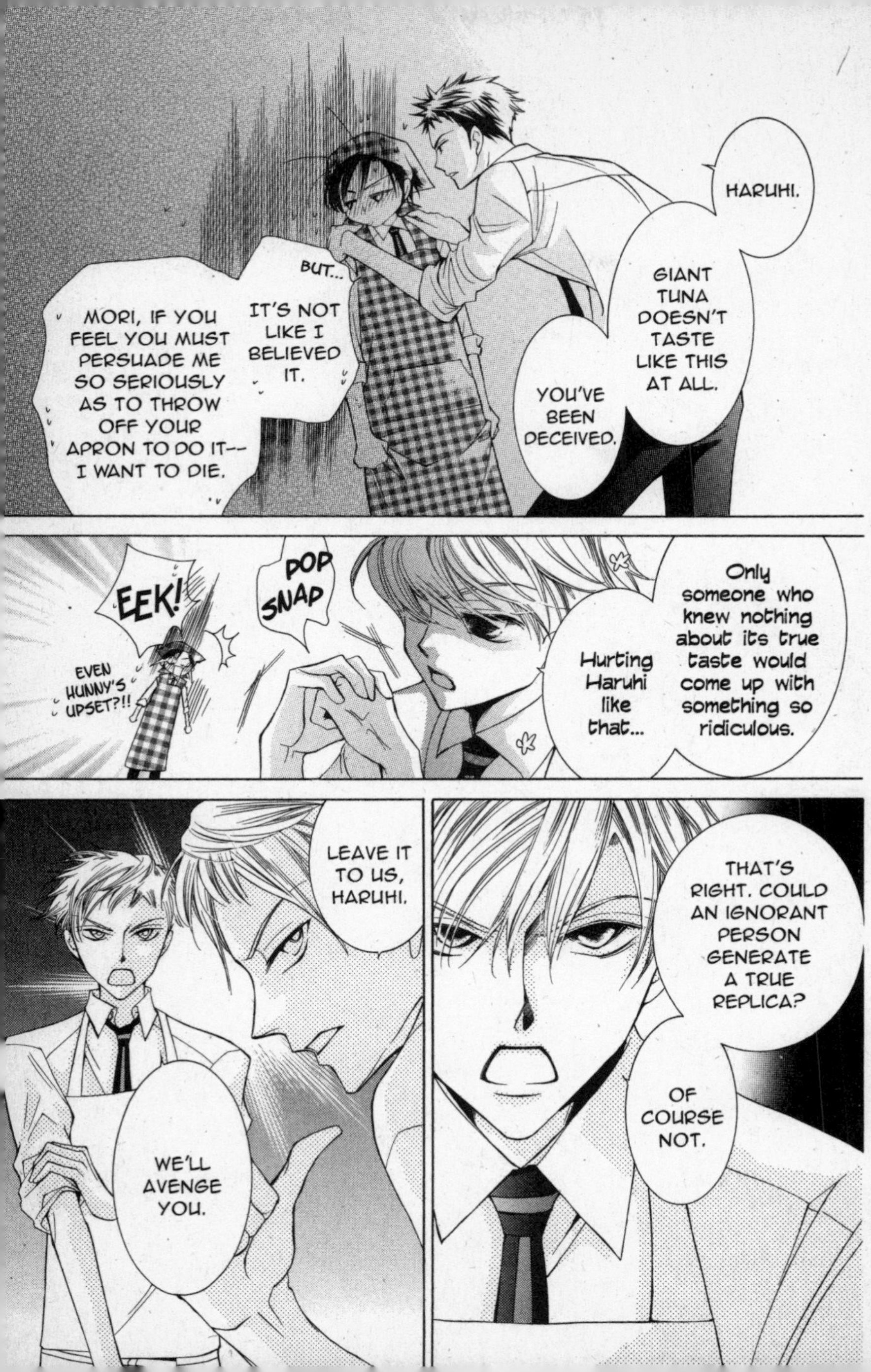
HARUHI.
GIANT TUNA DOESN'T TASTE LIKE THIS AT ALL.
YOU'VE BEEN DECEIVED.
BUT...
IT'S NOT LIKE I BELIEVED IT.
MORI, IF YOU FEEL YOU MUST PERSUADE ME SO SERIOUSLY AS TO THROW OFF YOUR APRON TO DO IT-- I WANT TO DIE.
Only someone who knew nothing about its true taste would come up with something so ridiculous.
Hurting Haruhi like that...
POP SNAP
EEK!
EVEN HUNNY'S UPSET?!!
THAT'S RIGHT. COULD AN IGNORANT PERSON GENERATE A TRUE REPLICA?
OF COURSE NOT.
LEAVE IT TO US, HARUHI.
WE'LL AVENGE YOU.

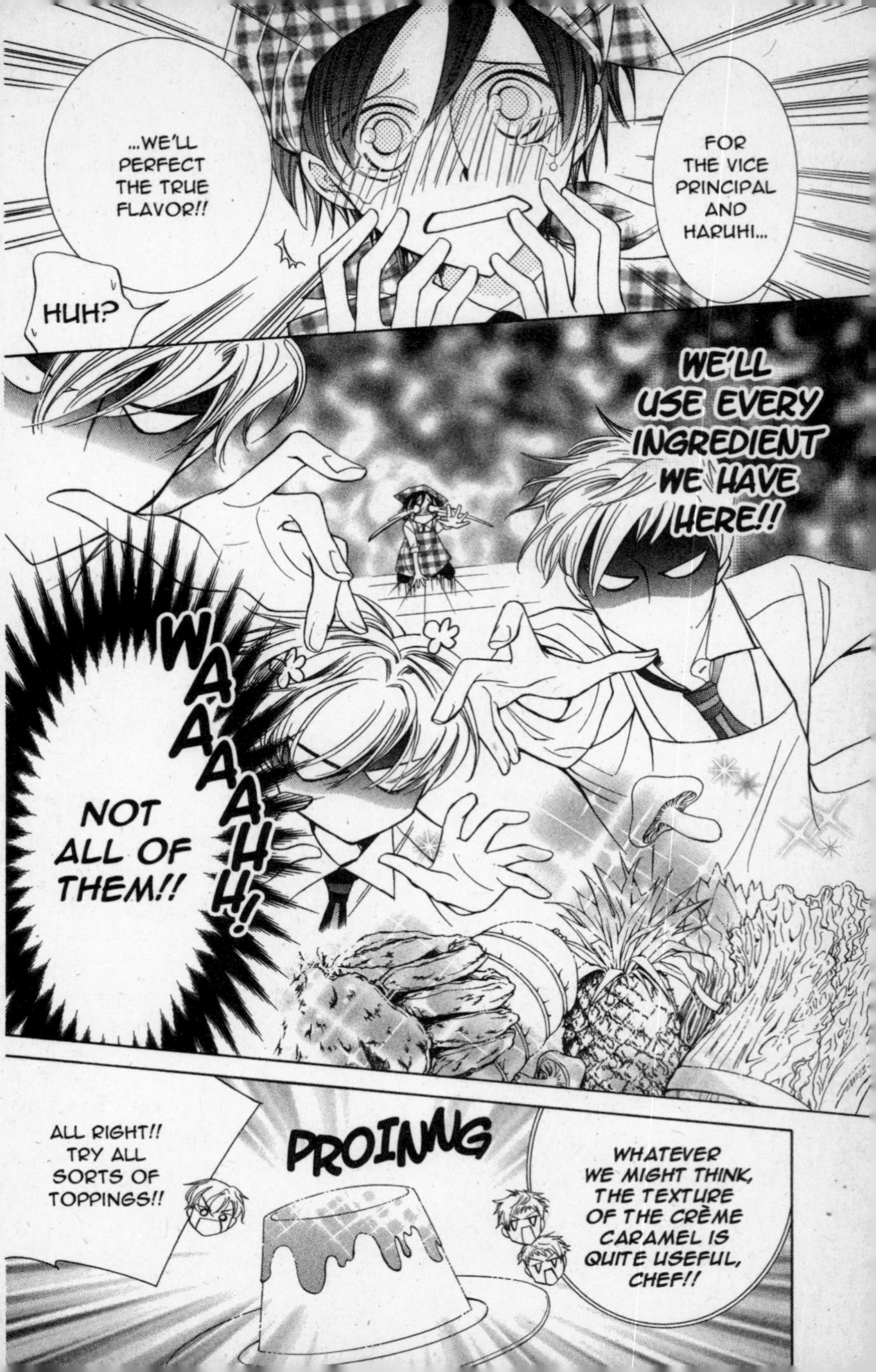
FOR THE VICE PRINCIPAL AND HARUHI...
...WE'LL PERFECT THE TRUE FLAVOR!!
HUH?
WE'LL USE EVERY INGREDIENT WE HAVE HERE!!
WAAAAHH!
NOT ALL OF THEM!!
WHATEVER WE MIGHT THINK, THE TEXTURE OF THE CRÈME CARAMEL IS QUITE USEFUL, CHEF!!
PROINNG
ALL RIGHT!! TRY ALL SORTS OF TOPPINGS!!

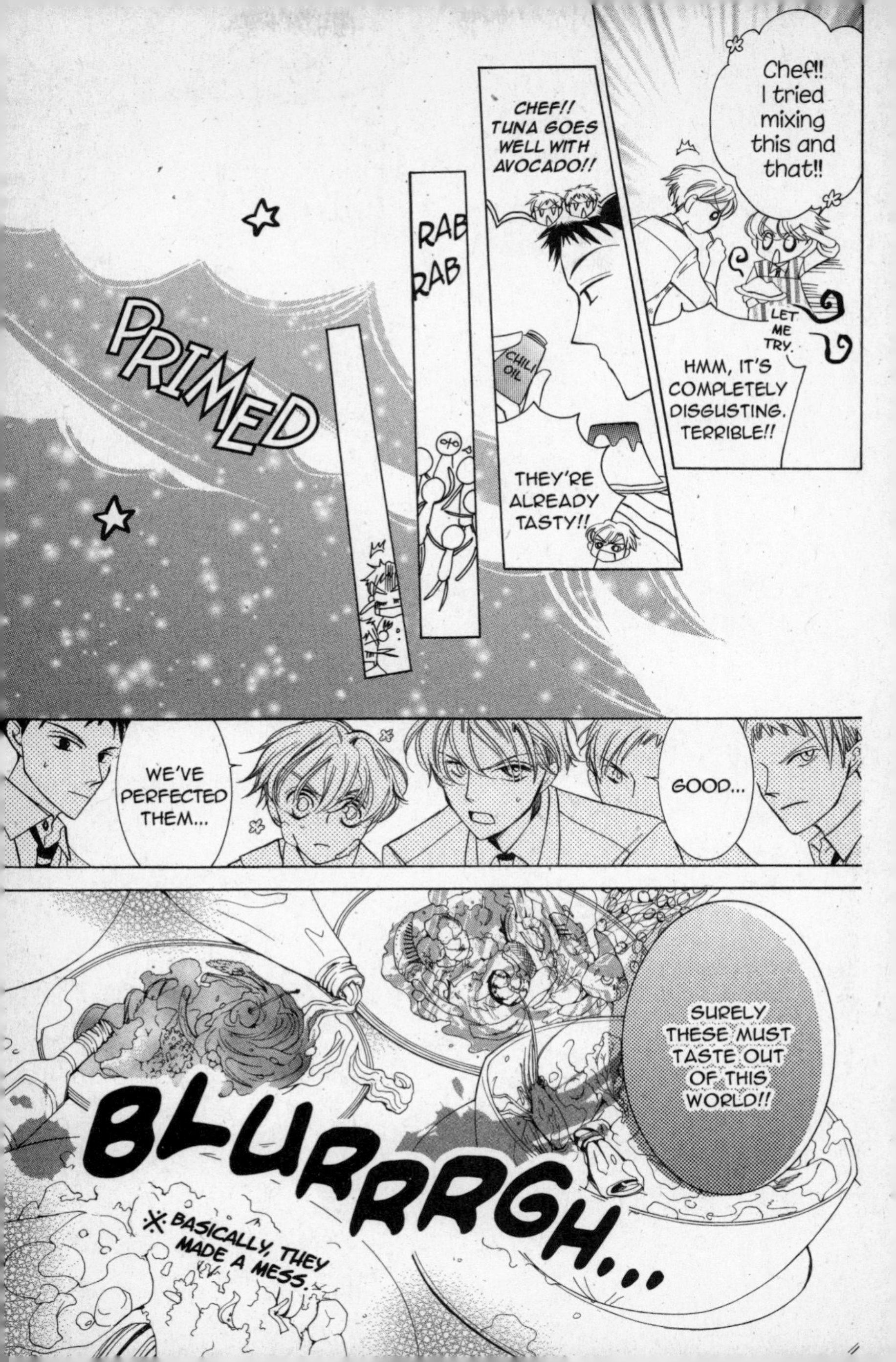
Chef!! I tried mixing this and that!!
LET ME TRY.
HMM, IT'S COMPLETELY DISGUSTING. TERRIBLE!!
CHEF!! TUNA GOES WELL WITH AVOCADO!!
CHILI OIL
THEY'RE ALREADY TASTY!!
RAB RAB
PRIMED
GOOD...
WE'VE PERFECTED THEM...
SURELY THESE MUST TASTE OUT OF THIS WORLD!!
BLURRRGH...
※BASICALLY, THEY MADE A MESS.

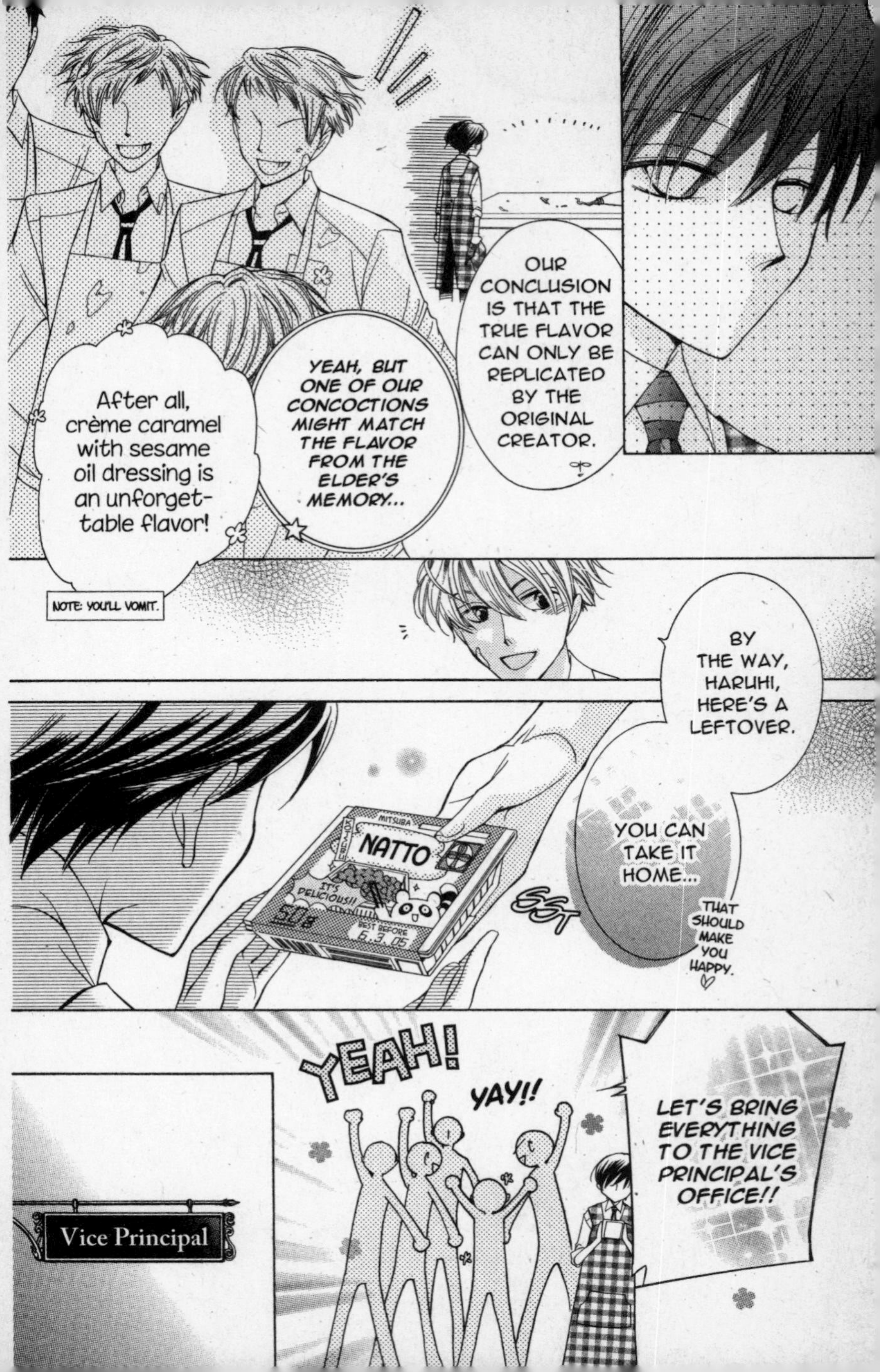
OUR CONCLUSION IS THAT THE TRUE FLAVOR CAN ONLY BE REPLICATED BY THE ORIGINAL CREATOR.
YEAH, BUT ONE OF OUR CONCOCTIONS MIGHT MATCH THE FLAVOR FROM THE ELDER'S MEMORY...
After all, crème caramel with sesame oil dressing is an unforget-table flavor!
NOTE: YOU'LL VOMIT.
BY THE WAY, HARUHI, HERE'S A LEFTOVER.
YOU CAN TAKE IT HOME...
THAT SHOULD MAKE YOU HAPPY.
SST
MITSUBA
NATTO
IT'S DELICIOUS!!
50g
BEST BEFORE 6.3.05
LET'S BRING EVERYTHING TO THE VICE PRINCIPAL'S OFFICE!!
YEAH!
YAY!!
Vice Principal

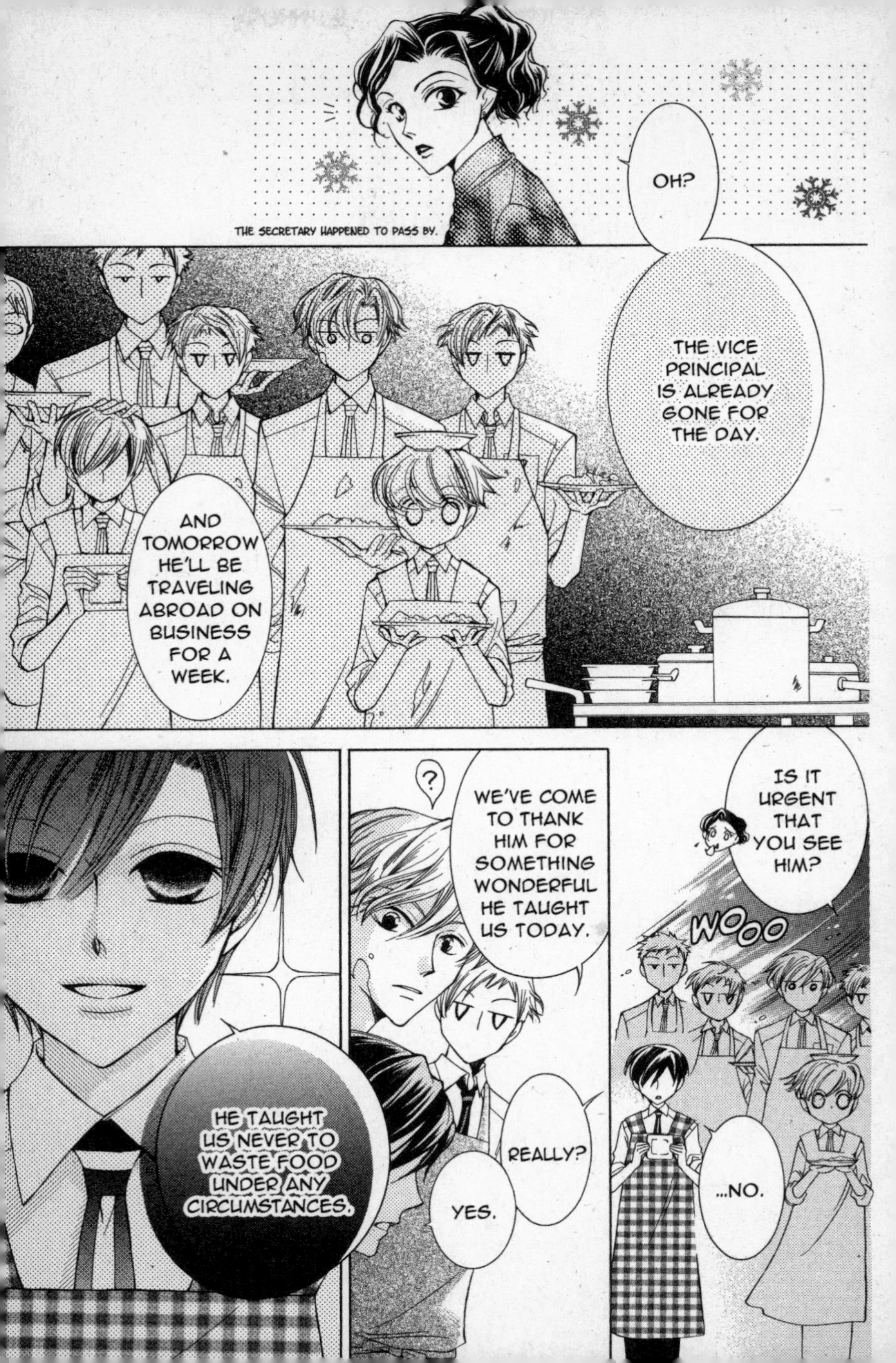
OH?
THE SECRETARY HAPPENED TO PASS BY.
THE VICE PRINCIPAL IS ALREADY GONE FOR THE DAY.
AND TOMORROW HE'LL BE TRAVELING ABROAD ON BUSINESS FOR A WEEK.
IS IT URGENT THAT YOU SEE HIM?
WOOO
...NO.
?
WE'VE COME TO THANK HIM FOR SOMETHING WONDERFUL HE TAUGHT US TODAY.
REALLY?
YES.
HE TAUGHT US NEVER TO WASTE FOOD UNDER ANY CIRCUMSTANCES.

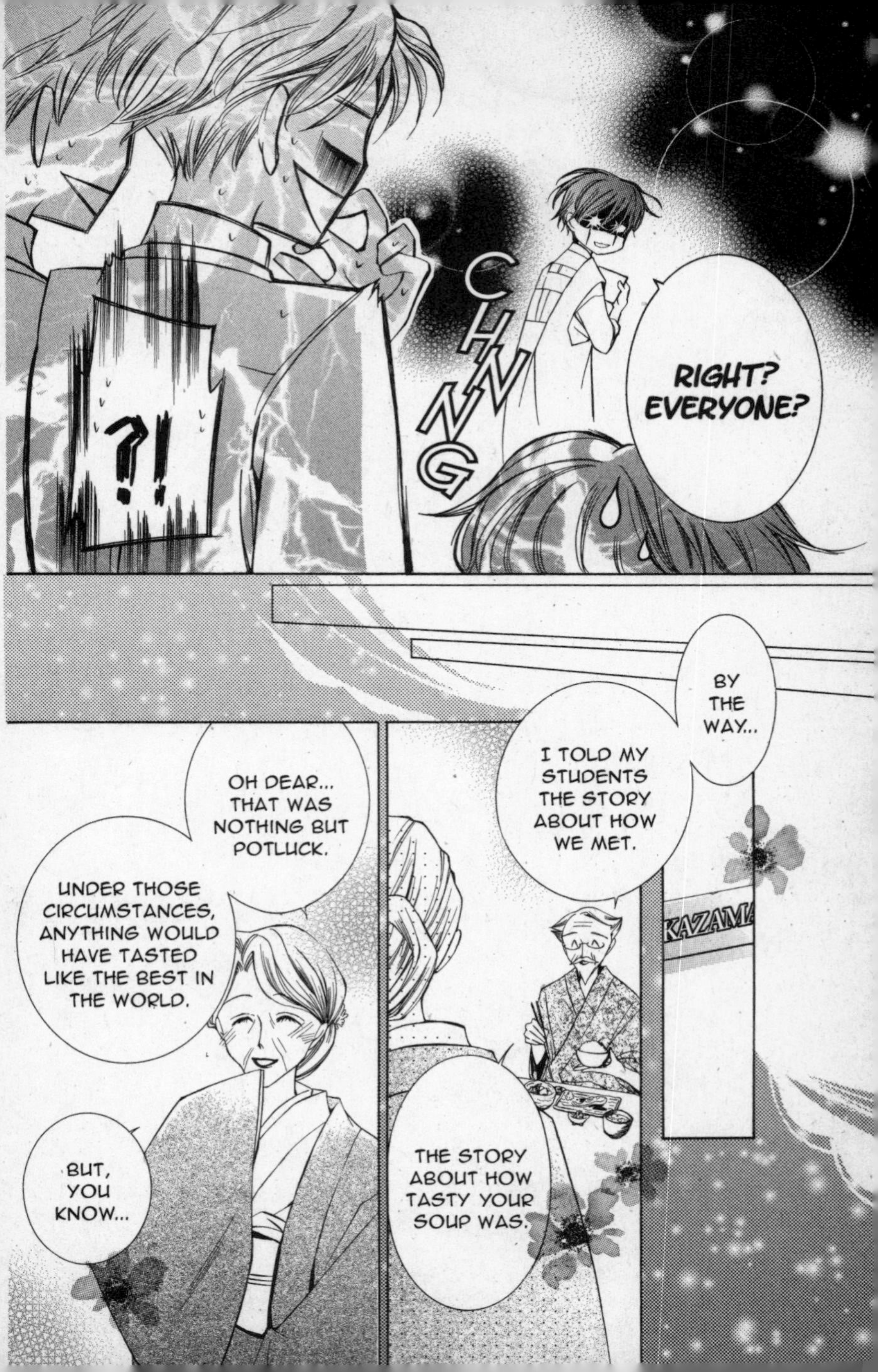
RIGHT? EVERYONE?
CHNNG
?!
BY THE WAY...
I TOLD MY STUDENTS THE STORY ABOUT HOW WE MET.
KAZAMA
THE STORY ABOUT HOW TASTY YOUR SOUP WAS.
OH DEAR... THAT WAS NOTHING BUT POTLUCK.
UNDER THOSE CIRCUMSTANCES, ANYTHING WOULD HAVE TASTED LIKE THE BEST IN THE WORLD.
BUT, YOU KNOW...

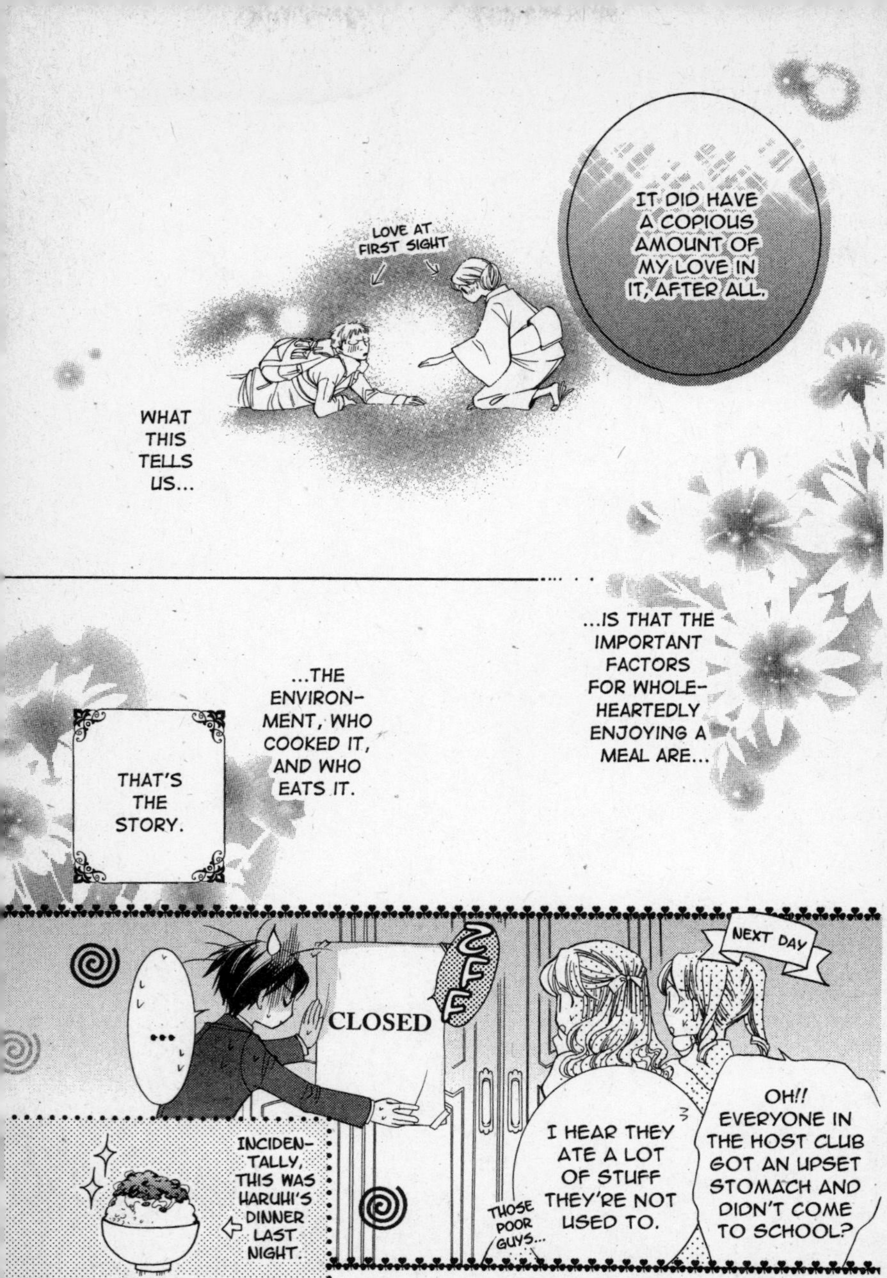
IT DID HAVE A COPIOUS AMOUNT OF MY LOVE IN IT, AFTER ALL.
LOVE AT FIRST SIGHT
WHAT THIS TELLS US...
...IS THAT THE IMPORTANT FACTORS FOR WHOLE-HEARTEDLY ENJOYING A MEAL ARE...
...THE ENVIRONMENT, WHO COOKED IT, AND WHO EATS IT.
THAT'S THE STORY.
NEXT DAY
OH!! EVERYONE IN THE HOST CLUB GOT AN UPSET STOMACH AND DIDN'T COME TO SCHOOL?
I HEAR THEY ATE A LOT OF STUFF THEY'RE NOT USED TO.
THOSE POOR GUYS...
ZFF
CLOSED
...
INCIDENTALLY, THIS WAS HARUHI'S DINNER LAST NIGHT.
RICE WITH NATTO

OURAN HIGH SCHOOL HOST CLUB VOLUME 6/THE END

☺ Special Thanks ☺

YAMASHITA, ALL THE EDITORS, AND EVERYONE INVOLVED
IN PUBLISHING THIS BOOK:
STAFF ↦ YUI NATSUKI, AI SATAKE, AYA AOMURA,
AKANE OGURA, YUTORI HIZAKURA
&
AKIRA HAGIO, NATSUMI SATO, MIDORI SHIINO, SHINOBU AMANO,
KEIKO TAKEUCHI, MIHO NAKAO
AND YOU, THE READERS!!! THANK YOU SO VERY MUCH! ⟿ B

EGOISTIC CLUB

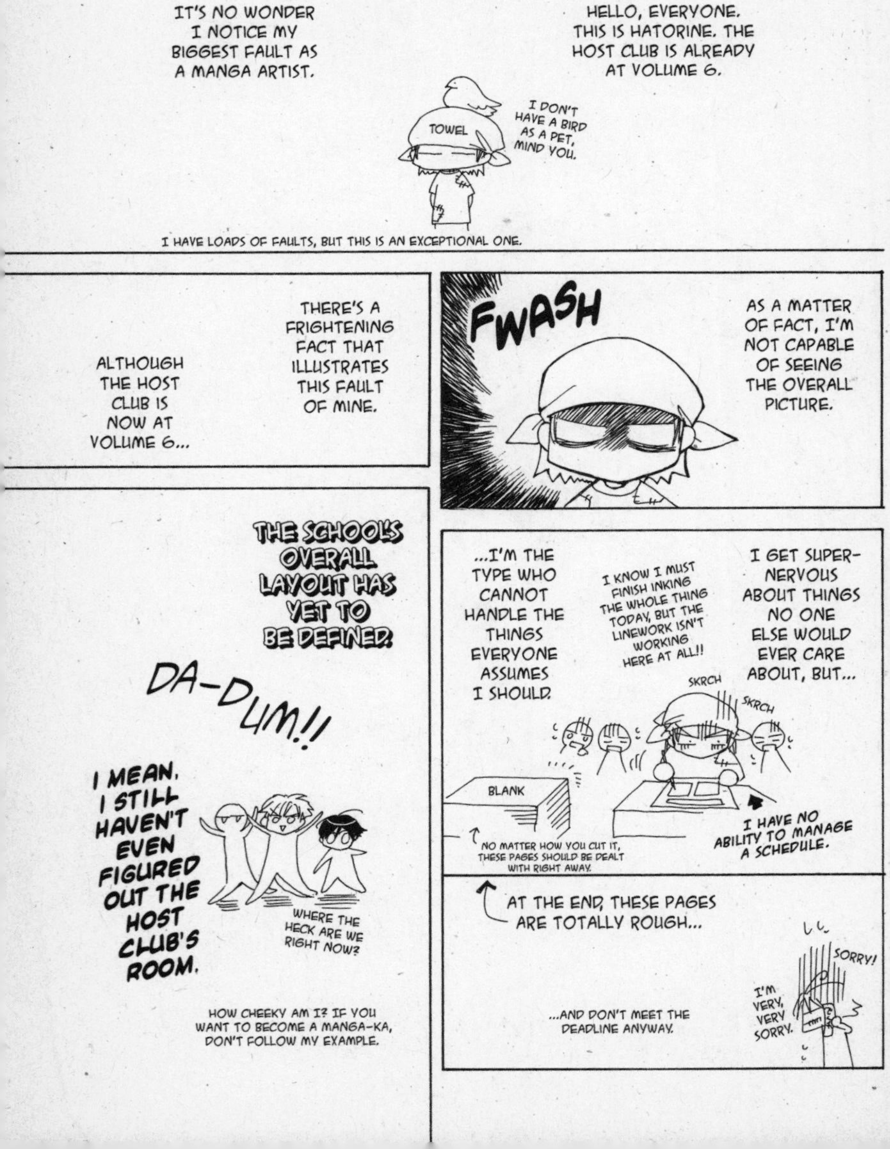

HELLO, EVERYONE. THIS IS HATORINE. THE HOST CLUB IS ALREADY AT VOLUME 6.
IT'S NO WONDER I NOTICE MY BIGGEST FAULT AS A MANGA ARTIST.
I DON'T HAVE A BIRD AS A PET, MIND YOU.
TOWEL
I HAVE LOADS OF FAULTS, BUT THIS IS AN EXCEPTIONAL ONE.
AS A MATTER OF FACT, I'M NOT CAPABLE OF SEEING THE OVERALL PICTURE.
FWASH
THERE'S A FRIGHTENING FACT THAT ILLUSTRATES THIS FAULT OF MINE.
ALTHOUGH THE HOST CLUB IS NOW AT VOLUME 6...
I GET SUPER-NERVOUS ABOUT THINGS NO ONE ELSE WOULD EVER CARE ABOUT, BUT...
I KNOW I MUST FINISH INKING THE WHOLE THING TODAY, BUT THE LINEWORK ISN'T WORKING HERE AT ALL!!
...I'M THE TYPE WHO CANNOT HANDLE THE THINGS EVERYONE ASSUMES I SHOULD.
SKRCH
SKRCH
BLANK
I HAVE NO ABILITY TO MANAGE A SCHEDULE.
NO MATTER HOW YOU CUT IT, THESE PAGES SHOULD BE DEALT WITH RIGHT AWAY.
AT THE END, THESE PAGES ARE TOTALLY ROUGH...
SORRY!
I'M VERY, VERY SORRY.
...AND DON'T MEET THE DEADLINE ANYWAY.
THE SCHOOL'S OVERALL LAYOUT HAS YET TO BE DEFINED.
DA-DUM!!
I MEAN, I STILL HAVEN'T EVEN FIGURED OUT THE HOST CLUB'S ROOM.
WHERE THE HECK ARE WE RIGHT NOW?
HOW CHEEKY AM I? IF YOU WANT TO BECOME A MANGA-KA, DON'T FOLLOW MY EXAMPLE.

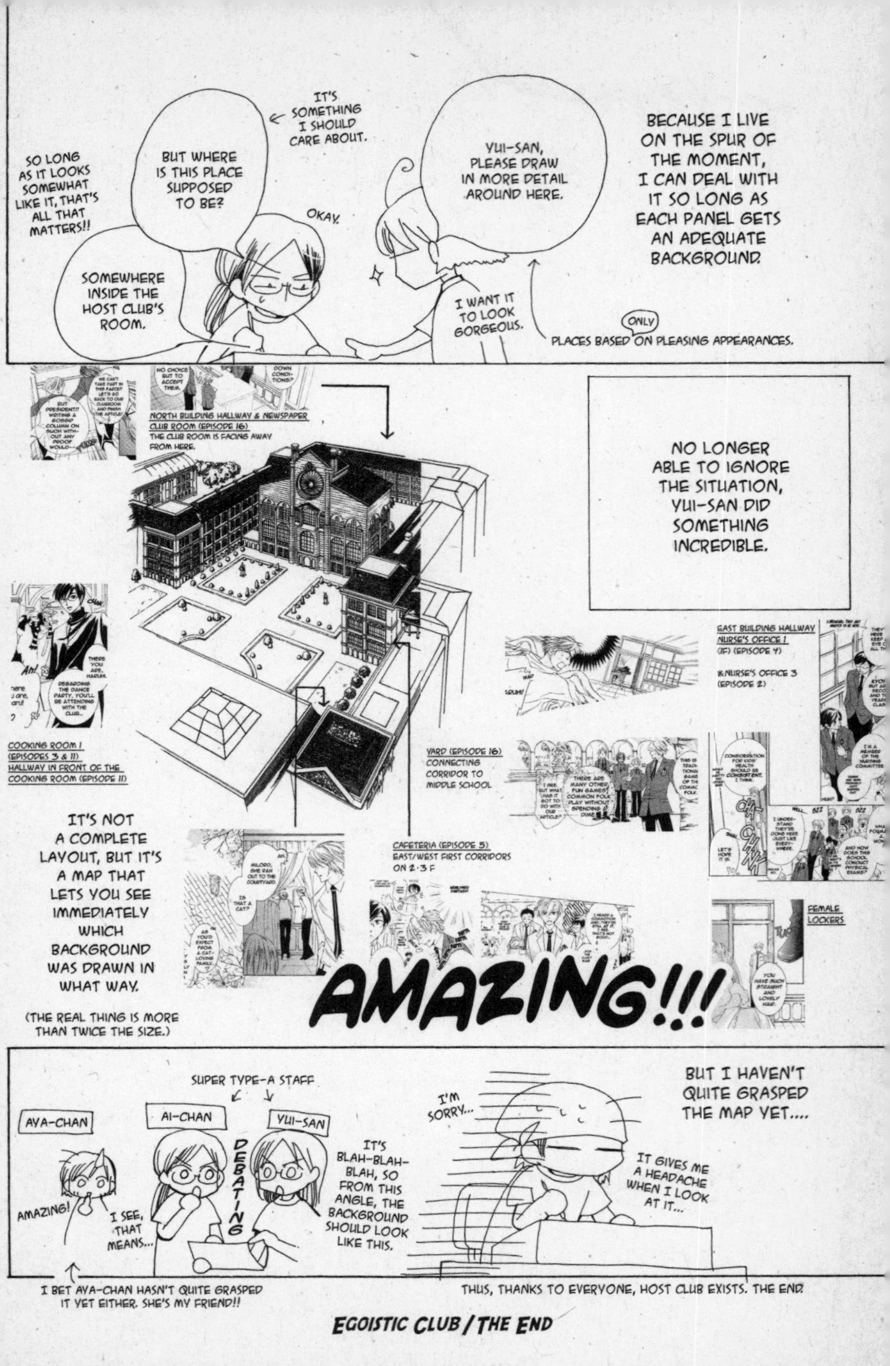
BECAUSE I LIVE ON THE SPUR OF THE MOMENT, I CAN DEAL WITH IT SO LONG AS EACH PANEL GETS AN ADEQUATE BACKGROUND.
YUI-SAN, PLEASE DRAW IN MORE DETAIL AROUND HERE.
I WANT IT TO LOOK GORGEOUS.
ONLY
PLACES BASED ON PLEASING APPEARANCES.
OKAY.
IT'S SOMETHING I SHOULD CARE ABOUT.
BUT WHERE IS THIS PLACE SUPPOSED TO BE?
SO LONG AS IT LOOKS SOMEWHAT LIKE IT, THAT'S ALL THAT MATTERS!!
SOMEWHERE INSIDE THE HOST CLUB'S ROOM.
NO LONGER ABLE TO IGNORE THE SITUATION, YUI-SAN DID SOMETHING INCREDIBLE.
NORTH BUILDING HALLWAY & NEWSPAPER CLUB ROOM (EPISODE 16)
THE CLUB ROOM IS FACING AWAY FROM HERE.
EAST BUILDING HALLWAY
NURSE'S OFFICE 1 (1F) (EPISODE 4)
&NURSE'S OFFICE 3 (EPISODE 2)
COOKING ROOM 1 (EPISODES 3 & 11)
HALLWAY IN FRONT OF THE COOKING ROOM (EPISODE 11)
YARD (EPISODE 16)
CONNECTING CORRIDOR TO MIDDLE SCHOOL
CAFETERIA (EPISODE 5)
EAST/WEST FIRST CORRIDORS ON 2·3 F
FEMALE LOCKERS
IT'S NOT A COMPLETE LAYOUT, BUT IT'S A MAP THAT LETS YOU SEE IMMEDIATELY WHICH BACKGROUND WAS DRAWN IN WHAT WAY.
(THE REAL THING IS MORE THAN TWICE THE SIZE.)
AMAZING!!!
BUT I HAVEN'T QUITE GRASPED THE MAP YET....
I'M SORRY...
IT GIVES ME A HEADACHE WHEN I LOOK AT IT...
THUS, THANKS TO EVERYONE, HOST CLUB EXISTS. THE END
SUPER TYPE-A STAFF
YUI-SAN
AI-CHAN
AYA-CHAN
IT'S BLAH-BLAH-BLAH, SO FROM THIS ANGLE, THE BACKGROUND SHOULD LOOK LIKE THIS.
DEBATING
I SEE, THAT MEANS...
AMAZING!
I BET AYA-CHAN HASN'T QUITE GRASPED IT YET EITHER. SHE'S MY FRIEND!!

EGOISTIC CLUB / THE END

EDITOR'S NOTES

EPISODE 22

Page 7: Most schools in Japan hold cultural festivals, or *bunkasai*, in the autumn. A bunkasai would be comparable to a student-led, daytime "Back-to-School Night" with exhibits and skits.

EPISODE 23

Page 37: *Wagashi* are traditional Japanese confectionery.

Page 42: The Host Club members are calling Haruhi a *shibu gaaru*, or "graceful girl." A shibu character is highly principled and exudes an air of refinement.

EPISODE 24

Page 71: The twins are teasing Tamaki by referring to the more recent Showa period (1926-1989).

Page 73: In katakana, *uesuto* can mean either "waist" or "west" as the spelling is the same for both.

Page 73: *Tenjiku* is an old Japanese word for "India."

Page 73: *Journey to the West* is a Chinese novel written during the Ming Dynasty (1368-1644). The Japanese title is *Saiyuki*, and it's the story on which *Dragon Ball* is based.

Page 80: The Host Club members use letters from Kanan Mitsuyama's name to spell out *mikan*, or "orange."

EPISODE 25

Page 100: *Iitomo* refers to *Waratte Iitomo*, or "It's OK to Laugh," a popular entertainment show that is broadcast daily on Japanese TV. Tamori is the host of the show.

EPISODE 26

Page 149: Oshin is the main character in a Japanese drama of the same name. Oshin is a girl from a very poor family who becomes a successful businesswoman after overcoming many obstacles.

Author Bio

Bisco Hatori made her manga debut with *Isshun kan no Romance* (A Moment of Romance) in *LaLa DX* magazine. The comedy *Ouran High School Host Club* is her breakout hit. When she's stuck thinking up characters' names, she gets inspired by loud, upbeat music (her radio is set to NACK5 FM). She enjoys reading all kinds of manga, but she's especially fond of the sci-fi drama *Please Save My Earth* and *Slam Dunk*, a basketball classic.

OURAN HIGH SCHOOL HOST CLUB
Vol. 6
The Shojo Beat Manga Edition

STORY AND ART BY BISCO HATORI

Translation & English Adaptation/Naomi Kokubo & Eric-Jon Rössel Waugh
Touch-up Art & Lettering/George Caltsoudas
Graphic Design/Izumi Evers
Editor/Nancy Thistlethwaite

Managing Editor/Megan Bates
Editorial Director/Elizabeth Kawasaki
VP & Editor in Chief/Yumi Hoashi
Sr. Director of Acquisitions/Rika Inouye
Sr. VP of Marketing/Liza Coppola
Exec. VP of Sales & Marketing/John Easum
Publisher/Hyoe Narita

Ouran Koko Host Club by Bisco Hatori © Bisco Hatori 2004. All rights reserved. First published in Japan in 2005 by HAKUSENSHA, Inc., Tokyo. English language translation rights in America and Canada arranged with HAKUSENSHA, Inc., Tokyo. New and adapted artwork and text © 2006 VIZ Media, LLC. The OURAN HIGH SCHOOL HOST CLUB logo is a trademark of VIZ Media, LLC. The stories, characters and incidents mentioned in this publication are entirely fictional.

Printed in Canada

Published by VIZ Media, LLC
P.O. Box 77010
San Francisco, CA 94107

Shojo Beat Manga Edition
10 9 8 7 6 5 4 3 2
First printing, May 2006
Second printing, October 2006

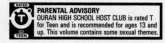

Tell us what you think about Shojo Beat Manga!

Our survey is now available online. Go to:

shojobeat.com/mangasurvey

Help us make our product offerings better!

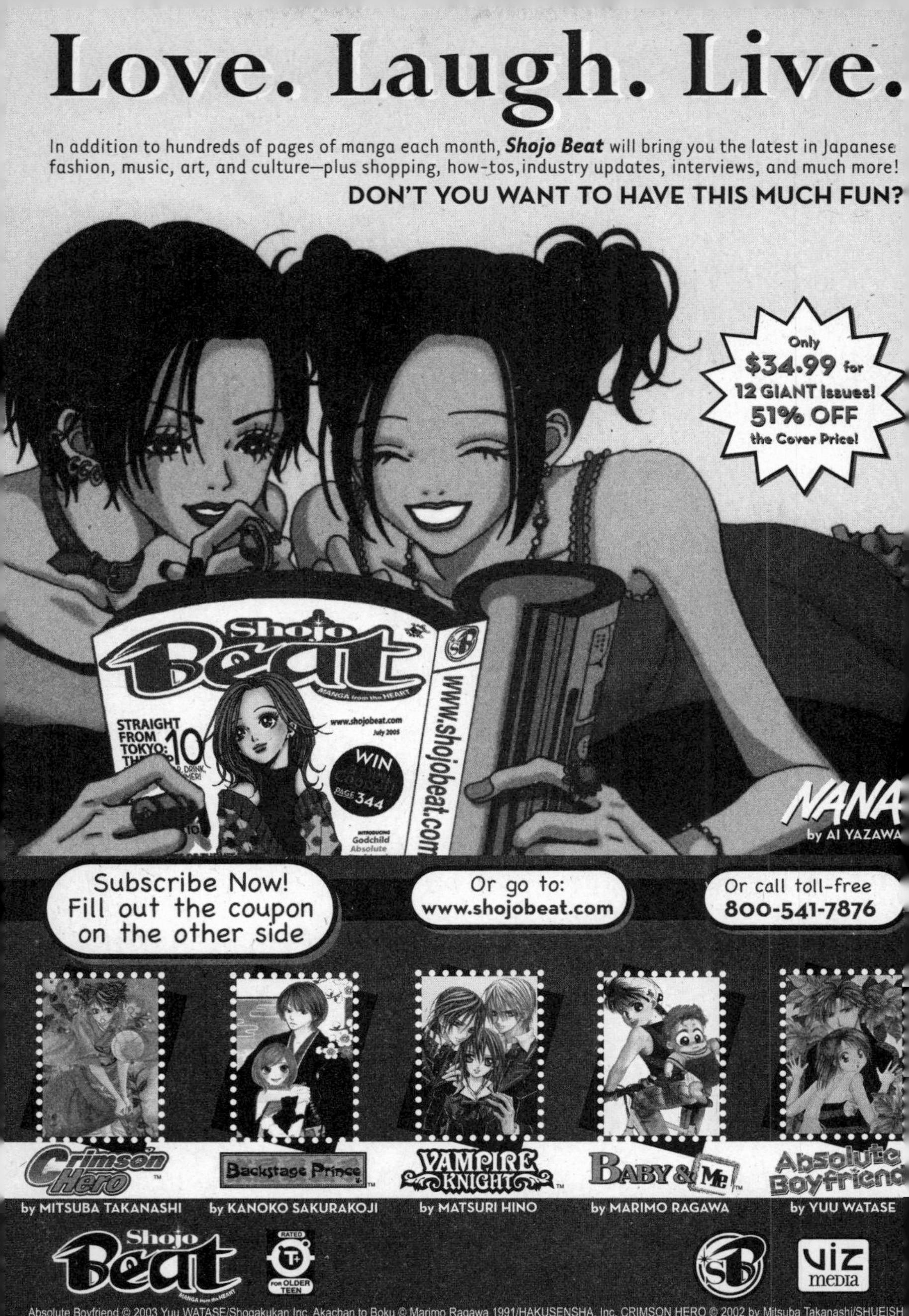
Love. Laugh. Live.
In addition to hundreds of pages of manga each month, Shojo Beat will bring you the latest in Japanese fashion, music, art, and culture—plus shopping, how-tos, industry updates, interviews, and much more!
DON'T YOU WANT TO HAVE THIS MUCH FUN?
Only $34.99 for 12 GIANT Issues! 51% OFF the Cover Price!
Shojo Beat
MANGA from the HEART
www.shojobeat.com
July 2005
STRAIGHT FROM TOKYO:
WIN
PAGE 344
INTRODUCING Godchild
Absolute
www.shojobeat.com
NANA by AI YAZAWA
Subscribe Now! Fill out the coupon on the other side
Or go to: www.shojobeat.com
Or call toll-free 800-541-7876
Crimson Hero by MITSUBA TAKANASHI
Backstage Prince by KANOKO SAKURAKOJI
VAMPIRE KNIGHT by MATSURI HINO
BABY & ME by MARIMO RAGAWA
Absolute Boyfriend by YUU WATASE
Shojo Beat MANGA from the HEART
RATED T+ FOR OLDER TEEN
SB
viz media